Megamedia Shakeout

The Inside Story of the Leaders and the Losers in the Exploding Communications Industry

Kevin Maney

JOHN WILEY & SONS, INC.

New York • Chichester • Brisbane • Toronto • Singapore

To my grandfather,

Victor Baldwin (1908–1993),

who would've wanted to know all about megamedia, asking as only he could: "How does this gon don thing work, anyway?"

This text is printed on acid-free paper.

Published by John Wiley & Sons, Inc.

Library of Congress Cataloging-in-Publication Data:

Maney, Kevin, 1960–
Megamedia shakeout : the inside story of the leaders and the losers in the exploding communications industry.
/ Kevin Maney.
p. cp.
ISBN 0-471-10719-0
1. Mass media—United States—Finance. 2. Mass media—
—Technological innovations. 3. Corporations, American. I. Title.
P96.E252U66 1995
338.4'730223'0973—cc20
DLC
For Library of Congress 94-43311
CIP

Printed in the United States of America
10 9 8 7 6 5 4 3 2 1

PREFACE

This book is about character.

Megamedia is one of the great dramas in business. It is an explosion of technology and opportunities described in terms such as information highways, 500 channel TVs, multimedia and digital communication. They're all related and all on the same stage, but there is no word that embraces all of the exciting things that are happening across communication, information, computer, and entertainment industries. To make writing and talking about the big picture easier, I'm calling this new industry *megamedia.*

While megamedia is an explosion, it's also an implosion. Companies from all corners of business are converging into the same market, forming allies with one another, battling against new competitors that never before crossed their radar. AT&T, Disney, IBM, Viacom, Microsoft, TCI, and Sega are all now in the same industry.

Megamedia is the play; the companies are the players. In this book, you'll read about the character of those players.

I've tried to single out the important companies swooping into megamedia and describe their strengths and weaknesses, long-term strategy, and culture. Most importantly, this book looks at the ability of companies to handle the immense changes that are still to come.

The book also gives you a picture of the leaders of the companies because strong leadership and vision seem to be keys to success in megamedia. You'll meet John Malone of TCI, Robert Allen of

AT&T, Ray Smith of Bell Atlantic, and some less well-known CEOs such as Marc Porat of General Magic and Ed McCracken of Silicon Graphics. I've tried to paint colorful pictures of them so you can understand not just what they do, but how they think.

Why emphasize character? It's the only way to get a handle on who in megamedia might win and who might lose through the next decade. Megamedia is moving rapidly; just try following the daily headlines—who's talking to who, which products were announced, what company is merging with what other company. Wall Street analyst reports aren't much help. They focus on the next quarter and judge success by the price of a stock. *Character* underlies all the little day-to-day moves that pop up in the news. By understanding a company's character, you've got a good shot at understanding how a company will deal with megamedia, and what its chances might be in the long run.

This book is for everyone. It may be the only place where you can get a complete picture of megamedia and its players. Most reports focus on isolated industries such as telephones or cable, which is the way Wall Street and journalists have looked at these businesses for ages. But megamedia is so much more—many major industries all now interlocking and blurring and competing. For the past two years, I've had a chance to cross old industry lines to find the intriguing players coming to megamedia from Silicon Valley, from Hollywood, from the Rust Belt, or wherever. That perspective should help you understand a major change coursing through our economic system. Something new—megamedia—is emerging. This book offers you a way to see it happening.

Investors large and small can use this book to help sort out where they should put their money. People working in these industries can come away with a better understanding of players who might someday be partners, enemies, or employers. Entrepreneurs can use this book to help think about opportunities.

This book is written to help anyone grasp megamedia—because megamedia will most certainly effect us all.

A few comments on my approach are in order. Quotes are from one-on-one personal interviews, unless otherwise noted. Occasionally, first-hand quotes are from group settings, such as press conferences, where I was present. While researching this book, I talked to top executives at more than 40 companies and interviewed another dozen independent consultants and analysts. Basic information about companies has come from interviews, corporate documents, news reports, and other sources where noted.

My focus is overwhelmingly on U.S. companies. The reason is that the United States, in general, is far ahead of the rest of the world in megamedia. But you'll find profiles of some of the international companies that are becoming important to megamedia, such as British Telecom, Rupert Murdoch's News Corp., Sony, and Sega.

My caveat to readers is that this industry is changing quickly. Information included here is as up-to-date as possible, but I don't doubt that some other merger or major product will be announced even as you read this book. Companies' long-term plans and corporate character should prevail over the latest news events.

Finally, thanks to John Mahaney for taking a chance on this project and to Myles Thompson for seeing it through. Thanks to *USA Today* for being supportive, and to Jim Cox and Paul Wiseman, two colleagues who made it possible for me to do this book.

Thanks to my children, Alison and Sam, for keeping me sane by playing during my breaks, and to my wife, Janet, for her never-ending faith in me.

If megamedia somehow allows us to spend more time with our families, it will all be worth it.

KEVIN MANEY

Alexandria, Virginia
February 1995

CONTENTS

1

COMPANIES GONE MAD

John Malone and Ray Smith lurched through Manhattan in the back seat of a limousine. It was 5 P.M. and they were on their way to be interviewed together on the television show "Nightly Business Report." That morning—October 13, 1993—the two had announced that their companies would enter into one of the most breathtaking mergers ever. Malone was chief executive officer of Tele-Communications Inc. (TCI), the nation's biggest cable-TV company. Smith was chairman of Bell Atlantic, the number-two regional phone company. The merger would create one of the most powerful communications and entertainment companies in the world—a company designed to crank the development of interactive, high-tech information highways into overdrive. By the time Bell Atlantic would absorb TCI and all its debt, the deal would be valued at $33 billion, more than any merger in history.

As the limo nosed through rush-hour traffic, Malone and Smith answered interviewers' questions on a cellular telephone. The two had been on the downhill side of a roller-coaster all day, and the normally hard-edged Malone and savvy Smith were not acting themselves. Not at all. In fact, a casual observer might have said they were acting, well—goofy. Like they were about to start playing with the electric windows and eating the peanuts set out on the wet bar.

"I got up this morning and looked in the mirror and I noticed my head was taking on a vague bell shape," Malone said into the phone, poking fun at Bell Atlantic's Bell System heritage. Smith chuckled. He'd heard Malone use the line a number of times that day. "We thought maybe we'd merge Liberty Media into Bell Atlantic and rename it Liberty Bell," Malone continued. Liberty was another Malone-controlled company that would be included in the Bell Atlantic–TCI merger. Smith was laughing. Malone paused. "Well, that's all my one-liners," he told the reporter on the phone.

The rest of the communications industry was not amused that day. While Malone and Smith were drunk with delight over their deal, executives at regional phone giants Pacific Telesis and BellSouth, at media conglomerate Cox Enterprises, and at upstart TV programmer QVC Network were meeting to discuss how to respond to the new Bell Atlantic–TCI monolith—a force that could change everything about their businesses.

Companies across the communications, information, and entertainment industries had been caught off guard. They were aware of the industry transformation that had begun early in 1993. They were buzzing about "technological convergence"—the supposed melding of televisions, telephones, computers, and content into one technology, one industry. Phone companies were beginning to buy cable-TV systems. Cable companies were testing ways to carry phone calls. Computer companies were looking at ways to put video on personal computer (PC) screens. Hollywood was thinking about selling movies over phone lines.

But the announcement by Malone and Smith took the convergence idea to a whole new level. In the nearly two-hour press conference that morning, Bell Atlantic and TCI had thrown down the gauntlet. They said they were going to create and deliver in a hurry the next generation of communications: interactive, 500-channel television, and two-way video communication. They were mapping the lanes of the information highway, then only beginning to be talked about. "Video games by wire, video shopping, video 800 numbers," Malone said at the podium. "Entertainment, TV on demand." They could do it by combining the strengths of a telephone company with the strengths of a cable company. Phone companies had sophisticated networks and lots of cash to spend. Cable companies had wired America with fat, coaxial cables that could carry all the wild new services that regular phone lines couldn't handle, and they had a working knowledge of the entertainment business.

"The capabilities do not exist in any cable company or any telephone company to do this," Smith said at the press conference. Malone chimed in, "The principal asset this company has is leadership. I think we will lead."

Over the next four months, the Bell Atlantic–TCI announcement drove other companies to action. Pacific Telesis, the phone company on the West Coast, said it would spend $16 billion to build a video information network in California. Nearly every other phone company unveiled some similarly costly, high-tech push. Viacom, a major cable-TV and entertainment company, and QVC fought each other to buy movie studio Paramount Communications—a battle that Viacom won. The companies said they wanted to make the entertainment needed to fill the 500 TV channels of the future. Regional phone company Southwestern Bell announced a $4 billion-plus alliance with the cable-TV arm of Cox Communications. The information highway was suddenly being spliced together at blinding speed.

The many moves were changing the communications industry so much and so rapidly that, by early 1994, Bell Atlantic and TCI started looking differently at each other. It was like an engagement that had gone on too long, giving the couple time to think of reasons not to get married.

On February 23, 1994, Malone and Smith met at the New York offices of Skadden, Arps, Slate, Meagher & Flom, Bell Atlantic's lawyers. They had talked on the phone the night before, right after the Federal Communications Commission (FCC) had ruled that rates paid by cable-TV customers would have to be cut 7 percent. The rate change could make TCI worth less to Bell Atlantic, and Malone wasn't willing to take less. Of that phone conversation, Smith said later, "I think we both knew."

What they knew was that the dramatic Bell Atlantic–TCI merger was dead. Malone and Smith talked it out at Skadden, Arps, but, from the moment they sat down, both had bluntly said that the deal wasn't going to work. Publicly, Malone and Smith blamed the FCC for a rate cut that made it impossible for them to agree on a final price. But the deal tanked because, in the four months since Malone and Smith had ridden through Manhattan telling jokes, the world had changed.

At their final meeting, neither Malone nor Smith talked about the real reasons behind their actions that day. Bell Atlantic had decided it no longer needed TCI's cable lines to be able to deliver services it wanted to offer nationwide—at least not at too high a price mixed with too much regulatory uncertainty. Smith would have loved to have closed the deal, but the realities of the technology projects that had popped up in just a few months' time allowed him to walk away.

On the other side, TCI, always a from-the-hip cowboy company, decided it could do things by itself if the alternative was to sell out for too little. Deep down, TCI felt it couldn't afford to be slowed by being permanently hitched to giant, bureaucratic Bell Atlantic—not if it wanted to continue to lead the way to a new era of home entertainment.

"One person said that I wanted to get the superhighway built and this was the world's best head-feint," Smith said, long after quieting the furor over the deal's collapse. Announcing the end of his talks with Malone had hit Smith hard personally. He had worked his butt off to sell the benefits of the deal to Bell Atlantic employees, Congress, and the general public. But he didn't backpedal for long. By late 1994, Smith was spinning his new strategy ever faster. Bell Atlantic was preparing an $11 billion digital information and entertainment system called BAnet and an interactive programming service dubbed Stargazer. He was putting together a video production alliance with two other Bells and Michael Ovitz, Hollywood's most powerful agent. BAnet would deliver Stargazer in Bell Atlantic's region, and, with other companies planning to wire the nation with new supernetworks, Bell Atlantic could roll out Stargazer nationwide by forming alliances and renting space on those supernetworks. No need to spend $33 billion on a cable-TV company anymore. After meeting with Wall Street analysts to talk about the collapsed TCI deal and Bell Atlantic's future, Smith said: "I'm energized again. The adrenalin is flowing. We have so many plans afoot we can hardly remember the TCI days."

At TCI, Malone also felt rejuvenated and more sure of his course. "We can do a lot of things now that we couldn't if we were going to be a part of Bell Atlantic," he said. For instance, he could dig deeper into a relationship with Microsoft, a company that wasn't thrilled about teaming with a big phone company. TCI and Microsoft quickly started spinning out ventures: an interactive personal computer channel for TV, and a high-tech television system test that may equal anything Bell Atlantic tries. Malone immediately began talking deals with many of the biggest names in the industry: Sumner Redstone at Viacom, William Esrey at Sprint, Wayne Huizenga at Blockbuster, Barry Diller at QVC. Malone was boarding a bullet train for the information highway. He wasn't going to get off until he had built an international communication and entertainment conglomerate, allied in all corners with immensely powerful partners.

By that time, one fact was clear: Bell Atlantic and TCI were heading down separate and possibly competing paths. The convergence concept had taken on a lot of new meanings. The pace and sweep of change had gone nuclear, and they haven't yet let up.

Information highways, 500-channel TVs, multimedia, communications megamergers such as Viacom's $9.5 billion deal to buy Paramount Communications—those are the hottest topics in business.

Nothing else is more vibrant, more dramatic, or more perilous. Whole industries are betting their futures on this new wave. Says Tom Peters, author of *In Search of Excellence* (Harper & Row, 1982): "You'd have to be an idiot not to believe that we're at the very beginning of something really big."

It's all part of a communications revolution. Companies and technologies are coming together to form a new industry that throws its arms around everything from Discovery Channel documentaries to palm-size personal computers, creating new ways to link people to information and entertainment.

The industry doesn't even have a name yet. The Wall Street firm of Goldman, Sachs has gamely tried out "communacopia"—a label that sounds more like a sexually transmitted disease than a high-tech industry. For better or worse, around *USA Today* we started calling the industry and the concept "megamedia." It's easier to say than "information superhighway," and it means something broader—content and machines as well as wires. In this book, I call this new industry/business/revolution "megamedia."

The events of this revolution are happening in a thunderclap. In a little more than two years—late 1992 to early 1995—the perception of communications and all the companies that touch it changed completely. Those two-plus years marked a turbulent break from the past. Companies altered their strategies and set off in new directions. New leaders took over and visibly led the charge. No set of companies ever changed so much, so fast, and the changes haven't ended. Big mergers, better technology, and new services will light up megamedia before this book can even be reviewed.

At the start of 1993, telephone companies were boring voice-communications utilities that couldn't come up with anything more exciting than "call-waiting." Within a year, they had started efforts to become futuristic video and information companies. TV shopping went from a low-brow, bowling-crowd business to a high-profile media star. A handful of computer companies that once focused on business customers moved toward becoming makers of Jetsons-like consumer television sets.

Through 1994, the revolution spread to more industries. Newspaper companies started thinking about how they might become information highway software creators. Catalog retailers ventured into electronic shopping. Wireless phone companies started realizing they could reach a mass market and push their once-expensive wireless phone service into average consumers' homes, maybe replacing traditional telephones.

"People have realized that things that tech guys like me have been talking about for a long time are actually coming true," says Nathan Myhrvold, head of research and development for software giant Microsoft. "It's causing something of a stampede to prepare for that." In 1990, Myhrvold started nudging his company to develop software for interactive TV. Now, Microsoft has several alliances with TCI and is bringing TV products to market.

Technology is driving the revolution. Two important developments have made all the difference in the world. They go by the names of "digital technology" and "broadband networks."

In digital technology, devices simply read information as a series of 1s and 0s, the way computers do. The old way to create and store information is called analog, which is usually the method in use when a mechanical device, like a phonograph needle, reads a continuously varying wave on a vinyl disk. The new way can be found in the nation's 40 million personal computers and in the audio compact disk (CD) players now found in half of all U.S. homes. The growing popularity of such machines has helped push companies to create or convert games, books, magazines, music, and other products into digital form. Any kind of information can now be stored digitally: movies, TV shows, phone messages, school homework assignments. The key is that when something is digital, it can be rearranged, cut apart, and mixed with anything else that's digital. A mail-order retailer can create a digital catalog that can be called up on a home computer. A shopper can look through photo layouts like those in the printed version; or ask the digital catalog to display only the brown pants that are available, or to transmit a video of a model wearing a particular outfit or set of jewelry; or request more printed information about the fabric, fit, or price. A digital catalog can be that flexible.

Ed McCracken, chief executive of Silicon Graphics Inc., tells a story of how flexible digital information can be. His company makes some of the hottest products in megamedia: computers and software that can store and manipulate three-dimensional graphics or video at blinding speed. McCracken didn't even know that Silicon Graphics equipment was used to help make the Clint Eastwood movie *In the Line of Fire.* Later, he found out that the producers had filmed Bill Clinton's campaign in action in 1992, then fed the images into Silicon Graphics machines to digitize them. The producers removed President and Mrs. Clinton and put the actors from the movie into the scenes. (Watch the movie. You won't be able to tell that the images were ever altered.)

Another important feature of digital information is that it can be compressed—sort of freeze-dried, actually—and sent across lines or over radio waves in a minimalist form. That's what's opening up developments such as 500-channel cable-TV systems. Approximately 10 digitally compressed TV channels can fit in the space of one normal TV channel. GM Hughes Electronics, for instance, is now selling a 150-channel satellite TV service called DirecTv. The service uses two $200 million satellites to transmit compressed TV channels to viewers—eight channels in the space of one uncompressed channel. Were it not for digital compression, Hughes would have had to launch 16 satellites to start DirecTv—an impossibly huge investment. "Compression made this a business," says DirecTv President Eddy Hartenstein.

Digital information becomes especially powerful when married to the other key development: the spread of high-tech broadband networks.

Those two little telephone lines coming into your desk phone are considered "narrow band." They can't even carry enough information to make your voice sound like it sounds in person. Your phone lines can carry one channel of medium-quality video if the signals are doctored by computers—hardly enough to spark a communications revolution.

But over the past decade, cable-TV companies have snaked their coaxial cables into 60 percent of U.S. homes and businesses. Long-distance phone companies (AT&T, MCI, and Sprint) have strung fiber-optic lines across the nation. Both coaxial cable and fiber-optic lines are considered broadband—they can carry hundreds, or even thousands, of interactive video channels, plus phone calls and computer data, at very high speeds. One example: A single hair-thin fiber-optic line can transmit 45 copies of *King Lear* per second versus just a few pages per second over old phone lines.

Local phone companies are spending about $100 billion to build networks that combine fiber-optics and coaxial cable and connect to every home or building. Cable companies are upgrading their networks, too. By 2010, most U.S. homes and businesses are expected to be hooked to broadband networks.

When the new broadband networks carry digital information, just about anything becomes possible. "The technology is taking down any barrier between fulfillment and imagination," says TCI's Malone. "There's hardly anything you could conceive of today in the information and entertainment field that you can't try. It's that kind of world."

What's possible? Movies on demand, interactive TV, video phone calls, long-distance schooling—new technology can do any of these today, although some capabilities are still mainly in labs or aren't quite down to a cost-effective price. Over the next few years, the technology will be tested, poked, and prodded by companies and customers. They will try to find the answer to the only question that could keep some of the technology from success: What will people really buy when they have access to all this stuff?

One other piece of the megamedia puzzle is the concept called convergence. It doesn't necessarily mean that computers, phones, and televisions become one machine doing everything, but it does mean that those technologies cross-pollinate to become something better.

An example of how convergence is supposed to work is Time Warner's Full Service Network project, referred to in-house as FSN. At the end of 1994, Time Warner's cable and entertainment division, which is 25.5 percent owned by phone company US West, turned on the high-profile test project in Orlando, Florida. It is a never-before-seen melding of parts. A computer system made by Silicon Graphics connects to a digital, multimedia switch built by AT&T—only the second switch of its kind ever built by the company. The switch sends a signal down fiber-optic lines and coaxial cable into a house, where a computerlike box (made by Scientific-Atlanta) plugs into an ordinary TV set. In some cases, on top of the box is a wireless phone from US West. The whole system is being set up and managed by the computer consulting arm of Arthur Andersen.

An FSN customer can turn on the TV and see a three-dimensional menu that looks like boxes on a carousel: one box is labeled "movies," another is labeled "shopping," and so on. Through the TV, the customer can watch regular broadcast channels or new interactive channels, or order a show or movie, which would appear immediately and cost a little extra. Or, the customer might play a video game against another Time Warner customer across town. Or, make a video phone call. Or, eventually, pick up the wireless phone, take it into the car, and use it while on the road. Almost all of those services and content were once separate. In Orlando, they're part of a whole.

"This is obviously not just an add-on to the cable company," says Tom Morrow, who joined Time Warner from US West to run a newly created unit called Time Warner Communications. "If you put a wireless phone on the set-top box and use the TV to look up phone numbers or do the video portion of phone calls, it's tough to say one thing is the phone business and another is the video business. Everything comes together in one set of services."

FSN and just about every one of the many projects like it need convergence to work because they meld pieces of several industries: cable TV, computer hardware, computer software, telephone, cellular, and retail marketing. No one company anywhere in the world knows how to do all those things. And that's what's driving the grand rush to form alliances, make investments, and merge.

Time Warner needs US West and other partners. Bell Atlantic lost TCI but vows to secure the knowledge and technology of TV and entertainment companies. AT&T has spun a dizzying web of alliances, from investing in software company General Magic to working on a test project similar to FSN in Castro Valley, California. Viacom bought Paramount and Blockbuster, with phone company NYNEX as an investor in the jelling monolith.

"In our wildest imagination, we can't sit here and think of all the possible combinations," says Jeffrey Kagan, president of a Marietta, Georgia, firm that has tracked the communications revolution. The mergers are not all going to work. Some will fall apart—several have already done so. Some will look silly in hindsight. "Some of these investments are going to turn out to be the eight-tracks of the '90s," Kagan says, conjuring up an image of the dead-end 1970s audio technology.

With its mergers and technology, the birth of megamedia is a big event. "It will change the world forever," says John Sculley, the former chairman of Apple Computer, who has had his share of highs and lows on the information superhighway. He and many others believe that megamedia, like other revolutionary technology, will work its way into the fabric of society. Think of the way cars changed everything from the way teenagers date to where people live. Or how the lightbulb extended work and play into the night, affecting everyone. That will be the scale of megamedia's impact. If you believe the grand visions of Sculley and others, video phones and computer communications could let workers live anywhere and still be nearly as effective as if they worked person-to-person in an office. Students in rural towns could do research at Harvard via desktop computers and fiber-optic lines. Businesspeople would be able to get any information—memos, up-to-the-second sales numbers, background on competitors, scientific studies—at any time, using wireless networks and computers the size of a Cracker Jack box. Workers and companies would become more productive and efficient than anyone can now imagine.

More rooted in today's reality, businesses in far-ranging industries are already trying out the early pieces of megamedia.

The "Sally Jesse Raphael" TV talk show first used video phone calls in mid-1993 as an inexpensive way to reunite the cast of "The Waltons" TV series for one program. In many ways, the two-way video was much more interactive than the usual one-way satellite video often seen on shows such as "Nightline." "It has such incredible possibilities," says Rose Mary Henri, executive producer of the "Sally" show. "It's definitely the wave of the future."

Chrysler is experimenting with selling cars via interactive advertising on television. The World Health Organization is looking into ways to use megamedia to monitor and perhaps arrest contagious diseases worldwide. Ice cream maker Ben & Jerry's has put desktop videoconferencing equipment in offices in its two Vermont plants to cut down on travel time between them. No industry can ignore what's happening.

Neither can entrepreneurs. No matter how megamedia emerges, opportunities will explode in communications, entertainment, and information over the next decade. Think about the early days of television, when two networks broadcast a few hours a day and the programs mostly mimicked those carried on the previous technology, radio. That's where the new megamedia technology is today—at the start of a business and cultural rocket ride. Nobody knows where megamedia is really going, any more than someone could have predicted Sega video games or MTV back when Milton Berle ruled the airwaves.

What are the very best things going to be? "We don't know what they are because somebody is going to invent them," says Joe Collins, president of Time Warner's cable-TV division, as he looks out at the future. Collins has learned to be open-minded. He recalls, in the early days of cable TV, telling Ted Turner that the idea for his CNN 24-hour-a-day news network was "a bad idea."

A lot is going on at once, which is why megamedia is tough to get a grip on. Features of megamedia's technology and services can only be imagined because they haven't yet left the lab and they've never before been known in human experience. The deals and maneuvers are tough to keep up with. Any given day can bring five or six megamedia announcements from major companies such as Microsoft, TCI, and AT&T. Clipping every headline would cramp your scissors hand.

A lot of companies and leaders ping-ponged through 1993–1994 and came out at this end with a vision embedded and a plan of action that had begun to move forward. One way to get ahead of all the coming megamedia events is to understand what drives those events. Look closely at the strategies of important companies, their views of the world, and the competitive pressures that are chasing them into new fields. Pick out leaders to watch: the more complicated, competitive, and messy the revolution gets, the more companies, employees, financiers, and the general public will rely on leaders who can articulate clear visions and rally people around them.

That's what this book is about—the forces, the strategies, and the leaders driving megamedia forward.

One important force shaping megamedia is the harsh lesson that companies learned about the speed of change over the past two years. To understand how various companies are approaching megamedia now, you have to understand the whipsaw events of 1993–1995 and how they shaped the way a generation of executives thinks about the future. Companies that got sucked into the megamedia vortex went through a period of time that rocked established ways of doing business. They cut themselves a modern slice of corporate hell.

That hell really started with John Sculley.

The chairman of Apple Computer stabbed at the arugula, shiitake mushrooms, and unrecognizable leaves on his salad plate in the subdued, swanky dining room of the St. Regis Hotel in New York. This was November 1992. Sculley barely paused to eat, between the words and sentences and insights that just kept coming to him. He spilled forth a whole vision of the world like an intense but carefully calibrated preacher. Sculley was talking about technological convergence. He described how the computer, telephone, wireless services, television, information, and entertainment industries were all flowing together—the very concept behind megamedia. But nobody else of Sculley's stature was talking about it, at least not so publicly and not with such conviction.

"It's tremendously exciting and it's not an evolution. It really is a revolution," Sculley said, ignoring the waiter softly laying a plate of salmon and exotic vegetables on the white tablecloth. "It's starting already. It's not science fiction." This would be, Sculley insisted, the passage from the Industrial Age to the Information Age—from the age of the physical to the age of the mental.

In that session and in many others around that time, Sculley laid out one idea that would become an important rallying point for the first blast of megamedia activity. He did a little arithmetic and figured that, by 2001, this revolution would create a worldwide telecommunications industry with revenue of $1.2 trillion, a worldwide computer and consumer electronics industry bringing in $1 trillion, and an information and entertainment content industry adding another $1.3 trillion. The total would add up to a global megamedia industry in 2001 of $3.5 trillion, about the size of Japan's entire economy in 1993. The figure stuck in the public's mind. A $3.5 trillion industry. *Wow!*

Sculley had reason to push his vision. Earlier in the year, he had "unveiled" Apple's Newton, a handheld combination of a computer, a telephone, and a paper-and-pen notebook. The trouble was, Newton wasn't even close to becoming a real product, and Sculley was taking heat for announcing what the computer industry snidely refers to as vaporware. He was fighting battles inside his company to get Newton developed and move Apple toward products such as computerized boxes that would plug into TV sets and handle interactive entertainment. Sculley had to convince Apple's employees and shareholders and just about everyone else that he was pushing the company in the right direction, getting ahead of a high-octane trend.

Over lunch that fall, Sculley was already talking about all content becoming digital. He talked about TV technology: "It will open up 600 additional channels because of compression." He described interactive shopping as "an entirely new way of commerce." He went on about wireless phones and pocket computers and amazingly realistic, visual ways of communicating, all letting people do their work from anywhere in the world. "It will probably have as much impact in terms of where people live in the 1990s and early 21st century as we saw when the interstate highway system came in during the 1960s," Sculley predicted. And all of this, Sculley insisted, was about to happen in a heartbeat.

Most of Sculley's peers didn't believe him. Sculley wasn't saying anything technologically improbable; everybody in the communications business knew that digital was the way to go in the future. Regional phone companies were laying some fiber-optic lines, which could carry high-speed digital transmissions. Barry Diller was about to take charge of QVC Network with a dream of creating digital, interactive TV services. Consortia of huge companies such as AT&T and NBC-TV were working on digital high-definition television, supposedly the TV set of the next millenium. Nathan Myhrvold, Microsoft's brilliant research chief, had written a legendary 31-page memo to Microsoft chairman Bill Gates saying the computer software company needed to get into TV. Goldman, Sachs's widely circulated "Communacopia" report had laid out the convergence concept for the financial community in July 1992.

But virtually none of Sculley's peers thought the technology or convergence would begin happening as quickly as Sculley was predicting. Not even close. US West, for one, looks back and admits that it thought of itself as a phone company at the time—an advanced, technology-oriented phone company maybe, but still a phone company. It wasn't contemplating anything like its $2.5 billion investment in Time Warner Entertainment, or a trial of interactive TV in Omaha, Nebraska, or a strategic push to become something new: a digital information company. Other phone and media company executives certainly weren't counting on overhauling their strategic plans within a year, and then overhauling them again months later. They were all talking evolution, not revolution. Sculley stood out there pretty much alone, the proverbial pioneer getting arrows in the back. But his beliefs thrust Sculley in front of industry audiences and eventually onto TV talk shows and into a role as the new Clinton Administration's high-tech sidekick. He sat next to Hillary Rodham Clinton while President Clinton gave his first speech to Congress.

Sculley's zeal would come at a price. He lost sight of Apple's day-to-day operations. The company's earnings and stock prices dove. After a decade of running Apple, Sculley wound up stepping down from his job as chairman in 1993. He then blindly took the chairman job at a convergence-oriented company called Spectrum, but quit four months later, claiming that Spectrum had allegedly misled him about the company's finances and prospects. Still, Sculley's words in late 1992 were a Paul Revere ride through the industry, sounding a warning that too few executives thought was urgent.

One exception was John Malone, the chief executive of TCI, who had long thought of himself as a high-tech big-thinker. Unlike Sculley, Malone preferred to do his big-thinking in obscurity. Malone is probably one of America's best-known executives today, but in the fall of 1992, most people had no idea who he was. That's the way Malone liked it.

While Sculley was talking, Malone was doing. If Sculley was the Paul Revere of the communications revolution, Malone was the guy who picked up a rifle and fired the first shot at Lexington and Concord. That shot was the famous announcement of 500-channel TV.

Malone picked the number 500 out of the air. On December 2, 1992, TCI said it was going to build digital compression technology into its cable operations, which served about 10 million TCI customers and another 4 million customers of related cable-TV companies, all spread across the United States. The technology would squeeze 10 channels' worth of video into the space normally taken up by one channel on a coaxial cable. A cable system built to handle 30 channels could carry 300; 50 channels, 500; 120 channels, 1,200. Malone happened to choose 500 when making the announcement. Whatever the exact number, that kind of capacity would be enough to broadcast a wide range of pay-per-view movies and top TV shows every night. The capacity would also make it economical to broadcast special niche channels, such as programming from Japan or Mexico, or to carry 25 college football games on Saturdays in the fall.

The system, Malone said, would be ready in January 1994—sooner than most industry watchers expected. And Malone was already looking past that launch date. "This is not the true multimedia future model," he said from his office the day of the 500-channel announcement. "It's a step in getting the public more into using interactive television, using a cursor on a TV screen and experiencing some of these services. I guess within a couple of years these boxes [the digital converter boxes that would plug into every TV set on TCI's new system] will evolve to be very smart and capable of doing a lot more things."

Sounding humbler than he really is, Malone suggested: "I think this will be a signal to the industry."

It was a signal, all right. For starters, the public sunk its teeth into the idea of 500 TV channels and wouldn't let go. It was a reaction no one expected, not even TCI. Malone had never said there'd be 500 versions of MTV, C-SPAN, and micro-niche channels like, say, The Cooking with Spam Channel. He was talking about 500 channels' worth of capacity, most of it carrying pay-per-view movies and sports. In the days following the announcement, network news anchors reported on 500-channel TV, comedy monologue writers made fun of it, editorial writers called for it to be used for education. The idea of 500 discrete channels of television—and a certain amount of loathing toward it—stuck to the public consciousness like an emphatic Post-It Note. If nothing else, the TCI digital compression announcement paved the way for general acceptance and understanding of a coming megamedia world.

It also caught the eye of programmers. Movie makers, infomercial companies, computer game makers, and on-line computer services—all started to realize that a 500-channel TV meant all kinds of new outlets for entertainment, information, and advertising. As the meaning of the 500-channel announcement sank in, TCI's public relations director, Lela Cocoras, fielded hundreds of phone calls from major programming companies and small-time entrepreneurs, including one person who wanted to start an all-Irish channel. The awakening interest was important. At that point, programmers were probably furthest behind in awareness of megamedia, and that was dangerous. Consumers buy programming, not technology. They sign up for a service because of the movies or ball games or shows it will bring them. All the 500-channel systems in the world wouldn't matter a bit if they couldn't be filled with enough high-quality programming.

If programmers didn't get the message when TCI announced 500 channels, they got another elbow in the ribs eight days later. Barry Diller is one of the smartest television and movie executives in history. He was head of ABC's prime-time schedule in the early 1970s and invented the Movie of the Week there. He ran Paramount Pictures for 10 years, then took charge of Fox, where he launched the Fox television network and put "The Simpsons" on the air. He left Fox in February 1992, saying he wanted to be an entrepreneur. On December 10 of that year, he announced he was putting up $25 million to buy into home-shopping channel QVC, and was becoming its chairman.

Reaction, especially in Hollywood, was nothing short of shock. Diller was expected to do something huge, like buy the NBC-TV network. QVC seemed so small-time, so lower-class. In the February 22, 1993, issue of *The New Yorker,* Ken Auletta wrote about the intimate details of Diller's decision to take on QVC and how it all traced back to Diller's purchase of an Apple PowerBook laptop computer. The PowerBook turned Diller on to the possibilities of technology, and Malone and Comcast's Brian Roberts convinced Diller that technology was taking cable TV to unfathomable new heights. QVC, at the very least, was going to be Diller's wormhole into that universe.

Hollywood went nuts. It had a long, open wound from ignoring video game technology in the 1980s. The most imaginative programmers in the world had missed out on what is now a $6 billion-a-year industry. They weren't going to miss another technological wave. Wild tales, probably apocryphal, popped up about runs on PowerBooks at Hollywood computer stores. Studio chiefs started having lunch with people like Gates and Sculley. The industry buzzed with the word "interactive," even if the studio people didn't know what it meant. Within months, many entertainment companies had formed some sort of interactive TV department. Viacom, during its fight to buy Paramount Communications, named Thomas Dooley to the new title of "president, interactive television." At The Walt Disney Company, the late Frank Wells, then president, and since-departed Disney Studio chairman Jeffrey Katzenberg formed a task force to study interactive ventures. Hollywood and others in the content business were well into their first information superhighway frenzy.

In other parts of the country, a different kind of high-powered group was feeling uneasy watching cable TV grab headlines. They were the suit-and-tie guys running the staid regional telephone companies—seven giant regulated utilities that were carved from the Bell System when it was broken up in 1984.

Phone company executives were feeling inferior as megamedia unfurled in early 1993. A lot of analysts and insiders were starting to believe that phone companies and cable companies were heading for war. Phone companies were going to get into the TV or video business, and cable companies were going to get into the phone or point-to-point communications business. The way it looked, two sets of wires were going to crisscross every city and town—one from a cable company and another from a phone company. The wires were going to compete head-to-head for every kind of communication and entertainment service, and the phone companies were going to lose.

Why? The phone companies were stuck—still are stuck—with billions of dollars' worth of skinny little "twisted-pair" phone lines going into 96 percent of U.S. homes and offices. The lines could barely carry one high-quality video channel, much less 500. It would be dangerously expensive to replace them, even though phone companies had lots of money. In 1992, each of the seven regional phone companies had $4 billion to $6 billion in cash flow, which is a measure of how much money a company has available to spend in a year. Phone companies also had great technology for switching signals from one customer to another. Still, the telephone companies were gagging on their twisted pairs.

By contrast, cable companies had coaxial cable running into 60 percent of U.S. homes and businesses, and that cable could easily transmit hundreds of channels of video and handle telephone-type voice communications. Cable companies had the high-capacity lines and a knowledge of entertainment programming. All they needed were the switches and the money to spend on new technology, and neither was expected to be that hard for cable companies to get. When they got those things, analysts figured, cable companies could eat the phone companies' lunch.

The two sides circled each other, not sure what to do and not sure there was a need to do anything. Their caution was shattered on February 10, 1993, when Gus Hauser agreed to sell his two cable systems in suburban Washington, DC, to phone company Southwestern Bell for $650 million. It was the first cable TV–phone company deal ever.

"We're doing something that has no antecedence in American business," Hauser said, referring not only to his deal but to a coming "confluence of industries" that he foresaw.

For cable and phone companies, Hauser's folding into Southwestern Bell was like a house from Kansas landing in Oz. In the flash of a single tornado, the landscape had changed. Many executives in both industries saw the beauty of combining rather than battling. Maybe more importantly, they got the idea that it was socially acceptable to merge. Bankers would finance it. Investors and employees would welcome it. Federal, state, and local politicians would, it seemed at the time, bless it. With that, phone company executives leapt aboard corporate jets and started scouring the cable industry for partners.

Some cable and phone executives had talked about deals before Hauser sold out, said Robert Morris of Goldman, Sachs, one of the most highly regarded telecommunications analysts on Wall

Street. After Hauser's deal, "Everybody was talking to everybody else." For example, Morris had heard that Time Warner Cable was jumping into talks with US West, AT&T, and "everyone else, too." Other analysts said Southwestern Bell had already talked to Cox Communications about a deal. Investors started betting that phone companies would pay premiums to buy cable companies. Within a month of the Southwestern Bell–Hauser deal, the price of nearly every cable company's stock hit a 52-week high.

Back to John Sculley. By that time, his message was hitting home. He was turning into the high priest of the communications revolution. He was helping shuttle a new term into public life: the information superhighway. He was calling on the Clinton Administration to set a farsighted goal for the superhighway's construction in the way President Kennedy had challenged the country to put a man on the moon. That goal may not have been realistic, but it got Sculley on even more talk shows.

The publicity fed the information superhighway concept into the mainstream. Behind the scenes, a lot of megemedia executives were punching the panic button.

So much was starting to happen. Entrepreneurial companies such as Interactive Network and TV Answer, now called EON, were getting attention for their embryonic interactive television systems, even though they were little more than expensive toys that let viewers play along with game shows or sporting events. Stock prices of any company that vaguely smacked of the information superhighway caught fire. The favorite interactive TV stock play at the time, QVC, went on a tear, rocketing from $37 a share on January 14, 1993, to $57½ on March 9. AT&T, which could already boast that its long-distance network was 95 percent fiber-optic, was readying a whole advertising campaign built around information superhighway concepts. One powerful promise was that working mothers traveling on business could tuck their babies into bed from a video telephone booth in a city thousands of miles away.

Politicians jumped in. Soon after the new Congress convened in January 1993, Representative Ed Markey, a Massachusetts Democrat who chaired the House subcommittee overseeing communications, called a high-powered hearing. Asked to testify were John

Sculley; Mitch Kapor, founder and former chairman of software company Lotus; and Craig Fields, former head of high-tech research for the Pentagon. For the first time, Congress looked seriously at what its role should be as the information superhighway developed. Sculley, Kapor, and Fields all told the subcommittee members that the superhighway was coming fast and would be the hottest issue of the next four years. "The technological pieces are in place," Kapor said to the sometimes bewildered-looking legislators perched on the huge mahogany dais in the hearing room. "What we need is political leadership."

There wasn't any. Industries and technologies were converging despite 50-year-old legislation and 10-year-old telephone industry court rulings designed to keep them apart. Market forces were ripping past political forces. Southwestern Bell had cut the deal for Hauser knowing that nothing like it had ever been approved by all the various regulatory bodies. The company pushed ahead, believing that it could convince regulators that the benefits of the merger should carry the day. That set the tone for the political backdrop through much of 1993. Megamedia companies decided to forge ahead while the politicians were still dazed. Companies were stirred to act even more quickly, to do their deals while they knew the rules.

The spring of 1993 belonged to cable companies. John Malone flashed to the forefront as the newest information superhighway celebrity. He quickly became known as a dark genius who had both breathtaking vision and the tough backroom power to make it happen. On April 12, Malone's TCI announced plans to spend $1.9 billion over four years to build a fiber-optic-based network in 37 states. The network would let about 9 million TCI customers get thousands of channels packed with pay-per-view movies and sports, home shopping malls, pay-per-use video games, and on-demand weather reports. It could also connect computers, letting them share information hundreds of times faster than when hooked over regular phone lines. TCI was not the first company to unveil big spending on fiber-optics, but TCI's plan was the biggest, the most aggressive, and the easiest to comprehend in terms of the services it would provide.

Malone, 500 channels, computers, information superhighways—the revolution was everywhere. *Time* magazine ran a cover story on it. On Sunday, May 16, 1993, both *The New York Times Magazine* and *Los Angeles Times Magazine* ran information highway cover stories. The L.A. *Times,* in the heart of the entertainment industry, focused on Malone and the television. New York's *Times,* in the home of the financial industry, centered its story on the phone companies—ultimately, the companies with the money to make it happen.

As if on cue, that very next Monday, phone company US West said it would pay $2.5 billion to buy 25.5 percent of Time Warner Entertainment. The deal included a 50–50 partnership in Time Warner's cable operation, which was second only to TCI's, and smaller stakes in the Warner Bros. studio and the Time Warner-owned movie channel, Home Box Office (HBO). US West was going to help Time Warner build the telephone portion of a fiber-optic test system to be set up in Orlando, Florida.

The deal was another turn of the ratchet—first Hauser at $650 million, then TCI's project at $2 billion, then US West–Time Warner at $2.5 billion. It ripped open a new fear among phone company executives. The notion of Southwestern Bell buying Hauser, a relatively small cable operator, was interesting. US West's locking up giant Time Warner Cable—that was something to worry about. There were only a handful of huge, well-managed, high-quality cable companies: TCI, Time Warner, Comcast, Cablevision, Cox. What if they all started pairing off with phone companies? What if you were a phone company executive who waited too long and the high-quality partners were all scooped up? How could you explain that to the board or to investors? In the spring of 1993, linking with a cable company seemed the best way for a phone company to break into the broadband, video world of the future. Three phone–cable partnerships were building cable systems in the United Kingdom and proving that the two kinds of companies could work together and learn from each other.

It also seemed certain that competing phone companies from other regions were going to buy cable operations in another regional Bell's backyard, just as US West had bought cable systems in NYNEX's territory. The only way to defend against that kind of encroachment would be to do the same thing: buy a cable operation in a competing phone company's territory.

Those were the kinds of thoughts humming through Bell Atlantic chairman Ray Smith's head as he watched the US West–Time Warner deal go down. He had met Malone a couple of years before, and Bell Atlantic and TCI were partners in a tiny venture in New Zealand. They wouldn't formally meet to talk about a deal until June 16, 1993, but Smith was already sure he and other phone companies needed cable partners, fast. "It became apparent to me that no telephone company and no cable company and no media company alone could experience the growth in media services and new markets that would be built across the country," Smith said. "We had to get a partner to fill in our core competencies."

Smith wanted TCI and he wanted Malone's genius—and he didn't want another phone company to get them. Within days after their first meeting, Smith sent Malone a four-page letter proposing to make a US West-like investment in TCI, or perhaps to merge the entire company into Bell Atlantic.

Cable executives were getting just as antsy to cut such deals. They seemed to be in the driver's seat; phone companies were scrambling to team with them, and cable values were soaring. But Malone and a few others started to worry that the triumph of cable would be temporary, for two reasons: politics and money. First, as debate slowly heated up in Washington, word was that the Clinton Administration was likely to regulate cable more harshly while easing up on phone companies—as it turned out, a correct prediction. Second, the dollar figures for building or buying the new technology were getting astronomical. Maybe TCI could afford to spend $2 billion, but few other cable companies could. Phone companies, though, could afford to spend amazing amounts of money. If released from restrictions, they had the capital to build systems that could blow a good many cable operators right out of the business. If teamed with a cable company, a phone company could become a sugar daddy that would fund all the wildest of TV dreams. Well before ever meeting with Smith, Malone told *The New Yorker* magazine, "I started telling [TCI Chairman] Bob Magness and the board that I felt we had to do a strategic deal with a phone company or we were going to have serious problems long-term."

Maneuvers along the telephone–cable-TV axis were by no means the only action in megamedia. As spring moved into summer, convergence and the information superhighway got hot everywhere.

At Symphony Hall in Boston, amid the classical nude statues that line the ornate chamber, Apple finally introduced its real, live, working Newton MessagePad—John Sculley's dream machine. Now that it was a real product, the Newton turned out to be the most advanced of a new group of devices called personal digital assistants, or PDAs. Among several others coming out around the same time were AT&T's EO Personal Communicator, and the Zoomer, jointly developed by Tandy and Casio. The PDAs were all a little different, but each was an attempt to put into the purchaser's pocket a computer that was as easy to use as an Etch-a-Sketch.

The first Newton was balky, had limited uses, and, at $699, cost too much. But it was, as only Sculley could say, a "product vision"—something radically new. Newton was convergence in the flesh. A computer by nature, it was designed to communicate via phone lines or cellular telephone networks—converging the phone and computer. Its pen-based screen and handwriting-recognition software was a convergence of computer and paper notebook. Newton wasn't going to burn up the global marketplace, but it certainly nudged it in new directions.

On other fronts that summer, Barry Diller's QVC had announced it would buy its one and only TV shopping competitor, Home Shopping Network (HSN), for $1.2 billion in stock. The deal boosted the profile of TV shopping. Most of the cable and phone companies had envisioned shopping as a mainstay of any new kind of interactive broadband system. Such a system should let customers shop via television as easily as they might shop using printed catalogs. Retailers and catalogers were starting to believe that, too.

QVC's bid for HSN wasn't just about shopping. It was a trumpet signal that Diller was definitely in the deal game. That was significant. Exactly two months later, Paramount and Viacom would announce that they had agreed to merge in a deal worth $8.1 billion.

Paramount, Diller's one-time employer, rushed into Viacom's arms in part because it was afraid of a raid by Diller and his backer, Malone.

Wireless communication started getting interesting around the same time. London-based British Telecom said it would buy a 20 percent stake in Washington, DC-based MCI Communications for $4.3 billion. The money would back MCI's plans to venture into wireless communication and cut other megamedia-related deals. Two weeks later, on August 17, AT&T announced that it would buy McCaw Cellular for $12.6 billion—a merger of the largest U.S. long-distance company and the largest wireless phone network. AT&T said the deal would move the company a giant step toward its goal of providing "anywhere, anytime" communication, whether by phone, computer, or Newton-like devices.

Wham! *Wham!* WHAM! The endless series of deals hit communication and entertainment executives relentlessly. It quickly started to seem that anyone who wasn't in on a multibillion-dollar deal was a wallflower, a dolt, a has-been. Some companies specifically decided *not* to join the dealmaking craze, and their images suffered in the media and on Wall Street. Chicago-based phone company Ameritech was one of those. "We think the future is going to unfold rather gradually," said Ameritech's chairman at the time, Bill Weiss. "We've paid a lot of attention to our basic business and we think that will serve us awfully well in the future." Whether a sound judgment or not, Ameritech got hammered for taking that stance during dealmania.

The momentum that cable companies had going into the summer of 1993 started losing speed on August 24. On that day, a U.S. District Court in Alexandria, Virginia, found in favor of plaintiff Bell Atlantic and overturned a key restriction in the Cable Act of 1984. That restriction had prevented phone companies from owning and providing video programming over their own networks. Basically, Bell Atlantic won the right to become a cable-TV company and compete with cable companies in its service area.

Before the ruling, a phone company was certainly free to build, in its region, a high-tech, fiber-optic network capable of carrying hundreds of video channels. But the economics would have stunk.

Under the Cable Act, only other kinds of companies, not the local phone company, could legally sell programming over a phone-company-built network. As an example, think of on-line computer services such as CompuServe. The phone company provides the line to connect to CompuServe, and CompuServe provides the electronic mail, forums, information services, and so on. The phone company doesn't make much money on that—it gets only the cost of a phone call. CompuServe makes the real money. The same would be true with video services traveling over phone company fiber-optic lines. Under Cable Act rules, the phone company could only carry some other programmer's video service and only make money on the transmission. In a model like that, phone companies don't have much incentive to spend the billions such high-tech networks cost. Phone companies would never make enough money as only carriers of other services.

The *Bell Atlantic* decision changed all that. If Bell Atlantic could be a programmer—and it had already been working on Stargazer to do just that—it could justify building a fiber-optic network. By selling Stargazer programming on the network, in competition with cable TV, Bell Atlantic could theoretically make big bucks. Judge T.S. Ellis ruled that Bell Atlantic was free to build a fiber-optic system, decide on the channels it will carry, create its own channels or programs, package the offerings, price them, and sell them. Right after the ruling, Bell Atlantic said it would construct such a system in Alexandria, wiring about 60,000 homes. Within two months, the company announced plans to spend $15 billion building systems of the same type throughout its service area.

The ruling applied only to Bell Atlantic. Every other regional phone company—the only companies held back by the Cable Act restrictions—soon filed similar suits in their own territories. "The walls are coming down and here's one of the bugles being blown," said Gus Hauser.

Once again, communications strategy was being flung in a new direction. Regional phone companies suddenly had a choice of paths to the video future. They could buy or join with cable companies to become programmers outside their territories—for most of 1993, that had been the way to go for ambitious phone companies—or they could decide to build multibillion-dollar systems in their own regions and try to become dominant video carriers and programmers on their home turf.

At meetings and high-level strategy sessions, Chicago-based Ameritech and San Francisco-based Pacific Telesis moved toward the stay-at-home strategy. US West in Denver and Southwestern Bell in San Antonio had already committed to buying into cable systems and expanding outward. NYNEX, based in White Plains, New York, and Atlanta's BellSouth moved slowly, seeming to opt for incremental change.

At Bell Atlantic's Philadelphia headquarters, Ray Smith had the planets lined up just right to explode in all directions at once. The plan was to build aggressively at home while buying cable systems as a way of spreading out nationally.

Smith pursued TCI like a blitzing linebacker homing in on a quarterback. He assigned a fact-finding team to spend two months sifting through every detail of TCI, from community cable licenses to bottom-line finances. "We had virtually all the information on every aspect of the company," Smith recalls. "They opened their arms to us. Probably in this process there were thousands of man-hours."

The team worked up what it thought were fair prices for every piece of TCI and Liberty Media, which was to be included in the deal. When the project got down to, as Smith puts it, "terms not resolvable," Smith and Malone went at it in a more intimate setting. On August 30, Smith and a small team met Malone and his small team in Portland, Maine, and spent the day haggling over final prices while plying the sea in Malone's boat. The two sides agreed on most price issues then, but Smith and Malone kept tinkering right through an all-day meeting in New York on October 12.

The next morning, Smith and Malone rocked the communications world with their merger announcement. Its impact cannot be understated. The merger took all the deals and maneuvering and strategy of the preceding year and slammed them into hyperdrive. Not only would the new company be huge and powerful, it would also mark a new standard for what it would take to compete in the next age. You better be big, you better be national, you better have a ton of money and talent—or you'll never beat this new player. By sheer size and clout, Bell Atlantic–TCI would be able to drive new technology such as interactive TV into the market, probably on its own terms.

"I saw very clearly that, had it happened, the deal would've really permanently shaped the domestic communications industry," Malone says in retrospect.

Almost everyone was certain that Bell Atlantic–TCI would ignite a wave of similar giant mergers. Stock prices of just about every kind of company that might be involved in such deals hit new highs in the days after the merger was announced.

Nobody realized that Bell Atlantic–TCI was more like a grand finale to an escalating fireworks show. After the big boom reverberated, the party came down to earth—temporarily.

Toward the end of July 1993, Martin Davis asked Barry Diller to lunch at Paramount Communications headquarters in New York. Davis was Paramount's long-time and volatile chairman. His company was sputtering and running out of time. Paramount was an entertainment giant. At its core were the Paramount film and TV studios, producing such hits as the "Wayne's World" and "Cheers" TV series. It also owned the New York Rangers hockey team, the New York Knicks basketball team, the Madison Square Garden arena, and a huge library of entertainment software. The company's financial performance, however, as Paramount's management had admitted to its own board of directors that spring, "lagged behind" the rest of the entertainment industry. When a company holding valuable properties lags behind, it becomes a ripe takeover target.

If anybody was going to launch an unwelcome bid for Paramount, it was going to be Diller, the QVC chairman backed by Malone and Comcast's Brian Roberts. Not so coincidentally, Diller had fought bitterly with Davis in the early 1980s when Diller, working for Davis, had run Paramount's movie studio.

Davis had already been negotiating to merge Paramount into another entertainment conglomerate, Viacom, run by Sumner Redstone. The last thing Davis wanted was for Diller to get Paramount. The lunch was tense for both men. Davis grilled Diller about rumors of a QVC bid for Paramount. Diller hid his intentions. The conversation turned hot. The lunch ended with Davis shouting, "I know you're coming after me!"

On September 12, Davis agreed to sell Paramount to Viacom. Eight days later, Diller hurled his own bid into the picture. The corporate battle royal raged through the fall and winter, packed with name calling, lawsuits, and a dramatic courtroom scene watched by millions on Court TV. Bizarre casts of characters joined in on each side. Viacom pulled Blockbuster and NYNEX into the deal. On QVC's side were BellSouth, Cox Enterprises, and Advance Publications, run by the Newhouse family.

By the time the fight had stretched into 1994, it had become a dull game of nudging Byzantine financial structures ever higher until one side gave up. On February 15, Viacom won, getting Paramount in a deal valued at around $9.5 billion.

The battle turned corporate strategists and CEOs toward yet another fork in the info road. "Paramount became a symbol of the battle for control of content that's going to be waged over the next decade," says Larry Gerbrandt of media analysts Paul Kagan Associates.

Aside from the anticlimactic conclusion of the Paramount drama, a handful of other important investment events occurred at the end of 1993 and the beginning of 1994. None was even close to the scale or wallop of Bell Atlantic–TCI or US West–Time Warner. In one deal, Southwestern Bell and Cox said they would contribute a total of $4.9 billion in cash and assets to create a joint cable-TV partnership. Long-distance company MCI said it would invest $1.3 billion in a fledgling wireless communications company called Nextel—a company that may yet compete against cellular phones in most major U.S. markets.

Less flashy but probably more important in the long run were announcements of multibillion-dollar construction plans by big phone companies. Pacific Telesis said it would spend $16 billion building fiber-optic-based networks throughout California, connecting to 5 million homes by 2000. US West unveiled plans of similar size and scope in its territories (the Rocky Mountain and Pacific Northwest states). Ameritech and BellSouth said they'd build such networks but announced more modest spending. Hand-in-hand, the companies all pursued their lawsuits to gain the right to sell programming on their own networks. The idea that nearly every city and town would get wired with phone company-owned broadband networks bent strategy yet again. As Ray Smith figured out, alliances with cable companies started to seem less important.

From that point on, 1994 turned into a year of retreat—a backpedaling that shaped strategy and leaders every bit as much as the overheated highway mania of 1993. The events of 1994 helped pull the information superhighway out of the realm of hype and into the real world.

Many factors drove the retreat, but the politicians pulled the trigger that shot it into motion. They finally started taking action, and the megamedia industry didn't like what it saw. The FCC, which regulates almost all communication services, lashed out at cable television companies. On February 22, 1994, the agency told cable companies they had to cut their rates 7 percent, the second forced rate cut in six months. The ruling would cut into cable company finances; Malone said it would slice $300 million out of TCI's 1994 cash flow. At the same time, both houses of Congress were seriously considering bills that would free phone and cable companies to get into each other's businesses and change the way the industries are regulated. But no one knew when the bills might pass—if ever—or what they'd end up saying. The big-picture message was that politicians were not just going to get out of the way and let megamedia happen. Not a chance.

The specter of regulation cast a chilling shadow on a number of deals. First, Bell Atlantic and TCI called it off; then, Southwestern Bell and Cox. Cablevision, a big New York-based cable operator, saw talks with several potential suiters swirl down the toilet. By mid-1994, the market for buying and selling cable-TV properties had ground to a dead stop.

Reality plowed into the technology, too. Time Warner's high-profile test of interactive TV in Orlando, Florida, scheduled to start in the spring, was delayed until the end of 1994. Other megamedia tests started up but fell far short of the hype of a year earlier. Microsoft's Nathan Myhrvold compared those first megamedia tests to the bizarre, always-crashing flying machines in old newsreels. "The trials will mostly be poor because they are first versions," he said. "But there will be some glimmers and insights that will make the next ones better." The public and investors, though, didn't always understand that.

John Sculley turned into a kind of personal barometer for megamedia. He had been ousted from Apple, had quit Spectrum, and had become the butt of industry jokes. "It certainly leads you to wonder how the gyroscope of a leader can seemingly spin out of control," said Jeffrey Sonnenfeld, a leadership expert at Emory University in Atlanta, who had followed Sculley's career. "You wonder if he wasn't drunk from all the publicity that made him into the multimedia guru." Sculley pretty much disappeared.

The go-go megamedia strategy had taken a beating in 1994. Many players started believing that deals and partnerships would work better on a smaller scale, tackling one chunk of megamedia at a time rather than everything at once. As the year wound down, some of the more low-key companies looked smarter. Capital Cities/ABC, for instance, had stubbornly refused to fire up any megamedia hype. The most powerful company in broadcast television had slowly formed small partnerships with the likes of computer company Oracle. It had formed a strong internal multimedia division that was watching out for the company's future but wasn't about to do anything drastic. "We are a long-term player and we'll be there when we feel comfortable," said Bruce Maggin, president of the multimedia division. "We may lose some opportunities to that and we have. But we'd rather let Bell Atlantic and Time Warner throw their money around."

Other companies waltzed into the picture when a mellower atmosphere prevailed. One was Microsoft. The company had been pumping up internal spending on megamedia research and development to $100 million a year. In the wake of the Bell Atlantic–TCI collapse, Microsoft tightened a relationship with TCI that had been forged at the top, between Bill Gates and John Malone. "We were getting together twice a month," Malone said, adding an oddly crude comment: "Bill's like my wife. He likes to start meetings at eight in the evening and go all night." By year-end, Microsoft and TCI were starting their own interactive TV experiment. Microsoft went on a megamedia tear, announcing partnerships with numerous companies and unveiling an on-line computer service.

By late 1994, an odd thing had happened. Change had become a way of life for any person or company involved in megemedia. Astounding deals came together as other huge deals came unhinged. Companies looked good, then they looked bad, or vice versa. QVC called off its deal to buy Home Shopping Network while pursuing Paramount. QVC lost Paramount, Barry Diller tried to merge QVC with CBS, QVC ended up being bought by Comcast, and Diller seemed to be out of a job. MCI and Nextel called off their deal, then tried to revive it, then watched it drift away. TCI and US West went on cable-buying sprees. Disney looked invincible, then lost two key executives and appeared vulnerable for a moment.

The die is cast. For at least the next few years, nothing will be predictable, stable, or easy. Companies that aren't prepared to deal with that won't get very far. The forces creating and driving megamedia have been set in motion over the past couple of years, and nothing will stop them.

2

THE MYTHICAL COMPUPHONAVISION SET

Let's get real.

A lot of people hear about technological convergence, swallow too much information superhighway hype, and believe that within a decade we're all going to be buying one amazing machine that does everything. Call it a compuphonavision set: a computer grafted onto a television grafted onto a telephone. It will be the only thing we need—our one-does-all information and entertainment appliance—and everything on it will be interactive multimedia. You want to be a couch potato? Tough cookies. Sit up, pay attention, and play along with that game show, choose the plot of that mystery program, and vote on which relief pitcher the baseball manager should put into the game.

It's not going to happen like that—certainly not now and probably not ever.

I've had a chance to see many of the important and unimportant tests of entertainment, information, and communication technology originating from companies such as Microsoft, Time Warner, Bell Atlantic, Hewlett-Packard, Nextel, EON, and 3DO. I've played with some of the most visionary systems and talked with the people who will shape how those systems develop and how they're used. Add all of those tests and visions together and sprinkle in a good dose of common sense, and the future of megamedia starts to come into focus. And it's not a future built around compuphonavision sets.

The machines won't fuse into one, but they'll borrow from each other so that, for example, a computer will be able to pull in video and a TV will store and change information like a computer. That'll make each separate device better. And as megamedia evolves, phones, TVs, PCs, and their hybrids will increasingly be served by the same networks and programming suppliers. A cable-TV company, for example, will be able to connect to any kind of communication device. Still, the devices will be different, look different, and be used differently. For the foreseeable future, each of the disparate devices will even mean something different to us emotionally. One of the best ways to describe that comes from Laurie Frick, marketing manager for Hewlett-Packard's interactive TV effort. "People are connected to the television through their hearts," she says. "People are connected to the personal computer through their heads."

So, for a long time, one device, a version of the television, will be the entertainment machine. It will be in living rooms and family rooms.

Another device, a version of the personal computer, will be the interactive information and transaction machine. It will be in businesses or home offices.

Yet another device, a version of the wireless phone, will be the communication gadget. That one will be in the user's pocket.

Here's how the best minds in the business think those pieces of megamedia will come together for users.

THE TV

Television will go through greater change than any other medium in the next decade. Yet, in many homes, 5 to 10 years from now, the corner of the room where the TV sits won't look much different.

We're not going to all suddenly heave our Sonys or Magnavoxes or whatever-brand televisions out the window. But the TV will become more of a monitor. The megamedia family of the future will have a TV set surrounded by a bunch of boxes, similar to the stereo components we pile up to hear music at its best.

The TV in 1999 or beyond will probably still be plugged into a VCR and a video game machine, much as they were at the end of 1994. But a couple of new components might be added. One would be what's known as the set-top box, about the size and shape of a stereo tuner or a slim VCR. Some, like those made by IBM, will have the power of today's Intel-486 desktop computers. Others, including those made by Silicon Graphics, might have enough additional computer power to create sophisticated 3-D images and do many tasks at once. Most users won't know the difference or care, except that Silicon Graphics-type boxes would likely cost more (whether bought or leased) and do more.

Expect any set-top box to come with a remote control that's very different from today's panel of buttons. Some will have a track ball and a clicker, sort of like a mouse on a PC, and maybe only two or three other buttons. Since almost all the controls can be on-screen, remote controls jammed with buttons for channels and volume may fade away. Other remotes will include game-control buttons like those on a Sega machine.

Next to the set-top box, there might be another box about the same size—a printer. Top models will be able to grab any image off the screen and print it, in sharp color, on plain paper. Smaller, cheaper models will print documents or images sent to it, almost like a fax machine. During a cooking show on an interactive TV channel, for instance, the cook might offer the recipe and a photo of the finished dish. Click a button on the remote control to order it, maybe for 50 cents, and the recipe would be zipped to your home and printed right there next to the TV set. Although applications for TV printers will have to get a lot sexier than that example before people will buy and install them.

What will be on this array of equipment? Pick up the remote control and hit the ON button. Don't expect one of the channels to immediately flash on the screen, as happens today. Instead, expect to first see some kind of three-dimensional graphic that identifies the available TV service and functions as a menu.

That first screen will introduce the TV service from the likes of Time Warner or TCI. The service will be something you subscribe to, like cable TV today. But around the turn of the century, you'll probably have a choice of many such services instead of just one, at least if you live in a big or mid-size city. One service, piped in over the coaxial cable line, might be offered by the local cable-TV company. Several other services will likely be available over a phone company-owned line, which will have to be either coaxial cable or fiber-optic. One of those TV services may be owned and operated by the phone company itself, like Bell Atlantic's Stargazer. But federal regulations will force phone companies to let just about any company use the phone lines to sell a TV service. All the company would have to do is lease space on the lines and hook its computers and video servers to the telephone network.

Again, the model for TV services will be closer to on-line computer services than to today's television offerings. In the on-line world, a user can plug a phone line into a PC, and the same line can dial up any service—CompuServe, Prodigy, America Online. In that model, the user pays a fee to subscribe to the service and a fee to the phone company for the line. The user might also subscribe to more than one service. That's how the model is likely to work in the TV universe.

How will users choose which service to subscribe to? Like the on-line services, the different TV services will contain much of the same core programming, yet each will eventually have unique offerings and its own personality. One TV service might be more family-oriented, full of educational shows and Disney films. Another might appeal to upper-crust types by offering access to ballet, opera, and financial networks.

The big umbrella services—the Stargazers, the Full Service Networks—will evolve into something new for the entertainment world. They'll become a combination of programmer, packager, and gateway to other networks.

As programmers, the major TV services will act something like today's broadcast networks. Maybe they'll create some programming of their own, like news reports or interactive video game shows. They'll buy other programming from movie and TV studios, video game makers, sports leagues, and similar sources. They may string together some of that programming on a traditional, linear channel, like USA Network. Or, they may sell the programs à la carte: buy a financial news report for 50 cents or a movie for $3.

As packagers, they'll be like today's cable-TV companies: each will put together a group of channels (MTV, CNBC, HBO, and so on) to offer to viewers. The kinds of channels offered might reflect the kind of viewers the service is after.

The gateway role is the most difficult to see clearly.

Today's best programming experts—the ABC, NBC, CBS, and Fox networks—want to remain whole. They understandably want to keep control of their programming. They don't want to sell pieces to a Stargazer so it, in turn, can be the one to offer pay-per-view versions of the latest episode of "Frasier" or repackage stories done by ABC News. Capital Cities/ABC, for instance, is working with computer company Oracle to set up its own video servers. ABC wants to be a traditional broadcast network, but maybe also a digital service that packages and sells à la carte and interactive versions of its programming direct to consumers.

The networks will likely get their way. They're too powerful to lose a programming battle to phone companies. A Stargazer or other TV service may then end up offering a gateway—an electronic, digital path—to the networks' TV systems. From the Stargazer menu, viewers might choose the ABC service, and the Stargazer computer would switch them over to the ABC computer. From there, viewers could buy ABC programming. Stargazer's computers would handle the transaction, keep track of what each viewer buys, and add it to a periodic bill. That's only one probable scenario. How megamedia will finally work is anything but settled.

By the way, the broadcast networks and cable networks aren't going to disappear. They'll still be there, running half-hour sitcoms and Olympics coverage and soap operas, chock-full of commercials. They'll produce the big hits that capture huge audiences, no matter how many channels and services are available on TV—shows like "Melrose Place" or events like the Super Bowl. They'll more than likely be available through any TV service that's offered. Not everyone will subscribe to the high-tech services, just as only 60 percent of homes get cable TV, and fewer have Nintendo or Sega. Plain old cable service will still be available and will cost less than a Stargazer-type service. Plain old over-the-air broadcasts will stick around, too, and they'll still be free. Old media never die, they just become less glamorous.

Let's go back to the redesigned remote control. Pick it up, turn on the new muscle-TV, watch as the TV service's graphical menu paints the screen. The remote will be something called an "air mouse." Point it at the screen and a little arrow appears. Move the track ball, and the arrow is guided in the same way that a mouse guides an arrow on a PC.

Point the arrow at the "channels" selection and click the "enter" button. Up pops a grid, much like the TV program grids in newspapers today, showing what's on each available broadcast and cable channel. Scroll through with the arrow, choose a channel, click, and it comes on. Want to channel surf? Set up a menu of the 10 to 20 channels you'll always want to zip through. Click into a surf mode, and you can flip through those channels by hitting the up- or down-arrow button. No more remembering that CNN is on channel 28, ABC on 7, MTV on 47.

In addition to the usual channels, some new kinds of linear channels will be tailored to extreme niches. TCI's John Malone semi-jokingly suggests there will be a Pet Channel. He and Microsoft are creating a computer channel. Magazine channels are on their way. Time Warner is working on one tied to its *Sports Illustrated* magazine. Others might get much narrower. An *Outside* channel? A *Black Enterprise* channel?

Click back to the main menu and click on "movies." Pick a category of movies you want to see, like Westerns or Tom Hanks films. Movie posters from that category might flip by on-screen as though they're in a 3-D Rolodex file. Click on a poster to choose the movie, which will begin a few minutes later. During the film, you'd have VCR-like control—pause, stop, fast-forward. Cost might be $3 to $4 a movie (more, for just-out releases). A hot title would never be sold out or need a reservation, as in video stores today.

Pay-per-view sports and other à la carte programming will probably work in similar ways. Another test gaining momentum is Your Choice TV (YCTV), which is TV service software developed by the creators of The Discovery Channel. Several cable companies have been testing YCTV and it seems to be on the way to becoming a successful product. YCTV lets viewers order the latest episode of a top TV series or soap opera within a week after its first run. Price is expected to be 50 cents to $1 for each program. The system also lets viewers browse for Discovery-type documentaries and order them on a pay-per-view basis, and it's working on packages of, among other possibilities, college football games. No matter where they live or what games are on national TV networks on a given Saturday, sometime in the next decade alumni may always be able to watch their alma mater play. "Television has always been appointment viewing and someone else was setting the appointment," says John Hendricks, president of Discovery Communications, which owns The Discovery Channel. "In the future, the viewer will set the appointment."

So far, none of this sounds very different from the television of today. It's mostly about entertainment, and the pay-per-view aspects are an on-line, electronic version of the VCR and video stores. That's why those kinds of developments are likely to happen and why they'll work and penetrate the marketplace. They're not really forging new markets. "Our belief is, we easily have to offer everything cable offers and things that are a natural extension of what people do today," says Lee Camp, who heads Pacific Telesis's hugely ambitious effort to deploy high-tech TV services to half its California customers by 2010. "To that, we'll bring the new experience of control and convenience."

Companies like Pacific Telesis think that TV can do more than its traditional role. A lot of executives have talked about grandiose services—entire MBA programs via interactive TV, virtual reality shopping, video family reunions, on-line video games played against people on other continents. Some of those may actually come around. If they do, it'll take another generation or two.

Other expanded services will probably come much sooner—within 5 to 10 years.

Even the more conservative companies chasing megamedia have put TV shopping near the top of their list. "Today's paper catalog shopping is a $50 billion to $70 billion industry," says Forrest Miller, corporate strategist for Pacific Telesis. "If we can get just a little piece of that, we'll be doing pretty well."

QVC and Home Shopping Network already are TV "stores," but their continuous stream of wide-ranging, preprogrammed offerings is pretty inefficient for most shoppers. You might have to watch for hours just to see if there's anything you'd like to buy. In the next few years, TV shopping might not get exponentially better. More shopping channels will surface, and some will be tied to specific retailers—Spiegel and Macy's, to name two that are already working on an electronic showcase. Others will aim at niche markets, like computer users. The channels will likely be tightly targeted versions of the QVC format. Shoppers would still have to sit and watch hosts show hours' worth of fishing equipment on the Zebco Shopping Channel.

Some catalogers will start offering their catalogs on-screen. In other words, the TV will deliver the same kinds of still images and text as are now in the printed catalogs, but shoppers could get the catalogs via TV instead of in the mail. The video catalogs would have some advantages over print. Buyers would be able to see a wider variety of products or many more photos of the same product, and could then order directly by clicking some on-screen images with the air mouse.

As TV systems get more powerful, video shopping channels and video catalogs will converge. QVC-type channels will get more interactive. Sitting in front of a TV, a customer can immediately order up a segment on men's shirts or women's jewelry, and place an order using the remote control. From the other end, catalogs via TV will start adding some full-motion video. Someone interested in a suit from Land's End could see a brief clip of someone wearing it. Think of the potential for a catalog if it were offered on a CD-ROM disk to be played on a computer. That's about what could come to TV over cable or phone lines. In the realistic future, however, despite wild promises from some companies, TV shopping isn't likely to get much more gee-whiz than that.

Two other new programming features are coming to a TV near you: over-the-wire video games and on-line database services. The first means that, instead of buying a video game machine and then buying or renting game cartridges, you could go through a service like Stargazer, click into a central video game computer, and pull down any of dozens of games to play. The Sega Channel is already up and running. It's a subscription service. Viewers pay about $12 a month to tap into it, and can then play any game on the menu any time, as much as they want. They can play solo, with a friend, or, at some point, against someone across town whose TV is plugged into the same network.

On-line services will have to change to stay legitimate parts of TV. Few people will want to send and receive electronic mail from their living room couches, trying to read it on a TV screen 10 feet away. We're not going to use TV sets to read. Still, all the big on-line services—especially Prodigy—are exploring ways to become part of TV's expanding universe. The bet is that they'll get into supplying supplemental information for television broadcasts, like detailed statistics that can be called up while watching sports events, or outtakes and background information about a classic film. It won't be easy though, for Prodigy, CompuServe, and America Online to use their success in computers to make it in television. In the business world, Bloomberg, a financial information service, is taking a plunge into video by creating a TV service for DirecTv, a 150-channel satellite service. Bloomberg Direct, as it's called, could lead Bloomberg in megamedia directions.

Amid all the programming, today's television has another important side: advertising. Among the toughest questions surrounding TV today are: If consumers gain much greater control over their TV viewing, will they completely zap around commercials? Then what will become of TV advertising? Madison Avenue doesn't have a clue what the answers are yet. A best guess, from people like BBDO ad agency executive Arnie Semsky, is that ads on the linear broadcast channels will still play the role they do today, although fewer people might see each commercial. In the interactive realm, ads will have to become bigger and better than they are now. They'll have to entice viewers to watch them by being either informative or entertaining. Chrysler might offer a TV service that lets car shoppers see videos of Chrysler cars, get impartial *Consumer Reports*-type information, and review prices advertised by local dealers. That's information. On the entertainment side, Coca-Cola might create a video game that showcases its product. Cutty Sark scotch is already taking a voyage into those waters. In 1994, it sponsored a 22-city tour featuring a virtual reality game that was set up in retail stores. Players sailed a Cutty Sark-style ship while battling attacking biplanes. The game, which cost $1 million to develop, could be a prototype for interactive game ads delivered through TVs or computers. The all-around good news is that, ads will have to become less of a nuisance to survive in the next age.

Beyond entertainment and advertising, TV will no doubt become a piece of the communications industry. An exciting possibility is that, a few years from now, we'll all be using TV sets and little video cameras to turn all our phone calls into video phone calls. But even the most enthusiastic players don't see that happening for a while. Tom Morrow, who heads the communications portion of Time Warner's Full Service Network trial in Orlando, sees TV's communication role this way: the set-top converter box will be able to be a base station for a wireless phone. Inside their homes, customers will flick a button and use the phone like the common, short-range wireless phones now in many homes, connected to regular phone lines. Morrow's wireless phone would send signals to the base station and the call would go out over the wire connected to the TV, whether the wire is from the phone or cable company. When the user leaves the house, a click of the button will turn the same phone into a cellular phone to be taken along. Calls would go out via wireless networks owned by or tied to the same company that wires up the TV system. Use the phone in the car, at the park, wherever. Both cellular and home phone calls would wind up on the same bill.

Video calls? They'll come around. The broadband networks will take away all the limits of 30 years' worth of attempts at videophones. Pictures could be clear and motion could be fluid, not herky-jerky like video calls over twisted-pair phone lines. Tiny video cameras could be set up next to TVs and maybe even today's home video cameras could take the pictures. But, for a decade or more, video calls will not be cheap. In homes, Time Warner's Morrow figures video calls will begin as a special thing average consumers do once in a while—on Mother's Day, when a baby is born. "They'll be something you set up in advance," Morrow says. Video calls are more likely to catch on in business first, via personal computers instead of televisions. That pattern is similar to the way long-distance phone calls were 20 years ago. Only when prices came down did consumer long-distance calls become common.

All in all, one of the most misunderstood phrases of the past two years has been "interactive television." It doesn't mean that we're all going to be wired to this demanding, brainy machine that won't let us just lay back and veg out. We're always going to want television to be primarily a passive device.

On the other hand, we sometimes forget that TV is already interactive to a startling degree. We plug in a VCR and play movies when we want and stop and rewind them. We take our own video with a video camera and play it back on the TV screen. We plug in Nintendo games and play highly interactive games. We watch QVC, then pick up the phone and call a number to order a product we see on-screen.

More than anything, the new TV technology is about making all those things easier, simpler, and, eventually, less expensive. See the movie without going to the video store. Play the game without paying $50 for a cartridge. Order the product without dialing a telephone number.

Maybe interactive TV will add a few new twists. Videoway, the cable-TV system in Montreal, is one of the most advanced in the world. For an added fee, viewers can get Videoway's interactive service. It's a fairly straightforward technology that basically knits four separate channels together to offer a single, seamless interactive program. During a big hockey game, Videoway viewers can flick back and forth among three different camera angles and one continuous instant-replay. Game shows can also become interactive. A host asks a question and gives four possible answers. Choose one. Astoundingly, the host tells you you're right or wrong, as if he's addressing you personally.

The service is remarkable and a lot of fun. But, like almost everything else about new TV technology, it's not for everyone and it's not a part of every program. It's just one other way to use a TV.

THE PERSONAL COMPUTER

A lot of companies, particularly those that make personal computers, say PCs will become the *real* endpoint on the information superhighway. To some degree, that will be true—at least for the information part of the new communications highways.

As megamedia rolls in, computers have one distinct advantage over televisions: they're a work tool. That means people are willing to spend more money on them than on home entertainment. Even individuals buying a PC for the home will spend $2,000 on a machine, hundreds more on software, and $20 or more a month on an on-line service. In an office, most users worry little about cost. They buy the hardware and software they need to do their jobs, and in coming years, they'll freely access any kind of service or communication network that will help them work more efficiently and better perform their jobs.

If cost is less of an issue when dealing with PCs, we'll be doing more amazing megamedia things on PCs sooner, but they will mostly be tasks related to information, work, and, possibly, education—not entertainment.

Unlike television sets, personal computers will physically change a great deal in the next 5 to 10 years, just as they've constantly changed over the past decade. One adage is that computing power has been doubling every 18 months. At that rate, around 2000, a single high-end desktop PC could have enough processing speed and memory to run the American Airlines Sabre reservation system, one of the biggest computing tasks in business today. It's enough power to make voice-recognition work and to easily store and manipulate video. Plug a machine like that into a fiber-optic line connected to the world, and you'll be able to do almost anything you can imagine.

Outside of the huge increases in internal power, the basic desktop PC will probably look pretty much the same as today's $2,000 multimedia computers. It will have a processor, a keyboard, and a monitor. The disk drives will be for optical CD-ROM storage disks instead of magnetic floppy disk drives, and PCs will routinely have stereo speakers mounted on them. There will be some changes. Tomorrow's PC will increasingly come with a small video camera on top. On the front will be an input jack for a microphone and an output for headphones. In the back, the modem connection will accommodate both twisted-pair phone lines and coaxial cable-TV lines.

Laptops, too, will be equipped for multimedia, with tiny speakers and possibly a tiny video camera. But laptops are meant to be portable, so communications will have to be portable, too. McCaw Cellular and IBM have built prototypes of IBM's ThinkPad laptop, a PC with digital cellular technology built in and a tiny antenna snapped on the side. As cellular networks evolve to handle computer data, cellular antennae will become common on laptops.

The new devices known as personal digital assistants (PDAs) or personal communicators will take the convergence of telephone and computer a lot further. Some of the better-known products are Apple's Newton, Motorola's Envoy and Sony's Magic Link. They don't have keyboards. Newton uses writing-recognition; Envoy and Magic Link have touch-screens that let users spell out words by tapping a tiny on-screen keyboard. The devices are equipped to connect to regular phone lines or cellular networks. They're not meant to be computers or telephones but something in between. A user can send or receive news, information, e-mail, and faxes over communications networks, plus store addresses and a personal calendar—even tap into an on-line computer service. So far, the products have sold poorly. They don't have enough power to work easily or well. But that will change and PDAs will gradually catch on.

Back to desktop PCs. By 1996, power users will be plugging super-fast PCs into broadband megamedia networks through cable TV or fiber-optic lines. In 10 years, that connection will be common.

What business and home users will realistically do with that kind of system is very nearly mind-blowing.

Look at it this way: when a PC is plugged into a cable-TV line, information can be transferred at speeds a thousand times greater than over a 9600-baud modem, the typical modem for midrange PCs linked to regular phone lines, says David Fellows, senior vice president of technology for Continental Cablevision. Continental is one of the first cable-TV companies to offer broadband connections to PCs. The huge increase in capacity "allows images to come down over the wire," Fellows says. "You can think of attaching video and voice to an interactive newspaper. You can do videoconferencing."

America Online, a top on-line computer service, bought Redgate Communications, a multimedia developer, in 1994. The idea, says America Online president Steve Case, is to use Redgate's skills to make on-line services do everything a CD-ROM disk can do—combine video, sound, text, and graphics in a speedy, easy-to-use format. "That's where we're headed," he says.

Sit down at a PC in coming years and tap into an on-line service. Instead of just getting Reuters' text news, which some services now offer, also pull up video clips generated by Reuters' just-started TV news operation. When looking in a medical library, get animated drawings of body parts. The broadband connections will also make all the power of the Internet available to just about anyone. The Internet is a high-speed, worldwide network of networks, connecting millions of corporate, academic, government, and commercial computer systems together. Someone operating a PC in Alaska could send e-mail via Internet to China, connect to a supercomputer in Minnesota, or join a computer party attended by PC users all over the globe. A broadband connection to the Internet would let a PC pull down whole books' worth of material off college libraries in seconds. On the seamy side, it's not hard to guess what might materialize on some of the Internet's sex-oriented networks once video can easily be exchanged.

Videoconferencing—the business version of video phone calls—will become an important and common function for PCs within a decade. Intel is working to have videoconferencing capabilities regularly built into PCs. Working with Compression Labs, which makes digital compression technology, Intel has created software that would let PC users turn a window on their screens into a video phone. Executives at phone company Ameritech are already using a version. Chairman Dick Notebaert keeps in touch with his college-age daughter that way. At PC Expo in New York, in June 1994, nearly every booth featured a desktop computer armed with a tiny camera and showing a video picture in a corner of the screen.

As videoconferencing systems get more powerful, businesspeople will use video calls as a more intimate way to talk, compared to voice-only telephone. One key feature is that a group of people could meet via video and share the same information on a computer screen—all while sitting at their own desks. Silicon Graphics has an internal companywide system like that. At least eight people can be visible in little boxes lined up along the top of the screen, while all see the same image on the main portion of the screen. The group can jointly review a software code or a marketing plan. They can even play games against each other. At 5:30 P.M. on most days, at the MIPS chip subsidiary of Silicon Graphics, groups of employees get on a flight simulator game together—each from his or her own desk—and try to shoot each other down.

Portable video calls are another matter. For a long time to come, video will only be able to be exchanged over broadband wired networks, not on wireless networks. Video takes up so much transmission space that cellular-type systems can't handle it—although someday, no doubt, they will.

Will people watch television on PCs? Yes, but not full-length *Lethal Weapon* movies or episodes of "Seinfeld"—well, maybe at 5:30 at MIPS they will. But there will be a role for real-time TV in a window on a PC, especially when it can be used as another information tool. Intel and CNN have launched a joint effort that would pump CNN's Headline News into any company's internal computer network. The Headline News broadcast feed would be picked up by a satellite set up by the customer, and the computer network would distribute the broadcast to employees' desktop PCs. Users would be able to call up the broadcast in a baseball card-size window on their screens. The service would be niftier than just a linear news show. Any user would be able to store part of the broadcast—

maybe up to 30 minutes' worth, which would be one whole cycle of the Headline News report—on his or her PC's hard-desk drive. Because key words and titles would be embedded in the broadcast, when the user wants to call up what has been stored, a menu of stories will pop up. Among the options: select which news stories to view and erase the others. Or, search the stories for specific topics, such as "health care" or "stock market," and call up only those stories. NBC and IBM are working on a similar service, called Desktop News, that would use NBC and CNBC reports.

There will soon be no technological reason why any TV broadcast couldn't be pumped into a window on PCs. Makes for some interesting possibilities. Sports writers could view a baseball game while writing a story, saving bits of video as "notes." Congressional staffers could search and store video clips from speeches broadcast on C-SPAN rather than saving just transcripts of text. Workers could view training videos while sitting at their PCs doing on-screen work as part of the exercise.

Since we're more used to sophisticated interaction with computers than with television sets, electronic commerce will probably come faster to the PC universe. A certain amount of commerce already rides on on-line systems and over the Internet. Consumers can order audio compact disks or computer software from on-line catalogs—which, at this point, are basically text lists. Businesses can order parts from GE Plastics over the Internet. Once services such as America Online go to multimedia, CD-ROM versions of catalogs will probably be available to PCs over broadband cable or phone lines. A Sears catalog could be thousands of pages long, offering great detail on every product and brief videos on, say, how to use certain power tools. A shopper finds what is wanted, clicks a few keys on the keyboard, types in a credit card number, and the item is ordered.

L. L. Bean is testing software called Acrobat, created by Adobe Systems. With Acrobat, a page from a catalog—photos, text, layout—can be transmitted to any PC, regardless of whether the receiving PC has software that would ordinarily be needed to reconstruct the same typefaces, colors, and so on, from the catalog.

It may sound like a subtle victory, but overcoming those obstacles will make electronic commerce happen more quickly.

A decade from now, computer commerce might really get interesting, especially if software made by General Magic catches on. General Magic wants its Telescript software to be embedded in megamedia networks to give computer users what General Magic calls an "agent." This agent, acting like a little digital assistant, could find and buy anything over the network. Say you want to buy something that's fairly hard to find—a set of goalie pads for ice hockey. You call up your agent and tell it what you want—size of pads, brand name you prefer, features you're looking for. You give the agent a budget of, say, $500. The agent takes off on the network and finds its way to computer systems of companies that sell goalie pads—systems also loaded with Telescript. The agent finds pads that fit your description and then comes back to your computer and shows the available choices, complete with pictures, prices, and other information. Type a command to place the order, and the agent zooms out to buy the pads, which will come in the mail. "It can create an electronic marketplace with no bricks and mortar," says General Magic CEO Marc Porat.

What are some of the best-bet markets for megamedia computing? Health care seems to be near the top of everyone's list. Ameritech is already deep into the Wisconsin Health Information Network, a multimedia network of 800 doctors and 15 hospitals in Wisconsin. The network allows doctors to share medical records, see X rays from a distance, get advice from other doctors on-line, and more efficiently file insurance forms. That kind of service is only the beginning. Multimedia health networks that can share full-motion video bring up the possibilities of remote medical care—a specialist at a large urban medical center being able to actually "see" a patient in a general practitioner's office in a small town, saving the patient a long trip. Hospitals are convinced that connected systems would allow them to share knowledge, administration, and other functions, all of which would cut costs. If megamedia can make health care better and cheaper, the market will grab onto the technology and run with it.

Education may be another big application. Bell Atlantic has vowed to spend up to $100 million to wire all the schools in its region to megamedia networks. Some other telephone and cable companies are making similar gestures. Megamedia could be a breakthrough for schools, if they can find the money to get into it and if teachers embrace it—both big if's.

Megamedia could make learning richer and more fun. For a geography lesson, computer and communications systems could let a class in Ohio make text and video e-mail contact with classes in all 50 states, asking each to send back information on their lives and surroundings. A high school class in Nebraska could tap into a UCLA marine biology computer to do research. Teachers at any level could create multimedia reports on what's going on in class, so parents could tap in and see the reports from a home or office PC.

No one knows whether such uses of megamedia will find their way into education. Privately, Bell Atlantic officials say that they aren't spending all that money to hook up schools simply out of generosity or to try to appease politicians. They figure that schools and parents will get hooked on megamedia and buy hundreds of millions of dollars' worth of network time, software, and programming from Bell Atlantic and other suppliers. It's not charity. It's an investment.

There are hundreds of other probable markets for megamedia computing. Home banking, long a flop, may finally come to pass. (For proof that people want to bank via PC, look at the popularity of home financial software Quicken—6 million users and growing. The company that makes Quicken was bought by Microsoft in October 1994, and Microsoft has big plans for home banking.) Telecommuting will get a brand new lift, once manager and worker can see each other on video rather than relying on phone calls and e-mail messages for contact. Real estate sales could be handled remotely. A couple in Boston, facing a transfer to Dallas, could tap into a computer network and view photos and videos of homes for sale in the Dallas area, get information on local schools and taxes, and see maps that show parks, airports, commuting routes, and shopping centers, as well as streets and highways.

Count on computers to clear the fastest path to megamedia, because that's where the money is.

THE TELEPHONE

Telephone *lines* have a multimedia future, full of video and data. But the telephone itself—the device that gives us instant, easy voice communication with something like 1 billion people around the world—isn't going to bulk up like that. Instead, it's going to slim down and get legs.

In the megamedia age, telephones will become cheaper, simpler, and more portable. AT&T's new corporate war cry—"Anytime, Anywhere!"—is what the whole voice communications industry is all about. Computers and televisions will provide power communications; phones will create ubiquitous communications. Sony is selling a cellular phone the size of a credit card. Competition is already driving down cellular call prices. New digital wireless networks are on the verge of making cellular phones as easy to use as a pay phone when "roaming" in other cities. Megamedia means never having to say, "I can't get to a phone right now." Unless, of course, you don't want to be found.

Not that everyone is going to suddenly buy wireless or cellular phones while wired phones go the way of the telegraph. But certainly a lot more people will use wireless phones or other kinds of portable communication devices within five years. A decade after cellular phones were first introduced, society is embracing wireless calling as more than a business or upper-class service. "I think society will adopt wireless as a given in five years," says James Dixon, president of wireless up-and-comer Nextel. "People won't accept wired communication any more than they do a rotary phone today."

Along the way, phones and phone networks will get smarter as voice communication technology increasingly meshes with computers. Different kinds of phone companies—McCaw Cellular, MCI, Bell Atlantic—are testing and pushing the concept of one telephone number for each customer, instead of a phone number for home, another for work, maybe another for a cellular phone and another for a pager. In the future, one number might reach all of those, thanks to computers and digital networks. Software in a network would find the person at the appropriate place. Say someone dials a golf pro's number during work hours. First, the network would send the call to the pro's wired work phone. No answer there? It would next try the pro's wireless phone, finding him on any of the 18 holes—or anywhere in the United States. Not available on the wireless either? The call could bounce to a pager, or, if his home is on the search list for business calls, the network would ring there. The entire search would be invisible to the caller and the receiver. The caller would only have to dial one number. The person on the other end would just hear a phone ring and answer it.

"Anytime, Anywhere!" is really not such a strange concept. Think of a phone call as software or content, like an audio CD. At home, we play our favorite CDs on a powerful, stationary home stereo. We take them into the car and pop one into the car's CD player. When walking in the park, we slide one into a personal stereo. Now think of phone calls being that flexible.

To take the possibilities a step further, over the next 10 years, say many phone industry executives, smart networks, competition, and consumer demand for portability will create a layered market that looks like this:

- Wired communication, the kind most people have in their homes and businesses, will always be the cheapest way to do voice-only communication. When people are at home or at their desks, they'll talk over wires.
- Personal communication services (PCS) phones could be almost as cheap as wired lines. PCS is a wireless technology being set up by phone and cable companies; unfortunately, it's coming along more slowly than many expected. Less powerful than cellular, it is also supposed to be less costly. PCS may become cheap enough so that some people will use it even inside their homes or offices. Others will mainly use it around town.

- Cellular phones, like the ones in use today, will be the next level—a little more expensive than PCS, but more powerful. Customers might want to be on the cellular network when they are outside of cities or traveling on main highways, or when they need to transmit computer data.
- Satellite phones will be the ultimate in portable voice communication. Motorola, for instance, is putting up a $3 billion to $6 billion Iridium satellite phone system. The system will allow calls to be made from absolutely anywhere in the world, even in the middle of the Sahara Desert. The rate will be $3 a minute.

The intriguing idea here is that one phone may someday be able to connect to any of those services. At home, plug the phone into a base station and it connects to the wired network. Take it traveling and it could access the least expensive network that could handle a call from anywhere, whether PCS, cellular, or satellite. Will it happen? Probably not in this decade, though maybe later. If one company were to own a full range of services, it might push such technology. But no one company is that broad today. Competition will keep the different kinds of services from completely converging in the near future.

Competition, though, is going to make each layer of service into a whole new ballgame for consumers.

In the wired world, nearly everyone now has one choice: the local phone company. That will change in big cities first and, eventually, in other regions. Some competition will come from cable-TV companies. In Rochester, New York, Time Warner's cable system has just begun competing on equal footing with Rochester Telephone for local phone service—the first situation of its kind in the United States.

Other competition may come from new local phone companies that start out by leasing lines and equipment from the existing phone company or cable companies. Long-distance competition started, in almost the same way. Ameritech, which wants to create a competitive market in its region so some regulatory restrictions will go away, is pushing that kind of plan. It wants to "unbundle" its telephone network so it can lease any combination of parts of it to newcomers. "If you want to take a piece of this and a piece of that and construct your own package, go do it," says chairman Dick Notebaert. To consumers, that would mean a number of companies would vie for the local phone service, much as MCI, AT&T, Sprint, and others fight now for long-distance business. The key unknown here is regulation. Congress and the FCC are in the throes of rewriting telecommunication law. A big part of their effort will be aimed at creating local phone competition, but when and how is still up for grabs.

In wireless phones, most customers now have only two choices: the local phone company and one competitor. That's going to change, too. PCS will compete against cellular for many of cellular's customers, and the federal government is awarding up to seven PCS licenses per city. On top of that, Nextel, backed by MCI, Motorola, and Comcast, is taking another route to wireless customers. Nextel is turning old taxi dispatch frequencies into digital cellular phone networks. The company plans to complete its systems in 45 of the top 50 U.S. markets within a few years. "There are going to be so many wireless phone providers going after the same customers," says Danny Briere, president of consulting firm Telechoice, "I can envision a customer in a car with nothing but wireless salesmen surrounding him or her."

The competition is expected to drive prices down and wireless phone use up. The industry had about $10.9 billion in revenue in 1993. By 2003, many analysts expect wireless revenue to hit $25 billion.

Where will the convergence of phones, TVs, and computers show up? In some of the smart wireless devices coming out, such as Motorola's Envoy or Sony's Magic Link.

Despite some ongoing experiments, the actual telephone device is not likely to get more complex. It won't turn into a screen phone, for instance. The phone is already a simple, elegant communication instrument that everyone is comfortable using. Megamedia gives it a chance to play on that strength.

It's easy to be skeptical about so much change coming to pass in so short a time. Even if technology can move at amazing speed, sometimes we can't. I keep a fascinating chart tacked up on my desk, for perspective. It's credited to Technologic Partners and is titled, "Time required for adoption of consumer products." According to the chart, TV was absorbed into society in a flash. The first TV sale was in 1946; eight years later, TVs were in 50 percent of U.S. homes. Among other technologies, adoption times get pretty long. VCRs, introduced in 1975, took 13 years to reach 50 percent penetration. Automobiles, first out in 1895, took 29 years to hit the 50 percent level. Cable TV, which started in 1948, took 39 years. Telephones were first offered in 1876 and needed 70 years to reach 50 percent penetration. Seventy years!

Then again, look what's happened since 1980. In 1980, there were no cellular phones. There was no personal computer industry. Very few offices had fax machines. Very few homes had VCRs. Cable TV was a small-potatoes business. Virtually no one had home video game machines. We were still fascinated by the simple game Asteroids at arcades.

Today, more than 15 million people use cellular phones. More than 30 million homes have PCs. Microsoft, in 1980 an unknown software company that had just struck its first deal with IBM, is one of the most powerful companies in America. Fax machines are an absolute requirement for any office. More than 85 percent of homes have VCRs, and the video rental business, not even imagined in 1980, brings in more than $14 billion a year. More than 60 percent of homes have cable, and new cable channels such as CNN and MTV are seen and known worldwide. Home video games are a $6 billion-a-year business. The $50 games couldn't have even run on a 1980 vintage mainframe computer.

The best minds in every industry touched by megamedia believe that changes just as big and profound are coming over the next decade. On the practical side, AT&T chairman Robert Allen believes the speed of megamedia's penetration rides on the shoulders of the companies faced with creating products and services "that people will pay for." General Magic Chairman Marc Porat is counting on something deeper happening. He says that people's demand for megamedia will pull it along. "In 10 years, kids today will be 20. They'll want to interact electronically in ways much richer than anything today," Porat predicts. "I think in 10 years developed cultures will change drastically."

Technology itself won't hold back megamedia developments. As late as 1993, some doubts lingered that technology could ever do so much at a price that would make economic sense. But now, the pieces are falling into place. Digital storage devices—hard disk drives, tapes, CD-ROM disks, or other kinds of units—will serve as the electronic warehouses, storing as much information as 10,000 or more desktop PCs. Linked to the storage units will be computer servers capable of dishing out video on demand to thousands of customers at once, and allowing them to stop or rewind or type in questions about a film's star.

The servers will feed into fiber-optic lines, and the programming will run through a multimedia digital switch that can send a signal to the correct home. Fiber-optics is a tested technology. The switches, called asynchronous transfer mode switches, are just coming out.

Once the signal reaches a home, a set-top box will convert it to a form the TV set can handle and display. The box, which will help with interactivity and store information, will be as powerful as PCs that cost $2,000 today.

Once it became clear that phone and cable companies were set on spending billions of dollars on high-tech networks, dozens of companies rushed in to develop better and better technology. The competition quickly started driving prices down. Says Ray Smith, chairman of Bell Atlantic: "I was worried two years ago that we'd be able to build our network. It doesn't scare me now. The American commercial engine gears up when it smells money, and it certainly has done that."

They're convinced over at Microsoft, too. "Over the past 20 years, performance of computers has increased 1 million times," says Microsoft's Nathan Myhrvold. "There's nothing to indicate that that's going to slow down. It will increase another 1 million times over the next 20 years. So 20 years from now, a computer problem that would have taken a year will take 30 seconds." Systems will become so powerful that virtual reality—the most advanced interactive application on today's industry scene—"will be overwhelmed by computer power," Myhrvold says. "Humans only have a certain number of nerve endings."

True, side issues may slow things—issues that involve humans, not technology. One of those issues is standards. Technology develops more quickly and becomes cheaper when there are universal standards. PC technology took off when most of the world agreed on the IBM design, for example. Standards let more people develop products and services that make use of the technology, which attracts more customers, which drives mass production, which pushes prices lower—and a big spiral keeps turning. But companies often fight over standards, and that's still happening across much of megamedia. Most companies are trying different versions of the technology, and each wants its version to be the standard. The faster companies iron that out, the faster megamedia will develop.

Security is another issue. Much of megamedia involves transactions done over wires—home shopping, ordering a movie, taking college exams, exchanging e-mail. What will be done to ensure the security of a credit card number sent through the network? How do you know someone at one end is who they say they are? Is there a way to do electronic signatures? These are some concerns that are still to be worked out.

In the broad megamedia universe, most companies now build their strategies on the assumption that the technology will happen. The side issues will come around, however painful the process.

The biggest unknown is consumer reaction. Nobody knows what people will buy or what they'll pay for it. At this point, knowing that would be like knowing about 900 numbers back when phones were invented, or knowing about Home Shopping Network at the dawn of TV. Consumers will decide what megamedia is and what it does. Time Warner and Bell Atlantic and everybody else can have their grand plans. But in the end, we're in charge.

It's hard to predict where megamedia will end up on a chart showing adoption of technology. If megamedia matches TV, the speediest technology to market, half of us will have it in eight years—sometime after 2003. We may be in for one wild ride through the 1990s.

3

BELL-HEADS NO MORE

THE TELEPHONE INDUSTRY

LEADERS TO WATCH: RAY SMITH AND BELL ATLANTIC

Ray Smith, the fiftysomething chairman of Bell Atlantic, can tell you that Eddie Vedder is the lead singer for the head-banging rock band Pearl Jam. With just a little coaxing, he'll do a dead-on imitation of Beavis and Butt-head. If Smith had to choose to do anything besides run a $13 billion telecommunications giant, he'd act in plays. He has, in fact, continued to appear on stage at a community theater near Philadelphia.

Although divorced, family counts a lot to him. Two weeks after announcing the biggest proposed merger in history—the ill-fated deal to buy TCI—Smith blew everything off his crammed calendar and flew to San Jose to coo and sigh over newborn Annecy Genevieve Smith, his first granddaughter. "She's a perfect baby," he said at the time, preferring to talk about her rather than John Malone. "I have four kids and I've never seen one like this."

Smith is terrifically funny. He is terrifically impatient. He is a master schmoozer—one of the few telecommunications executives who is actually liked by state regulators, news reporters, members of Congress, and a good many competitors. He is neat, sharply dressed, and fond of interesting ties, but he likes to be seen with his jacket off and his sleeves rolled up, fulfilling the image of a hard-working manager.

In his smallish, unremarkable office at Bell Atlantic's Philadelphia headquarters, Smith fumes about internal bureaucracy. He praises the practical. He sets audacious goals, like saying that Bell Atlantic, long a company dominated by engineers and lawyers, must become a world-class entertainment company—fast. He's also hopelessly hooked on management gimmicks. Over the years, he has encouraged subordinates to carry blue poker chips in their pockets to remind them to focus on blue-chip priorities. The headquarters hallways are plastered with posters blaring management-guru sayings such as "Empowered to Delight the Customer." Smith has sent an endless stream of managers to attend motivational seminars.

From any perspective, Ray Smith is a confounding, atypical phone company executive. And all the rest of the executives at all the other phone companies have, at some point, looked to the heavens and thanked God for creating him.

Smith has become the Christopher Columbus of the telephone industry. He's willing—desperate, actually—to be first to explore new markets and the new routes necessary to get to those markets. Far from feeling threatened, most competing CEOs are grateful. "We're happy to let Bell Atlantic do what it's doing," says Ameritech CEO Dick Notebaert, who would rather take his company on a safer, more low-key ride to megamedia. Smith and Bell Atlantic are far out front on a risky trip into unknown territory. Other telephone companies, to a great degree, measure their strategic moves against Bell Atlantic's. If Smith guides his company in one direction with some success, other phone companies either follow or learn from that. If Bell Atlantic hits a storm and sinks—well, better them than us, competitors think.

That's the way it has been time and again during recent years. Bell Atlantic, which operates in Delaware, Maryland, New Jersey, Pennsylvania, Virginia, West Virginia, and Washington, DC, filed a roll-the-dice lawsuit in Alexandria, Virginia, seeking to be allowed to own and sell video programming within its mandated telephone region. The suit challenged federal laws that kept phone companies out of the programming business in their regions by arguing that the law violated Bell Atlantic's right to free speech—an unconventional constitutional argument that no other phone company had dared to try. Bell Atlantic won, gaining a head start into the TV programming business. Within a year, all other regional Bell companies had filed similar lawsuits in various cities in their own territories. By the end of 1994, most of the others had won.

Bell Atlantic took a shot at the concept of the phone–cable megamerger. It proposed to buy TCI for around $30 billion. While the deal was pending, other phone companies rushed to try to strike deals with major cable companies. When the TCI merger fizzled, so did the megamerger strategy for the industry. Smith said he had come to realize he didn't need to spend all that money to get where he wanted to go. Other CEOs then agreed—although, to be fair, a few had thought all along that the TCI bid was nutty.

Examples go on. One of the latest, unveiled in May 1994, is Bell Atlantic's farsighted $11 billion flexible network architecture, to be built in 20 major markets by 1999. This scheme gets the company's video service off the ground today, not sometime in the future, and coincides with building new megamedia networks and hedging against changes in technology. If the plan works, it should let Bell Atlantic put in new networks as demand evolves and as the networks make economical sense. Most other phone companies' plans call for either racing ahead to build the best technology now, or holding back and moving cautiously. Bell Atlantic is the first to try an aggressive but flexible approach. Don't be surprised if others imitate aspects of the plan.

To grasp the gist of where the telephone industry is heading in megamedia, watch Smith and Bell Atlantic for their triumphs and their foibles. "We are the most aggressive RBOC [regional Bell operating company]," Smith says. "We're a long-standing, 125-year-old company with a great tradition that is changing quickly, and the culture of TCI is the way we're moving—getting leaner, stronger, quicker. Though we've worked hard, we're only halfway there."

In a sense, Smith's Bell Atlantic has been fearless in a time of fear for the regional phone companies and other local telephone players such as GTE and Rochester Telephone. In 1993 and 1994, they had to rethink the very meaning of the kind of companies they had to become—no longer local carriers of phone calls and data, but broad-based technology, information, and entertainment companies. Over the next decade, they'll have to successfully carry out that transformation or risk a fate that echoes that of the big railroad companies at the dawn of the jet age.

In the megamedia universe, no set of companies faces more strategic challenges than the regional phone giants. And no set of companies will be more important to how and when megamedia comes to market.

What are the biggest challenges?

Crumbling Empires

When the old Bell System was broken apart on January 1, 1984, it was divided into seven local telephone companies and AT&T, the long-distance company. The seven companies—Bell Atlantic, US West, Pacific Telesis, Ameritech, NYNEX, SBC Communications (previously Southwestern Bell), and BellSouth—got monopolies within their regions and would not compete against each other. Only a smattering of independent local phone companies, such as Rochester Telephone or Southern New England Telephone, intruded on the Bells' territories. Even then, one company always had a monopoly wherever it operated. Rochester Telephone controlled Rochester, New York, for instance, while the surrounding regional Bell, NYNEX, stayed out.

For most of the decade after the Bell System broke up, the monopolistic walls stood secure. The seven Bells got at least 90 percent of revenue from local phone traffic and the access charges that long-distance companies pay to local phone companies to connect long-distance calls through local networks to individual customers. The seven protected companies grew at a steady, slow pace over the years.

That's all turning to mush. Local access companies such as Teleport have created a booming business of stringing private lines to connect high-volume phone users like factories and office buildings directly to long-distance companies. Customers of Teleport and similar companies save money by bypassing the local phone network. The effect on regional Bells has been that some of their biggest and best customers have been getting siphoned away.

Cellular networks are taking away some other business, and threaten to do more damage. AT&T owns McCaw Cellular, the nation's biggest wireless company. AT&T–McCaw plans to drive cellular prices low enough to compete with local phone service and connect McCaw customers to AT&T's long-distance network, again bypassing the local phone company and swiping revenue from access charges.

Now comes a new threat. Big cable companies are getting into the telephone business, competing directly against the local phone monopolies. Time Warner has been the most aggressive in the United States. TCI, Comcast, and Cox have built and run cable systems in the United Kingdom, where cable companies have been offering competing phone service since 1993—and sucking away up to 25 percent of British Telecom's customers in areas where cable-phone service has been turned on. Those cable companies (and others) want to do a repeat in U.S. markets. So far, state and federal regulations have made that difficult, but the regulations are loosening. Cable companies are getting ready.

Big-time local phone competition is coming. To keep up, the regional phone companies are going to have to offer better service than their competitors, or be able to beat them in price wars. The only way to do either will be to build megamedia networks, which can offer top-of-the-line services and are cheaper to operate than current local phone networks. In light of the threat they're facing, phone companies' megamedia moves are a counteroffensive. Hope you didn't think they were building their new networks out of the goodness of their hearts.

Antiquation

To varying degrees, the phone companies have two current problems: antiquated technology and antiquated people.

The technology anchor is mainly those deadbeat twisted-pair phone lines. They were fine for phone calls. They were even fine for computer connections for a while. But in the new age, communication is going multimedia. People will increasingly exchange information using video, sound, text, or combinations of all three—and they'll want to do it at eye-blink speeds. Twisted-pair phone lines can't handle those operations, but phone companies own twisted-pair lines running into some 90 million U.S. homes and 10 million U.S. businesses. The lines are worth billions of dollars. Switches and other equipment that make the network go are worth billions more, but they add little capacity to handle video or multimedia traffic. Most of the phone company networks are rapidly becoming obsolete.

Phone companies need to find a way to slide from twisted-pair to broadband networks of fiber-optics and coaxial cable. They'll have to do it in a way that doesn't torpedo their balance sheets by writing off billions of dollars' worth of existing equipment while spending billions more on new stuff. Yet, they'll have to act quickly enough to keep up with competitors—mainly the cable companies, which are building their own advanced networks.

Regarding their people, phone company organizations are bloated and, until a few years ago, virtually everyone in management at all seven regional phone companies had nothing but phone company experience. That's changing. All the Bells have been cutting people and management layers, but they've only just begun. They'll have to get leaner and move faster to face the new competition. Many of the Bells have been aggressively hiring people from the computer industry, Hollywood, cable-TV companies, and Madison Avenue. But the majority of top management still has little experience outside the monopoly telephone arena, at a time when their companies are getting into a whole new world.

Regulation

Local phone companies were set up as monopolies, so they were set up to be heavily regulated. The regulations are going to weigh down phone companies, even if Congress passes updated telecommunications laws.

Through 1995, phone companies face a long list of no-no's that make ventures into megamedia more difficult. Unless they win Bell Atlantic-style court cases, none of the regional Bells can own and sell video in their own regions. They can't transmit anything—voice, data, video, or music—across long-distance boundaries. Only long-distance companies like AT&T and MCI can do that. They can't build megamedia networks in their regions until they get permission from the FCC and, usually, from state regulators. Applications to both are typically lengthy ordeals. All of the current rules are at least 10 years old, and some of them date to 1934.

One bit of good news for phone companies is that many likely competitors—including other phone companies, cable-TV companies, and AT&T—are burdened by some similarly complex set of regulations. Congress will try to cut through the bureaucratic tangle for all megamedia companies, and it will likely pass laws that let phone companies get into megamedia businesses more freely. But nobody's expecting too much.

The better news is that the regional phone companies have a handful of gigantic strategic advantages: money, technology, territory, and access.

Money

The Bells are rich. Each of them has annual operating cash flow of more than $4 billion. Every year, Bell Atlantic, for instance, has about $5 billion flowing through the company that it can spend on things like technology, research, new network construction, or acquisition of other companies. Add the seven regional phone companies together and they have a whopping $32 billion or more in cash flow each year, dwarfing the cash flow of any other industry getting into megamedia. That's a lot of wallop.

One caution: The Bells have to be very careful about using that money. Phone company shareholders count on stability and reliably fat dividend payments. The Bells can't suddenly dive into risky growth strategies, spend big, and chance having to cut dividends. Their stock prices would collapse. Their shareholders would revolt. If new competition or an economic recession wilts the Bells' earnings, they could find it harder to pump so much cash into megamedia.

Technology

The Bells may be stuck with low-tech twisted-pair lines, but everything else about their networks is top-shelf technology, including switches, billing systems, and computers that monitor reliability in the networks. The phone companies are comfortable with technology and are used to deploying the newest and best. That should help them to grasp and use megamedia quickly.

Territory

Each phone company has a continuous, connected territory. Cable companies all have scattered, isolated territories. That's a big plus for phone companies. It will be much more efficient and productive to build one big megamedia network versus many small ones.

Access

The regional phone companies are already doing business with and selling services to almost every household and business in the United States. Phone company bills—and the messages and advertising they can carry—land in almost every mailbox. Those are powerful contacts that can't be matched by any other industry. In an effort to turn their corporate names into recognizable brands, Bell Atlantic, Ameritech, and NYNEX have been using logos and ads on bills and other messages that reach their huge customer base. Those brands would, presumably, come to stand for reliable, high-tech communications. That image would become valuable, helping the phone companies to stand out and catch the eye of consumers in a hotly competitive arena.

In the ways they're using their strengths to meet the challenges of crumbling empires, antiquation, and regulation, the regional telephone companies have a lot in common. They all know they'll have to spend their money and use their technology to build broadband megamedia networks somehow, someday. They're all pushing for laws that let them act more like competitive companies than regulated monopolies within their territories. They want to be able to quickly and easily set prices, build networks, and get into new businesses. They've all decided they need to be allied with some kind of content provider. US West has Time Warner. Bell Atlantic, NYNEX, and Pacific Telesis all have joined in a venture with Hollywood agent Michael Ovitz. BellSouth, Ameritech, and Southwestern Bell are getting together with Disney.

Beyond that, the companies diverge. In some ways, they are very different. And Bell Atlantic definitely stands out there alone.

Stargazer

To get a glimpse of Bell Atlantic's ultimate target, spend an afternoon with Larry Plumb. He's the head of communications for a group called Bell Atlantic Video Services Company, in Arlington, Virginia, and he's probably had more practice explaining Stargazer than just about anybody else. Stargazer is Bell Atlantic's programming service, a totally new business for the company and a brand name it hopes will become as well-known as HBO or Showtime. Stargazer apparently will become the core of Bell Atlantic's new venture with NYNEX, Pacific Telesis, and CAA, though terms are sketchy.

Walking through what Stargazer is, how it will be transmitted, and what people will do with it is a good way to look at Bell Atlantic's plans for the future. It even helps explain BAnet, the company's flexible network.

The first stop in Plumb's building is a room plastered with posters from old movies such as *Spartacus* and *Dracula*. At one end of the room are two large Sony TV sets on tall metal stands. Hooked to one TV is a PC-size box with a phone on top—a kind of jerry-built, first-generation interactive set-top box. Plugged into the other TV is a sleeker black box, closer to what is beginning to go into the market. The box on each TV set is linked to nothing but ordinary twisted-pair phone lines. The lines go into the telephone network. When someone dials in—mimicking an on-line PC service such as Prodigy—the boxes can tap into a Bell Atlantic test computer that's acting as a video server.

The technology at work here is called ADSL, short for asymmetric digital subscriber line. ADSL uses computers to cram one reasonably good channel of video over a regular phone line. Plumb dials one of the Sony TVs into the Stargazer computer. When it answers, he punches in an ID number using the telephone keypad, and goes through a menu similar to many phone-mail systems. He looks in a guidebook for the code of the video he wants to see, then punches in that code. The book lists 60 or so movies and shows, from *Sleepless in Seattle* to *George of the Jungle* cartoons. Plumb chooses a Bon Jovi music video. It pops onto the screen in a few seconds and looks as good as anything that comes in over cable-TV lines or the airwaves. It is real, working video on demand, using technology available today—no small feat.

"This changed a lot of people's thinking," Plumb says. "It allowed us to go out and start talking to Hollywood studios and be taken seriously. It's a market-entry technology."

The ADSL version of Stargazer and BAnet has its limitations. The obvious one is that most people don't want to punch codes into a phone to order videos or movies. Another is that a whole video signal doesn't fit down phone lines. ADSL squeezes it to its barest elements, transmitting only the incremental pieces of the picture that change—leaving the background, for instance, on the screen as long as possible. Video that's fairly static (TV news, most movies) looks great. Video that has fast camera pans or scene changes (basketball games, action movies) can fuzz out and look strange. A computer has to work four minutes to create one minute of ADSL video, so live broadcasts are out of the question. Plus, ADSL signals can travel only a mile at best from where they're generated, without breaking up.

A second generation of ADSL will fix some of those shortcomings in 1995–1996. It will make access easier and live broadcasts possible. That should be enough to allow Bell Atlantic to start making Stargazer, transmitted over ADSL lines, available to consumers in some areas. In fact, that's part of Bell Atlantic's flexible network plan. Because ADSL signals would travel over existing phone lines, a Bell Atlantic video service could be deployed quickly, and Stargazer may become the first video-on-demand system up and running commercially. An ADSL version of Stargazer won't blow anybody's socks off, but it might lure some early-adopter customers. At a minimum, it will give Bell Atlantic a crucial head start in the business, learning what customers want, how to make the system work, how to market it, and how to develop programming.

To see the real Stargazer, the one that could someday challenge cable TV, Plumb moves to another room outfitted with a big-screen television. The TV is tied into a computer and laser-disk player that run the Stargazer demo. "This is our concept car," Plumb explains. "It's our lifesize clay model."

Plumb picks up an air mouse, a wandlike remote control that has only a couple of buttons. He points it at the screen and clicks to power up Stargazer. This version is full of graphics to lead viewers around the system. One main visual metaphor is an elevator. Say you want to move from the movie section of Stargazer to a shopping section. Click, and what appear to be elevator doors close briefly across the screen, then let you off on a graphical street. Point the air mouse to move past the stores on the street—J. C. Penney, Sharper Image, Eddie Bauer. The different "floors" of Stargazer include Entertainment, Shopping, Learning, and Assistance. "We believe we need an assistance desk," Plumb says, clicking to call up a little window that will someday show live video of someone akin to a megamedia operator. "That's in case you get lost or need help."

Back on the Entertainment floor, the viewer "walks" past three-dimensional images that lead to other kinds of programming. Some go into linear channels like CBS, ESPN, or Discovery. Others go into music videos, video games, and travel videos. Others move past different genres of movies. Click on a movie title and up pops a brief preview and pricing information. Next to that is an ad for a local pizzeria. Want to order a pizza to go with that movie? Click on menu items to order pepperoni, onions, whatever, then click to order, and wait for the delivery person to knock on the door.

Anybody who ever used a computer would find it easy to use Stargazer, although Plumb says the system needs to be made even easier. "Anybody has to be able to go into this with a two-minute learning curve, no manual," he says.

Stargazer is a complete megamedia programming system. It's an operating environment, the way Windows is an operating environment for PCs. It's a packager of networks and pay-per-view programming, like cable TV today. Into that it will roll commercial activities, like shopping and banking. Eventually, Stargazer may be a programmer itself, producing its own movies or shows the way networks like ABC do, or creating new kinds of interactive services no one has even thought of yet.

That's where the CAA venture comes in. CAA, led by enigmatic Michael Ovitz, is the most powerful talent agency in Hollywood, representing a broad range of stars, including Kevin Costner, Sylvester Stallone, Steven Spielberg, and Eric Clapton. CAA has branched out from its base business, it brokered the deals when Sony bought Columbia Pictures and Matsushita bought MCA, it orchestrated an advertising campaign for Coca-Cola and produced the TV commercials, and it puts together movie packages, assembling screenplay, director and stars from CAA's client list, then sells the complete package to a movie studio.

Smith started talking to Ovitz in 1994, after Ovitz had already been talking with NYNEX and Pacific Telesis executives. "It became clear to me that if we could join with CAA, NYNEX, and PacTel, we had the dream team," Smith says.

Under their agreement, the three Bells will pool their video programming efforts into one jointly-owned company. In a second jointly-owned company, they'll develop technology to deliver megamedia programming. Each of the three Bells will contribute $100 million in cash or assets to launch the operations. Bell Atlantic, which was furthest along in developing video services, will contribute more assets, while the other companies will put up more cash.

Ovitz's CAA will act as a superconsultant to the two joint enterprises. CAA will help hire executives and buy programming, but that's just the beginning. "The regional Bells need to be plugged into Hollywood, and Ovitz is the plug," says Rob Agee, editor of Interactive Television Report. "In one fell swoop, they have instant access to the major studios in Hollywood."

The three Bells say that their programming future is tied to the CAA-guided entities. Stargazer, in fact, may become the programming service offered by Pacific Telesis and NYNEX. The new entities may become powerful factors, given the Bells' money and Ovitz's connections. In the long run, though, the deal doesn't seem to mean the Bells will necessarily act in unison. As megamedia develops, the partners will have very different needs and visions for how they want programming to develop.

Keep in mind that Bell Atlantic is already a driving force in megamedia. It's not going to step aside and let a modestly-funded joint venture dictate the company's future. Stargazer and Bell Atlantic's push into entertainment will move forward one way or another. Time will tell whether the new entities play a leading role.

How this powerful version of Stargazer will get into homes is the second half of Bell Atlantic's flexible network. ADSL and twisted-pair lines won't be good enough—Stargazer will need broadband lines. A combination of coaxial cable and fiber-optic lines will be used first. A fiber-optic line will carry the signals from Bell Atlantic computers and switches into neighborhoods, where the line will connect to boxes that distribute the signals to a few hundred coaxial cable lines that run into nearby homes. Over time, Stargazer may skip the switch to coaxial cable and travel on fiber-optic lines that run right into homes and businesses—a more powerful but more costly set-up that Bell Atlantic will build as demand and economics for megamedia get stronger.

Bell Atlantic has hired AT&T to build most of the BAnet system. General Instrument, IBM, and others will make set-top boxes—as powerful as many PCs—that will decode the Stargazer signals and run the graphics and games and other services. Oracle has signed on to create the computer software that will run Stargazer, sorting and sending out movies and home shopping transactions and any other kind of programming.

Stargazer is a decidedly consumer-oriented product aimed straight into homes. It is actually separate from Bell Atlantic's network—the wires and switches of BAnet will be important to deliver Stargazer, but neither BAnet nor Stargazer will depend on the other for survival. By law, Bell Atlantic's network has to be open to any programmer. If other companies want to send a Stargazer-type system over Bell Atlantic's network, they can. They pay the cost of transmitting over Bell Atlantic's wires. Ray Smith thinks that five or six major programmers will compete over phone company-owned lines in every big market. He points out that more than 100 programmers applied to use what will be the company's first megamedia system, in Alexandria, Virginia—"a big surprise," he says.

The flip side is that Stargazer can travel. When other phone companies build their broadband networks, they too will have to let anyone use them. Bell Atlantic plans to sell Stargazer within its region over its own network, and outside its region over other phone companies' networks. That's unique. By late 1994, none of the other phone companies had moved decidedly toward creating a programming service that they'd sell outside their regions.

BAnet

While Stargazer aims at consumers in their homes anywhere, BAnet will take on the business market in Bell Atlantic's region—a business-heavy area that handles dense telecommunications traffic. The high-speed BAnet network will carry computer data and phone calls for businesses at better prices. As for other kinds of services, the network "will take true interactive multimedia training into large businesses," says Stuart Johnson, group president for video services at Bell Atlantic. "It will do telecommuting with true interactive two-way video to homes."

All in all, the cost of building the network will run $11 billion to $15 billion, spread over five to six years. That sounds like an incredible amount, but it'll probably turn out to be only a couple of billion dollars more than Bell Atlantic would've normally spent over that time frame to upgrade and maintain its networks—a heck of a lot less than Bell Atlantic would've paid to buy TCI.

Other Ventures

Bell Atlantic has been taking a few other interesting steps that show how it will wrap the company in and around megamedia. Realizing the need to lure creative developers of programming and services into its orbit, the company built, in Reston, Virginia, one of the most advanced digital production centers. The center includes digital studios, interactive TV equipment, demonstration centers, and just about every high-tech device anyone would need to create interactive TV shows, new generations of video games, or new kinds of TV channels. The plan is to have developers rent space in the facility, work there, and eventually ease into a relationship with Bell Atlantic. Like Stargazer, the facility is supposed to become part of the venture with CAA.

On the regulatory side, Bell Atlantic is having more success than just about anybody in cutting deals with states to open a path for the company to develop information highways. The biggest successes so far: New Jersey and Delaware, which have agreed to innovative schemes that cap prices for customers while letting Bell Atlantic build megamedia networks.

To round out the company, Bell Atlantic keeps investing in wireless networks and international businesses. The most striking deals are a $1 billion investment in Iusacell, a Mexican cellular phone company, and a plan to merge Bell Atlantic's wireless operations with NYNEX's wireless business to create a giant in that industry.

The Helmsman

All of those moves, all the aggressiveness of Bell Atlantic, go back to how Ray Smith thinks and how he sees megamedia unfolding. No one else in the telephone industry has been more convinced that megamedia is coming quickly.

"You have to believe the markets are going to expand tremendously," Smith says. "There are a lot of indications that will take place. The computer generation is now coming forward—the twenty-somethings—and boomers are retraining themselves into computer jocks. The market will be dominated by people who want to use intelligent terminals to manage their lives. People will want to shop at home if they can do it conveniently. QVC has 5,000 people taking orders as fast as they can. That's a noninteractive, rudimentary service. If you had easy billing and a way to browse through the video equivalent of catalogs, it would grow stupendously. It would be a major substitute for the way we shop today.

"All you have to do is make some very modest estimates as to how revenues will begin to drift and you can get excited about what will happen in 1995, '96, '97, '98, '99." The only new telecommunications business opportunity Smith has ever been more certain about came around 10 years ago, and that was cellular phones.

Smith's ability to digest all that's going on and see ahead of it might come from his college days at Carnegie Mellon University in Pittsburgh. The school had two major programs that were essentially side-by-side on campus: an engineering school and a drama school. "We called them fruits and vegetables," Smith recalls. "I was a vegetable because I was an engineer. The fruits were the drama students. So there was a kind of convergent thinking there. The kind of people you knew and your fraternity brothers—you were sitting around with engineers and drama students, not just engineers." It made Smith look beyond the borders of technology and consider more of a worldview. It also sparked his ongoing affair with the theater.

After college, Smith joined the Bell System and went on a swift but fairly unremarkable career-long journey up the Bell ranks. In 1985, he was named Bell Atlantic's chief financial officer. In 1988, Smith was told he'd ascend to the company's top spot in a year, when then-chairman Thomas Bolger retired. That gave Smith a year to do some deep thinking about where Bell Atlantic would have to go during his reign.

Smith thinks by writing. "Good, solid, boring writing," he says, "but it's pages and pages. When I'm trying to think of strategy and the big picture, I'm not just talking it or reading others' briefings. I write what I think it is." He tends to chew around ideas with the company's technology experts or with its legal and regulatory staff. He travels a lot and meets and talks with other leaders, such as Intel chairman Andrew Grove, Vice President Al Gore, and George Lucas, film producer and king of technology in Hollywood. Then Smith comes back and writes. "It forces me to figure out what people are saying and what I'm really thinking," he says.

When he started thinking about the future, there was no megamedia epiphany. This most aggressive, gung-ho phone company CEO first latched onto megamedia for defensive reasons. "It doesn't sound sexy," Smith says, "but I concluded that our communication network had to deliver every kind of information that was ever going to exist (including video), or we'd be at a disadvantage." The last phrase is a CEO euphemism. What Smith believed was that if Bell Atlantic didn't replace its twisted-pair copper lines with broadband digital networks, the company was going to get its butt kicked before the end of the century. Smith did not start out by thinking that Bell Atlantic's golden opportunity was to become a TV programmer.

Smith's vision for Bell Atlantic evolved over about three years. First came the idea that the network had to be advanced enough to deliver full-motion, high-quality video, and that would mean building fiber-optic lines, digital switches, and all the attachments. But regulatory roadblocks would have to be shattered. Bell Atlantic launched a flurry of legal maneuvers. Among them was the case brought in Alexandria.

While helping to prepare the case—again, a task that involved writing—Smith came to understand the value of content in the coming age. "We wanted to be a programmer, a producer, and sell it. Of course we did!" he says. At first, Smith was thinking purely about information content, such as news reports or financial data. Not until 1993 did Smith believe Bell Atlantic had to get into entertainment, too.

As Bell Atlantic built more digital and fiber-optic technology in 1991, the rest of the picture became clear for Smith. The system would need computer servers to store and send movies, news, and other content to consumers. Because servers could easily manipulate content, the system could be interactive. And if it were interactive, Bell Atlantic could sell video on demand and create TV shopping malls. "I drew up cartoons—had to draw them myself—to explain it to people inside and outside our business," Smith says.

Inside Bell Atlantic, the technologists, who had been kicking around these ideas with Smith, were excited and ready to drive ahead. Operations managers were harder to convince. They didn't want to change. Smith believes that a vision tag-line adopted in 1991 helped break through managers' jammed thinking. The vision: "To be the world's best information and communications company."

Says Smith: "That word 'information' drove us. When having strategic planning reviews, people would say, 'That's great for communications, but where does information come in?'" The word "entertainment" has since been added to the vision.

The TCI deal in 1993 would have made a great leap toward Smith's vision. But the deal's collapse didn't change the vision or Smith's resolve to chase it. These days, Smith has defined four markets for Bell Atlantic, and the company is pursuing all of them. Smith says he is absolutely sure they will be good businesses beginning in the next few years. The businesses, and his terms for them, are:

1. "Anywhere, anytime communication"—wireless devices that can send and receive voice, data, or video, and the concept of having one phone number that can find someone at home, at the office, or on a cellular phone.
2. "Information at your fingertips"—electronic mail, computer networks, handheld computers that can communicate over wireless networks, video communication on computers.
3. "Entertainment redefined"—video on demand, on-line video games, huge selections of sports and programming.
4. "Virtual shopping mall"—interactive home shopping using a PC or TV set.

If any part of the strategy worries Smith, it's entertainment, which is furthest from Bell Atlantic's traditions and core capabilities. It is a rat's nest of egos, intellectual property rights, and contracts. The competition will be companies such as The Walt Disney

Company, Viacom, TCI, Capital Cities/ABC—basically, the best in the world at producing entertainment. Bell Atlantic has steep mountains to climb. That's why it turned to CAA for help.

"Can we combine the skills of Disney and Warner and Bell Atlantic and all kinds of companies and be in this and produce it? The answer is probably yes," Smith says. But he quickly adds that the key question is: "Can we do it on a timely basis? I certainly hope so."

This area will be a big part of Smith's next few years. He says he is now spending "a stupendous amount of time" on content, especially entertainment. That means learning, forming partnerships, hiring talented people, possibly even buying or investing in entertainment companies—though he says that doesn't include major acquisitions like buying a movie studio. Deals will be narrowly targeted, more like individual projects. Bell Atlantic, with guidance from CAA, may begin financing movies to be produced at its Reston digital studio and distributed by Stargazer—in essence, acting like a Hollywood studio.

In other areas, Bell Atlantic's overall megamedia strategy is set. Smith will have to adjust it as regulations or technology change. He'll spend some time helping the company to create alliances and to make acquisitions to meet its goals.

Will Bell Atlantic succeed? Its ambitions are huge. It is now one of the world's best local phone companies. No doubt it can build its high-tech network and become one of the world's best all-around communications companies. But Bell Atlantic wants to develop into something far greater, reaching lightyears beyond its current business borders. It strains imagination to think of a phone company finding success in entertainment and home shopping.

Yet Bell Atlantic has shown it is willing to be aggressive and take risks. It's much further into megamedia—all aspects of it—than any of its sister companies. Bell Atlantic will make the big reach. Some things may elude its grasp—maybe TV shows, maybe something else. But it's likely to do well in some surprising new areas. It will continue to lead its industry and to be an ever more interesting company.

A gigantic ambition? "Sure it is," Smith says with a shrug. "That's what visions are supposed to be."

US WEST: COWBOY CULTURE GOES BIG-TIME

Richard McCormick is 2,000 miles and a few lightyears away from Ray Smith. Tall, lanky, stiff, quiet, the chairman of Englewood, Colorado-based US West is nothing like Smith's butter-smooth ball of energy. He's married, a father of four, a telephone man since joining AT&T in 1961 as an engineer in Kansas City. When he wants a little excitement, McCormick gets on his Harley-Davidson motorcycle after work and rides off to dinner somewhere.

He doesn't seem to have the megamedia vision thing, at least not when you talk to him. When he runs down US West's biggest moves, he sounds like a proud parent awed by his children's accomplishments, not a driving force who made it all happen from the top down. "I'm kind of a laid-back, low-key, sleepy guy," McCormick admits. "I'm not a publicity seeker. I think I'm a consensus builder. I believe in putting the best team of people together and letting them take the credit. If I have to settle a fight, I'll settle it, and I think I'm capable of making the hard decisions."

His purpose comes down to this: "I like to get the strategy right and have our actions speak instead of our words."

Somehow, it works. If any regional telephone company is going to race Bell Atlantic for first place in the megamedia marathon, it's US West. Over the past few years, under McCormick, US West has pulled together a forward-looking management team of people from inside and outside the phone business, developed a bit of a cowboy culture that's willing to break from the industry pack, and struck alliances with key outside companies—a combination that is launching the Rocky Mountain regional Bell into a new era.

US West has one key advantage that so far has pretty much eluded Bell Atlantic or any other telephone company: it has piled up a wealth of real, working television experience, thanks to strong relationships with two of the leading entertainment companies in the world, Time Warner and TCI.

US West has a lot of megamedia projects under way. It is helping Time Warner turn its cable systems into interactive TV and multimedia communications networks. It's building its own megamedia networks within its region. It's working on digital projects in the United Kingdom. The foundation underneath all those projects is the interaction between US West and Time Warner or TCI.

The interaction works on several levels, not just as a way to trade knowledge of phones for knowledge of TV. "Time Warner is tremendously entrepreneurial and creative, while we at US West have a history of running a highly technology-driven business," says Tom Pardun, the US West executive managing the company's alliance with Time Warner. "We're trying to learn from and take the best of both companies."

The Time Warner alliance is certainly at the forefront of anything US West does in megamedia. As of late 1994, the alliance was the only standing telephone–cable megadeal. In May 1993, US West paid $2.5 billion for a 25.5 percent stake in Time Warner Entertainment. That gave US West 50 percent control and joint management of Time Warner Cable, the nation's second biggest cable operator behind TCI. Just as importantly, it handed US West 25.5 percent of the powerful Warner Bros. movie studio and 25.5 percent of the Home Box Office (HBO) premium movie channel, both Time Warner properties. That made US West the first phone company to own hands-on stakes in high-caliber programming companies.

The structure of the deal has helped make it work. Ask anyone—analysts, insiders, competitors—and they'll say that the alliance has come together beautifully. Skills from the two companies seem to complement each other. Managers have been getting along, and top-level executives have meshed strategy and vision. US West has enough power to feel like a confident insider at Time Warner, but not enough to threaten any of the Time Warner units or plow under their cultures. "We're stirring together two ingredients and they won't be the same after they're stirred and they can't be taken apart," says Tom Morrow, who's in a unique position to see this mixture. Morrow worked for US West for years and helped US West decide to make the Time Warner investment. Then he went over to the other side, joining Time Warner Cable to help it get into the telephone business.

US West and Time Warner have discussed altering the financial structure of US West's investment, but both companies insist that won't change or hurt their growing relationship.

The first frontal assault on megamedia by US West–Time Warner is the Full Service Network (FSN) in Orlando, Florida. An interactive TV and communications network, FSN is mostly a Time Warner project, a prototype for rebuilding all of Time Warner's cable systems. US West is putting together the telephone portion of FSN—and learning from Time Warner.

Separately, in Omaha, US West is running a TV test system that's similar to FSN. The Omaha project is primarily US West's, although Time Warner has influenced it. One small but tangible influence: Time Warner is putting Hewlett-Packard printers next to its Orlando interactive TVs to print coupons or messages. After seeing that innovation, US West decided to put the printers in Omaha, too.

"We think of the two tests as fraternal twins," says US West's Pardun. "We're taking the best data from the two trials and sharing the information."

What's ahead for the alliance? US West will continue helping Time Warner get into the telephone business. It's already building voice telephone capabilities into Time Warner's cable system in Rochester, New York—the first city that will have true competition between cable and phone companies for local telephone traffic. Elsewhere, Time Warner will advise US West on the phone company's roll-out of interactive TV within US West's region. The companies haven't said much about how US West might use its stakes in Warner Bros. and HBO, but, among other possibilities, those companies can be expected to work with US West to develop interactive products—maybe an HBO movies-on-demand system or a Warner Bros. Studio Stores shopping channel. US West is working on an interactive service that will let viewers look at movie listings, see trailers and interviews with stars, and buy related products. The service will run on both US West and Time Warner networks.

Count on US West's money to help Time Warner expand its holdings in cable or megamedia-related businesses. Look for the pair to be buyers throughout the rest of the 1990s. US West has shown it will also be a cable buyer on its own. In the summer of 1994, it paid $1.2 billion to buy two prime cable systems outside Atlanta. The systems happen to be adjacent to big Time Warner cable systems in Atlanta. By operating the systems together, US West and Time Warner will be able to create telephone service to compete against the local phone company, BellSouth. The pair of companies could also more efficiently build an interactive TV system by spreading it across the Atlanta area.

By the end of 1995, US West was rumored to be negotiating to buy a number of huge cable companies. Some of the rumors had it buying Cablevision Systems, which operates on Long Island, next to Time Warner's big cable system in Queens, New York. Another had US West buying Continental Cable, which is strong in New England. Still another said it would buy Viacom's cable holdings, which are worth more than $2 billion.

If US West completes one of those big deals, the US West–Time Warner alliance would likely become the number one U.S. cable company, ending TCI's long reign at the top.

The switch would be a little ironic. US West's relationship with Time Warner is obvious. Yet US West has a subtle relationship with TCI that's almost as valuable.

The two companies' headquarters are only a few miles apart in suburban Denver's busy office-park sprawl. "It's a good relationship, one both companies have worked hard on the last five years," McCormick says. "We've gone from almost no contact then to full-fledged partners in the U.K." McCormick is referring to Telewest, one of the biggest cable TV companies in the United Kingdom. Telewest is also one of the U.K. cable companies that offers phone service over its network, competing against British Telecom. US West and TCI jointly own and operate Telewest. US West's positive experience with Telewest was a huge factor in US West's decision to pump $2.5 billion into Time Warner.

By the way, US West doesn't own a stake in TCI and probably never will. Many of TCI's cable systems are in US West's territory, and regulations prevent US West from owning cable operations in its region. As of late 1994, direct investment in TCI would only become a regulatory and financial mess for US West.

Still, the two will likely do more together. They've long been partners, along with AT&T, in a venture that has been testing movies on demand in Littleton, Colorado. "We do discuss options in the U.S.," McCormick says of John Malone and TCI. "Though we'll compete in some places, I believe we'll be partners elsewhere."

Whatever they do together, there's no doubt US West keeps absorbing knowledge about television from TCI and benefits from being able to have strategic discussions with Malone, a CEO who ranks among the most aggressive in all of megamedia. For a long time, that will help keep US West ahead of the curve when it comes to getting into video.

One other slice of US West shows how it's been smart about learning new businesses early. In 1994, in the U.K., it turned on the world's first commercial PCS phone network—a partnership with Cable & Wireless, a U.K. phone company, called Mercury One-2-One. PCS is a digital, wireless phone, like cellular phones but cheaper to operate. PCS will likely come to the United States in 1995, and US West will once again have a head start.

A good deal of US West's megamedia strategy is aimed outside its territory, with partners. That makes sense, considering that US West's operating territory is the most spread-out and sparsely populated of any of the regional Bells. Its states are Arizona, Colorado, Idaho, Iowa, Minnesota, Montana, Nebraska, New Mexico, North Dakota, Oregon, South Dakota, Utah, Washington, and Wyoming. Not exactly urban, information-intensive areas. That means that the potential of its markets is limited, so US West has to look outside to become a major communications player. It also means that competitors will be less likely to invade many of US West's markets, at least not until after they've marched on riper markets in places like California and New England. By that point, US West may have already built megamedia systems in its top markets—US West has, after all, announced one of the more aggressive construction plans. Its interactive TV system in Omaha will soon pass 60,000 homes and it is building systems in Denver, Minneapolis-St. Paul, Boise, and Portland. Plans for building in dozens of other cities are ready. At this point, only Bell Atlantic and Pacific Telesis are spending more and building faster.

Still, the new networks may be the least of what US West brings to this party. The company's rich experience and first-class friends may give it the best chance among phone companies to develop the touch and feel, the services and programming—the software—that will turn wires and computers into a business. None of that is lost on Chairman McCormick. In his aw-shucks Midwestern way, he simply says, "I feel very good about the position we're in."

PACIFIC TELESIS: FORTRESS CALIFORNIA

Think of California as a communications-age jewel. It has some of the busiest information and entertainment centers in the world—Los Angeles, San Francisco, San Diego. It has Hollywood. It has Silicon Valley. Its population looks at new gismos, and new ways of doing things, a little differently than people anywhere else. Says Pacific Telesis chief strategist Forrest Miller: "Early adoption is a way of life here."

Pacific Telesis (PacTel) is the telephone company for California. For now, it owns the state, in telecommunications terms. To conceptualize PacTel's megamedia strategy, picture this: the company is racing like hell to build the equivalent of a communications-age fort around California, hoping it can get the moats, the gates, the walls, and all the battlements secured before the barbaric invaders (we know them as cable-TV companies) come crashing in to pillage the place.

Sometimes, even the people at Pacific Telesis talk about their strategy that way. "Nobody ever won a war by abandoning their home territory," says Lee Camp, the vice president in charge of megamedia for PacTel.

The company calls its plan "California First." It is the speediest megamedia network construction project of all, outgunning even Bell Atlantic in raw dollars, pace of connections to homes, and concentrated, single-minded intensity. PacTel plans to spend $16 billion through 2000; its goal is to make information superhighway-type services available to half of all homes in California by the century's end. As the construction gets up to speed, it is passing 2,000 homes a day, 700,000 a year. The PacTel folks aren't being diverted by venturing outside their regions or by developing sophisticated programming services like Bell Atlantic's Stargazer. Un-unh. They're sticking to what they know (building networks) and the place they know (California). Full speed ahead.

It's a huge gamble. Maybe PacTel can win California. Then it will have a terrifically strong base from which to expand in future decades. Maybe by sticking close to home it will avoid embarrassments that might blast holes in companies like US West and Bell Atlantic.

PacTel's strategy pivots on geography. Besides California, the company's territory includes only one other state, Nevada, which brings in less than 2 percent of PacTel's revenue. California hasn't exactly been cooking in the first part of the 1990s thanks to a stalled economy. But over the long haul, the state is certain to be an economic monster. "It's quite an engine," says Miller, a big man stuffed into a small office chair in a conference room in the San Ramon, California, complex where most of PacTel's megamedia group works. "That's an advantage and a disadvantage. The advantage is, these are terrific markets. The disadvantage is, that's not lost on other people."

The strongest cable operators in the country—TCI, Time Warner, and the newly merged Cox Cable and Times Mirror Cable companies—all have major franchises up and down the state. All have big video and telecommunications plans for California.

"If we're going to be faced with competition relatively early," Miller says, "we're going to have to take care of that first. The greatest risk is sitting still."

Miller and his team believe they're alleviating some of the risk in the all-out plan by building a network that can start saving PacTel millions of dollars in operating costs right away. Fiber-optic lines, the backbone of the new network, are far more trouble-free than copper lines. PacTel is also equipping the network with loads of diagnostic hardware and software, which should help the company fix problems more easily and more cheaply. As Miller sees it, the network could allow the company to employ fewer repair people, dispatch fewer trucks, and lose less business because of downed lines or switches—all adding up to a system that pays for itself even before the futuristic interactive services come on line.

Once the network is in place and interactive TV turns into reality, PacTel seems—for now, anyway—to want to be mostly a transport company, not a programmer. Lee Camp's group had been working on interactive TV models along the lines of Stargazer before entering into the nascent venture with Bell Atlantic, NYNEX and CAA. Pacific Telesis is trusting its programming future to that venture. The company has never made the same kind of commitment to programming as Bell Atlantic or US West. "If certain [interactive TV] services play to our skills, we'll provide them," says strategist Miller. "But you won't see us going out to buy a Paramount. We're more likely to design information services, like work-at-home software and systems."

Telecommuting is an example of how California First applies to more than hardware. Commuting is a particular problem in the state. The clogged freeways of Los Angeles and the choke-points between San Francisco and Silicon Valley are famous nationwide. PacTel is pushing the concept of telecommuting by putting together packages of services for telecommuters using today's technology and by trying to work at cultural change, within companies, that will make working from home more acceptable. Once megamedia networks make two-way video meetings possible, look for that push to accelerate.

In another sly little way, PacTel intends to turn a California problem into its own strategic advantage. Through the 1990s, the state has been disaster-prone—earthquakes, fires, mud slides, riots. In general, during disasters, cable-TV systems are much more likely to go dead than phone systems. Telephone systems are more reliable and are stocked with back-up components and redundant systems that cable doesn't use. If electricity goes out, the cable system goes out. But phone networks don't. They carry their own power—just enough electricity to make a phone ring and carry the signal. Cable systems can't do that yet. As competition heats up against cable companies, Pacific Telesis fully intends to make sure Californians associate PacTel with reliability during the kinds of nightmares that the state will surely face again.

Even when it comes to alliances, PacTel is sticking to California. CAA is a Hollywood company. Its other information superhighway venture is with *The Los Angeles Times.* The alliance is developing information services, such as electronic classifieds and business listings, that would be accessed through PacTel's new network.

Its wireless strategy and ways to marry it to megamedia are all focused on the state. PacTel made the unique move, in 1994, of spinning its international cellular business into a separate company, now called AirTouch. Current focus is on the coming PCS phones. PacTel aims to win licenses within California.

A lot can go wrong with PacTel's megamedia strategy. In almost every way, the company is leaving itself wide open to danger.

What if the savings from the self-diagnosing network are overstated? It definitely stretches believability that the company could spend $3 billion a year building the network and somehow come out saving that much by cutting staff and making fewer repairs.

What if the company builds too fast, putting in expensive networks long before applications and customers emerge to make them profitable? PacTel is not giving itself the flexible leeway of Bell Atlantic, which might let the Eastern giant adjust if markets evolve more slowly. PacTel doesn't have the rounded approach of US West's investments inside and outside its home turf and in some programming, all of which could cushion such a blow.

PCS is no sure thing. Pacific Telesis has abandoned a proven competitor in wireless—cellular phones—in favor of a potentially strong but completely unknown service that's still being buffeted by regulatory winds. How long will it take to get PCS up and running? How much will it cost? How much of an edge will it have on traditional cellular? No one knows the answers yet.

One very real possibility PacTel faces is price wars. If plane loads of competitors plan to come to California to build megamedia networks that will tap the state's riches, there's sure to be a battle based in part on prices—much like a decade ago, when AT&T, MCI, Sprint, and others first unleashed long-distance competition. Price wars usually affect hardware, whether it's a high-tech network, personal computers, or VCRs. The way to get around price wars is to have some kind of special programming or service—software—that can't be duplicated. By putting a whole lot of its eggs in the hardware basket, PacTel could get badly damaged if price wars break out. Perhaps anticipating that possibility, PacTel has hired an executive who has some experience fighting price battles. In mid-1994, David Dorman was named chief executive of the Pacific Bell division. For 14 years, Dorman had previously been at Sprint.

Price wars will probably be a part of the wireless phone business, too. PacTel may start up PCS networks throughout the state, but PCS phones will compete against established cellular phones and against another kind of wireless phone network being built by Nextel in most parts of California. Profit margins may get pretty thin in that business in four or five years.

On the one hand, Lee Camp is right: Pacific Telesis has to defend California, no matter how many competitors come barging in. If PacTel can hold onto the state, then it can expand. As Camp says, "After all, the plan is California First, not California Forever."

On the other hand, if the walls of PacTel's Fortress California don't hold, the company has nothing to fall back on.

AMERITECH: MOST LIKELY TO NEITHER SUCCEED NOR FAIL

Dick Notebaert can barely contain himself. Ameritech's chairman is like that—high-energy, a far cry from mellow and gracious Walt Weiss, who retired from Ameritech and handed Notebaert the top job in 1994. What seems to get Notebaert going are little entrepreneural ventures that pop up within Ameritech, no matter how small or silly. One is basically a voice-mail greeting card that can be sent to a loved one. Another is a computer program called WinGopher, which a small group at Ameritech developed to help people find their way around the Internet, the humongous and complex worldwide computer network. Talking about those ventures, Notebaert bounces in his seat; his voice rises, his hands gesture.

He gets even more ebullient when he starts describing Ameritech's work with Intel. Intel is developing and selling PC hardware that lets people make video phone calls using two PCs linked over regular twisted-pair phone lines, and Ameritech is one of many communications companies helping. The video is crude and choppy, but it works. Notebaert has one of the PCs on his office desk. He wants to get one for his daughter, a college student, so the two of them can keep in touch via video. "And now I want one in my home," he says. "You're going to get used to having things like that in the workplace, and you're going to want to have them at home."

It's not hard to see what fuels Notebaert's motor. He likes a freewheeling organization that will pounce on opportunities. He wants to take megamedia to the business market first, believing that almost all new technology migrates from business to consumer markets. For the rest of the 1990s, two motives will drive most of Ameritech's megamedia strategy: retooling into a lean, competitive company, and chasing the business market.

Doesn't sound too exciting? It's not—by design. Ameritech's megamedia effort might be described as "carefully aggressive." The company, which operates in Illinois, Indiana, Michigan, Ohio, and Wisconsin, has a basic philosophy that megamedia will evolve slowly, not at lightning speed. There's no rush. The company hasn't tried to buy any cable companies. It hasn't invested in a movie studio. It hasn't unveiled any $10 billion-plus network construction projects. Its only programming venture is an alliance with Disney and two other Bells. As of this writing, the companies have revealed little about the alliance.

But Ameritech hasn't been sitting on the sidelines. It's spending a fairly modest $4.4 billion to connect 6 million customers to megamedia networks by 2000. It has struck a few low-key alliances—the one with Intel, and another with General Electric to create information services that could travel the network. It would be hard to find a better programming partner than Disney.

Most of Ameritech's other moves are off the beaten path, quite different from those of its sister companies. Ameritech aims at doing things that make good business sense today, while starting the company on a straight and well-paved path to the brave new future.

That approach seems to make Ameritech the company most likely to neither succeed nor fail. It's simply not taking the big risks that could either vault it into a leadership role or blow it out of the water. Most likely, Ameritech's plan will prove to be a solid, prudent way to move ahead while avoiding big potholes. That's just where Notebaert wants to be. "People have said we'd be left standing by the side of the road," Notebaert says, ever-confident that the Bell Atlantics and US Wests have overdone it. "Now they're saying maybe we're right."

One way Ameritech has gotten ahead of its peers has been by reengineering (to use a popular term) the way the company works on the inside. None of the internal operations of the other regional Bells seems as well-managed, lean, and entrepreneurial, or better structured to handle competition when it emerges.

Weiss started that change in 1990–1991. "The Board and I decided that something had to happen or we were just going to be a tired old telephone company 10 years or 20 years down the path," Weiss says. "In February of 1992, the top 30 people in our business met off-site in The Breakers in Palm Beach, Florida. On Sunday night, when we started our conference, I said that we're about to do something that we have never contemplated before. We're going to destroy our company and rebuild it." The goal was to break down the old Bell structure, which divided the company up by regions and focused on the network—a utility company's approach to business. The process that started in Palm Beach spread back to Ameritech's Chicago headquarters and was communicated to teams across the company. A year later, in February 1993, Ameritech sacked the regional approach and divided the company up by products and services, such as small business services, consumer services, and cellular. The focus changed from the network to customers. The company started sliding away from being a utility and moving toward becoming a competitive organization.

The transition hasn't been easy, but Weiss is sure that it's making a difference to Ameritech's future. "We came from a history of entitlement," he says. "The only way you are going to have security in the future is if you earn it in the marketplace every day; so your entitlement is based on what you contribute to the company, not your right to be here. It has made an absolutely marvelous difference. There is more energy in our business today than I have sensed in my 43 years."

Notebaert is trying to take the changing culture he inherited and move it deeper into entrepreneurship. He has helped bring in dozens of people from other, competitive industries. Patrick Campbell, who came in as executive vice president of strategy and business development, was hired from Sony-owned Columbia TriStar Home Video. Jack Reich, hired from MCI, came aboard as president of multinational accounts. "These people really change our perspective," Notebaert says. At the same time, Notebaert is furiously watering any seeds of entrepreneurship that spring up in the company. He tells anybody who will listen how one group came up with the idea for WinGopher "and somebody just said, Do it. There's all this creativity just bubbling up."

Ameritech's approach isn't as visible or enthralling as Bell Atlantic's whirlwind creation of enormous webs of megamedia networks and products. But over the long haul, it may be nearly as important. If Notebaert can follow through on the internal makeover, Ameritech might be well-positioned to react as changes happen in the marketplace. Flexibility will be built into the company instead of into the network.

The other side of Notebaert's strategy is a focus on business—specifically, business within Ameritech's region. "Everything written in the media deals with consumer home entertainment—how you get into the home," Notebaert says. "We agree with that and we've announced our infrastructure to reach into consumers' homes. But we also say, everything starts in the workplace, whether it's a VCR, a cellular phone, or even something as mundane as central air conditioning."

Ameritech's megamedia network will pass businesses *and* homes, but business will be the first to connect to it and use it and pay for it, Notebaert believes. The Intel videoconferencing PCs are aimed at business first; so are the Ameritech–General Electric information services and electronic commerce. The company has developed the Wisconsin Health Information Network, a multimedia system that connects more than 800 doctors and 15 hospitals, allowing them to trade information on patients, look at X rays from afar, and—especially—fill out and file insurance forms electronically. Ameritech believes the health care industry will be a long-term driver of megamedia networks. The business of setting up health care networks is turning into an exportable sideline: Ameritech is building and operating a health care network in Nashville, Tennessee, which is within BellSouth's region.

Ameritech is making other moves toward megamedia and competition. It has been the most vociferous regional Bell in calling for open competition for local phone traffic and long-distance calling. The company has been actively trying to break its network into pieces that could be leased to companies that want to offer alternative phone service. For example, say a local cable-TV company has lines running around town but no switches and no capability to track calls for billing customers. Ameritech would want to lease its own switches and billing services to that cable company, letting competition in but ensuring Ameritech gets a cut of the action. At the same time, Ameritech is demanding to be allowed to offer long-distance service. Again, its confidence about letting in local competition or getting into the highly competitive long-distance arena goes back to Ameritech's new, competitive internal culture.

For the most part, though, look for the company to stay home and stay cautious. Its Midwestern region is rich enough to support a good megamedia market, but not rich enough to lure intense competition the way California or New England will. (Time Warner and MCI, however, have plans to invade Ameritech's turf.) If the company stays on course, everything seems to point to a steady, growing, solid, and reasonably dull future. That is, unless you talk to Dick Notebaert. He will no doubt find a lot more thrills to send him bouncing out of his chair over the next decade.

NYNEX: A TICKING TIME BOMB

When it comes to megamedia, NYNEX comes off as the flailing Bell.

NYNEX has tried a lot of things in its effort to line up for the future, but few of them—not even its $1.2 billion investment in Viacom—have helped much. The exception has been NYNEX's moves outside the United States, mostly in the United Kingdom and Asia. At the rate it's going, NYNEX should probably close up shop in New York and New England and just run an international company.

That's a bit harsh, but all I had to do was listen to Alan Bennett to know that NYNEX is going to have a hard time dealing with megamedia. NYNEX thought it was being smart by hiring Bennett to be president of interactive entertainment for the company. Bennett has a long TV-industry pedigree, having run TV stations and syndicated programming companies. That would make NYNEX the only telephone company to put a TV entertainment guy in that kind of lofty position. It's the kind of person the phone companies should hire—somebody with a completely different perspective and entertainment expertise to jostle those technoid, engineering minds.

Bennett, a wiry speedball of a man who talks fast and walks fast, landed at NYNEX in 1993 and ran into a brick wall. He has tried to freshen up the company's ideas about interactive television and programming, but he feels he's having a very frustrating time. The telephone people have fought the outsider. "It's like the white corpuscles coming out to attack," he says.

Bennett's experience fits with the bigger NYNEX picture. The company seems to know what it should do in megamedia, so it takes a lunge at some aspect of it, then falls short and lands on its noggin.

To back up for a moment, NYNEX is the phone company for New York, Connecticut, Massachusetts, Maine, New Hampshire, Rhode Island, and Vermont. It is, by any measurement, the least efficient and least productive regional phone company. It had suffered under a muddy leadership situation. Long-time chairman William Ferguson was so low-profile he was almost invisible. Frederic Salerno, the vice chairman, has been more visible but always seems to be apologizing, not leading. Ivan Seidenberg took over as chairman in April 1995. "He is a breath of fresh air," says Steven Yanis, analyst at Kidder Peabody. But Seidenberg will have a tough time turning around NYNEX.

NYNEX has the fewest cellular customers, except for Pacific Telesis, which spun off its cellular operations into a separate company. Its megamedia market trials are among the skimpiest of all the phone companies. Its plans for new network construction are sketchy at best, at least as far as anyone at NYNEX has described them in public. Its biggest announcement has been a plan to wire about 330,000 homes in the Boston area for interactive services.

Meanwhile, the company is sitting on a ticking time bomb. Its region, especially the New York-to-Boston corridor, is one of the most densely populated telecommunications hubs in the world. That could be good for NYNEX, except that all kinds of companies are planning to take bites out of the region's telephone traffic. That includes alternate access companies such as Teleport and new wireless company Nextel. Both are already operating in the New York area. Cable-TV company Time Warner and its partner, US West, have discussed buying Cablevision. Together, they would cover a good deal of metropolitan New York with a network that could be upgraded to compete for phone service. To top it off, regulators in New York State, where NYNEX has 64 percent of its phone customers, are among the most aggressive at encouraging telephone competition.

Add up the pieces, and of all the regional phone companies, NYNEX seems to most desperately need a successful megamedia strategy.

Salerno keeps saying that the kind of moves other Bells have made—big cable deals or gigantic construction projects—are too expensive and too risky. NYNEX is, finally, trying to renovate its internal operations along the lines of what Ameritech has done. But, in general, NYNEX thinks it has a better way.

What way is that? One answer is: going international. NYNEX has bought and built cable systems in the United Kingdom for probably one-third less per subscriber than the going rate for cable systems in the United States. NYNEX is now about even with Telewest for the title of biggest cable company in England. The U.K. cable systems have been growing in value and becoming increasingly profitable, which is all to NYNEX's credit. But TV opportunities in the United Kingdom are minuscule compared to those in the United States. Is NYNEX getting all it can out of the U.K. experience so it can import TV knowledge back to possible U.S. markets? No. NYNEX is the only phone company involved in U.K. cable that's going it alone. US West is in Telewest with TCI. Southwestern Bell is in a U.K. venture with Cox Cable. Those companies are learning cable TV from the best and are building TV industry relationships. They're also learning how TV and phone cultures might mesh—good to know if your phone company might someday buy TV operations. NYNEX is getting too few of those lessons from its U.K. systems.

NYNEX is also about to go into cable TV in Thailand—again, by itself.

NYNEX's most daring and visible megamedia venture is its investment in Viacom. It put up the money during Viacom's battle against QVC to take over Paramount. The investment helped Viacom win. NYNEX got two seats on the newly merged company's board of directors.

But NYNEX didn't get much else. It doesn't have any defined control, like US West's share at Time Warner Entertainment. There were no promises to create programming for NYNEX, no prearranged working relationships that might let the companies trade knowledge. Most analysts felt NYNEX made a bad investment, putting up too little money to gain any real clout at Viacom. Even top executives at Viacom imply they don't quite know what to do with NYNEX. Salerno, who fought to get NYNEX to put its money into Viacom, may have been passed over for the chairman job because of the deal, say NYNEX insiders.

NYNEX never seemed to know what it wanted with Viacom. It often has said that the investment would guarantee that programming from Viacom and Paramount would be available for whatever networks NYNEX might build. But that's a pretty thin reason. It assumes TV shows, movies, and entire TV channels will become tied up so they can only be broadcast over certain networks, like the Fox network's deal to tie up NFC football games. That's not likely. Federal rules prevent some of that from happening, and programmers will almost always want to sell their goods over as many networks as possible. NYNEX's argument is like saying Safeway should start investing in food purveyors in case the day comes when, for example, Heinz wants to sell its ketchup through only one chain of grocery stores.

NYNEX and Viacom have announced that they will work together on joint projects. The first will be to create interactive versions of Viacom-owned networks MTV, VH-1, and Nickelodeon. The project has yet to get off the ground, and neither company has offered details about what it will do.

NYNEX is also part of the alliance with Bell Atlantic, Pacific Telesis, and Michael Ovitz's Creative Artists Agency. The venture may be one of NYNEX's best shots at pulling itself out of its megamedia hole. The alliance is creating two companies that will develop megamedia programming and technology to be shared by the partners, that should give NYNEX access to Bell Atlantic's Stargazer interactive TV service and to programming secured by Ovitz.

Seidenberg is another ray of hope. Within NYNEX, Seidenberg was the executive who hitched the company to the CAA alliance. He also forged alliances that will give NYNEX more clout in wireless telephone businesses and negotiated for new, more flexible regulations in the states in which NYNEX operates. Compared to Ferguson and Salerno, Seidenberg is a strong leader and dynamic personality. He seems to know what he needs to do. "My job is to pick up the ball and get NYNEX repositioned a lot faster than we would've hoped," he said on November 17, the day he was named to become chairman.

He offered a few clues about how he'll run NYNEX. He seems to prefer relationships like the CAA partnership better than hard investments like the Viacom deal. "The corporation of the 21st century will be built on virtual relationships," Seidenberg says. He'll continue to flatten NYNEX operations and try to get rid of bureaucracy. He'll drive NYNEX toward businesses outside NYNEX's region; he aims to have outside businesses represent half of NYNEX's revenue in 7 to 10 years.

Bennett may be able to rally behind Seidenberg. NYNEX's TV chief seems to earnestly want to move ahead in megamedia. He has many of the same ideas that are heard around Bell Atlantic or US West. He's enthusiastic about megamedia and he definitely has big-time ambition: "I'd like to be the NBC, CBS, and ABC of the 21st century," he says of NYNEX and its partnerships with Viacom and CAA. He says the company has been working quietly, behind the scenes, at a lot of pieces of interactive TV. And he tries to talk up NYNEX as a company that's been unjustly criticized for lagging behind.

Yet, as he says all that, it's hard not to hear the frustration in his voice.

BELLSOUTH: A HUGE, RICH, WELL-RUN QUESTION MARK

Bill Retterson, BellSouth's lanky and very Southern senior vice president for broadband services, is at his first major cable-TV industry convention. It's an eye-opener. Singers croon old tunes from movies at the American Movie Classics booth. People play loud video games at The Sega Channel. Rock music, sound effects, and the chatter of carnival-voiced barkers blare from every direction. Stimulation is everywhere, and Retterson wants some of it for his company. "We're seeking alliances with the technology and entertainment industries," Retterson says. "We won't try to build everything ourselves. We just don't understand this." He waves his arm to indicate the cacophony all around the show.

Genial as Retterson sounds, he hasn't sent many invitations for anybody from technology or content companies to sit at BellSouth's table. The company is a curious dark horse in megamedia. It is a huge, rich, well-run, technologically savvy telecommunications company. Its internal megamedia strategy includes building new networks and owning content. Yet it can't seem to get off its collective butt and really *do* something. A few moves BellSouth has made—including an option to invest in QVC's failed bid to buy Paramount, and the development, with IBM, of a computerized cellular phone called Simon—lost their sizzle before they even got out of the frying pan.

BellSouth resembles a well-trained army massed at megamedia's border. Nobody, including BellSouth's leadership, seems to know whether, when, or how it might charge in. The company is certainly being cautious. "We believe in [the interactive multimedia] future," BellSouth chairman Don Clendenin wrote in the company's annual report. "We are committed to making it happen for our customers—in the disciplined way our owners expect."

BellSouth is the biggest regional phone company, whether measured by number of phone lines (19 million) or annual revenue

($16 billion). Its nearly $5 billion in annual cash flow could help the company pay for almost anything it might want to buy. BellSouth's region, which covers Alabama, Florida, Kentucky, Louisiana, Mississippi, North Carolina, South Carolina, and Tennessee, is growing and pumping up BellSouth's telephone business. Yet the region isn't population-dense or attractive enough to lure the kind of competition that will move in on other areas.

BellSouth, the biggest wireless operator among regional Bells, runs cellular service inside its region and outside. It has foreign operations in places like Germany, Venezuela, and Australia. The company is good at selling high-cost services, such as call-waiting or caller ID, and it has built top-notch technology into its network. Reasonably lean, it is considered to be well-managed.

All of those qualities could set the company up for great success in megamedia. It would seem to be in position to make dramatic moves and carry them off.

Instead, BellSouth has dabbled. Most strikingly, it bought options to invest about $500 million in QVC during QVC's fight to take over Paramount. When QVC lost to Viacom, BellSouth was left holding options on a home shopping company whose stock had fallen far below the option price. BellSouth let the options lapse, and QVC wound up being sold to cable operator Comcast.

During the phone companies' big push to buy cable-TV operations, BellSouth bought a small piece (22.5 percent) of an insignificant Texas cable company called Prime Management. It helped IBM develop Simon, a cellular phone with a small screen that can be used to send and receive messages and keep personal date books. The product has had an underwhelming response. BellSouth has been maneuvering to build a broadband prototype network in Brentwood, Tennessee, but that venture hasn't gone far. It has jumped into a programming partnership with Disney, Ameritech, and Southwestern Bell, but that hasn't done much either.

And yet . . . and yet . . . BellSouth keeps talking a big game.

"We feel the interactive media future that has been predicted by all the gurus is real and is going to occur," BellSouth chairman Clendenin said in an interview. "There may be some debate about when this country will get into high-scale interactivity, but we want very much to be part of that.

"We need to get involved on both sides of the equation," Clendenin continued. "We need to be a networker, both inside and outside our region . . . and get involved in getting content—interactive shopping, interactive entertainment."

Retterson, the broadband strategist, says there are real plans behind such talk; BellSouth just hasn't wanted to tell them to anyone. "We don't want to be part of the hype. We don't see a benefit in telling our competitors what we're going to do," Retterson says. "That doesn't mean we don't know where we'd go first, or have business models."

How about some hints, Bill? Well, he says, BellSouth probably won't be buying any big cable companies in the near future. "We've been through every cable company and we can't work with that," he says. Cable systems cost too much for too little benefit, he believes.

The company will build fiber-optic and coaxial cable networks within its region, but won't spring for an all-out rebuilding project like the one in Pacific Telesis's future. It will develop high-tech networks as demand for broadband services increases.

BellSouth will definitely be looking for more alliances, especially in programming. It had really liked the idea of being a part-owner of a merged QVC and Paramount, and feels a strong need to buy into that kind of software. "We're still looking to fill that void," Retterson says. "We're not panicking."

So BellSouth could yet do something interesting in megamedia. It could even do something astounding. But its actions so far make one wonder whether BellSouth will do anything before it's too late.

SBC COMMUNICATIONS: COULD BE GREAT . . . BUT RUNNING OUT OF STEAM

Ed Whitacre could have been running the model 21st-century communications company by now. Brilliant international holdings.

Cable TV in strong U.S. markets. A solid phone system within the region. And a plan to pull them together into a sharp megamedia strategy.

But after a heady start, Southwestern Bell—renamed SBC Communications in October 1994—stalled out. It has fallen back somewhere behind Bell Atlantic, US West, Pacific Telesis, and Ameritech in the race to assemble holdings on the new frontier and present a smart-looking strategic face to the outside world.

That outcome is kind of odd. Whitacre's SBC hasn't seemed like the kind of company that would give up after a setback. Whitacre, SBC's chairman, is a humorous, straight-shooting Texan who doesn't particularly like the media spotlight. He may be the best manager among all the phone company chairmen. Whitacre runs a lean corporate office in San Antonio and doesn't shy from competitive situations. That shows in the kind of company he has put together. SBC gets about one-quarter of its revenue from competitive businesses such as cellular phones—more than any other regional phone company.

For years after the Bell System breakup, SBC was the least imaginative Bell company. It stuck to the telephone business in its boom-and-bust oil region of Arkansas, Kansas, Missouri, Oklahoma, and Texas. Whitacre has changed that. Starting in the late 1980s, the company bought Metromedia Cellular, which doubled its wireless business, and eventually became known as the best cellular operator among the regional Bells. It invested $1 billion to buy 10 percent of Mexico's telephone company, Telefonos de Mexico, which operates next door to SBC's territory. The value of that investment has more than quadrupled. Along the way, the company was one of the first to get into cable television in the United Kingdom, jointly operating a cable company with Cox Cable and offering TV and telephone service over the same network.

In February 1993, Whitacre cut the deal that shook the telecommunications world: SBC agreed to buy Hauser Communications for $650 million. It was the first phone company–cable deal. It would give SBC 225,000 cable-TV customers in two high-income Washington, DC, suburbs. The contiguous suburbs would be a perfect place to try selling phone service over cable, if regulators would go along.

It was the deal that set off the panic that led to US West's investment in Time Warner and Bell Atlantic's run at TCI.

Then Whitacre put together the deal that would have surely vaulted SBC into the megamedia stratosphere. The company was to have teamed with its U.K. partner, Cox Cable, to create a U.S. cable-TV venture worth about $5 billion. As announced in December 1993, SBC would have put $1.6 billion in cash and assets into the venture for a 40 percent stake. Cox would have spun its 21 cable-TV systems (worth $3.3 billion) into the venture, and kept the other 60 percent. The partnership would have created the sixth-biggest cable-TV company, with enough size and clout to compete against the biggest TV players. The combined company would then have gone after other cable properties, most likely Times Mirror's, in an effort to become the third-largest cable operator. The deal was structured as elegantly as US West's investment in Time Warner. The pieces all seemed to fit. The deal was on the brink of creating a new megamedia force.

And it fell apart—for a lot of the same reasons that Bell Atlantic and TCI called off their merger. The cable-TV rate cuts ordered by the FCC played havoc with the value of each side's investment. Strategies changed to make phone–cable deals less necessary. SBC, from all indications, got cold feet and walked out. That was in April 1994. By June, Cox had moved on to pursue its growth strategy by itself, eventually buying Times Mirror's cable properties for $2.3 billion.

SBC pulled back after that. It closed the Hauser deal and began operating the systems around Washington, the first phone company to have its very own cable plant. But then it disappeared from the inside chatter about who is looking to buy which cable companies. In fact, SBC supposedly started looking for ways to sell the Hauser systems.

In the meantime, SBC didn't unveil much of an aggressive megamedia network construction plan. Its biggest announcement was that Microsoft would supply technology for a low-key, 2,500-household test of interactive TV in Richardson, Texas. SBC also signed to be one of three regional Bells in a sketchy programming partnership with Disney. Otherwise, the company went stone-cold in mid-1994, announcing no significant ventures, alliances, or strategic moves in megamedia.

To be fair, competitors haven't been pouring into SBC's territory to challenge its telephone business or build a lot of high-tech networks. The company has been under less pressure to make aggressive moves than many other regional phone companies.

Still, for now, SBC seems to have run out of steam. At the very least, it has lost its momentum in megamedia.

But don't write off SBC. It should be an interesting company to keep an eye on. Whitacre has absolutely shown that he is ready and willing to make unusual or even risky investments, such as those in TelMex and Hauser. The company probably knows competitive business as well as any other regional phone company, thanks to a culture steeped in battles on cellular and other fronts. Plus, SBC is gaining TV experience that is second only to US West's, through its U.K. cable system and, now, the Hauser systems.

If SBC gets moving again, look for its investments to be among the smartest of any phone company's deals. Although, if it doesn't get moving again soon, SBC may risk needing more than smart deals to help it catch its peers.

GTE AND ROCHESTER TELEPHONE: TWO PLAYERS TO WATCH

The local telephone industry universe is pretty limited compared to, say, the computer or media industries. Seven gigantic regional companies dominate the picture. Right behind them is GTE, which is actually bigger than any of the Bells but not quite so visible. After that, the field of high-impact players shrinks pretty quickly. Here are two interesting players to watch as megamedia unfolds.

GTE

The company has annual revenue of $20 billion. Its operating cash flow is $5 billion a year. It has 17 million phone lines and cellular operations in areas covering about 30 percent of the U.S. population.

GTE is clearly a company with resources, clout, and conservative management. It hasn't made any strikingly bold moves into megamedia, and most likely won't.

That doesn't mean GTE has sat on its hands. Chairman Charles ("Chuck") Lee has said that "a critical part of our strategy is to position GTE for the emerging opportunities in telecommunications." The company was one of the first to test a broadband interactive TV system in a community. The consumer trial, in Cerritos, California, started in 1988. Unfortunately for GTE and for the whole concept of interactive TV, the system was rudimentary and had too few offerings to truly stimulate a lot of interactive use. The test drew a lot of bad press in late 1993, most of it saying that the Cerritos experiment proved that nobody wants to interact with a TV set. All it really proved was that nobody wants to interact with a bad interactive TV system.

But GTE learned from Cerritos—that's what the experiment was for—and the company is aggressively building new megamedia systems in four key markets: Thousand Oaks, California; St. Petersburg, Florida; Honolulu, Hawaii; and the Virginia suburbs of Washington, DC. Those systems will cost about $250 million and should be up and running by late 1995. GTE has plans to build similar networks in 66 markets over the next decade.

GTE plans to get into video services and possibly programming, although it hasn't made any major moves in either direction. It did develop, at Cerritos, something called Main Street, an interactive on-line service something like Prodigy, but delivered over broadband lines and aimed at TV screens, not computers. It offers electronic encyclopedias, shopping, news, and video games. Main Street has already met with some exportable success: Continental Cablevision is putting Main Street on cable systems serving about 500,000 homes.

GTE has one major advantage over the regional phone companies: much less regulation. It doesn't have to win a court case to own or sell programming. It can have long-distance operations—in fact, it used to own the Sprint long-distance company. It can get a head start on the regional Bells in those businesses.

However, GTE has a disadvantage: it doesn't have one big contiguous region like the Bells do. Building and running a megamedia network in a huge region of connected states will cost less than having to construct separate, smaller megamedia networks in pockets across the country. GTE is spread from the tip of Maine to southern California. It covers a lot of rural territory and smaller cities, not many major markets. Economies of scale aren't going to work in GTE's favor.

GTE will probably stick around in the middle of the pack in the telephone industry—not a leader, but not lagging behind either.

Rochester Telephone

Good things can come in small packages, even in the land of telephone giants. Rochester Telephone serves only 1.5 million customers. Its biggest operation is serving its home turf, Rochester, New York, where it has about 330,000 customers. Its annual revenue is about $1 billion.

Yet Rochester Tel has already vaulted ahead with a megamedia first. In mid-1994, it reached a deal with its New York regulators to open the Rochester region to telephone competition while stripping away the most cumbersome rules governing Rochester Tel's business. Time Warner, the Rochester-area cable-TV company, plans to offer phone and cellular service in competition against Rochester Tel. That will make Rochester the first place in the country to get true battling phone service, and Time Warner may take away some Rochester Tel customers. But because Rochester Tel would no longer be a monopoly, regulators won't keep a lid on its profits and will let the company more freely expand into other businesses. That's the kind of deal Ameritech, for example, has been trying to win in its Midwest region.

The move says a lot about Rochester Tel. It's an aggressive, entrepreneurial company that has been willing to stay ahead of the telecommunications curve. Until huge rebuilding projects like PacTel's came along, Rochester Tel could boast one of the most advanced phone networks anywhere. Now, the company sees opportunity in the communications business, and it wants to grab it.

"We want to be bigger and operate businesses outside Rochester, New York," says Catherine Duda, a spokeswoman for Rochester Tel. "We'd like to expand through acquisition. We have no specific plans or deals on hold, but the [new regulatory] structure will permit us to act nimbly, whether we're buying or partnering."

One deal has already popped up: Rochester Tel said in October that it plans to buy WCT Communications, a long-distance phone company, for $110 million.

Sharon Armbrust, an analyst at consultants Paul Kagan Associates, has always liked Rochester Tel's chances in a competitive market. "They're one of the most progressive in saying, 'Come at us, and we want at yours,'" she says. "That's an expression of confidence."

4

HOW MANY CHANNELS DID YOU SAY?

THE CABLE-TV INDUSTRY

LEADERS TO WATCH: JOHN MALONE AND TELE-COMMUNICATIONS INC.

John Malone is fast becoming the Henry Ford of the Communications Age, and he's not all that comfortable dealing with it.

Since mid-1993, Malone's square-jawed face has glared out from stories about megamedia in *Fortune, The New Yorker,* and every major newspaper and newsmagazine, and on network TV news broadcasts. He is an entrepreneur who, like Ford and his Model T, is bringing a life-altering, historic new technology to the masses.

Using cable giant TCI's clout and his own considerable will, Malone has been working to drive digital, interactive TV into consumers' homes, giving an average family more communication power than anyone could have imagined a few years ago. For that, Malone has been called before Congress, asked to make speeches, and wooed at powerful dinners. When he steps into a Chamber of Commerce lunch in his home base of Denver, a crowd congeals around him, some asking for autographs.

Malone, chief executive of Tele-Communications Inc. (TCI) and the most powerful single figure in megamedia, both loves and hates this clamoring. The part he loves is recognition as the genius leader of a communications revolution. "All he wants is credit for being the smartest guy on the planet," a cable TV executive who is allied with TCI once told me. Malone has an ego that could fill Denver's Mile High Stadium, but it's all focused on the cerebral. He doesn't want people to fawn over him. He doesn't own a monstrous mansion or fancy cars. He doesn't manage his company simply to drive the stock price as high as it can go, even though Malone's wealth is almost completely tied to TCI's stock. Instead, he wants every echelon of business and society to admire that brain of his. He wants the best and brightest to laud him for his vision and strategy.

But the accolades and public gawking bump up against another side of Malone. He's kind of shy, really. A big, stocky man, he's also blunt and crude and awkward in public, a cross between a Marine and a geeky engineer. He's one of the most private CEOs ever, rarely letting even his closest business associates meet his wife, Leslie, or come to his house, or go out on the sailboat he keeps off the Maine coast. TCI staffers tell of Malone's going to dinner in Atlanta with Ted Turner, a hugely popular and recognizable figure, before Malone was so well known. Turner got relentless attention—people went up to him, photographers followed him. Malone came away saying, "I don't know how Ted lives like that."

So Malone, in his mid-50s, struggles against his fame. If he had merged TCI into Bell Atlantic, Malone vows he would've tried to slip off to the sidelines and let Ray Smith run the show. He was serious about it. I ran into Malone in the men's room during a conference held soon after the Bell Atlantic deal was announced. I asked if we could go somewhere and talk about his plans. He replied, "Nah, talk to Ray. He's captain of the ship."

Now Malone is structuring TCI so he can take a half-step back from it. He says he wants more time with his family, more time on his boat, more time away from stress. It may not seem that way, considering TCI's nonstop deal activity. But TCI's new structure, which makes headquarters into a holding company for four distinct businesses run by their own executives and issuing their own, separate shares of stock, "will allow me to do what I like to do, which is be a little more strategic," Malone says. "And I won't have to do things I don't like, which is a lot of public visibility, a lot of lobbying, that kind of thing." Then he thinks for a second and says with a tinge of regret mixed with a shade of pride: "Y'know, I'm still gonna be a personality. I draw crowds."

Over the next decade, Malone's inner friction may be the one thing that could bump him out of the lead position on the information superhighway. When a leader gets as hot as Malone, everyone watches for a fall. But anyone looking for him to tumble because of bad strategy or foolish deals will have a long wait. Instead, keep an eye on the escape routes—something that takes Malone off to start a new company or play a less intense role. He was willing to sell all of TCI to Bell Atlantic—in part, to get out of the limelight. He might do it again.

Until Malone makes such a move, if he ever does, he'll continue to be a major force shaping megamedia. And he'll continue to play the role he's had for the past decade: leader of the cable-TV industry.

The industry will need all the leadership it can get as it looks for a way through the challenges of the next few years. Keep in mind that, until a few years ago, cable television was anything but a glamorous business. It was mostly about stringing coaxial cables and figuring out ways to squeeze a little bigger profit margin out of a fairly static business. Cable companies have been monopolies in their service areas, and most have acted accordingly. The technology had not been all that exciting. The big players were not tremendously dynamic.

The industry, in a big way, has gotten lucky. For decades, it has been crisscrossing cities and towns with coaxial cable, then running it down to each house, drilling through a wall, and hooking this cable right to the TV set. It was the best kind of cable to carry the number of video channels that cable companies wanted to send into homes. By 1994, those cable-TV-owned coaxial cables were hooked to more than 60 percent of U.S. homes, and they ran past more than 90 percent. Many cable companies had replaced main lines running into neighborhoods with fiber-optics, mainly because they would cost less to maintain than copper coaxial cable.

As it turns out, that architecture of fiber-optic main lines connecting to coaxial cables that run into houses is great for all the programming and services that are emerging in megamedia.

With a little help from new technology—digital compression and computerized set-top converter boxes—that system can carry 500 or more channels' worth of television, handle interactive shopping or video game playing, and send movies or TV shows on demand to individual homes. Add some multimillion-dollar switches to the network and the cables can carry phone calls, too. Installing switches and boxes and compression on existing wires to get to megamedia will be far easier and less expensive than the phone companies' task of building whole new networks from scratch.

That bit of serendipity has put the cable industry on the edge of both huge new opportunities and the greatest competitive onslaught it has ever seen.

The opportunities will come from using cable systems to try to grab a much bigger share of consumers' entertainment and communications spending. People aren't going to spend a lot more money or time on visual entertainment, no matter how electrifying megamedia becomes. People just don't *have* a lot more money or time. But the smart people in cable figure they can carve out business from other industries. For instance, by investing in technology, a cable operator will soon be able to offer movies on demand or something close to it. That could take money and time from video rentals. Or, cable may sell video games over cable lines. TCI and Time Warner have helped start The Sega Channel, which is doing just that. If consumers play games via The Sega Channel instead of buying individual cartridges of games, the cable operators would get a cut of money from a segment of entertainment that was previously beyond their reach.

On the communications side, cable companies see that, by adding switches and devices that let signals go two ways over their coaxial cables, they could carry phone calls and take some money from the phone companies.

They've found that if PC users get a special cable modem and hook their PCs to a cable-TV line rather than a phone line, the PCs can send and receive data about 1,000 times faster. Even more attractive, a PC hooked to cable is always connected to the on-line service, just as a TV is connected to cable channels as soon as the TV is turned on. No more dialing in through a modem to access an on-line service—a process that takes a couple of minutes and prevents customers from using the services as freely as they'd like. Linking PCs to on-line services is a growing business already, among some cable operators. Cable companies never before got any part of that money.

The flip side is that phone companies are coming after the cable-TV business. Pacific Telesis, US West, and others are building broadband networks that can carry everything cable lines can carry—maybe more. They are planning on taking money and market share out of the cable companies' hides, as well as from video renters, video game sellers, and so on. It will be the toughest real competition the cable industry has ever had to face.

The leading cable companies—TCI, Time Warner, Cox, Comcast, Cablevision—are all very different. More importantly, they are much more than just cable-TV companies. They generally have a variety of other holdings in media, entertainment, and communications. Yet they and the rest of the cable industry share some weaknesses and strengths that will loom large as the remaining years of the 1990s unfold.

Cable's Weaknesses

Too Small and Spread Too Thin. Compared to the telephone industry, the cable industry is a ragtag bunch. The biggest company, TCI, has around 15 million customers, which is about the number of residential customers served by a regional Bell company. But after TCI, the numbers slide off quickly. The seventh-biggest cable company has about 1.5 million customers. The smallest of the seven Bells has ten times that many.

The smallness of cable companies means they don't have nearly the amount of spending money telephone companies can generate. Their cash flow could never keep up with $10 billion megamedia construction projects, for instance. The size of cable companies also means they may not have the ability to borrow as much as phone companies or raise as much money by issuing shares of stock.

Not that cable companies don't crank out the cash. They do. TCI's annual cash flow is approaching $2 billion. In the past, big cable companies have had enough money to expand their systems and make investments in programming. But megamedia may prove to be a much more expensive game that will require big bucks just to stay at the table. Only the top few cable companies might be rich and powerful enough. In fact, Viacom decided to sell its cable division to a joint venture led by TCI because the company felt the division was too small on its own to keep up with the changing times, says Viacom CEO Frank Biondi. Viacom had been the 12th largest cable operator, serving about 1 million customers. Consider the chances for the dozens of cable operators smaller than Viacom.

Size is only part of the problem. Each cable company's operations are scattered all over the country, often in tiny pockets. If they were massed all in one place, like regional Bells, it would be more cost-effective and easier to build megamedia systems and distribute programming and services. Time Warner's cable is somewhat concentrated in a few major metropolitan areas. But TCI's cable is strewn across the nation, a lot of it in rural towns and second-tier cities.

Regulatory Hell. Cable TV has got to be one of the biggest regulatory headaches in history. Federal laws and FCC rules have leaned heavily on cable companies, dictating what kind of businesses cable companies could get into, whom they had to sell their programming to, and, lately, how much they could charge for their services. Congress has promised to pass new laws that would lift some of the regulatory burden. But new laws will likely be structured so regulations go away only when a cable operation faces true competition in a region. As long as a cable system has a monopoly, it will probably be governed by regulations designed to keep it in check. Because competition will take some time to emerge, cable companies may have to deal with tough federal rules for years. Restrictions will be a drag on their ability to compete.

The other regulatory burden has local origins. Cable companies have to win licenses—and, often, get approval for changes in cable operations or service—from every municipality in which they operate. Most of the time, the relationship with local governments isn't difficult. But it's time-consuming and laborious, and usually involves a fee to the local governments. A cable company can serve hundreds of individual communities. The need to deal with all of them is a competitive disadvantage. Potential competitors such as phone companies will be free of that burden.

A Bad Rap. Cable companies will run up against one other problem that's spongier than the hard facts about size or regulation: Many cable operations don't have good relationships with their customers.

To be blunt, a good many cable companies have a history of arrogance in customer relations—an attitude of, "We're your only choice, so we'll help you when we get around to it." Response to customer calls for service can sometimes take days or even weeks. Compared to phone systems, cable systems are built with less protection against outages. They blink out often enough to rile subscribers and, perhaps, worry potential computer or phone customers. Besides, the reason the FCC slapped cable companies with mandatory price reductions was that too many cable operations, in the absence of competition, had been soaking customers. If you don't believe cable companies have a reputation problem, just ask potential competitors such as phone companies and Hughes's direct broadcast satellite TV service. They invariably say that the number-one reason they think they can take market share from cable is that many consumers hate their cable company and would sign up with any alternative.

Given that reputation, the issue of a brand for a cable company gets cloudy. Big cable companies are well behind phone companies in trying to establish a corporate identity and brand name. Local cable operations are often known to consumers under a local brand name or a name left over from some earlier ownership. Many consumers can't name the corporation that owns their local system.

Thousands of people subscribe to United Artists cable and don't know that TCI owns it. Thousands of New Jersey residents buy Suburban Cablevision's service. They never knew it was owned for years by Maclean Hunter, and probably don't know it was bought by Comcast.

To consumers, names like TCI and Comcast mean little. That lack of recognition will hurt those companies as competition revs up. A strong national brand name can help marketing efforts and differentiate a company. But until cable bucks up its customer service reputation, maybe companies are better off not creating and then getting stuck with a brand name that might carry negative feelings into the next decade.

Overall, although cable industry weaknesses can seem ominous, more than likely they will only slow big cable companies, not stop them. In the long, tough fight over megamedia, cable companies will have some serious strengths that phone companies or other kinds of competitors may never be able to match.

Cable's Strengths

A Broadband Head Start. In many metropolitan areas, cable already has the kind of megamedia wiring that phone companies are only beginning to build. As mentioned earlier, fiber-optic main lines run from the cable "head end," where satellite feeds from all the different networks are collected and pumped into the cable system, down to neighborhoods or clusters of homes. There, the TV signals are switched into coaxial cable lines, which carry them into individual homes. Phone companies will spend billions of dollars to duplicate that setup.

Digital compression started to trickle into the cable-TV market in 1994–1995. It will squeeze up to 10 channels of video into the space on a cable normally taken up by just a single channel. It will give many cable systems a capacity of 400, 500, or more channels. And that will let cable companies strike at megamedia right away, not sometime in the future. Compression over the broadband cable lines will let cable offer movies and popular TV shows in a "virtual on-demand" mode. That means that a two-hour movie might play continuously on eight different channels, each starting 15 minutes after the other. At whatever time a viewer tunes in and decides to pay for a movie, the start will never be more than 15 minutes away. The systems will also give cable operators room to offer pay-per-view sports, niche TV networks, and lots of home shopping. Building compression into a cable system will cost hundreds of dollars per subscriber. But it won't cost as much as building a whole new broadband network.

The next step is to make cable systems two-way, which would be the start of interactive TV and telephone calls over cable. About 8 percent of cable systems were two-way in 1994. John Malone is, of course, biased about cable's capabilities: "We can bring telephony services of higher quality and lower cost to the public long before telephone companies can bring video services to customers. We do have the best technology and I think we can get there fastest."

Nimbleness. Small size can be an advantage. Cable companies may not have the cash and clout of phone companies, but they have speed. They are lean. They have few layers of management and little bureaucracy. They are, at heart, entrepreneurial companies willing to go after new opportunities. They can make decisions quickly and change direction on a dime—traits that will help a great deal over the next few years as megamedia goes through many twists and turns on its way to market. Ray Smith, who has worked hard to slim down Bell Atlantic's decision-making process, says that on a scale of 1 to 10, measuring a company's nimbleness and risk-taking spirit, Bell Atlantic is a 6. He rates TCI a 9.

Small size has one financial benefit. Investors in cable companies don't expect steady earnings growth or dividend payouts. They know the company will plow profits back into the business for the sake of growing the overall company. If earnings dive temporarily because the company made a big investment, shareholders don't bail out or call for the heads of management. That allows cable companies to take financial risks. Phone companies won't have that luxury. Their investors have put in their money expecting steady, unspectacular growth and little risk. That will keep phone companies from moving as aggressively into megamedia as they might like.

Knowledge of TV. Wires and technology only make megamedia possible. Programming and video services will make it a business. Here, cable companies have a whopping lead over competitors.

First of all, video has always been cable's business. The companies have an entertainment orientation and entertainment relationships. They have an institutional feel for what works on TV and what doesn't.

A more important factor: cable companies own programming. Turn on the TV in any cable system. Flick around the dial. After getting past the broadcast networks—ABC, CBS, NBC, and Fox—almost every other channel is at least partially owned by cable companies. QVC is owned by Comcast and TCI. Turner Broadcasting—home of CNN, TNT, The Cartoon Network, and more—is backed by TCI and Time Warner. The Discovery Channel is part-owned by TCI and Cox. MTV, VH-1, and Nickelodeon are owned by Viacom. Black Entertainment Television, Court TV, ESPN, and American Movie Classics all have cable owners. Having a piece of assets like these will be a potent weapon. Not only will programming assets become more valuable as megamedia increases demand for content, but today's successful programmers are likely to develop new kinds of programming for the next age.

Cable has other kinds of content relationships, too. Time Warner also owns Warner Bros. Studios, a major movie maker, and the Time Inc. magazines, which could become fodder for electronic products. TCI has made investments in Hollywood studios and plans to expand there. Cox owns newspapers. All of these related businesses will give cable a window on content matched by few other industries.

On to the Superhighway. Given its strengths and weaknesses, where is the overall industry going next? The biggest trend is toward consolidation. Cable companies know they'll need some kind of critical mass to hack it in megamedia. Cable consolidation really got going in 1994. Cox bought Times Mirror's cable systems for $2.3 billion. Comcast bought Maclean Hunter's U.S. systems for more than $1 billion. TCI bought Norfolk, Virginia-based TeleCable for $1 billion. A lot more buyouts are coming, probably until the industry gets down to four or five major players controlling almost all of the nation's cable systems.

Another side of consolidation is clustering—pulling together contiguous cable territories to form big cable–communications entities. Cable companies will trade, buy, and sell systems to create clusters.

Cable companies will diversify. They'll continue to buy into or create new programming. They'll venture into wireless phone service, whether cellular or PCS. They may dabble in other types of businesses. They'll invest in on-line computer services such as Prodigy or America Online. TCI bought 20 percent of Microsoft's fledgling on-line service, The Microsoft Network.

The big players will continue to push new technology into their cable systems. Digital compression will roll out slowly, adding hundreds of channels of capacity. Many systems will add a return path, which will give cable a two-way capability and allow it to offer on-line computer services, video games, interactive shopping, and other services. A return path eats up about four channels' worth of space on a cable system—a lot if a system has only 40 channels, but no problem if it has 400 channels. Cable operators in major communications centers like New York and California are hot to add switches to their systems so they can offer telephone service as early as 1995.

Along the way, the major companies will continue to add fiber-optic lines to their systems, pushing fiber closer to the individual homes served. The less distance signals have to travel on coaxial cable, the greater their capacity for carrying more channels and services, and the better the reliability of the overall cable system.

Some of the companies will experiment at the horizons of megamedia. Time Warner is doing that in Orlando with its Full Service Network. TCI is doing it in Seattle and Denver with Microsoft's help.

And out front of almost every trend in the industry will be John Malone's TCI.

Dimensions of the Leader. TCI is the most powerful company in cable and possibly in all of television. Its strength radiates from the size of its cable-TV operations plus its unmatchable combination of holdings, alliances, and friends.

The cable side of TCI, run as a nearly-independent company by Malone's chief deputy, Brendan Clouston, has been assembled by acquisitions over the years. Now that TCI has reabsorbed Liberty Media and cut other deals, TCI-controlled systems were reaching about twice as many cable subscribers as the company's closest competitor, Time Warner, at the end of 1994. TCI's biggest systems include those in Chicago, Denver, Hartford (Connecticut), and San Jose. The company has at least 20 percent of the total cable-TV market.

That's enough clout to make almost anything happen in the industry. TCI can practically guarantee the success of a new cable channel or service by putting it on all its systems. It can, and has been trying to, create de facto standards for technology such as digital compression and digital set-up boxes. Since TCI is so big, technology companies such as General Instrument and Scientific-Atlanta will usually build to whatever specs TCI wants.

The money from all those cable operations lets TCI be a constant investor and builder. It spent $100 million on its digital compression facility and digital studio outside Denver, opened the spring of 1994. It is in the middle of spending $2 billion on megamedia networks—fiber-optic lines, two-way cable, and so on. And TCI has the money to keep buying other cable systems, adding to its power plant.

The other side of TCI is programming. Most of it falls under the Liberty Media subsidiary, run almost independently by Peter Barton. It is an amazing string of assets, most of which can be traced to investments TCI made years ago to help programmers get started—a way to ensure that cable TV would have a wide variety of programming to fill its pipeline. TCI owns stakes in Turner Broadcasting, Discovery Communications, Home Shopping Network, QVC, The Family Channel, Court TV, Black Entertainment Television, American Movie Classics, Encore movie service, and a line-up of regional sports networks. That makes TCI the most influential TV programming company this side of the four broadcast networks.

What won't be found among the assets listed in TCI's financial reports is a third important aspect of the company: its friends and partners. The company has gotten close with many of the most powerful people who will play roles in megamedia. It is creating a computer channel and running a megamedia test system with Microsoft, an outcome of a developing relationship between Malone and Bill Gates. Rupert Murdoch of News Corp. keeps in constant touch with Malone, and News Corp. and TCI have a couple of joint ventures. Somewhere, in some way, TCI is running tests or is involved in joint ventures with: AT&T, US West, Dow Jones, Knight-Ridder, Intel, IBM, General Instrument, Sega, Time Warner, Comcast, Carolco Pictures, and Disney. Although none of these is a permanent ally, the list shows TCI's reach. It has solid relationships across more industries—all of them potential megamedia players—than perhaps any other company in any industry.

TCI's biggest liability is also not on its balance sheet. For a company of its size and importance, it has suffered an outrageous and long-running string of public relations and lobbying debacles. Its relationship with Congress and the FCC has always been antagonistic. Witness Malone's off-the-cuff but stupid remark to an interviewer for *Wired* magazine in mid-1994. Malone said he could build information highways more quickly if someone would "shoot [Reed] Hundt"—the FCC commissioner. Imagine how that helped TCI's cause in Washington.

Among the general public, TCI often comes across as a power-hungry company bent on cornering the cable-TV market. Even among peers, TCI's reputation as a brutal competitor can hurt it. During the battle between Viacom and QVC to buy Paramount, Viacom filed suit against TCI and Malone. (TCI was backing QVC's bid at the time.) The suit alleged that TCI had used "bully boy" tactics to manipulate the cable industry, such as threatening to drive down the value of rival programmers by dropping them from TCI's systems. The suit further damaged TCI's reputation and helped keep TCI out of the Paramount fight.

Everything TCI is, Malone built—from its high-tech bent to its programming muscle and even to its coarse character, which is, after all, a reflection of the man at the helm.

The company's roots go back to 1952, when rancher and cottonseed salesman Bob Magness—still TCI's chairman—sold his cattle to build a cable-TV system in Memphis, Texas. Magness built other systems in Montana, Colorado, and elsewhere in the West. By 1970, TCI was the tenth-largest cable operator in what was still a minor industry. It sold its first shares to the public that year.

John Malone, meanwhile, had been laboring in the old Bell System. He had grown up in Milford, Connecticut. His father was an engineer at General Electric. His mother was a teacher. He has one sister. In his youth, Malone was a gifted science student and a pretty good athlete. His sports were soccer, track, and fencing. He got into Yale, graduated with a B.S. in electrical engineering/economics, and started working for AT&T at its prestigious Bell Labs in 1963. Over the next four years, he piled on academic degrees: a master's in industrial management from Johns Hopkins; a master's in electrical engineering from New York University; a doctorate in operations research from Johns Hopkins. To this day, around TCI's glass-and-concrete tower outside of Denver, employees call the boss "Dr. Malone."

The education and Bell Labs experience made Malone comfortable with technology. His next step taught him about business: a stint at McKinsey & Company, the premier management consulting firm. He worked there until 1970, when he took a group vice president job at General Instrument (GI), maker of equipment for cable-TV systems. The GI job introduced Malone to Magness, who hired Malone as TCI's president in 1972. Malone's mission from the start was to make TCI big enough to challenge the three networks: NBC, CBS, and ABC.

Through the 1970s, TCI operated on a shoestring out of a Denver headquarters that could only be described as a warehouse. Cable was mainly a rural service, importing network-TV signals to areas that had poor reception. In the late 1970s, as HBO caught on, cable started turning into a major-market business. TCI went on an acquisition and building binge, moving into markets such as Buffalo, Pittsburgh, and Chicago. Malone saw only one way for cable to do well in big cities, where reception of network TV was good: cable would have to offer more of its own special channels. He started investing in programming—mostly passive investments that would help entrepreneurs such as Ted Turner stay in business.

John Hendricks was trying to start The Discovery Channel around that time. "I ran out of money in February 1986," he says. "No one would invest in the network. I had read that Malone said the industry ought to invest heavily in programming because that's what drives consumer interest. I had nowhere else to turn. I gave John Malone a call. He was immediately responsive. He sent a VP to meet with me and within a month advanced us half a million dollars to keep us afloat and an outline of a deal for later investment."

By the early 1990s, TCI was the biggest player in cable TV and its programming. Malone was looking for the logical next step—something that would drive the industry to a new level of power and profits, the way programming did in the 1980s. The industry had experimented with crude interactive TV and two-way technology before: Qube, in Columbus, Ohio, was the biggest test. By the 1990s, computer chips and digital compression were starting to make it possible to build two-way cable systems that could be truly useful and easy for consumers to operate. Malone saw it as the point on the horizon to drive toward.

In 1992, he launched TCI into megamedia, saying the company would spend some $2 billion on high-tech networks, would develop digital set-top boxes, and would start to invest in new high-tech programming and services, like The Sega Channel, Interactive Network, and tests of movies on demand.

Malone seems to be the perfect man for his time. His combination of high-tech know-how and business savvy are hard to come by. "Here in one man is the ability to recognize technology in its minutiae as well as its bridge to strategy," says Richard Green, president of Cable Labs, a cable industry research group. Malone is also an extraordinary dealmaker. By one count, during his time at TCI, Malone has bought, invested in, or started joint ventures with 650 companies. His deals break new ground for complexity—a Malone hallmark by now. He is comfortable owning bits and pieces of many things, covering all possible angles, but controlling little. "I have an investment mentality," he says. "The phone companies have a control mentality." He's also comfortable running a joint venture with a company in one market and competing with the same company elsewhere.

Besides bad PR, Malone's weakness is day-to-day management. He's a strategist, a thinker. The rest escapes him. At the ground level, many of TCI's cable systems have not been well-run. Malone doesn't talk much about that.

These days, in fact, Malone is getting further away from the daily business of cable TV. He's trying to get above that, see to the edges of technology, and steer TCI through the 1990s.

Where are TCI and Malone going next?

First of all, Malone says, the company will do just fine without the Bell Atlantic merger, which these days seems an eternity ago. The regional phone company would have given TCI solid financial backing and high-tech expertise. Malone's more than willing to forge ahead without them.

"I always respond to a challenge and this is a challenge," he says, sitting on the L-shaped couch in his office at TCI headquarters. It's a fairly simple place with a modern look and windows that show the Denver skyline poking up from the prairie in the distance. Malone's small desk area is adorned with a model sailboat but not much else. "We built this company from zero. The last three to four years were the first in my business career where we've had any money. We're used to not having money. Used to having to go find the money to do every deal, to use creative financial logic to build assets. It's not really threatening to me."

A taste of that creative financial logic: TCI is restructuring itself into four operating units, each issuing its own new classes of stock. One unit is the cable operation headed by Clouston. The second is programming run by Barton. The third is international investments and operations run by Fred Vierra. The fourth is TCI's investments in new technology and programming ventures headed by Larry Romrell. In the past, the price of TCI's shares had been held down because of the company's mix of assets. For example, investors who would normally pay a high price for programming companies were scared by the cable division's big debt and low net income. By cutting loose four focused units, Malone believes investors can buy into the part of TCI with which they feel most comfortable. Malone is betting the strategy can boost the overall market value of TCI by as much as 50 percent.

If share prices soar, TCI will more easily be able to buy other companies using stock instead of cash. That could propel TCI into a whole new acquisition binge.

TCI itself will turn into a holding company, keeping a majority of shares in the four divisions. Malone will remain TCI's president and CEO, overseeing the four companies. He'll make sure they continue to operate in synch, so new programming ventures benefit from the clout of the cable operations.

The structure also gives Malone more distance from the day-to-day operations and some escape hatches. He could sell TCI's share of any of the divisions, or he could buy one of the smaller ones for himself and ride off with it, leaving behind some of the most visible and regulated portions of TCI's portfolio.

Malone can boost TCI's financial situation on his own, but technology is a different story—especially on the telephone side. "It's one area we'll have to fortify," Malone says. To do that, he is reaching out to a partner: Sprint.

In October 1994, Sprint, TCI, Comcast, and Cox announced a telephone partnership. The venture will bid on and buy PCS wireless phone licenses and build wireless systems in cities across the United States. As another part of the venture, Sprint will help the three cable members get into the telephone business. Sprint will supply technology and expertise (and possibly money) to build and market telephone systems. In return, Sprint can connect its long-distance network to local customers through the cable companies' lines, saving money by avoiding high access charges typically imposed on long-distance companies by local phone operations. "There's no question this venture is huge to TCI and its shareholders," says TCI cable chief Clouston. "It means TCI as a company can stand alone and build its core business. It's an answer to the question, 'What's your telephone strategy?' We can play offense. We're going to be in the telephone business on the local level, as we must be."

On paper, the partnership looks impressive, and it may turn into a highly successful venture. At this point, in the earliest phases of putting the venture together, there is a caveat: The partnership was thrown together quickly in heated times. Companies that wanted to bid on PCS licenses had to have alliances intact and paperwork ready by October 28, 1994. That drove companies to act, even if they wanted to forge deals that went beyond PCS. As the deadline loomed, TCI was talking with AT&T and possibly MCI about a similar deal. Comcast had a relationship with MCI and at first tried to work with that company. Cox may also have been casting for partners. It was a game of musical companies. In a way, Sprint, TCI, Comcast, and Cox happened to have sat in the same chair when the music stopped.

Also, keep an eye on Malone and Sprint chairman William Esrey. Both are hard-headed, horn-locking, domineering leaders, and observers say they don't get along the way Malone and Bell Atlantic's Ray Smith did. Could be interesting to see if they can work together.

Malone's Future. Malone's angle on megamedia is to build the networks first—systems that can handle hundreds of channels, interactive TV, and two-way communication. The programming and services will follow. "We'll put in place a platform so with a little more effort or energy we can experiment with things we think might be businesses," Malone says. "If the public's not interested in that product, it gets the yank."

Malone wants to play a direct role in figuring out and developing next-generation programming and technology. That's where the new venture capital subsidiary comes in. "It's really taking some of these technologies and ideas and embryonic businesses and supporting and being involved in them and developing them," Malone says. "It may range from joint ventures with other large companies to putting a few million dollars into some inventor's idea to see if he can make it into a viable business. I think that's going to be a big business for us and it's something I'm very much personally interested in. I'm excited about it. We see a lot of undercapitalized little guys who have good ideas and don't know how to get from where they are to economic viability."

Basically, its' the same role Malone played for the early cable programmers, repeated in a new environment.

TCI is beginning one relationship that scares the pants off just about every player in megamedia, and that's its alliance with computer software powerhouse Microsoft. It's difficult to say where that might go. Malone and Microsoft chairman Bill Gates are like two dominant bulls butting heads. They've had trouble reaching agreement on any kind of broad deal in the past, but they've started working together on specific ventures. They are creating an on-line service and a cable-TV channel that will focus on PC hardware and software. They are running an interactive TV test together in Denver, possibly a first kiss that will lead to TCI's use of Microsoft's operating software to run its megamedia network.

"I think they're likely to be the best guys around," Malone says of Microsoft. "We're going forward and I expect they'll be very heavily involved in a lot of things we do in the future and I think they expect that too."

Malone, by the way, had been meeting with Gates as often as twice a month in 1993. But, Malone says wryly, "I've spent less time with Bill since he's gotten married."

In the future, what else can be expected from Malone and TCI?

They'll be buyers of or investors in more cable systems. "I'm an opportunist," Malone says. "If a deal becomes attractive, I'll do it." But some of the more fantastic aspirations sometimes tagged on TCI—like buying a major Hollywood studio—probably aren't in the cards. First of all, TCI won't have that kind of money to spend. But, Malone says, "We really are very interested in working with studios to create new service offerings worldwide. And if the price of doing that is us making some kind of investment, we might do something. But we don't regard ourselves as competent to own studios and never have. We think it's a game for professionals in that field."

Malone doesn't rule out backing one of his allies if it tries to buy a major asset like a studio or TV network. Malone says he would back Ted Turner, who may very well try to buy something big, whether a film studio or broadcast network. Turner is clearly one of Malone's favorite subjects. Malone visibly lights up at the mention of Turner's name. "There's only one Ted Turner," he says. "No comparisons can be made. We'll try to support Ted in anything he wants to do. Ted needs periodic challenges to keep him young."

Malone will continue to deal with his personal issues, too. He's been cutting back his workday, often spending just five hours in his office when he's in Denver. He's trying to spend bigger chunks of time with his wife at their vacation home in Boothbay, Maine, and on his boat. When he's in Maine, he instructs his staff not to call him. Malone is pushing more responsibility over to Clouston and Barton, and trying hard to put them in front of the public and in front of the people in Washington, so those two become the faces of TCI. That way, maybe Malone will feel he can stay in the game, hovering at some high level, above the fray, looking forward for TCI—instead of scoping out a handy exit.

TIME WARNER: SHOOTING FOR THE MOON

Jim Chiddix quit school during his senior year at Cornell University to go to Hawaii and work on a sailboat. He still looks like he could be captain of some fishing vessel, thanks to his graying beard, rugged features and stout body. For no particular reason, the move to Hawaii eventually led him to the cable business there. He ended up running the Honolulu system in the early 1970s. "I've grown up with the cable industry," Chiddix says. Along the way, he learned cable TV's technology and architecture.

Now Chiddix spends most of his time in an office overlooking train tracks in Stamford, Connecticut. He is Time Warner Cable's vice president of engineering and technology and the leading architect of Full Service Network, Time Warner's $3 billion to $5 billion bet on the future. For years, Chiddix has been thinking about turning cable systems into megamedia networks that would transmit interactive TV, video phone calls, and hundreds of channels of programming. He was saying it in speeches in the late 1980s. As a low-tech, low-cost preview, he put together Time Warner's test system, called Quantum, in Queens, in New York City. Quantum had capacity to carry 150 channels' worth of programming in analog form, not digital. Quantum allowed Time Warner to offer virtual on-demand movies and video, and new niche-market channels. Customers in Queens started reacting to cable TV and pay-per-view movies in a whole new way—a way that suggested they'd buy and use more programming if they could control when and how they'd get it.

"It struck a chord within Time Warner," Chiddix says. "In essence, Time Warner is a company that owns intellectual property. New ways to distribute intellectual property add value to it. This is not just about cable TV."

Time Warner chairman Gerald Levin agrees. Time Warner is mainly engaged in creating entertainment and information products. Warner Bros. makes movies and TV shows. Time Inc. publishes magazines and books. Warner Music Group is one of the world's largest record companies. HBO both packages and makes movies and TV shows. Cable TV pulls in just one-seventh of Time Warner's total annual revenue. Yet Levin believes that the developments in cable can become a booster rocket for the rest of Time Warner's enterprises.

"Content is, and will remain, king," Levin says. "But what people fail to see is that broad systems of distribution are the power behind the throne." Pushing technology to create new and better distribution, like video on demand or electronic news stands, is becoming Time Warner's megamedia strategy for all its news and entertainment units, not just for cable TV. And getting there first is an important element of that strategy. By creating the most advanced technology, Time Warner can find out what consumers will buy and create next-generation programming ahead of competitors. At the unveiling of FSN on December 14, 1994, in a Sheraton hotel in Orlando, Levin compared the effort to Home Box Office, CNN, and MTV, which were all among the first to exploit cable TV technology. "Sooner isn't only better. Often, it's everything," Levin said. "FSN will drive home this lesson with unforgiving velocity."

Levin has turned into the chief cheerleader for the Full Service Network, or FSN. Over lunch in a small, plush executive dining room at the top of Time Warner's headquarters in New York, he rarely stopped talking about FSN. It is his number-one priority within the company. He is willing to spend billions on it, even though Time Warner still groans under heavy debt. To help FSN along, he has sold chunks of his company to US West and Japanese electronics firms Toshiba and Itochu.

Levin believes the FSN systems themselves will be a great business, especially once they start carrying phone calls, too. Perhaps more importantly, Levin says, people using the networks might watch more Warner movies if they can get them without driving to a video store. Or, they might listen to Warner music on a pay-per-listen basis, instead of tuning in free radio, or interact with an on-line service run by Time-owned *Money* magazine to get help managing the family's finances. Any of those activities would pump new money and new life into Time Warner's products. The contact with consumers who electronically interact with Time Warner products would let Time Warner learn more about its customers, so the company could improve its products, tailor them, and make them even more attractive. Levin is sure all of this will happen better and cheaper and faster for Time Warner because it is one of the few players that will own both the content and large-scale megamedia networks. "It is our manifest destiny," Levin says.

The first Full Service Network is just beginning to operate in Orlando, Florida, in a test involving about 4,000 customers. Of all the tests of new television technology, FSN is the most celebrated and scoffed-at—probably because Time Warner is shooting for the moon. It is putting in a system of fantastic power, at a fantastic price. The set-top boxes alone, which are built by Scientific-Atlanta and based on high-performance Silicon Graphics computers, at first cost more than $2,000 each. It will take a lot of $3 movies to make up for that. The digital video storage system, also being put together by Silicon Graphics, will have to have enough memory to store 500 two-hour movies, Time Warner says. How much is that? The equivalent of the memory in more than 10,000 desktop PCs. The Orlando system has the most advanced digital switch available. The switch, made by AT&T, can handle video phone calls as well as voice calls and data traffic. Time Warner claims that more lines of computer code went into FSN than were needed to put a man on the moon. Engineers reinvented everything about TV, even speeding up the time it takes for an infrared signal to get from a remote control to the set-top box once a button on the remote is pressed.

Consumers who turn on TVs hooked to Orlando's FSN first see a navigation system that's the most eye-popping yet devised. It should be. Silicon Graphics computers are famous for creating Hollywood special effects, including the dinosaurs in the movie *Jurassic Park* and the visual tricks in *Forrest Gump.*

Turn on FSN—using a specially-designed remote control that has extra buttons—and the system software takes a few seconds to load into the set-top box. Then, on the TV screen, up pops a navigation system called Carousel. It's a visual guide to the network. Boxes—labeled movies, sports, shopping, games—twirl slowly around the screen as if on a Lazy Susan.

The system is simple to use and learn. Members of the media attending the Orlando unveiling were ushered into hotel rooms equipped to get FSN. Anyone who tried it immediately understood how to call up movies or games or move around the system.

FSN's high-powered system offers real, working video on demand—for now, mostly Warner Bros. movies. Viewers select the movies box off the Carousel to see lists of available films. Highlight a listed movie using the remote and see a preview. Hit a button to order. Price in the Orlando test is $2.95 a movie, though Time Warner is experimenting with prices. While watching the movie, viewers can stop it, watch something else, turn the TV off, play a video game and later go back to the movie exactly where it was stopped. Hit fast-forward and the movie jumps ahead but the picture remains clear. Same with rewind. It's more responsive than a VCR.

Turn to the shopping feature on FSN and enter a three-dimensional mall, again created using Silicon Graphics software. Move past stores such as Spiegel, The Nature Company, Warner Bros. Studio Store. Hit a button to go "inside" and see videos of specific products. Order products by hitting another button and punching in a credit card number.

Some games using Atari's Jaguar system are available over the FSN system, and some of the games can be played against another FSN user in another house. A Hewlett-Packard printer can print coupons or ads or capture images off a TV show or movie.

Other features will be coming to FSN. CNN, ABC, NBC and *Time* magazine are teaming to create a video and print news on demand service. Users could pluck individual video news reports off the service. Warner Music Group is developing a music shopping and video service. A group at FSN is creating an educational service aimed at schools. Musician Todd Rundgren is working on an interactive music service that would let users create their own mood music.

The partnership with phone company US West will help bring telecommunications to FSN. US West bought 25.5 percent of Time Warner Entertainment for $2.5 billion. The main part of that deal gives US West half of both the equity and the management of Time Warner Cable, which is the nation's second-largest cable-TV company. By tapping US West's expertise and technology, Time Warner plans to add several communications services to FSN. One is plain old phone calls—voice conversations that are spoken into the same kind of telephones now installed in homes, but travel over cable network lines instead of phone company lines. Another is PCS service. FSN lines will also be able to hook personal computers to on-line services.

The plan is for FSN networks to eventually carry video phone calls. A tiny camera atop a TV set will transmit the pictures. The person on the other end will appear on the TV screen. The network is also expected to handle videoconferences for businesses at rates much lower than such services charge today.

For now, most of the telecommunications services are held up by federal and state regulations. As issues get sorted out in coming years, there's no reason to think FSN won't play in all those areas.

The grand FSN plan starts with the Orlando test. It's the only place Time Warner is building the full-fledged system. It will be the place where Time Warner tries to figure out what consumers will want enough to pay for in the next age, and what services make economic sense. In the meantime, the rest of Time Warner Cable won't be sitting on its hands. The company is rebuilding all its cable systems, imitating the fiber-optic lines and basic architecture used in the Orlando system.

"It's going on as we speak," says Joe Collins, the gruff president of Time Warner Cable. "It's the main part of our investment over the next four years. It will transform our systems from the historical tree-and-branch architecture to a [two-way, switched] system ready for FSN."

The strategy is that, by the time Orlando shapes up into a complete business, Time Warner's other cable systems will have what is basically an FSN skeleton built and ready to go. "When we're ready to roll out FSN applications," Collins says, "they can ride in on that architecture. We'll be prepared for the day we go into the FSN business."

By the way, the FSN wiring—even without the expensive set-top boxes and digital servers—will expand the capacity of Time Warner-owned cable systems to 150 or more channels, so Time Warner can begin offering virtual movies on demand and other innovations before FSN comes around. "We don't have to deploy FSN until it becomes a market," Chiddix says.

FSN leaves one big question open: Has Time Warner built something in Orlando that's too far ahead of its time? A lot of Time Warner watchers believe FSN technology costs too much to become a business. Some have mocked Orlando as "Qube 2," saying it will be a 1990s version of the interactive TV system that Time Warner Cable's predecessor, Warner Amex, tested and ultimately shelved in the 1970s and 1980s. Time Warner management is under tremendous pressure from shareholders to make FSN pay off. Many of them believe FSN has diverted Time Warner's focus from software, the company's core strength.

Levin, Chiddix, and Collins, of course, disagree. They believe that the cost of the technology they're using will drop like a rock over the next few years, when items such as digital storage devices for movies go into mass production. By the time Time Warner is ready to roll FSN into its other markets, such as New York, Houston, and Memphis, the technology will be economically viable. If it generates just $8 to $10 more a month in fees from consumers, they figure, FSN will turn a profit.

Here's a slightly different observation: maybe the financial success of FSN ultimately doesn't matter. The strategy may yet turn out to be strong for the whole of Time Warner, even if FSN flunks and the Orlando set-top box gets buried next to the old clunky Qube control box.

By plowing head-first into its high-profile FSN test, Time Warner has stimulated the development of megamedia in general. Competing cable and phone companies have moved on their megamedia plans a little more quickly because they've seen Time Warner coming on strong. Technology companies such as Silicon Graphics and AT&T are developing and testing products in Orlando that can be used to build other megamedia systems.

The faster megamedia gets built and the better those systems work, the more the demand for high-quality content to put on those networks will increase. And that's Time Warner's bread and butter. Warner Bros. is the most consistently successful movie and TV show producer in Hollywood. *The Fugitive* and the sit-com "Murphy Brown" are only samples of its products. Time is perhaps the premier news-gathering operation in the country, considering it owns *Time, People, Sports Illustrated, Fortune,* and *Southern Living.* That kind of high-quality software will be needed to fill megamedia pipelines, whether they're built by Time Warner, TCI, Bell Atlantic, or whomever.

Plus, the FSN effort has prodded the content parts of Time Warner to think about next-generation software. The print media group might come up with a hit interactive magazine based on one of its titles. Warner Bros. could develop interactive games based on its top movies. As Joe Collins often says, the best applications for megamedia haven't been invented yet. The FSN push is getting the pieces of Time Warner to think that maybe *they* could invent them. Who knows—megamedia products often cross the old lines separating media; maybe FSN will help Time Warner create the internal synergy that has eluded the company ever since Time Inc. and Warner Communications merged in 1990.

Maybe Qube 2 isn't such a bad way to describe the Orlando test. The original Qube, started in Columbus in 1977, also created a brand new kind of pipeline that had to be filled. It opened up more cable channels than ever before, and made the system nominally interactive. The system let Warner experiment with programming that nobody had tried before—sometimes out of desperation, just to have something to put on the system. Qube tried airing videos of rock stars and called it Pop Clips. It eventually became MTV and was sold to Viacom. It also tried a children's network, which became Nickelodeon, also later sold to Viacom. The people who developed

Qube and learned from it have turned out to be an outstanding class of leaders who are now running next-generation projects at a number of companies. Some of those executives still within Time Warner are James Gray, vice chairman of Time Warner Cable, and Robert Pittman, CEO of Time Warner Enterprises. Outside the company, there's Larry Wangberg, who is taking Times Mirror into interactive TV; Scott Kurnit, who is leading Prodigy's charge into megamedia; Tom Freston, chairman of MTV Networks; and Robert Morton, executive producer of David Letterman's TV talk show.

Qube is long gone, but its legacy has turned out to be enormously important. Orlando's FSN project may well be heading down the same kind of rough road that derailed Qube, but the trip should help make Time Warner a winner in the coming age.

COMCAST: FATHER, SON, AND COMPANY

Ask Ralph Roberts about his son, Brian, and the mellow old founder of Comcast puffs up and glows. Brian is only in his mid-30s, but he is Comcast's president and chief strategist. He's also the cable-TV industry's freshest leader, rocketing to the forefront because of his quiet thoughtfulness and headline-grabbing moves, such as Comcast's startling mid-1994 bid for shopping network QVC.

"He's very articulate, knowledgeable, sincere—there's no sham about him," Ralph Roberts says of Brian, who is sitting a few feet away, looking embarrassed. "He has the capability to blend people together. You can see it in the company and in the industry. MCI calls and respects his opinion. He's on Turner's board at Ted Turner's request. He's the NCTA's [National Cable Television Association] choice to talk before Congress. He's been on the good side of so many issues. He makes marvelous presentations for the financial world." At that, Ralph Roberts grins, realizing his fatherly excesses, and says: "I'd personally vote for him—and so would his mother."

Ralph Roberts' comments might otherwise sound like so much biased bologna, except that just about everyone who has dealt with Comcast agrees. They'd add a few other Brian Roberts' traits to the list: shrewd, competitive, financially savvy. And for all his reputation as one of the nicest guys in cable, Brian Roberts can bust kneecaps when cornered. Some say he could develop into a less snarly version of TCI's John Malone, which certainly would make Comcast's future exciting.

Ralph Roberts, now in his 70s, founded Comcast with partners Julian Brodsky and Daniel Aaron in 1963. They started with a cable operation in Tupelo, Mississippi, and just kept building and buying cable systems. By the late 1980s, Ralph Roberts had made Comcast into one of the nation's top five cable companies. It developed some of the best customer relations in the cable industry. To this day, most of Comcast's cable operations remain strong.

Brian Roberts is taking Comcast to the next level, making it into a megamedia company. Since becoming Comcast's president in 1990, he has plunged the company into the wireless telephone business—the first major cable company to make a move into wireless. When Comcast owned 16 percent of QVC, Roberts lured Barry Diller to run the network, turning QVC and Comcast into instant forces in cable programming. Roberts has bought more cable systems to give Comcast more clout, and has helped develop a go-go culture at Comcast that's ready, willing, and able to storm into new businesses.

Brian Roberts doesn't have an overarching, synergistic vision or grand strategy for Comcast. He wants to keep Comcast independent, not sell out to a phone company. He believes in the new communications technology and sees that it's where Comcast must go. Beyond that, he's mostly an opportunist. "It's a business to share in the future," he says, sitting at a table in the company's new headquarters in central Philadelphia. "We're willing to invest in ideas. Fortunately we've built a very strong, financially secure business so that we can afford to take some risks and venture into areas that need development or nurturing."

Up to now, Comcast's "risks" have been well-chosen beauties, financially and strategically. They're worth looking at, one-by-one.

Cellular Phones

Comcast went on a buying binge in 1992, picking up Metrophone and Amcell, two big cellular phone providers in the Northeast corridor.

Comcast is now the fourth-largest cellular provider in the United States, and cellular is about one-fifth of Comcast's revenue. The cellular buy has been an amazing investment. Comcast's cellular operation grew 50 percent in the first half of 1994 versus the first half of the previous year. It grew 45 percent in all of 1993.

Strategically, adding cellular was like firing a competitive lightning bolt into the company. Unlike cable, cellular is a tough, battling business. Comcast's cellular unit has learned to compete well, matching or beating its adversary's market share in almost every market. The company, from the beginning, has moved executives around so cable people get to sit in cellular's hot seat, and that may turn out to be one of the best returns from the cellular investment. Cable TV is going to become competitive, and managers who get a preview should perform better when those days come. "When you don't have a lot of competition, you're much more relaxed than when you have a lot of competition," Ralph Roberts says. "The old relaxed ones suddenly become sharp as tacks when they know their life is at stake."

One other benefit from cellular: cable companies are moving into providing telephone service. Comcast, which is joining the alliance with Sprint, TCI, and Cox, is the only big cable company that has actually been in the telephone business, learning about switching, marketing, billing, and all the other ins and outs.

Digital Wireless Communications

Comcast bought about one-third of startup Nextel when Nextel was little more than a neat idea. Nextel had been buying licenses to radio frequencies once used for taxi dispatches. Its plan was to put in new digital technology that could let those frequencies carry wireless phone calls, data, and messages in most of the nation's top markets. The big hurdles would be money and clout. Brian and Ralph Roberts called on MCI chairman Bert Roberts (no relation). Comcast persuaded MCI to invest $1.3 billion in Nextel and become a partner, giving Nextel the cash and brand name to make its plan a reality. Snags have meant that the partnership with MCI is apparently dead. Nextel will probably be a pretty good business anyway, and it will give Comcast another door into the wireless market.

Hard to say what will happen to Comcast's relationship with MCI. The Comcast Robertses had never met MCI's Roberts before the Nextel deal. Afterward, they talked about each other as if they were good friends and allies. Now Comcast is aligning with Sprint. It would be sad news for Comcast if MCI turns its back.

Programming

Comcast's programming side is in turmoil. To hear Comcast talk about it in the past, that piece of Comcast revolved around Barry Diller. Diller, who had run TV networks and movie studios, is one of the most successful entertainment executive ever. The Roberts plan was to draw Diller into cable TV's camp, then help him use QVC to build a mainstream programming empire that would feed cable's pipeline. Diller's bid to buy Paramount was part of that plan. His plan to merge QVC into CBS in July 1994 was not. Comcast didn't like it. To protect its investment in QVC, Comcast bought it all, with help from TCI. It ripped Roberts' relationship with Diller, who is expected to quit.

Brian Roberts now says he doesn't need Diller. QVC, sans Diller, will be a good business for Comcast. "The core business has grown 15 percent to 20 percent every year since 1986 or '87," Roberts says. "Most of the people running it have been there since then." He calls the purchase "a defining moment for Comcast."

Yet Comcast is left with no angle into mainstream programming. The company owns small stakes in Turner Broadcasting and E! Entertainment Television. It has also helped start The Golf Channel, a promising cable niche network. But the company is going to have to search for another way to get into big-time television. "We're still looking for a major play, which eventually we'll have," Ralph Roberts says. Hard to say which companies or people the Robertses might have in mind.

Brian Roberts is wildly interested in on-line computer services, both connecting users via cable lines and owning the services themselves. Comcast, like a lot of cable companies, is testing technology that lets on-line service users plug their computers into cable lines instead of phone lines. The connections could be a new source of revenue for cable operations and, Roberts says, the technology opens opportunities to create whole new kinds of computer services. "The computer content people are who we ought to be nurturing," he says.

Comcast plans to set up a venture capital unit, operating like Malone's model at TCI. "It's what I did 30 years ago," Ralph Roberts says. "We'll look for young people with new ideas and help them develop them. We may hit 1 out of 10."

One thing Comcast hasn't done is launch a big, high-profile test of megamedia technology. It probably won't. That may put Comcast a half-step behind TCI and Time Warner, but Brian Roberts has an interesting philosophy here. Comcast brings in about $1 billion in annual revenue, much less than TCI or Time Warner. Instead of spending on a major test, Roberts would rather wait until megamedia technology is ready and can be bought, essentially, off the shelf. "We've found that when somebody invents the equipment, they come knocking on our door so fast," Roberts says. The approach won't make Comcast a technology or megamedia programming leader, but it's probably the smartest one for the company.

Comcast does have one major problem. On the information superhighway, it is a little Mazda Miata right smack in the path of an oncoming 18-wheeler named Bell Atlantic. The companies' headquarters are blocks apart in Philadelphia. About 30 percent of Comcast's cable subscribers are in Bell Atlantic's service area. Almost all of its cellular operations compete against Bell Atlantic. Comcast executives were quaking in their loafers when it looked like TCI and John Malone were going to join Bell Atlantic. Comcast won a reprieve when that deal fell apart, but Bell Atlantic is still charging into Comcast's businesses. Brian Roberts says Comcast can compete against much-bigger Bell Atlantic by moving faster and being innovative, and he cites Comcast's success in cellular—it splits most markets 50–50 where it competes against Bell Atlantic. But make no mistake: Bell Atlantic is going to make Comcast's job hard, whether in TV, phones, wireless, computer connections, whatever.

Along those lines, Comcast may need some financial help to keep up with megamedia developments. Comcast has long been one of the most financially sound companies in the cable business, with low debt and lots of cash on hand. But that won't be enough to keep making major deals such as Comcast's $1 billion purchase of Maclean Hunter's cable systems and its $2 billion QVC buyout in 1994. Brian Roberts says he'll consider bringing in financial partners whenever necessary. He and finance whiz Brodsky landed the California Public Employees' Retirement System to help fund the Maclean Hunter deal.

One of Comcast's competitive weapons in megamedia will undoubtedly be its culture. Ralph Roberts and his partners have stayed together for 30 years. It may sound corny, but they set a tone of integrity, honesty, trust, and stability that permeates the company today. Says Ralph Roberts: "We go out of our way to make this a big issue around here: You should like your job." It means that good people come to Comcast and stay. Employees can try new things without fear of failure. Anybody in the company can stop by a top executive's office to explain an idea or problem. Its corporate culture will help Comcast continue to be a fast-reacting opportunist as megamedia unfolds.

Still, a lot of how Comcast fares will depend on Brian Roberts. He wants to stay independent and he wants to make Comcast the fleet-footed entrepreneur of megamedia; the bug on the big companies' necks; the next MCI, a company Brian Roberts clearly admires. He wants to continue to take Comcast in new directions, placing bets all around the megamedia table. "Hopefully we'll be risk takers," Roberts says.

So far, Roberts looks like he's got the knack. The early investments in cellular, QVC, and Nextel were brilliant moves that were far ahead of the pack. Roberts is considered a strong day-to-day manager within Comcast. And he showed, when he busted Diller's move to CBS, that he can joust with the big boys. Could be that, in the next decade, Brian Roberts will really make his father proud.

COX: A FAMILY DYNASTY JUMPS INTO MEGAMEDIA

Jim Robbins is pumped. A big man wearing a tie picturing school buses, the president of Cox Cable talks as if he's ready to jump out of his shoes to get at cable TV's future.

"For the next 10 years and probably longer, we've got a whale of a business here, provided the government doesn't continue to do absolutely stupid things," he says, taking a jab at recent cable regulation. But isn't he worried about potential competition from phone companies? "Hey, I'd love to work against the phone companies," Robbins says. "I can run circles around competition that's been a protected monopoly for 100 years."

The bravado comes courtesy of the June 1994 deal that sealed Cox's place among the top cable companies and handed it a role in megamedia's future. Cox paid a whopping $2.3 billion to buy cable systems owned by Times Mirror. If not for the deal, Cox executives have said they might have found their cable operations too small to stay in the game—and probably would have sold them. Instead, in one blast, landing Times Mirror rocketed Cox into the top tier and gave Robbins a second life.

A big reason Cox took the $2.3 billion leap was the dawning of megamedia. Cox believes that cable systems can evolve into interactive broadband pipelines more quickly and easily than phone company systems, and at far less cost. "It's what drove us to the Times Mirror transaction," Robbins says.

Besides, Robbins points out, the move is consistent with Cox's 100-year history. James Middleton Cox, a high-school dropout, got the family dynasty rolling by buying the *Dayton Daily News* in 1898. Then he bought more newspapers. When radio was new, Cox jumped into it, starting WHIO in Dayton, Ohio, in 1923. In television, Cox built the first TV station in the South in 1949. One of the first media companies to buy into cable when that was new, Cox picked up the Lewiston, Pennsylvania, system in 1962. "One of the hallmarks of the company's success," Robbins says, "is it has not shied from new technology."

Cox Enterprises, still owned and run by James Cox's descendants, today owns 20 TV and radio stations and 18 newspapers, including *The Atlanta Journal and Constitution*. Its Manheim Auctions is the world's largest automobile auction company. Before the Times Mirror deal, Cox served 1.8 million cable subscribers. After adding Times Mirror's 1.2 million subscribers, Cox Cable became a separate publicly traded company, although about 80 percent of the shares are owned by Cox Enterprises.

For the most part, Cox doesn't bring anything earthshakingly new to the megamedia party. Its officials talk about many of the same plans that others do: telephone over cable, movies on demand, interactive services, video phone calls, and so on. The company, like others, is running a couple of broadband test systems—one in Omaha, Nebraska, and another in Irvine, California.

Cox should have a couple of advantages when it wades into the phone business. Big Cox and Times Mirror systems sit next to each other in Southern California, so Cox now has one huge 600,000-subscriber contiguous region from San Diego to Orange County, just south of Los Angeles. The cluster of systems in this high-density, communications-intense area should give Cox a no-brainer entry into the phone business. "It has the nearest-term revenue and market potential for us," says Cox Cable's top telephone executive, David Woodrow. Plus, Cox maintains a relationship with phone company SBC Communications. The two jointly operate a cable system in the United Kingdom, and they've maintained U.S. ties after a big cable deal between them fell apart in April 1994. Look for SBC to help Cox on the phone side.

Programming, for now, is a Cox Cable weakness. It has a smattering of video programming assets, but nothing to celebrate. It owns 24.6 percent of Discovery Communications and a production company called Rysher Entertainment, plus a few other minority stakes in programmers. As part of the Times Mirror deal, Cox put $100 million into a new video programming unit one-third owned by Cox and two-thirds owned by Times Mirror. It'll take a while to see whether that turns into much. "We'll continue to search for programming investment opportunities that make sense," Robbins says. He says he "feels strongly" that a major cable company needs to own a strong programming arm.

Cox Enterprises' media assets might spice up Cox Cable's megamedia plans. The Atlanta newspapers, for instance, are already offering an on-line service over Prodigy, and that has spurred Cox to test Prodigy over cable lines in San Diego. Robbins says that maybe even Manheim Auctions could develop an interactive car pricing and buying system. But have the different Cox divisions gotten together to talk about this stuff? "Well, not as much as we should," Robbins admits.

Cox Cable has solid, prudent management and a nimble culture. It won't go nuts trying to spend money on megamedia, but it should be able to react to changes as they come.

If nothing else, Cox Cable has size and clout. Its 3 million subscribers should help it negotiate for programming. The cash from the systems should help finance technology. The newly public stock can help fund more deals—and Cox says it will look to buy more cable systems. Parent Cox Enterprises, which has annual revenue of $2.5 billion, will always be standing by.

Cox will probably never be one of the most aggressive cable companies punching into megamedia. "We'll experiment in a modest way, but we won't bet the company on it," Robbins says. And it has a long way to go to become as diverse and well-rounded as TCI or Comcast.

Cox won't ever be far behind its competitors, and as long as Robbins is around, it will never lack in enthusiasm.

LE GROUPE VIDÉOTRON LTÉE: C'EST INTERACTIVE

Chicoutimi is a heck of a place to look for the future of television. On the banks of the chilly Saguenay River, it is the northernmost city of any size (population: about 58,000) in the Canadian province of Quebec. By the fall of 1995, mostly French-speaking residents of Chicoutimi will be the first to get hooked to Universality Bidirectionality Interactivity (UBI), an ambitious interactive TV system assembled by Le Groupe Vidéotron Ltée.

While U.S. companies have made a lot of noise about interactive TV and run endless tests, Vidéotron has slipped off to the north and quietly made it happen. Vidéotron's Montreal-area cable system has had elements of interactivity since 1990. UBI will take the technology several steps further. No cable TV company is close to matching Vidéotron's experience in creating and marketing interactive television.

"The Canadians have done some brilliant work," says Bill Samuels, president of ACTV in New York, which sold technology to Vidéotron for its system. "They certainly can be called missionaries in this area."

Outside of Canada, Vidéotron is barely known. André Chagnon started the company in 1964. He built his first cable system in northern Montreal and part of Laval, just outside of Montreal. Chagnon has a taste for technology, and in 1974 he put up one of the earliest cable systems capable of handling two-way signals. He was experimenting with interactive TV in Quebec around the same time that Warner Amex was trying out Qube in Columbus, Ohio.

Chagnon made his mark with a system he calls Vidéoway. Introduced in Montreal in 1990, Vidéoway is a real, commercial, and successful interactive cable TV system. It's nowhere near as advanced as Time Warner's experimental Full Service Network, and it doesn't offer video on demand. But it does take TV to a new level.

The heart of Vidéoway is technology that "personalizes" television. One side of the Vidéoway remote control is lined with four buttons that let viewers interact with certain shows. During broadcasts of Montreal Canadiens hockey games, Vidéoway customers can use the buttons to flip between three camera angles and a continuous instant replay. During game shows created for Vidéoway, viewers can play along as if they're part of the show. The host seems to respond directly to the viewer, saying an answer is right or wrong. The effect is startling. The interactivity is used on children's shows (answer questions, like what letter "dog" begins with), exercise shows (choose the intensity of the work-out) and news broadcasts (choose to see more business news and skip sports, for example).

The technology is fairly simple. For one interactive show, four channels of video come into the Vidéoway terminal atop the TV. Hitting the four buttons actually flicks between four channels, all transmitting synchronized but different tracks of the same show. Answer a question right or choose a certain kind of news to see, and the terminal switches to an appropriate track. The switch from one track to another is seamless, unlike when changing channels, so the show appears to be one broadcast.

Beyond interactive video, Vidéoway offers video games, home shopping, classified ads, and information services such as weather, phone directories, and text news. It's essentially an on-line computer service adapted to television.

To get Vidéoway's interactive offerings, consumers buy Vidéoway's cable TV service and pay another $4 to $15, depending on what level of service they choose. About 26 percent of Vidéoway cable customers get interactive services. That's 325,000 interactive customers, and they use the interactive services an average of 13 hours per week. The success of the services has given Vidéotron valuable experience in this emerging business.

UBI will take the company further, mostly by offering more and better services. UBI will not offer video on demand. But it brings in a range of partners to build services companies such as Time Warner are only testing.

Vidéotron owns 30 percent of UBI, which is being set up as a joint venture. The other 70 percent was sold in chunks to Hydro-Quebec, Canada Post, Loto-Quebec, National Bank Canada and Hearst Corporation, the only U.S. company in the consortium. National Bank Canada, for example, developed a home banking system for UBI. Cost to users is $4 a month. Hydro-Quebec, the province's power company, has created a way to let UBI customers use the service to control household appliances and save on energy costs. Hearst has added electronic phone listings, which lets users make restaurant reservations, buy tickets, and shop as well as look up phone numbers.

To get UBI up and running, Vidéotron has had to rebuild its cable network to make it two-way and add bandwidth. IBM has built UBI's TV set-top boxes using the speedy PowerPC computer chip. The service will cost as much as $500 a home to install, but Vidéotron says the investment will pay off. Its experience shows it will.

"Very few people were optimistic about Vidéoway," Andre Caron, at the University of Montreal, told *Interactive Age.* Caron helped Vidéotron research the market for UBI. "Basically, what we found is that people perceive the (Vidéoway) technology as user-friendly, an expansion of TV." That's why consumers want and buy the service.

Vidéotron is rolling UBI into 34,000 homes in Chicoutimi in 1995. Through 2002, the company will take the service to 1.5 million homes in Montreal and Quebec City.

Megamedia players would be smart to keep an eye on Vidéotron. For one, it's a window on the future. Hearst joined the UBI partnership because Vidéotron is a "quantum step" ahead of anything being done in the United States, say Hearst executives.

Another reason to watch Vidéotron is that it doesn't plan to stay only in Quebec. The company has already begun to move toward franchising the Vidéoway approach. It plans to sell Vidéoway to cable operators in the United States and other parts of the world. A megemedia company anywhere may wake up soon to find these Canadians in its backyard.

CABLEVISION AND JONES: TWO POSSIBLE SURVIVORS IN A CONSOLIDATING INDUSTRY

In 5 to 10 years, there may not be much "et cetera" in the cable industry.

The industry, as it evolves beyond traditional cable TV and into a broad communications and entertainment business, is becoming far too important and profitable to stay so fragmented. It will also take a lot of capital and clout to keep up with the top-tier companies. The big guys will aggressively push to get bigger, so they'll be buyers of other companies and systems. A lot of medium-size and little guys will find it harder to stay competitive on their own, so they'll be sellers. Consolidation of the industry, which began in a big way in 1994, will rev faster and faster. Now, something like 50 companies divide up about 85 percent of the cable TV market. In a decade, that 85 percent will be dominated by four or five powerful national companies and a few big independent regional companies. Some mid-size companies may stay independent but become partially owned by and allied with one of the majors. The rest of the market will fall to scattered rural mom-and-pop operations that will mostly look like old cable-TV companies, not high-tech megamedia firms.

The buyers, and ultimately the major companies, will likely be the ones I've profiled here: TCI, Time Warner, Comcast, Cox. Some of the phone companies might join them—especially, it seems US West.

The rest of the industry will be fascinating to watch as companies maneuver to join one camp or another, or gussy up their systems to lure buyers, or break off pieces to sell separately. A couple of companies—Cablevision Systems and Jones International—may be interesting because they're more colorful than most.

Cablevision

In a relatively short time, this Woodbury, New York-based company will cement its future as a strong regional independent, sell out to another company, or crash and burn at the hands of competitors.

Cablevision's crafty founder and chairman, Charles Dolan, already blew it once. Around the time the Bell Atlantic–TCI deal was announced, when cable stocks were at sky-high levels, Dolan was reportedly talking with several companies about selling Cablevision. The companies included Time Warner and Bell Atlantic. But Dolan supposedly demanded too high a price. His stock was in the 60s. He wanted a price in the 70s. Nobody would pay it. Then, as telephone company–cable deals unraveled, cable stocks plunged. By 1994, Dolan would've been lucky to get in the 40s for Cablevision.

Dolan stopped trying to sell and moved on to try a strategy of making Cablevision into an independent regional powerhouse. The company's main asset is the world's most attractive single cable system. It covers all of Long Island and has almost 700,000 subscribers. It rakes in the highest revenue per subscriber of any cable system anywhere. Many of its customers are upscale and well-educated, just the type who would buy interactive information services, movies on demand, and other coming products and services. In recent years, Cablevision has built two-way, fiber-optic, digital technology into the system, so it is nearly ready to carry interactive services and telephone calls.

By itself, the system could be a good business for years to come. It could also become a base, along with Cablevision's Yonkers, New York, system, for regional expansion. In fact, in Yonkers, which touches the northern edge of New York City, Cablevision has built a new high-tech, 110-channel operation that is offering subscribers the ability to choose individual cable channels and pay only for those. Dolan has said he may invade other New York suburbs with similar offerings, to compete with the established cable companies in those areas. As an added regional gambit, Cablevision and a partner, ITT, are paying $1 billion to buy New York's Madison Square Garden (MSG) from Viacom. MSG includes the famous 20,000-seat arena, two pro sports teams—the Knicks (basketball) and Rangers (hockey)—and MSG Network, the largest regional sports channel on cable.

If Cablevision can keep competitors out of Long Island while inching into nearby territories, Dolan may create a successful, independent regional company.

On the flip side, if Cablevision isn't the absolute best at delivering TV and communication service, competitors are going to come charging after those attractive Long Island customers. Time Warner and US West, which own the huge New York City cable system next door to Dolan, are chafing to get into Long Island. Phone companies NYNEX and Bell Atlantic would like to be selling TV service there, too. Meanwhile, MSG has long been a barely profitable entity.

If competition gets too tough on Long Island and his expansion strategy doesn't work, Dolan could always just sell out. He'd probably keep the programming division at Cablevision, called Rainbow Programming Holdings, producer of the Bravo and American Movie Classics cable channels. Dolan, nearing age 70, could dance away.

But what if the price isn't right? Tough-guy Dolan has shown his willingness to hang on and fight if he doesn't get his way.

Jones

"For the past three years, I have not even considered myself to have been in the cable business," Jones International chairman Glenn Jones said in 1994. "I've been in the business of the extension of the human mind."

That's a pretty good introduction to Jones, the cable industry's only philosopher-entrepreneur. "I almost hired a vice president of philosophy one time," Jones says, "but my people talked me out of it."

It might be easy to giggle at Jones as he says such things, wearing a double-breasted suit with wild pink tie and matching hanky, his glasses atop his helter-skelter hair. But his approach has worked in the past and may be Jones International's ticket to the future.

No telling how much of that future will depend on operating cable-TV systems. Glenn Jones was one of the earliest cable operators, starting out in Georgetown, Colorado, in 1967. He built Jones InterCable into what is now one of the top 10 cable companies, serving about 1.6 million customers. Its systems are top-notch, and they're getting early training in competition: Jones's Alexandria, Virginia, system is preparing to battle Bell Atlantic, which is making Alexandria its first interactive TV market.

But cable doesn't seem to be where Glenn Jones's heart is anymore. Oh, he loves where megamedia is heading, but mostly because of what it can do for people, not because owning the networks is a great business opportunity. "We're talking about a self-empowerment technology that has never existed before," he says.

Much more of Jones's energy is focused on the odd but growing programming side of Jones International. It is an all-out effort at no-nonsense educational programming. The main piece of it is Mind Extension University: The Education Network, which Glenn Jones started in 1987. The network, known at Jones as ME/U, is the first real shot at distance education—adults can use it to get real college degrees from schools such as George Washington University, the University of Maryland, and the University of Arizona. ME/U broadcasts videos of lectures from affiliated colleges. Students register with the universities, pay tuition, buy the books, and take exams monitored by ME/U-hired proctors. Often, the students set VCRs to record the lectures, then watch when they have time. And people do use it. Hundreds have by now been awarded degrees through ME/U, including a woman named Tracy Smith in Homer, Alaska, who got her MBA from Colorado State University via the cable network.

In 1993, Jones launched a second network, dubbed Jones Computer Network. It operates similar to ME/U, but focuses on computer training and computer courses. It offers a degree in computer science from George Washington University.

Glenn Jones has done a lot with crude means of interactivity—registration by mail, exams by proctor, courses recorded on VCRs. Now he's fired up about what real high-tech interactivity could do for his concept. Students could register and take exams by interacting through a TV or personal computer, and see videos on demand instead of having to program a VCR. Jones has hired Bernie Luskin, who had been president of Philips' interactive CD-ROM unit, to bring interactivity to ME/U and Jones Computer Network. Jones and Luskin see all kinds of possibilities for distance learning, worker retraining, and personal improvement courses.

"It's a huge market and a huge opportunity," says Luskin. And it's a profitable business. Glenn Jones notes that ME/U and Jones Computer Network collect fees from cable operators that carry the channels, plus a share of tuition fees, book sales, and other charges. Some of the network's broadcasts also carry some advertising. "It's a multiple revenue stream, which is better than most networks," Jones says.

Jones didn't say that he'd sell his cable systems, and maybe he won't. But he also didn't say that cable operations were important to his future. Maybe after doing battle with Bell Atlantic in Alexandria, Jones will decide that programming is the place to be.

5

MAKING IT SING AND DANCE

THE MEDIA AND ENTERTAINMENT INDUSTRIES

LEADERS TO WATCH: FRANK BIONDI, SUMNER REDSTONE, AND VIACOM

Frank Biondi has a hell of a job to do. The chief executive of Viacom has to stitch together the newly merged Viacom and Paramount companies and make a $9.5 billion deal pay off. He is also pulling Blockbuster Entertainment into the mix as it merges into Viacom. Plus, he has to please phone company NYNEX, which invested $1.2 billion in the merged company. Then, in the long run, Biondi has to steer this monolith through the changes that megamedia will bring to the entertainment business.

If Biondi can make it work, the potential is awesome. Viacom could become the most exciting and interesting entertainment company of the next decade. Viacom owns: Paramount movie and TV studios; Blockbuster video rental and music stores; channels MTV, VH-1, Nickelodeon, Showtime; publisher Simon & Schuster; six amusement parks; pieces of Spelling Entertainment, Discovery Zone play centers, USA Network; and a stake in the development of a new broadcast TV network called United Paramount. To get an idea of what it might do, look at how Viacom could slide a hot project up and down a delicious media food chain.

Start at Simon & Schuster, the book publishing house that came as part of Paramount. Say it publishes a hot novel. Paramount's film studios make the movie version. Blockbuster, the world's largest video store chain, rents and sells the video. Then the movie plays on Viacom's Showtime movie channel, and on a new movies-on-demand service over Viacom's megamedia test system in Castro Valley, California, or on networks being built by NYNEX.

The movie has a sizzling soundtrack, so it's sold at Blockbuster-owned record stores. The music videos from the album play on Viacom's MTV and VH-1 networks, and the songs play on the company's 14 radio stations.

As technology develops, mix Blockbuster's skill in retailing with MTV and video on demand, and get a channel that lets consumers order music videos and buy the album by hitting a few buttons on the remote control.

The movie's stars appear on Viacom's *Entertainment Tonight* or are guest stars on Paramount's *Deep Space Nine.* The movie becomes a sitcom filmed at Paramount's TV studios. To complete the circle, the sitcom's star becomes famous and writes her autobiography for Simon & Schuster!

Don't get the wrong idea—Viacom doesn't plan to force so much perfect synergy on the merging companies. It doesn't want to be so stiffly integrated that its movies would *only* play on Showtime, for example. In fact, it hopes to be able to sell its software to any outlet, even if it might compete with some other part of Viacom. The company has an impressive batch of assets. If they can start plugging into one another, all the better for Viacom. Paramount's movie studios, for example, are going to produce family movies bearing a Nickelodeon label, and some of the Paramount-owned amusement parks will build Nickelodeon-based attractions.

"We wake up every morning and mentally pinch ourselves in awe of what has transpired the last 12 months," Sumner Redstone, chairman of Viacom, said in December, 1994. "This three-way merger is far outstripping the potential we originally envisioned for it." Redstone is the tenacious dealmaker who built the company and won the Paramount merger fight. He and Biondi have a tight relationship—Redstone calls him "my friend and partner"—and Redstone completely trusts Biondi to run the conglomerate he's built.

Besides all its tangible assets, Viacom has a few intangibles going for it. One is the attitude of MTV Networks, which operates MTV, VH-1, and Nickelodeon and is moving into movie production. MTV Networks may be the most innovative TV programming unit working today. Most importantly, its hip, young slant will help Viacom win over next-generation consumers—the very people who will be the first to desire and pay for megamedia. Who knows how MTV Networks may influence the more staid Paramount units joining Viacom.

Another intangible is the clout of Paramount's production capabilities. Paramount is one of a handful of major, global film producers and distributors. For Viacom, it's a magnet for world-class talent and projects. They'll not only make movies and shows at Paramount, but the people and projects may then filter into other parts of the company. At an entertainment company, Biondi says, "You need motion pictures to be the locomotive."

The biggest question mark, really, is Biondi. Can this handsome, likable, somewhat dull guy pull it off? Can he handle the many factions of Viacom and build the company into all it could be in a rapidly changing environment? Just after the merger with Paramount, multimedia executive Ted Leonsis joked: "If he can do it, we should probably send him to Bosnia."

It's possible that Biondi is one of the only executives who *can* do it. Perpetually tanned, athletic, and attentive to his wife and daughters, Biondi is a nice guy through and through. He believes in open communications and in earning loyalty by treating people fairly. When talking about the merger, Biondi is as concerned about people as he is about money or assets. His door and phone line are open to subordinates. He spent a lot of time massaging egos and easing fears after the deal was done. "There was a lot of free-flowing anxiety," Biondi says. "Fortunately it didn't last too long." When he made the hard decision after the merger to fire Richard Snyder, the man who built Simon & Schuster into a publishing powerhouse, it was because Snyder was a cutthroat, divisive manager who didn't fit on Biondi's team.

Biondi is a practical manager who finds creative people and then lets them do their jobs. He has no interest in deciding what TV shows to air or demanding new endings to films. Under straitlaced Biondi, for instance, MTV developed its often-raunchy style and has used it to grow into a worldwide supernetwork.

Biondi does not plan to force a vision on the company—and it would probably be a mistake if he did. "I came from business school 10 to 15 years ago when you needed a master plan," Biondi says. "Here we're in seven or eight lines of business and there's not a universal strategy for each of them. You have to allow division managers to develop a strategy and my job is to see the intersections or roadblocks."

Biondi has perspective. In the late 1970s, cable television was a wide-open pipeline that was practically empty. It carried broadcast stations to homes that wanted better reception. It had nothing new to offer consumers, nothing unique to cable that took advantage of its technology. Then Home Box Office (HBO) came along. Biondi helped run it.

"Lots of people were saying, 'Eh, it's not for everybody, it's not such a big deal,'" Biondi recalls. But it turned into a big deal. The first premium movie channel caught on, and it became the "killer application" that made cable TV special. HBO is credited with launching the cable industry into a new age of growth and power. The lesson: "When a killer app [application] is on everybody's doorstep," Biondi says, "not everybody sees it. Some say maybe yes, some say maybe no."

Now a new pipeline is opening up, the way cable did two decades ago. This time it's the digital, interactive, broadband networks being built by cable and phone companies. What the new pipeline needs is a killer application. Biondi believes he knows how to try to find it, or at least how to recognize it when it rears its head. Then maybe he can repeat the HBO story.

So Biondi has a good shot at forging ahead to megamedia once the dirty work of merging is finished and the next age beckons.

Biondi will have one powerful force on his side: a meteoric market for "software." In this case, software means the content that people see, read, hear, or play on all kinds of technology: movies and TV shows, documentaries, music, news, books, financial information, video games, magazines, sports, school lunch menus, and on and on. As most software company executives watch megamedia unfold, a confident smirk curls up on their faces. They know that high-quality entertainment or information can be valuable in any new medium. A good action movie, for instance, will earn money in theaters, in video stores, on a movies-on-demand TV system, in an on-line interactive game adaptation, or on any other "platform" that comes along. The most important thing for these companies is to keep producing *good* movies, or news reports, or whatever is their forte.

To software companies, megamedia will become a new distribution technology, one that lets people order a range of entertainment over broadband networks. History has shown that any successful new distribution technology vastly increases the market for software.

Take VCRs. In 1981, when VCRs were in only a few million homes, movie studios mistook the devices for a threat. Studios waged a battle to prevent videos from being rented. The studios lost—a good thing for them. The video rental boom that followed has heaped additional revenue on hit moves long after they've left theaters, and it has rescued films that bombed in first-run release. Now, 48 percent of all movie studio revenue comes from home video rentals and sales.

Megamedia is going to do the same thing for software, although potentially on a grander scale because it could become such a powerful technology. Here's an example of what megamedia could do for one small slice of the software industry.

On most Sunday nights, about 30 million people watch *60 Minutes* on CBS. Those are all the people who both want to see the show and are able to be in front of their TV sets when it comes on. Nobody knows how many people would like to see *60 Minutes* on a given Sunday but can't. Maybe they're doing homework or visiting with relatives. Some experts estimate that would-be audience at 10 million people. Only a small percentage of them remember or bother—or know how—to program their VCRs to record the show for later viewing.

If video on demand becomes as easy as changing channels, those 10 million otherwise-occupied people could see the show whenever they had time—and maybe pay $1 for the convenience. The audience for *60 Minutes* would increase by one-third. The value of the show would get a huge boost through increased advertising fees and additional revenue from the pay-per-view charges.

On a broader scale, megamedia will create huge capacity for carrying and delivering software. Companies building the networks will need to fill their pipelines with software, igniting demand. And because many companies will be competing to deliver software to consumers in any given region, there will be bidding wars for the best and most unique software. We've seen some of that already. In 1994, the Fox network paid $1.6 billion for the right to broadcast NFL games for four years. Profits from broadcasting the games themselves will never come close to that amount. But NFL games are unique and popular, and owning them differentiates Fox in a highly competitive TV industry.

It's very likely that software companies could do nothing different and still profit from megamedia. They could simply continue making *Terminator* movies or publishing *The Philadelphia Inquirer.* There will always be good markets for good software.

Yet software companies have learned—usually the hard way—not to ignore technology. The most stinging lesson had to do with video games. Hollywood kissed them off as a fad, even though the studios would have had the talent and technology to do well in the business. Video games became a $6 billion-a-year industry, and only some of that money is trickling to Hollywood studios.

Software companies also know that content doesn't always translate easily from an old technology to a new one. Charlie Chaplin, master of the silent screen, could never figure out how to make a "talkie." Scores of hit radio shows bombed on TV in the 1950s. Knight-Ridder lost $40 million trying to put text news on TV screens in the 1970s. Today, most books can't easily be turned into best-selling CD-ROM products for computers.

Now, megamedia is looming. The difference in the best software companies in the next decade will be how well they prepare for it.

Software companies seem to be thinking about megamedia in different ways. On one end of a spectrum is The Walt Disney Company. Although Disney is dabbling in more high-tech projects than most people realize, it has been thumbing its nose at the flurry of spending on megamedia. "We are not investing in the superhighway," Disney CEO Michael Eisner told a conference on information highways. "What we have, they [networks, cable channels, and so on] will need. As long as they exist, we will have someone to sell our products to."

At the other end is Time Warner, which is mostly a software company but is now spending up to $5 billion to build its own megamedia networks.

In the middle is a strategy that calls for getting to know the technology while still concentrating on software. Some companies are doing that by hiring people from high-tech fields. Hollywood studios have been hot to recruit multimedia software programmers. On a higher plane, Hollywood's top talent agent, Michael Ovitz, hired Robert Kavner to help his clients get into multimedia. Kavner was an executive vice president at AT&T, where he ran the company's megamedia efforts. Hearst Corporation, which publishes magazines such as *Cosmopolitan* and *Esquire,* hired Al Sikes, former chairman of the FCC, as its new media director. Other companies are building labs or making modest investments in technology companies, or forming alliances with multimedia firms.

Viacom stands in that middle ground. It considers itself to be a software company, period. It's not going to become a technology company. But its test system in Castro Valley, California, may give Viacom a leg up on competitors.

Castro Valley is a quiet little suburban-sprawl community on the east side of the San Francisco Bay. A lot of the residents work in high-tech companies all around the Bay area, sometimes commuting an hour each way. The population is generally upper-middle-income and well educated.

In 1993, Viacom formed an alliance with AT&T and started to build and run a digital, interactive cable system in Castro Valley, as a way to test both technology and programming. The system is similar to those being built by Time Warner, Bell Atlantic, and TCI. AT&T is doing almost all of the technical work. Viacom has been quite purposely along for the ride.

"We've gotten closer to the technology than anybody," says Robert Meyers, Viacom's vice president of corporate development, who is in charge of Castro Valley. "From our standpoint, Castro Valley is a model to learn from. To create future programming, you've got to know what the guts are of the system."

Viacom's role in Castro Valley is to exercise the technology AT&T is building. That means pumping new kinds of cable channels and programming through the system. "Nickelodeon has definitely felt like it's been held back by the concept of a channel," Meyers says of Viacom's children's cable network. "They've already started a magazine and done video games and gone international. Now they can do this." "This" might include putting interactive Nickelodeon games on the system, or "multiplexing" Nick into a series of more narrow channels, each aimed at a specific age group.

Viacom will also experiment with something it's been calling Showtime Anytime. It would be movies on demand, but by subscription. For one monthly fee, viewers could choose to see any or all of the movies on Showtime's menu for that month—and see them on demand, whenever it is convenient. It's an interesting strategy. A subscription movie service with a limited menu should be cheaper to operate and require much less powerful technology than an on-demand service that replicates a video store, offering thousands of titles all the time. And a monthly subscription brings in a stable revenue stream, compared to consumers' choosing and paying for three or four à la carte movies each month.

Other units of Viacom are beginning to look at how they can use and learn from Castro Valley. MTV may offer some kind of video on demand or an interactive shopping channel. It's already experimenting with a home shopping show, "The Goods," which may be a prototype. Paramount's smallish interactive division has developed a couple of CD-ROM entertainment guides—coincidentally, with AT&T's help—and they would be put on the system. An on-line service may be devoted to *Star Trek*, a property owned by Paramount. Meyers has only begun to talk to Simon & Schuster about how publishing could use the system. One idea involves an on-line service that would let readers send e-mail to authors or request book reviews.

NYNEX, by the way, is not involved in Castro Valley at all. Also, Viacom is likely to sell its cable operations to raise money to pay off debt. If it sells cable, Biondi says, Viacom will either keep the Castro Valley system or reach an agreement to continue to take part in the tests there.

"The most important thing is, Castro Valley will get our people thinking about how to program for these networks," Meyers says. To spur that along, Viacom is also building a digital, multimedia production studio in New York, not far from the company's headquarters. Adds Meyers: "We'll be a hell of a lot smarter as a result of Castro Valley."

Learning the technology is also helping Viacom anticipate other, subtler issues that are likely to come up as megamedia develops. One of those issues is control and placement of programming on other companies' megamedia systems—something most software companies will have to wrestle with. Suppose Viacom develops a package of MTV channels: regular MTV; an MTV on demand, which lets viewers choose videos to see; an interactive MTV shopping channel; an MTV information service, which lets users get reviews of releases, documentaries on rock stars, and so on. Viacom will want that package to be available over other companies' megamedia systems, like Bell Atlantic's Stargazer. Stargazer may have its own ideas about how it wants to organize its system. It may want all the shopping channels on one menu, all the information services somewhere else, all the regular channels in a third spot. Maybe Stargazer even wants to put top-drawing individual programs in a place where viewers could buy them à la carte; it might want to strip out MTV's popular "Beavis & Butt-head" to sell separately. Viacom doesn't like any of that. It wants all the MTV-related products to be packaged under the MTV brand name, and, ideally, placed in the first menu people see when they turn on Stargazer. "The brand is not an individual show," says Ed Horowitz, Viacom's senior vice president of technology.

Horowitz, who is Viacom's chief high-tech strategist, sees lots of challenges in creating an identity and winning viewers in a world of hundreds of channels and choices. He's reaching into Viacom's media grab bag for help. He figures that TV will get more like radio is today, with dozens of niche selections that have to battle for recognition and market share (he calls it "guerrilla niche warfare"). Who would know better than Viacom's radio people how to handle that kind of market? The company owns 14 radio stations. Horowitz has them looking at how Viacom can market TV channels in a 500-channel universe.

Blockbuster should prove an interesting addition to Viacom. At first, it might look like adding the company is nothing but a short-term debt-repayment move. Blockbuster, a hugely successful entity, is pulling in excess cash that can help Viacom pay for its massive mergers. Blockbuster's primary business of renting videotapes seems destined for doom as movies-on-demand services come around.

Over the past few years, though, Blockbuster was smart enough to see that future possibility. Like a man told he has a disease that could kill him in 10 years, Blockbuster hustled to find cures. It invested in movie studios, sports teams, and children's play centers in an effort to turn Blockbuster into a rounded entertainment company and brand name. The strategy is working. Blockbuster has as bright a future as any operation heading into megamedia. It could become an important part of Viacom, possibly assembling a Blockbuster movie channel or sports channel or creating a music-on-demand system using its music retailing operations. Interestingly, when Blockbuster was organized into Viacom, both Showtime Networks and Paramount Parks (which operates theme parks) were made part of the new Blockbuster Entertainment Group. Clearly, Blockbuster will be an important part of Viacom.

At the top, Biondi views all this megamedia maneuvering with a hint of detachment. He is leaving most of the work to Horowitz, who, like Biondi, was a key HBO executive in the 1970s and 1980s.

Biondi is ever the practical CEO. He wants to stay on course, building brands and products that can migrate to megamedia, while keeping enough of a finger in the new technology to understand it.

"Our approach is to be essentially software providers," Biondi says, sitting on a lone chair in the middle of his office. The office is not extravagant. A polished desk sits at one end next to a potted fig tree. A couch and chairs are laid out in the center area. Windows run the length of the room, and the ledge is cluttered with athletic trophies, knick-knacks, and many, many framed photographs of his family. "Somewhere along the line, when the information highway reaches critical mass, we'll be able to deliver our software over the highway." Biondi adds: "The information superhighway, from my perspective, as a big market, is 5 to 15 years out."

Biondi is more occupied right now with the shorter term, between now and 5 years from now. Mostly, that has to do with the merger and with managing the bargeload of debt Viacom took on to buy Paramount. Debt is the main thing that could kick Biondi in his management shins. It threatens to keep Biondi from spending on new products and strategic directions just as megamedia gets uncorked. Biondi says he isn't worried about it—although he could hardly be expected to say otherwise. He has been selling off pieces of the merged company to raise money to pay off debt. And he's been drawing on his past experiences to manage the situation. Biondi navigated HBO through massive changes when that operation had little money in the 1970s, and he guided Viacom out of monstrous debt in the late 1980s after Redstone bought the company. "We'll concentrate our resources on businesses we feel we know something about and on good opportunities," Biondi says. "We won't make a lot of marginal investments."

He's also pushing to bring in new revenue from overseas, where Viacom has been successfully opening markets for its networks. MTV, for instance, is now one of the best-known TV programming brand names on the planet, right after CNN. Nickelodeon is moving into other countries. Paramount's movies will join Biondi's overseas marketing drive.

Who can say what else might pop up. Redstone has been said to be interested in adding one of the three big TV networks to Viacom's portfolio. Stay tuned.

All in all, Biondi has Viacom just about where a software company wants to be. It has loads of strong programming, it has great brand names like MTV, it reaches young audiences, it has a world-class movie studio—and it has a sound strategy for understanding and getting started in megamedia. If Biondi can slog through the merger aftermath, he'll be ready to hop on the information superhighway when it comes into view.

For now, he can afford to be the way he always is: reserved, pragmatic.

"No one knows what the [megamedia] market's going to look like till the dust settles," he says. "And we're in a stage now where a lot of dust has been kicked up. There's a lot of hope and a lot of fear and a lot of opportunity in the air."

CAPITAL CITIES/ABC: EVOLUTION OF A DINOSAUR

A feeling of quiet strength hums through the halls of Capital Cities/ABC's New York headquarters—and that's really saying something. In the late 1980s, the three big broadcast TV networks—ABC, NBC, and CBS—were gasping for air. They were being called dinosaurs. Cable TV was driving them to the tar pits, sucking away a third of their prime-time audience. They were losing money, changing owners, and cutting costs and people.

But the dark days are over. Megamedia is around the corner. Far from finding themselves fat lumbering targets in the next decade, the networks are seeing that they have a number of strong assets that may serve them well, including powerful brand names, sophisticated video news organizations, and a knack for finding or creating programming that can appeal to millions. "The network should be much more confident about its role in the future than it would've been even a year or two ago," says Bruce Maggin, Capital Cities/ABC's executive vice president for multimedia.

None of the networks has talked much about its plans for multimedia or interactive television. CBS seems to have done almost nothing to move into those fields. NBC has been a little more aggressive, putting together interactive video news tests and working on building its cable channel, CNBC, into the premier video business news operation.

Capital Cities/ABC seems to be the most aggressive; it is forming alliances, running tests, and developing an internal strategy for megamedia. The company's plans show what could become of the three old-line networks if they don't sit on their hands through the rest of the 1990s.

Capital Cities bought ABC in 1986 for $3.5 billion, with help from superinvestor Warren Buffett. The combined company owns radio stations, eight TV stations, and a $1 billion (in annual revenue) newspaper and trade journal publishing division. It owns 80 percent of cable sports network ESPN—which also operates ESPN2—and stakes in Arts & Entertainment Network and the Lifetime network. The ABC network, by far the biggest and most important part of Capital Cities/ABC, has its ups and downs, depending on what shows are popular in a given season. But its news division has been a consistent top performer, aided by stars Peter Jennings and Ted Koppel and the dean, David Brinkley. The company's total revenue tops $5 billion a year, and it has more cash on hand—and more purchasing power—than almost any other media company. The company has said it could easily swallow an $8 billion acquisition.

Maggin is supposed to figure out where ABC goes from here. He has spent much of his working life at ABC. Over the past decade, he has mostly helped the network find new markets for its programming, such as sales of videotapes of ABC-produced shows or news broadcasts. He plans on doing the same sort of thing over the next decade, but it's going to get a lot more complicated.

In his office at the 77 West 66th Street headquarters, Maggin dives right into the five areas he'll be chasing for ABC. They are markets he is fairly sure will pan out as the new technology comes along.

The first area is what he calls *interactive programming*—a fairly low-tech version of interactivity developed by a few start-ups such as NTN and Interactive Network and on-line computer services such as Prodigy. Some kind of added, interactive programming would ride into homes along with regular ABC broadcasts. During the Academy Awards, for instance, a game would pop up just before each category is announced, letting viewers choose who they think will win the Oscar. The viewers could enter their answer using a remote control and win points for correct answers. Data about each viewer's score would ride back to the game company, and top-scoring viewers might win prizes. In other versions of these kinds of systems, the content is added information instead of games. It might be background information about characters in a soap opera. Confused viewers could call it up while the show is in progress to find out who's done what to whom in the past.

As a way to get into interactive offerings, ABC started a service in October 1994 on America Online. Users can get information about ABC, or play games, but it won't be on the TV screen in conjunction with broadcast programming—not yet anyway.

Basically, those kinds of interactive technology are ways to add a level of contact with audiences to ABC's otherwise linear, one-way network broadcasts.

Maggin's second area is *multimedia software,* mainly games or CD-ROM disks. ABC's brand name could give instant credibility to a CD-ROM product. Maybe ABC could do a CD-ROM based on Koppel's "Nightline." Or a video game might be based on the "Roseanne" TV sitcom. Maggin says ABC would hire software companies or enter into joint ventures to create such products.

A third push will be to take ABC out of homes and into *multimedia technology* used in amusement parks and shopping mall kiosks. Perhaps ABC could lend its dramatic expertise and its brand name to a virtual reality ride. "Take Luxor," Maggin says, referring to the Las Vegas hotel that includes a virtual reality amusement park. "The technology is terrific but the story-telling is awful. People get bored with that." More immediately, ABC has developed a traveling electronic sports show. Using electronic images, a participant might walk across a balance beam a couple of inches off the floor—but to the person on the beam, it would look like he or she were walking from one of the World Trade Center towers to the other.

A fourth area is *time shifting.* ABC is taking part in tests with Bell Atlantic and Discovery Communications' Your Choice TV. Both are testing systems that let viewers see popular TV shows a day late or a few days late, at almost any time they want. A viewer who misses "NYPD Blue" on Tuesday night could see it at noon on Thursday for a fee of around $1. A few clicks of the remote control would order the show. "I'm very bullish on TV-on-demand," Maggin says. What will work best are "just aired, just promoted television shows that you'll see on a television medium."

The last area Maggin is exploring for ABC is a way to enhance network programming with extra choices via *interactive TV*. His example: Peter Jennings does a story about Russia on ABC's Evening News. It is given only a few minutes of air time, but hours of video were shot for the story, including interviews and background scenes. On a powerful megamedia system, a viewer who sees Jennings' story could click a remote control to ask for more information. Maybe the viewer would like to see some of that excess footage, or maps showing Russia's hot spots, or a list of other stories ABC News has done on the same topic during the past month.

Those five areas, Maggin says, play to ABC's strengths. ABC owns and knows how to create programming. It has a great brand name and an exceptional video news unit. "There are only three or four organizations in the world that can create worldwide, in-depth news," Maggin says. Looking at TV in the next decade, he adds: "Perhaps the greatest resource this company has is its news division."

One of Maggin's chief concerns is the positioning of ABC and its programming on any upcoming megamedia networks. The concerns are similar to Viacom's. If a Stargazer type of system creates its own menus and categories, where does ABC fit in? Will Stargazer want to sell on-demand versions of individual ABC shows? Will it want ABC's network broadcast to be lumped in a menu with the other major networks? Maggin says those issues will be tough to figure out. He likes YCTV for hit shows. Yet ABC is working with Oracle to develop its own interactive, multimedia video server. For sports, news, and some other programming, the network may prefer that when a Stargazer viewer clicks on ABC, the viewer gets connected (in a split second) to ABC's server, which then can offer all of ABC's programming and services in a package. "We must maintain the integrity of our brand," Maggin says.

Basically, ABC has the tools, the culture, and the money to be an important programmer in megamedia. No matter how much megamedia slices up the country into niche markets, free mass-market TV is not going to disappear. The nation will always want to unite around a few great, shared experiences. In music, millions of us buy the latest Rolling Stones album even though there are thousands of other CDs available. In books, John Grisham's novels sell out while thousands of other titles stay on store shelves. In television, no matter what else is available, we'll want to make sure we catch that wonderful sitcom when it airs for the first time, so we can talk about it at work the next day. Or maybe it's the Olympics we tune to, or another "Lonesome Dove" miniseries. It's hard to see how any other company outside of the networks will be able to consistently assemble and broadcast that kind of programming anytime in the next decade. Better yet, the big networks can now make and own unlimited amounts of their own programming. Limitations were lifted in 1994. Ownership of high-quality programming will be the networks' best hedge against erosion, by new technology, of the power of network-style broadcasting. Capital Cities/ABC is making a brilliant move in that arena: It plunked down a $100 million investment in DreamWorks, the entertainment company being formed by film producer Steven Spielberg, former Disney executive Jeffrey Katzenberg, and music mogul David Geffen. The deal should ensure that ABC gets some of the most creative programming of the late-1990s.

At the very least, network TV is looking like a healthy business. In fact, the networks' renewed vigor has drawn outside interest. Several companies are looking to buy a network. Within a few years, one, two, or all three major networks could conceivably change hands. But Capital Cities will likely hang onto ABC, and Maggin believes the network is doing the right things for the future. Says Maggin: "We're a long-term player and we'll be there [in megamedia] when we feel comfortable."

THE WALT DISNEY COMPANY: THE POWERHOUSE

You might know the characters from the movie *Aladdin:* Robin Williams' Genie, Princess Jasmine, Jafar. If you have kids, you also can recite most of the dialogue in the movie and may find yourself inadvertently singing pieces from the soundtrack. For a couple of years, *Aladdin* was everywhere, and that shows why Disney says it is going to be a software powerhouse even if it doesn't dive headlong into megamedia.

Analysts at NatWest Securities ran through an exercise about *Aladdin.* In its worldwide theatrical release, the movie raked in $440 million. In the fall of 1993, the videotape of the movie went on sale and became the all-time best seller: more than 24 million tapes were sold. Since mid-1993, Disney has turned *Aladdin* into a restaurant and stage show at Disneyland, a parade at Walt Disney World, some of the most popular merchandise at Disney stores, a Sega video game, a top-selling music album, a record-setting ice show, and two half-hour TV specials. NatWest figured that all the incarnations of *Aladdin* generated 27 percent of Disney's operating income in 1993. If that sounds impressive, keep in mind that Disney's 1994 follow-up, *The Lion King,* was an even more stupendous hit at the box office and no doubt will beat *Aladdin's* sales in videotapes and related merchandise. Keep in mind, too, that Disney owns the 5 best-selling videotapes ever: *Snow White and the Seven Dwarfs, Aladdin, Beauty and the Beast, 101 Dalmations,* and *Fantasia.*

Disney is the strongest programming brand name in the world. Its collection of copyrights is the most valuable anywhere. Disney movies, characters, stories, music, and other offshoots can step into any medium that ever will be invented. If megamedia creates powerful new ways for entertainment to reach consumers, it will only expand the ways Disney can make money from its properties. One example has already popped up: As digital compression expands the capacity of cable-TV systems, TCI will roll out a premium pay channel called Starz!, which plans to air first-run movies. TCI has signed a deal giving it early access to Disney movies through 2004. The value of the deal for Disney is estimated at around $1 billion.

Yes, Disney chairman Michael Eisner has been publicly recalcitrant toward the rush to megamedia. But who can blame him? He's in the driver's seat. Every megamedia-related company would like to do business with Disney, whether to buy its movies or programming to transmit over networks, or to develop interactive games or shopping channels, or even to make some kind of strategic investment in the company. Disney will never be left out. The megamedia players will line up outside Disney's door. Eisner can pick and choose the best paths and alliances for his company. And he won't have to gamble Disney's money. At one information superhighway gathering, Eisner put Disney's attitude this way: "When in doubt, don't invest."

Of all the executives in Hollywood, says former Time chairman Nick Nicholas, "Eisner is closest to being right."

But don't get the impression that Disney is lounging poolside and lazily sipping cocktails with little umbrellas sticking out of them. The company sees what's coming, and it's getting ready.

Disney's rich history is part of its strength. Walt Disney and his brother Roy started their animation studio in 1923 and made the first Mickey Mouse cartoon in 1928. The studio created its first full-length animated film, *Snow White,* in 1937. *Fantasia* and *Pinocchio* followed. Disneyland opened in California in 1955. By then, the company and its characters were popular around the globe.

After Walt's death in 1966 and Roy's death in 1971, the leaderless company temporarily lost its way. The movie *The Love Bug* would be its last big hit for 15 years. The legendary animation division nearly dissolved. The company started to turn for the better just before Eisner was brought in from Paramount in 1984 along with Frank Wells, who became Eisner's number-two executive and his right-hand man. They also brought along Jeffrey Katzenberg, and the trio launched ambitious grown-up film divisions, re-energized the animation group, and went on an expansion tear.

The 1990s are shaping up as a Disney golden era. Disney is now Hollywood's biggest single movie producer, releasing around 60 films a year under brand names such as Hollywood Pictures, Miramax, and Touchstone Pictures. Each new animated feature has been bigger and more profitable than the one before, starting with *The Little Mermaid,* then *Beauty and the Beast, Aladdin,* and *The Lion King.* The company continues to increase its annual investment in movies, which hit an amazing $1.4 billion in 1994. All along, it has remained one of the most efficient producers of films, making them for about 25 percent less than the industry average.

But the company is not just about films. It's also a major producer of TV shows, including the hit "Home Improvement." More importantly, as the *Aladdin* spinoffs have shown, Disney is already multimedia—and nobody is better at using characters and stories from films as fuel to rev up other outlets.

Disney's theme park division is about the same size as its film unit. Most of the theme parks use the Disney characters to develop rides or just to lend atmosphere to the park. Its Disney Channel takes Disney products into homes over cable-TV systems. Disney operates a record company and a magazine division. It is planning to build 500 Disney stores worldwide, all selling clothes, toys, home furnishings, and accessories featuring Disney characters. Even Disney's ice hockey team leverages a film property: it's called the Mighty Ducks, after a Disney film by the same name, and the name and logo have made the team one of the most successful sellers of jerseys and hats in all of sports.

Disney may be prudent about technology, but it's not afraid of it. In December 1994, the company formed Disney Interactive, which will develop interactive games and educational software for PCs and Sega and Nintendo machines. Those are proven markets that Eisner can feel comfortable investing in. The new unit is creating titles based on Disney characters and building on the success of Disney's computer software group, which had become the fifth-largest developer of entertainment software for PCs by the end of 1994. Disney has produced a handful of CD-ROM titles, including "Disney's Animated StoryBook: The Lion King," a hot seller during 1994s holiday season. The "Lion King" game required a major commitment: Fifteen animators created 2,000 new cells, and two musical numbers were added to the original score, all for creation of the game. Meanwhile, an internal task force is studying interactive TV technology, and a top-secret unit is supposedly at work developing high-tech virtual reality rides for Disney theme parks. Such rides might someday let customers sit inside a machine that lets them enter a computer-generated version of a Disney film. Fly with Peter Pan. Swim with Ariel the mermaid. Such rides could open up, as they sing in *Aladdin,* "a whole new world" for Disney parks.

In coming years, expect Disney to continue to churn out the movies that drive the rest of the company, and to find the most inventive ways to send its characters scurrying into other profitable areas.

Disney may buy one of the three major broadcast TV networks. In late 1994, it negotiated to buy NBC but the deal died. Although a network would be a weighty new asset for Disney, it's not likely to change much about the company's basic strategy. Disney will always be primarily a software company. If it shifts from that, it's in trouble.

Disney is the only major film studio that's still independent, and that sometimes fuels rumors that the company will be bought. Disney is probably too big to be bought by anyone else. An acquirer would have to pay about $35 billion, almost four times the price Viacom paid for Paramount. Disney may, though, sell a stake to a telephone or cable-TV company, the way Time Warner sold a chunk to US West. In the summer of 1994, Disney announced a programming venture with Ameritech, Southwestern Bell, and BellSouth—possibly a prelude to a deeper relationship with one or more of those regional Bells. Again, though, nothing like that would likely change Disney's strategy nor its outlook for the next decade.

There are a couple of negatives to watch for at Disney. Foremost is the management situation.

Frank Wells died in a helicopter crash in early 1994. He was the company's dealmaker and Eisner's chief adviser. He was also Disney's point man when evaluating new technology. No one has yet stepped in to fill those very important roles. About two months after Wells's death, Eisner had quadruple-bypass heart surgery. Eisner returned to work within weeks, and soon after forced out Jeffrey Katzenberg, who has been given a great deal of credit for turning around Disney's animation division. The successful triumvirate is down to one. Eisner may carry on just fine by himself. He is, after all, the master architect of today's Disney. But a lot of people are watching to see whether Eisner slips.

The second negative has more to do with perception than reality. Disney has had problems on a few fronts, particularly the miserable financial condition of EuroDisney in France. But none of those setbacks has mattered to investors or allies because of the astounding success of Disney's animated films. Those films have become the new face of Disney, and the company has developed an air of invulnerability around them. Each one grosses more than the one before. Each gets better reviews. Each spins off more products and sucks in more licensing money. Each gives people more confidence in Disney and sends the stock a notch higher.

What would happen if one of the films were to perform so-so, or even poorly? The mighty image of Disney would take a drubbing. Everyone would point to Katzenberg's departure and say the animation group can't make it without him. The company would seem fallible again. Investors who went on Disney's long ride up might use such a flop as an excuse to bail out. Potential partners might back off, perceiving that perhaps Disney had lost it. The reality is that a less-than-great film probably wouldn't mean a thing was wrong with the company's internal strengths. Still, perception counts for a lot when negotiating contracts or fending off competitors or takeovers.

Disney hasn't had to sweat such a problem yet, and maybe it won't for a while. For now, Eisner still looks like a Genie, ready to zap Disney's magic into every little blip of megamedia.

KNIGHT-RIDDER: DARK HORSE OF THE SUPERHIGHWAY

Outside the window, snow-capped mountains jab into the clear blue sky. Roger Fidler taps his mouse a couple of times and the screen of his Macintosh computer fills with something that looks like the front page of a newspaper—except it has computer icons and little bits of video tacked onto it. It's the experiment Fidler has been laboring over in Knight-Ridder's Boulder, Colorado, media lab for the past couple of years. He hopes this experiment will save his industry.

The newspaper industry is a deer frozen in megamedia's headlights, soon to be creamed if it doesn't get moving. Magazines are being a little more quick-footed. Yet, any way we look at it, the business of creating and selling printed news is in for a rough transition as megamedia develops. Fidler's work is an attempt to get ahead of the changes in how people might get news and information in coming years.

But Fidler's project is still far from anything that might really be a business for publishing companies. Fidler thinks for a second and then hits on what is both exciting and damning about what he's working on: it's pretty much beyond today's human experience. "It's not reading," he says. "We don't have a term for what this is."

The product itself is a prototype of an electronic newspaper given the fictional name of *The New York Current.* For now, it runs on the Mac. But Fidler's group is creating the paper to run on next-generation machines—powerful, lightweight, notebook-size computers resembling Apple's Newton. On the Mac, clicks of a mouse control the newspaper. On a Newton, it would be taps of an electronic pen, or perhaps voice commands.

Call up the *Current* and it resembles the front page of many newspapers. Fidler believes print newspapers are familiar and easy to use, so he has tried to adapt the best of the medium to the electronic *Current.* The front page is actually a news digest highlighting the day's top stories, and a guide to what's inside. Click on a front-page story to open to a bigger story. Along the edges of the *Current* are icons and indexes that give access to other "sections"—sports, or business—or start up video or audio portions of the paper, which are used to enhance the text stories. A story about President Clinton might have a button that offers a video clip of his speech the night before. A music CD review might have a button offering a minute of a song from the album. Other buttons on stories would offer deeper information on a topic. The history of Israel might be consulted after reading a news story about political struggles there.

The newspaper would be delivered into the computer by plugging the device into a cable-TV or phone line, or perhaps dialing into a news service over cellular phone systems. The computer could get any newspaper from anywhere. Someone from Dallas who is traveling to Toronto could plug in and pull up that day's *Dallas Morning News.*

Other things Fidler's newspaper may do: speak the news, so "readers" could hear it while driving; print out stories or ads for scissorless "clipping"; make the print larger for people with poor eyesight. The *Current* has a place for advertising. Tiny ads show up along the bottom of each page. If an ad catches your eye, click on it and see a full-screen version. A restaurant ad may show photos of the dining room, the menu, including daily specials, and directions for driving there. Personal ads might include video clips.

Will something like the *Current* ever become a marketable product? Nobody knows. Its best feature is that it gives Knight-Ridder and other print media companies a tangible way to think about what they can or might do, and to ask the right questions about where they're going. Early on, Fidler made the decision to open his lab to the newspaper industry, citing a feeling that newspapers will probably all sink or swim together. Since then, says Peggy Bair, who is number-two at the lab: "Hordes of newspaper people from all over the world have come through here. There are so many questions in this field and so few answers. People are grabbing onto this concept."

Ultimately, Knight-Ridder hopes the lab will help it become the leader in whatever happens next. Perhaps, if Fidler develops a hit product, Knight-Ridder could wind up in the business of selling its software and format to other newspaper companies.

In general, executives in the newspaper and magazine industries have a collective knot in their stomachs. They see megamedia coming but don't seem to know how to get ready, how much to spend, or how quickly to move.

One thing on their side is that traditional print newspapers and magazines are actually among the most efficient and interactive ways for consumers to get news and information. They are easy and familiar to use. By flipping pages and skimming headlines, readers can quickly find stories of interest and skip the rest—an easier interaction than any CD-ROM publication. Print products are portable. They are inexpensive. Media executives add all of that up and conclude that printed products are not going to go the way of stone tablets anytime soon.

A counterpoint, though, is that electronic media will start to hurt print media in some narrow but painful ways. Classified ads, a major source of revenue for newspapers, are already edging into online computer services. That trend will continue. Consumers will find it much easier to type in a car model and price range and have a computer search for the right classified ad, instead of peering through pages of teeny text. That might be the siphon that pulls other kinds of ads—and eventually, news and information—off of paper products and into electronic transmission.

If they can figure out how to use them in megamedia, newspapers and magazines have some important assets. They create software—good, solid, unique content backed by brand names that people know and trust. In fact, writer and consultant George Gilder has called newspapers the information highway's dark horse because many people dismiss them, yet they happen to have some of the world's best and biggest information-gathering operations anywhere. Newspaper journalists are experts at choosing, sorting, and editing news—a service that will be in demand as increasing amounts of information rain down on us all. The same attributes would apply to leading magazines like *Time, Business Week,* or *PC Magazine.*

Megamedia networks are going to need content, no question. To print media executives, that could spell a great new opportunity to sell their software.

As yet, no great megamedia strategy seems to have sparked the print world. Knight-Ridder is only one print company taking a roundhouse swipe at megamedia. Otherwise, across the industry is a smorgasbord of approaches, an indication of the confusion. Here are some examples:

- Times Mirror, publisher of *The Los Angeles Times,* is making a major commitment to video programming. It sold its cable-TV systems to Cox Enterprises, then put $200 million into a joint venture with Cox that will create cable channels. The first will be Outdoor Life Channel, based on Times Mirror magazines such as *Field & Stream* and *Yachting.*

- A number of newspapers are developing on-line products that may be the beginnings of a new kind of news and information service aimed at local markets. Cox Newspapers, publisher of *The Atlanta Journal and Constitution,* has developed its version, called Access Atlanta, with the Prodigy on-line service. *The Washington Post* is working with computer software company Oracle. America Online offers

Chicago Online from *The Chicago Tribune* and on-line versions of *The San Jose Mercury News* and *The New York Times.*

• Magazines are mostly taking the CD-ROM path. *Newsweek,* owned by the Washington Post Company, puts out the most innovative translation of a magazine into CD-ROM. *Newsweek InterActive,* published quarterly, is treated like a periodical instead of just a compilation of past *Newsweek* stories. *PC Magazine* is doing something similar. Its parent, Ziff-Davis Publishing, has been the most aggressive magazine publisher in creating on-line services and CD-ROM products that spin out of the company's publications.

The Tribune Company is doing a double back-flip into the megamedia pool. The company owns *The Chicago Tribune, The Orlando Sentinel,* and Fort Lauderdale's *Sun-Sentinel,* and a string of TV and radio stations—pretty standard stuff for a media company. Over the past couple of years, it has shoveled $200 million to $300 million into megamedia ventures. It bought Compton's New Media, the biggest interactive CD-ROM publishing company. It bought a small stake in on-line computer service America Online. It started a home shopping show featuring Joan Rivers, and a cable-TV channel called ChicagoLand TV, which uses *Tribune* newspaper staffers to feed a 24-hour local news network.

Tribune Company's basic strategy is to build a first-rate news organization and finance it by giving it multiple outlets. The splayed investments are a way to make sure the company has a piece of the outlets that become good businesses, although Tribune may find itself kissing a lot of frogs—and spending a fortune—before landing a prince or two.

A gallery of print media companies are sitting on the sidelines, taking a Disneylike approach: we'll create good software, and megamedia delivery companies will come to us. In the short run, those companies may seem wise. None of the moves into CD-ROM or online services or cable TV programming is likely to become much of a business for print media companies for some time. They'll probably even be money losers. But as the decade rolls along, print publishers had better make sure they're doing enough to get to know the technology, the way Disney is making sure it knows what's coming. That will be the only way to be ready for opportunities when they become apparent.

Knight-Ridder is among the leading candidates to gain that understanding of megamedia and find ways to use the new technology. The company is the nation's second-largest newspaper publisher. Its properties include *The Philadelphia Inquirer, Miami Herald, Detroit Free Press,* and *San Jose Mercury News.* Knight-Ridder owns a handful of operations that will give it windows on megamedia. One is a cable-TV system—a partnership with TCI, which should give Knight-Ridder access to TV visionary John Malone. It also owns Dialog, a computer information retrieval service, and Knight-Ridder Financial, a financial industry news and information service. It has launched an hour-long cable-TV news show that spins out of *The Philadelphia Inquirer* newsroom, and an on-line service from its San Jose newspaper.

Fidler's lab is the only venture by a major newspaper company that looks well beyond today's technology. "We're building dream cars," Fidler says. "We're talking about technology that's five or six years away. Nobody yet knows how people will use these things."

Among other key issues, the lab has helped the company think about how to include and sell advertising in an electronic newspaper. Fidler's work has given Knight-Ridder a way to talk to Madison Avenue about the concept and show ad executives a demo. Some of the company's editors have cycled through the lab to start trying to figure out how to write, edit, and present news over megamedia systems. Fidler has met with cable-TV executives to talk about how to transmit these newspapers, and how to get the handheld computer devices into consumers' hands so they have a way to buy the newspaper. All of that will give Knight-Ridder a head start.

Could the lab turn out to be a boondoggle? Sure. Knight-Ridder has gone down that road before. In the early 1980s, the company tried its hand at what it thought was the future of newspapers: putting text of news on a TV screen. Viewtron, as it was called, was horrendously boring and expensive. Knight-Ridder lost at least $40 million before shutting down the service.

But in the age of megamedia, sitting still may be the worst offense. Fidler believes his project can become Knight-Ridder's competitive advantage. And that could be key. "The question is not whether there will be newspapers of some kind in the future," he says. "The question is: Who will publish them?"

RUPERT MURDOCH'S NEWS CORP.: WORSHIPPING THE SUN GOD

There is only one true global media baron. Too bad his company could be destined for oblivion.

That may seem like an odd thing to say about News Corp., the $12 billion company built and controlled by Rupert Murdoch. More than any other company, News Corp. is intertwining the twin trends of megamedia and globalization. After a few years of struggling, the company has been on a roll, making some brilliant strategic moves that show Murdoch has a clear view of the decade to come.

But the danger comes to light in the comments of others. Viacom's Sumner Redstone admiringly says Murdoch is the number one risk-taker in the world. Ted Turner calls Murdoch a mad genius. Many say Murdoch is the only business person who John Malone fears and respects as an equal. But all that praise is for Rupert Murdoch. None of it is for News Corp. or its operations or any of Murdoch's lieutenants. Murdoch's peers know that News Corp. is Murdoch and Murdoch is News Corp. When Murdoch, in his mid-60s, is no longer there, the company will most likely no longer be there, either—at least not the powerful, unpredictable company so many competitors have come to know and hate. It is News Corp.'s fatal flaw for the next age.

That's not to say that Murdoch won't be a great player in megamedia while he lasts.

Murdoch has assembled an awesome basket of assets that allows him to reach more than two-thirds of the world's television households and touch yet more people through movies and newspapers. In television, News Corp.'s most powerful operation is Fox

Broadcasting, the fourth-biggest broadcast network in the United States and the only network that has been able to challenge the power of ABC, NBC, and CBS. Also in the United States, News Corp. owns fX, a fledgling cable TV channel, and a handful of local TV stations. In other parts of the world, Murdoch's television power is concentrated in satellite-delivered TV. In Great Britain, his company owns half of BSkyB, a booming satellite TV service worth more than $6 billion. In Asia, News Corp. owns 63.6 percent of Star TV, which can beam television channels to 3 billion people from China to Israel to India.

The core of News Corp.'s software operation is Twentieth Century Fox. One of the top movie studios in Hollywood, it has been the producer of *Mrs. Doubtfire, Speed,* and Arnold Schwarzenegger's *True Lies.* The studio includes Twentieth Television, creator of "X-Files," "NYPD Blue," "Picket Fences," and "The Simpsons," a show that has become a huge international hit.

In printed products, News Corp. controls most of the major newspapers in the United Kingdom and Australia and owns *The New York Post* in the United States. The company owns *TV Guide,* the highest-circulation weekly magazine in the United States, and owns giant book publisher HarperCollins, which has recently marketed books by Michael Jordan, Margaret Thatcher, and Dan Quayle.

On top of all that, News Corp. owns a handful of small technology companies, including the Delphi on-line computer service. The company even owns half of Australia's biggest domestic airline.

If you're looking for some line of thinking that connects all those assets, don't bother. There is no grand strategic plan involved here. Murdoch is an opportunist. If something looks like a good deal and he has the money, he buys it—usually by paying more than anyone thinks the property is worth at the time. "News Corp. is what it is today because I never pretended to know in advance which course developments will take," Murdoch told *Forbes* magazine. "If ten years or so ago we had attempted to chart on paper the destiny of our company, we would never have anticipated the 30 very diverse acquisitions we made on four continents, almost all of which arose from unique and unanticipated events."

Murdoch built his company one piece at a time. He had inherited a newspaper company in Adelaide, Australia, from his father,

Keith Murdoch, who had become something of a famous journalist in Australia and England. Interestingly, before the elder Murdoch died, he had been managing a newspaper empire, though he owned little of it. When Keith Murdoch passed away, almost all of his empire vanished.

From the beginning, Murdoch has been a driven, obsessive, and combative man. He is blessed with the kind of charm that could melt butter from 30 feet away, and he uses it often on employees, competitors, and world leaders. But the charm is a tool. It has its purposes. Underneath, Murdoch is a hard tyrant who will belittle underlings and turn his back on long-time friends or colleagues as business dictates. He tolerates no challenge to his power. Murdoch has often told listeners, "My past consists of a series of interlocking wars."

He bought newspapers and TV stations across Australia in the 1960s, then started buying media properties in Great Britain and the United States in the 1970s. Murdoch's name became synonymous with down-market journalism as he pumped sex and crime stories into his media. In the 1980s, News Corp. bought the Fox studio and launched the Fox network. The person who ran Fox for Murdoch in those days was Barry Diller.

At the beginning of the 1990s, News Corp. went on its biggest acquisition binge of all, snapping up magazines and the publishing houses that became HarperCollins. The company also launched BSkyB. The satellite service began life as a serious money-loser. At that point, News Corp. had bought too much, was losing too much money, had too much debt. News Corp. came close to collapsing and didn't pull out of its nosedive until 1993.

Now, though, the company is cruising. Its global reach is its clearest strength. Time Warner, TCI, Viacom, and even AT&T are just beginning to play on a field so broad. Those four companies, in fact, have determined that their greatest potential for growth in the mid-1990s will be selling U.S.-created software and communications services in Europe and Asia. In that respect, News Corp. is already two steps ahead of the most impressive megamedia companies.

The biggest potential winner in News Corp.'s arsenal of delivery systems may be Star TV, especially as China moves to a more open economy and its 1.2 billion citizens gain access to television sets. In 10 months in 1993, Star TV's audience grew 279 percent. The system offers a handful of English-language, American-made TV channels and movies. More importantly, Star TV can aim regionalized channels at China or India, for instance. The system has started beaming Mandarin-language versions of its sports and music video channels across Asia. For now, Star TV is losing $20 million a year. But Murdoch's investment looks like it will pay off big-time by late in the decade.

Software, though, is what powers News Corp. And Murdoch is showing that he sees how to serve software across a global table, making money on the same product over and over again. A great example is Murdoch's investment in football.

In December 1993, Murdoch's Fox television agreed to pay $1.6 billion to broadcast NFL games for four years, yanking professional football away from CBS. It was a seemingly outrageous bid, and Fox lost $100 million on the broadcasts in 1994–1995 in the U.S. market. But the deal means so much more to Fox than just a series of Sunday afternoon programs. First, the NFL games blasted the Fox network into the big leagues. No other single stroke had done more to put the network on equal footing with ABC, NBC, and CBS. More than a dozen local TV stations changed their affiliations to Fox from CBS because of the football deal. That gives Fox a bigger potential audience for its other shows and adds to its clout when seeking new programming.

Then there's the global side to the NFL deal. Murdoch also got 49 percent ownership of the NFL's World League—not just TV rights, but ownership. The new version of the World League will start play in the spring of 1995 with six teams from Europe. The first try at a World League flopped in 1992 when it tried to combine European- and U.S.-based teams. This time around, Murdoch will be broadcasting games worldwide—on BSkyB, Star TV, and other systems—and his ownership stake will keep him working to make sure the league makes it. By the time this first contract between the NFL and Murdoch runs out in 1998, Murdoch may become the single most powerful figure in professional football, and football could wind up as one of the world's richest sports.

Murdoch plans to use sports to glue together his worldwide media hodgepodge. Besides football, he's trying to create a new global professional golf tour that would rival the PGA. His ally in the venture is Australian golfer Greg Norman. Murdoch has also paid $400 million for British soccer rights, $155 million for rights to North America's National Hockey League games, and $375 to start an Australian rugby league. It's all software the world will watch.

Globalization seems to be in Murdoch's blood. Megamedia, however, may prove a little more elusive. As Murdoch says, he has no grand plan. The pieces of News Corp. don't fit as neatly as the pieces of, say, Time Warner or Viacom might. When it comes to things that may be important in megamedia, News Corp. has some yawning holes. It has no software brand names that have the strength of Disney or MTV—important for selling software over many technologies and distribution channels. The company owns no wired networks, so it has no capability to get into interactive TV services or the telephone business.

News Corp. also doesn't have a partner that may help in megamedia. Murdoch has an ongoing relationship with TCI's Malone and the two have made some minor moves together. News Corp. is working with British Telecom to develop interactive TV services. Yet for the most part Murdoch isn't good at sharing power. He follows his vision and no one else's. Don't expect him to sell a major stake in News Corp. to a phone company, for instance.

And yet Murdoch is not blind to megamedia, as shown by his relationship with a man named Gregory Clark. An Australian physicist, Clark was a research star at IBM. He worked for the company in the United States and in Australia. He had been IBM-Australia's director of science and technology development. He and Murdoch got to know each other through mutual friends.

"We started having social chats about optimizing the use of content," Clark says. "It evolved from there. I got really interested in content, online services, the information superhighway. I became more aware of how important content was going to be."

In September 1994, Murdoch asked Clark to join News Corp. and become president of the News Technology Group. Before that, News Corp.'s megamedia efforts had been scattered around the company—an on-line *TV Guide* in one corner, CD-ROM products somewhere else. Clark is pulling them together and developing a big-picture strategy.

For now, a lot of Clark's efforts are focused on Delphi, a second-tier on-line computer service that News Corp. bought in 1993. "We have big plans," Clark says. "We consider it so important, we'll invest whatever is required to make it a viable online business."

Delphi will do a lot of the same things competing services do, but Delphi will eventually carry a lot of content produced by News Corp. and Fox. Clark says that may include on-line versions of company-owned newspapers, an education or research service from HarperCollins, and forums and information about hot Fox TV shows. The service will become a way for News Corp. to experiment with the future. "There will be an emphasis on delivering in an interactive way data or content related to our content," Clark says. "If we can get it right, it's going to be really important. We're going up the learning curve."

Most tellingly, Clark seems to have Murdoch's ear. The two confer often. Clark has Murdoch thinking about how to spread News Corp.'s software across many technologies, not just across continents. Clark has Murdoch's pledge of money and resources to develop interactive products. The two men, for instance, have hired top talent for Delphi, including Alan Baratz, Delphi's new CEO. Baratz is another former IBM executive—he helped build the technological foundation for what is now the Internet.

In fact, Delphi may be the operation to watch to see if Murdoch can take full advantage of megamedia. If Delphi flops—and it may—Murdoch's company won't look like it has much of a chance of keeping up with the Viacoms and Disneys. If Delphi turns into an exciting service that challenges established online computer services—America Online, CompuServe and Prodigy—News Corp. should be on its way to winning at megamedia.

Still, no matter what News Corp. accomplishes these next few years, it will suffer from the fact that it is totally dependent on the will of one man. There's a story that illustrates the hold that Murdoch, often referred to within the company as the Sun God, has on News Corp. In the late 1980s, Barry Diller had worked with Murdoch to develop the Fox network and run the Fox studios. By 1991, the pair was succeeding beyond anyone's expectations. In the book *Murdoch,* author William Shawcross writes:

> By 1991, Diller still liked and admired Murdoch. He thought him absolutely honest and clear-sighted. But he was continually astonished by the way in which Murdoch ran the company through the "pull" of his own personality. "I often had to fight the desire to join the people who were worshiping the Sun God," said Diller later. "It's a hard fight. He knows it and he's quite good at using it."

That year, Diller told Murdoch he wanted to become an equity partner in News Corp. Murdoch said no, telling Diller, "There is in this company only one principal." By February 1992, the best executive Murdoch ever employed left the company.

Murdoch circles the globe endlessly, in large part because he needs to physically show up at his operations to make decisions and boost morale. That's how weak many of News Corp.'s managers are.

As long as Murdoch is alive and doing business, his power and aggressiveness and vision are News Corp.'s strengths. But Murdoch's weaknesses are also News Corp.'s weaknesses. Murdoch's reputation, for instance, continues to be down-market. Fox network runs some of the most lewd shows on broadcast television. Murdoch's newspapers tend to be working class and sensationalist. Murdoch is struggling to break out of that mold and reach broader audiences.

Most of all, though, the danger to News Corp. is that it someday will be left "Murdoch-less." That may not happen for a decade or longer, but unless Murdoch lets others in, News Corp. won't be a powerhouse for the ages. Maybe it will stay together and sputter through the next era, looking for a soul. Or maybe it will break apart, leaving pieces scattered across the globe.

BARRY DILLER AND TED TURNER

When people discuss content for the next communications age, the names of two men in their 50s come up again and again. One is Barry Diller. The other, Ted Turner.

Both are brilliant innovators who have stunning track records. Diller has run the ABC-TV network and Paramount's film studio. While working for Rupert Murdoch, Diller created Fox's TV network. Then he went on to buy into and run QVC. Turner built Turner Broadcasting from scratch, created the first cable-TV superstation (WTBS), then started CNN, TNT, The Cartoon Network, and Turner Classic Movies. He has also bought a couple of midsize Hollywood studios.

Both men are desperate to do something bigger and better. Each wants to own and run one of the top five or six content companies in the world. At that, they will probably be successful.

But if I were to make bets on these guys' long-term success in the megamedia world, I'd say this:

Turner will hit paydirt.

Diller will fizzle.

I've interviewed both Turner and Diller. I've talked to dozens of people about them. I've studied their companies. And when the pieces are put together, Diller, to me, comes out looking like the most overhyped executive of our time.

That's not to denigrate Diller, believe it or not. Diller is one of the best ever at running operations that produce or deliver mainstream, general-audience programming—movies or TV shows that will be seen by 100 million people worldwide. He is credited with giving the go-ahead to "Roots" in the 1970s, backing the colossal Indiana Jones movies, and putting "The Simpsons" on the air. That's what Diller is good at and that's what he will be good at in the future. No one would be surprised if Diller were to end up running a giant mainstream content company that churns out innovative, high-quality hits for network TV and multiplex movie theaters. That would make Diller wildly successful in the entertainment business.

But since taking control of QVC in December 1992, Diller has acquired a sheen that goes beyond entertainment. He is being labeled as the man who would marry mainstream programming sense to new TV technology, especially 500-channel, interactive cable systems. But that's not Diller. It's not what he knows or likes. There's a funny flaw in the anecdotes that describe how Diller bought a PowerBook laptop computer in 1991 and had some high-tech epiphany: he obviously had never used a computer until then. Diller does not come across as a leader who quickly grasps the benefits of new technology.

More telling is that, in two years of running QVC, Diller did nothing dramatic toward that company's future. When he took over, it was a well-oiled TV shopping machine already moving more upscale. Diller added a few dashes of panache to the network and created a second channel, Q2. But he didn't take TV shopping to some new level, or plow into developing interactive versions of QVC, or migrate QVC into other electronic media such as on-line computer shopping services or CD-ROM catalogs. QVC's earnings growth, regularly in double digits just as Diller came aboard, trailed off during his watch. The company's stock price zoomed from the mid-30s just before Diller to the mid-70s when Diller-hype swept Wall Street in 1993, and then withered back to the mid-30s by mid-1994. Investors were no longer willing to bet on the Diller sizzle.

On a more personal level, Diller is an executive out of the old Hollywood school, where it was not uncommon for arrogant, self-centered bosses to micromanage creative products, berate employees in public, throw tantrums, and fight with their peers and superiors. Diller is famous for all of that; one tale has Diller hurling a videotape at a staffer. The staffer ducked and the tape knocked a hole in an office wall. That's not the kind of executive who will build bridges to megamedia, which is becoming a cross-industry collaborative business. Diller's style may work in Hollywood, but it won't work around companies like AT&T or Compaq.

Diller's plans remain focused on broad-scale entertainment. QVC had always been little more than a springboard. He tried to buy Paramount and failed; tried to merge with CBS and failed. Now Comcast is buying QVC and Diller will likely quit, worth about $100 million as he walks out the door. Diller will find a place atop one of the big-name entertainment companies, do very well there, and concern himself little with set-top boxes, interactive TV, and home shopping.

Ted Turner strikes me as a very different kind of executive. Yes, he is a garrulous loudmouth who, in a recent interview, carried on about violence on TV and about the federal government while tossing out several references to "my wife Jane"—actress Jane Fonda. Turner is also mercurial. "You never know what Ted's going to do next," says TCI's John Malone with a chuckle. "That's Ted."

But Turner has honed the skills that will work in megamedia. Most importantly, he has shown that he can see the future of a new programming pipeline and run with it.

That's what he did with satellite technology and the cable pipeline in the 1970s. Turner owned a local TV station, WTBS, in Atlanta. He realized that cable was a wasteland of open capacity hardly being used for anything. He also was the first to see that he could bounce his locally assembled programming off satellites and make it available to cable operators nationwide. That gave Turner Broadcasting its jump-start: the WTBS superstation.

Again, seeing that open pipeline, Turner had the vision to understand that it could handle a 24-hour news network that people could tune into whenever they wanted news. CNN, perhaps cable TV's greatest programming innovation, was born. Now, it's so powerful, it influences world events.

These days, Turner is ahead of almost everyone else in understanding the value of software and exploiting it. He bought MGM's film library in 1986 and began pumping its classic movies, such as *Yankee Doodle Dandy,* into WTBS and, after its launch in 1991, TNT. He bought animator Hanna-Barbera's library in 1991 (*The Flintstones, Huckleberry Hound*) and put the cartoons on WTBS, TNT, and The Cartoon Network, a new outlet he started in 1992. He bought the Atlanta Braves baseball team and Atlanta Hawks basketball team because they are software—the games can be shown on WTBS and sold to the broadcast networks or other outlets. After buying movie studios Castle Rock Entertainment and New Line Cinema, Turner had amassed a library of 3,700 films, perhaps the biggest collection ever. He launched another outlet, the Turner Classic Movies channel.

All of the Turner-owned software gets mixed, cut up, repackaged, and pumped into all of the Turner-owned outlets, plus others such as videotape sales and CD-ROMs of CNN's coverage. Turner once told *Forbes* magazine, in typical off-color Turner style, that his

John Malone (left), CEO of Tele-Communications Inc., and Ray Smith, CEO of Bell Atlantic, shake hands on October 13, 1993, after announcing the merger of their companies. The ill-fated deal unleashed a megamedia frenzy at major corporations.

SERVICE
NETWORK
COMPACT
DISK
FACSIMILE
MACHINES
TELEVISION
PERSONAL
COMPUTER

MCI

Top Left: Time Warner CEO Gerald Levin (left) and US West CEO Richard McCormick chat during a news conference announcing their $2.5 billion partnership. The alliance became one of the most effective in all of megamedia.

Bottom Left: Another broken engagement: MCI chairman Bert Roberts (left) unveils a $1.3 billion investment in wireless telephone upstart Nextel, run by Morgan O'Brien (right). The deal fell apart in mid-1994, leaving both companies vulnerable in megamedia.

Microsoft CEO Bill Gates (left) and Hewlett-Packard CEO Lew Platt share smiles at a mid-1994 press conference introducing a new H-P computer. Gates is trying to retool his company to make a leap into the next age of technology; Platt has already done that at H-P.

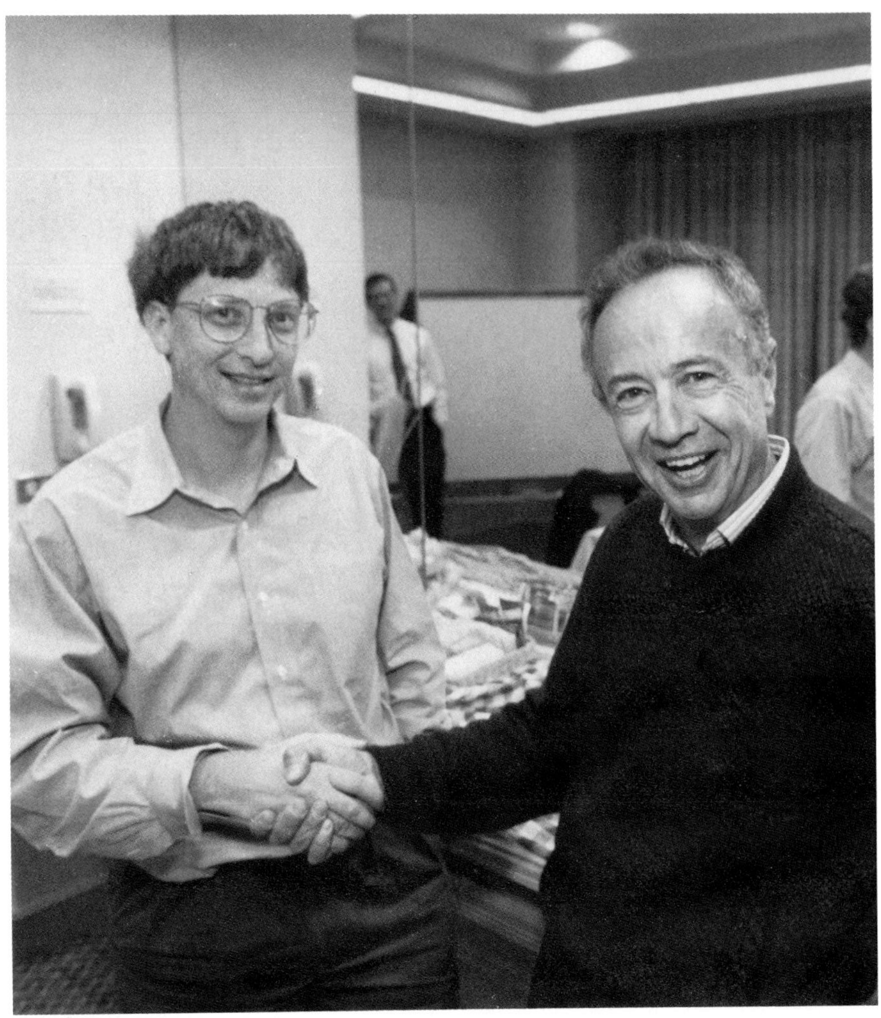

The power team of the 1990s: Gates and Intel CEO Andrew Grove. At the end of 1994, 80 percent of all personal computers were running on Intel chips and Microsoft operating software. The two executives control the destiny of the PC industry, which is facing a tough transition into the next age.

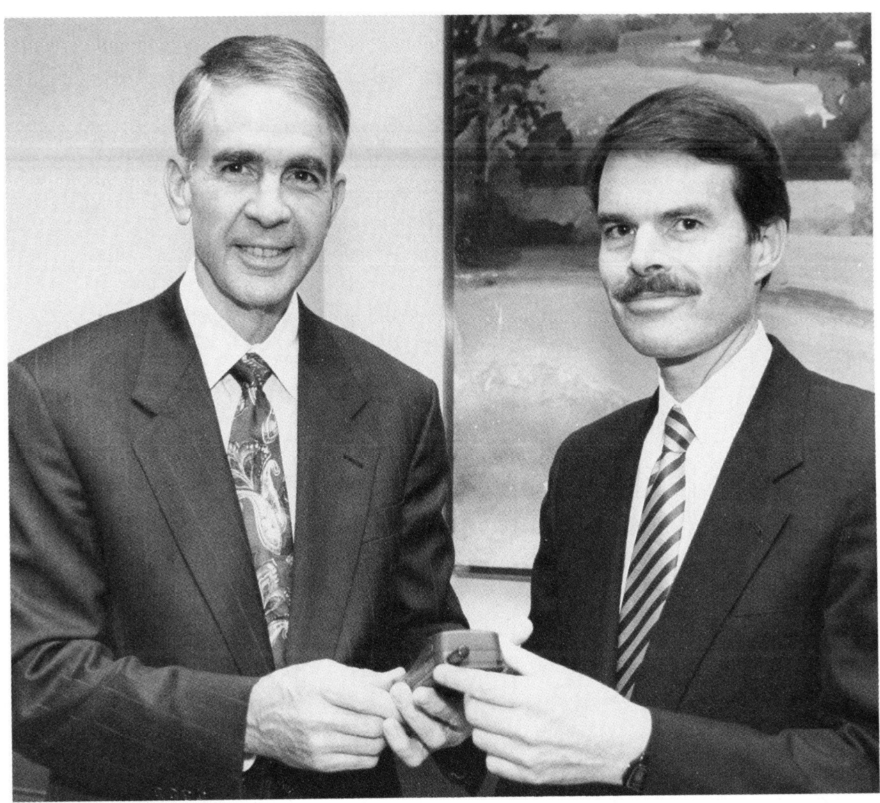

Robert Allen (left), chairman of AT&T, and Craig McCaw, founder of McCaw Cellular, created one of the most awesome powers in communications. AT&T was already huge, good and growing. Then it bought McCaw, the biggest and best cellular phone company. The deal will help AT&T dominate megamedia.

Ted Turner (left) and Barry Diller are the two most famous players in the content business. Turner is on the rise and has been launching networks more often than most people buy socks. Diller failed at two takeovers, then watched Comcast buy his company, QVC.

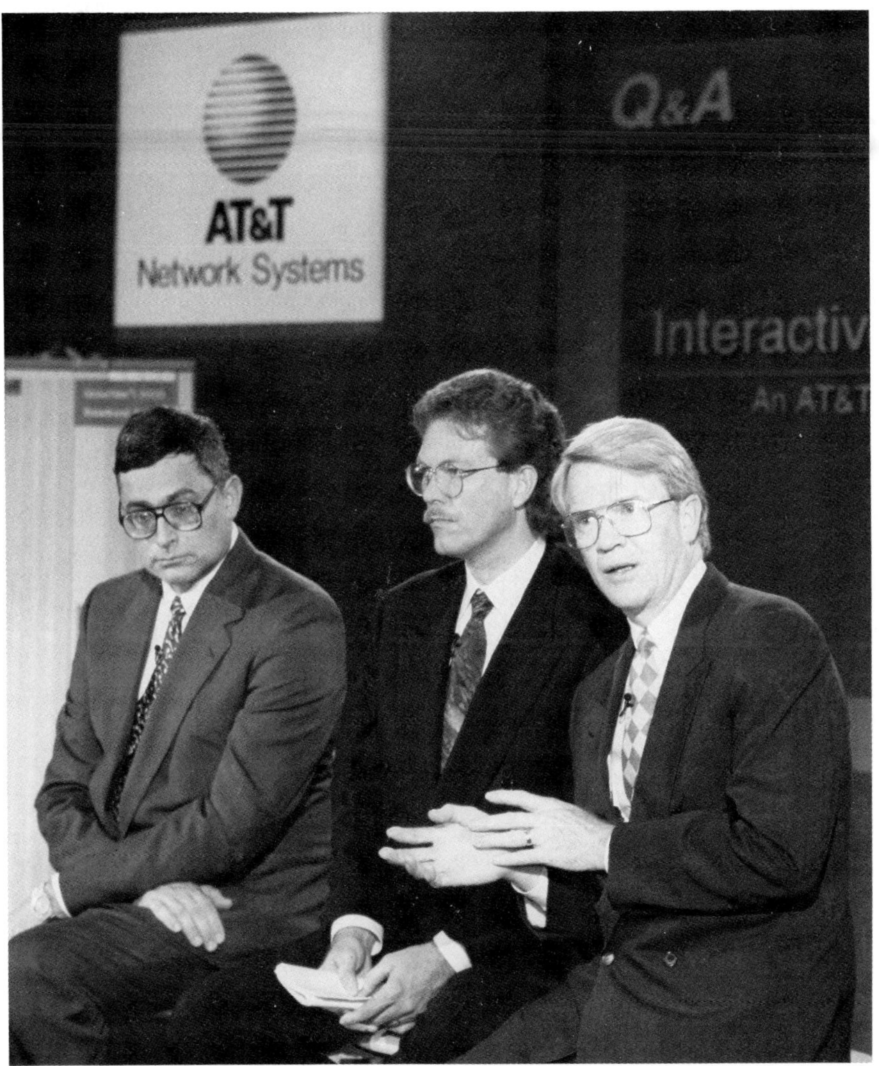

Ed McCracken (right) turned Silicon Graphics into an emerging force in megamedia. The company's software and computers helped make Jurassic Park and Forrest Gump, then became the guts of Time Warner's Full Service Network. Here, McCracken is announcing an AT&T-Silicon Graphics alliance with Dan Stanzione, recently made head of Bell Labs, and James Barton, a Silicon Graphics vice president.

US West's McCormick (left) cut a deal with Sam Ginn, CEO of Air-Touch, to merge the two companies' wireless operations. In the fall of 1994, the megamedia frenzy focused on wireless and forced companies into numerous desperation alliances.

company's approach is like chicken farming: "Modern chicken farmers, they grind up the intestines to make dog food. The feathers go into pillows. Even the chicken manure they make into fertilizer. They use every bit of the chicken. Well, that's what we try to do over here with television products, is use everything to its fullest extent."

Interestingly, when Turner talks about wanting to buy a major broadcast network or major studio and become a top-five media player, his reasons center on software. Only the biggest players, Turner often says, can afford to buy the best software—NFL games, the Olympics, first-run movies, TV shows from top producers. He wants to get his hands on the best software so he can package it, repackage it, and repackage it again.

All in all, Ted Turner and the company he built know how to think for the next age. When new pipelines open up—whether 500-channel cable systems, high-tech phone company systems, interactive TV, whatever—Turner will no doubt know how to look at them and see revolutionary ways to use them. As megamedia outlets emerge, he'll find new ways to sell software to the public. If any established player is going to break new programming ground in megamedia, it will be Turner.

Already, Turner Broadcasting is probing high-tech possibilities. It's in a joint venture with Intel to create a news-on-demand service. Stories that appear on CNN would get coded and sent via satellite to computer systems at corporations. The systems would store the stories digitally. Workers at PCs equipped with Intel video chips could call up the stories they want to see and view them in a corner of their computer screens.

In a nod to the expanded TV pipelines that are coming, Turner is reportedly considering an art-film movie channel—a narrow niche channel, but one that an elite adult audience might be willing to pay for.

Ted Turner has experience at some other essential megamedia-age skills. For more than a decade, he's had to constantly work with partners. TCI and Time Warner are major investors in Turner Broadcasting, and they have an active voice in the company. Turner has learned how to manage those partners and sometimes outmaneuver them, although at times the partners have frustrated him. As megamedia evolves, companies like Turner's will increasingly need to work with partners.

Turner can be a hands-off manager, especially when he gets into a business he knows little about. After buying Castle Rock and New Line, for instance, he worked hard to keep the creative studio chiefs on board, then stayed out of their way. He tends to do that with all of Turner Broadcasting's holdings—he'll watch things and comment, but he usually doesn't micromanage. With all the networks and production operations Turner Broadcasting owns, Turner only views a couple hours of TV a day. "I watch CNN investigative reports and certain programs," he says. "I have sets on in my office all the time but I'm only monitoring them. It's work."

He pauses, then grins and adds a touch of Turner humor: "I watch the Braves a lot too, but that's work . . . well, it's less work when they're winning."

6

THE MOST VALUABLE ASSET ON EARTH

THE LONG-DISTANCE COMMUNICATIONS INDUSTRY

LEADERS TO WATCH: ROBERT ALLEN AND AT&T

"Welcome Back Bionic CEO" says the sign over Bob Allen's desk inside AT&T's headquarters, which is tucked next to woods in quaint Basking Ridge, New Jersey. Allen, AT&T's chairman and chief executive, has just returned to work after hip replacement surgery. Cartilage in the hip had deteriorated, leaving him in pain much of the time. Now he's got a new titanium part in there that works great. He's back in the office earlier than doctors had planned. "I can dance," he says, doing a quick shuffle on the low-pile carpet. By the time you read this book, Allen will be back on the golf course, clipping a couple of strokes off his 10 handicap, thanks to his first pain-free swings in ages.

In the meantime, Allen will be making AT&T into the single most powerful company in the world.

Do a double take if you have to, but that's what's happening. No company in any industry is better positioned to reap rewards from the global megamedia explosion. The genius of AT&T is that it is a relatively neutral company that has the best communications technology and the biggest and best communications network. No matter who wins in megamedia, most of the players will want to—or will have to—do business with AT&T. No matter what information highway applications turn into hits, AT&T benefits—as long as the new applications mean that overall communication traffic increases. Unless it royally screws up, AT&T is the only company that really can't lose in megamedia.

"AT&T is doing all the right things," says Tony Robertson of Alex. Brown & Sons, one of a chorus of financial analysts praising the company. "The marketplace is changing rapidly but Allen is taking that on head-on."

If the sheer strength of AT&T's network and technology aren't enough, the company can reach into a knapsack full of other high-caliber weapons. It now owns McCaw Cellular, the nation's biggest wireless phone company and probably the most innovative in its industry. The AT&T brand name is the strongest communications brand in the world, giving the company an automatic edge wherever it uses that logo. Its management ranks are deep and talented, even though it recently lost multimedia chief Robert Kavner and computer chief Jerre Stead. And AT&T has money. Lord, does it have money: $67 billion in revenue in 1993, probably topping $70 billion in 1994. Operating income is more than $6 billion a year. Annual cash flow is more than $7 billion. Anything AT&T needs as it vaults into megamedia, it should be able to buy.

The company is also—and this is very important—highly competitive. It is nothing like the monopolistic Ma Bell of old. In the decade after the 1984 breakup of the Bell System, AT&T shed 140,000 jobs, wrote off $25 billion in restructuring charges, and broke itself into 22 divisions. For a $70 billion company, it is lean, fast, and hungry. It has won the Deming and two Baldridge prizes for quality, a feat unmatched by any company. The changes are Allen's doing—his legacy at AT&T. "I give Allen credit," says Bert Roberts, CEO of AT&T's toughest foe, MCI. "He's shifted that company from a monopoly orientation to a much more competitive organization."

AT&T is the leading member of the long-distance communication industry. Although AT&T has a lot of other kinds of business, the transport of phone calls and data over its worldwide network hauls in 60 percent of the company's revenue. For now, AT&T has only two main competitors in long-distance: MCI and Sprint. AT&T controls about 65 percent of the U.S. long-distance market.

All three of the big long-distance companies should be beneficiaries of the megamedia trend. Like AT&T, both MCI and Sprint have built high-capacity fiber-optic networks that can carry anything from today's phone calls and faxes to tomorrow's multimedia videoconferences and interactive movies.

Megamedia will drive more traffic—and traffic that is a lot more profitable—onto all those long-distance networks. For example, two collaborating managers who might now only talk by telephone will, in five or six years, add video and shared computer information. That's additional traffic for the network because the video and data take up more space on the network—more lanes on the information superhighway—than a simple phone call. The long-distance companies can charge higher rates to transmit high-bandwidth communication such as video. Another example: People now play video games by buying cartridges and plugging them into home machines, a complete zero of a market for long-distance companies. Soon, they'll play games by tapping into on-line service such as The ImagiNation Network and possibly playing against a friend in another state—over long-distance phone lines.

Think of the long-distance companies as megamedia's long-haul carriers. To give the information highway metaphor a good bludgeoning, long-distance companies own the interstate highways that connect local road systems. Any kind of information that has to be shipped from one region to another would likely travel over highways owned by AT&T, MCI, or Sprint. The companies would charge a toll—less for compact cars (phone calls), more for 18-wheelers (multimedia or video). Megamedia is a broad technological wave that should increase traffic—and tolls—on the highways in a lot of ways. It'll mean the creation of better, faster, and cheaper cars (multimedia computers, interactive TVs, pocket phones), so people will want to drive more. It will create new kinds of services and stops along the routes, like the shopping malls or giant theme parks, or grand office complexes that lure even more people onto real highways. (That would be the equivalent of interactive home shopping channels, video-on-demand TV, and multimedia telecommuting systems.) The whole shebang should then feed on itself. Efficient highways and cars allow people to move farther from their offices and other amenities, adding more traffic to the highways. Similarly, information highways and their services will mean that people can move to a mountain cabin in Idaho and "work" in Chicago and "shop" in Dallas and catch every New York Yankees baseball game. Communications networks will ship all that interstate and international traffic over long-distance company lines to computers and TV sets.

The networks that AT&T, MCI, and Sprint have already built are the first real, live pieces of megamedia. They are waiting for the rest of the pieces to catch up and feed the networks' business. The networks are 95 percent or more fiber-optic. They can carry digital information and virtually anything megamedia can bring their way. The networks are up and running, but are mostly carrying voice-only phone calls, which is like using a fully equipped aircraft carrier only to go bass fishing.

The one smudge on long-distance companies' pretty picture is a threat of increased competition. One way or another, the seven regional Bell companies will win the right to get into the long-distance business. As of this writing, they cannot sell long-distance—cannot ship calls from one "local area" to another. That was part of the consent decree that governed the breakup of the Bell System. Either Congress will soon pass a law that removes those barriers, or the Bells will kill the consent decree in court actions. Then seven well-financed, experienced telecommunications companies will charge into the industry.

At the very least, the Bells will eat at long-distance market share within their regions—Ameritech will ship a call from Chicago to Milwaukee instead of having to send it over long-distance company lines. At worst, the new competition will fire up price wars. No matter: AT&T, MCI, and maybe Sprint shouldn't get hurt badly because their main assets are their networks. It would take years and billions of dollars for a regional Bell to create anything like the existing networks.

AT&T will have the least to fear of any of the long-distance companies. Not only does it have the biggest network, but it has the broadest base of other kinds of business ready to take advantage of megamedia. Other telecommunications companies fear AT&T.

AT&T is an odd bird in U.S. business history. A year after Alexander Graham Bell invented his "electrical speaking telephone," he formed Bell Telephone Company in Boston. He won a court order, in 1879, barring Western Union from infringing on his telephone patents, ending early competition in the business. Three years later, Bell Telephone bought Western Union's huge electrical equipment manufacturing arm, Western Electric. The company and the telephone market took off.

Contrary to popular belief, the Bell System wasn't always a government-mandated monopoly. As Bell's patents expired in the 1890s, other companies raced into the market and competed fiercely against Bell Telephone. In 1899, the company changed its name to American Telephone & Telegraph, moved headquarters to New York, and started aggressively buying rivals. By 1913, AT&T was so big and so dominant, it was forced to decide to either agree to be governed by federal regulation or face antitrust action. It chose regulation. Any competitors left were too small to get in AT&T's way. Over the next 70 years, the company grew into the all-encompassing, monopolistic, powerful Ma Bell that so many people remember.

Today's AT&T is not really a continuation of the 120-year-old company. It's more like an offspring of Ma Bell, a second generation. In 1982, the company settled a Justice Department antitrust lawsuit. Under terms of the settlement, the old Bell System was broken into eight parts on January 1, 1984. Seven parts became the seven regional Bell companies—the local phone businesses. The eighth part became today's AT&T. In the settlement, the company was smart enough to keep the two pieces of the business that have allowed its successful evolution in the next age: the long-distance network, and equipment manufacturing. It also kept Bell Labs, one of the best research labs in industry.

Who gets credit for seeing the future back in the early 1980s? A young Bob Allen. At the time, he was a vice president known for excellent analysis. He was put in charge of a task force to look at AT&T's future and report on how best to structure the government settlement. When the company stunned the business world by spinning off the huge local businesses while keeping long-distance and manufacturing, it was acting on recommendations made by Allen's group.

The choice didn't look so good at first. AT&T limped through the 1980s. It went through grueling change as it learned to be competitive, laid off masses of workers, and failed in new businesses such as personal computers. It groped for an identity, a structure and a strategy that would carry it forward. Only in the mid-1990s did AT&T really find its way. And that way revolves around the company's all-important network.

AT&T's network is a little hard to visualize. It's not like a giant factory or a library of movies that someone can point to and say, "There, that's what it's all about." It is largely fiber-optic cable, underground and undersea, in a web across the United States and connecting to 270 other countries. The lines are governed by 135 supersophisticated switching machines—computers that guide signals to their correct destinations. A single switch can shuffle a half-million calls an hour. The whole network carries 175 million calls worldwide every business day and rakes in $40 billion a year in tolls. The undersea cables alone would circle the equator five times. All AT&T's phone lines laid end-to-end would stretch 2.75 billion miles, just about the distance from here to Neptune.

As far as AT&T knows, no one has ever calculated the actual worth, in dollars, of the entire AT&T network. As one clue, the company says that, over the past nine years, it has spent, on average, $2.6 billion a year on growing and improving the network. That's $23.4 billion. The entire network is probably worth a few times that.

Allen describes his network in a series of superlatives: "It is the most capable, most flexible, largest, most used, most adaptable, most technologically advanced network in the world," he says. "It's not the only one, but it's the largest and we believe it's the best." You could also put it this way: AT&T's network is possibly the most valuable single business asset on earth.

And the network is especially valuable because, as discussed earlier, it's essentially ahead of its time. It will be able to carry just about anything megamedia throws at it. In fact, to live up to its value and potential, AT&T must find ways to drive megamedia traffic onto the network—the sooner, the better.

And there you have the core strategy driving everything AT&T will do over the next decade. As the company continues to expand and upgrade its network, all the other activity at AT&T will spin from the desire to put more traffic on the network. To understand every move AT&T makes, keep that in mind.

At first glance, for instance, AT&T looks like it has been spraying its resources all over the megamedia map, often with questionable degrees of success. AT&T bought a little Silicon Valley company called EO, and the two built the EO handheld personal communicator—a cross between a cellular phone and a computer. It could make wireless calls, send wireless faxes, exchange electronic mail, store calendars and address books. Why would AT&T do an EO? "The more useful we make [new communications] devices, the more volume we add to the network," Allen says. The EO weighed as much as a hardcover dictionary and cost almost $2,000. It flopped and EO went out of business in 1994. Was that a big setback for AT&T? No. The real goal was to hasten the creation of these little communicators, and, in turn, spur new traffic for the network. EO accomplished that by introducing the products to the public and taking an early stab at creating a market for them. AT&T would've preferred to have made tons of money from selling the EO devices. But that was never the main point. The goal was to get people using devices that would cause them to communicate—and use long-distance networks—in ways they never had before.

The same strategy applies to AT&T's work on several interactive TV tests. One is a test of movies on demand with TCI and US

West in Littleton, Colorado. Another involves interactive TV tests with Viacom in Castro Valley, California, and GTE in Manassas, Virginia. AT&T wants to stimulate development of those systems and help make them big hits so people across the country will want them. The movies and interactive services will have to be shipped from the people who create them to the cable or phone companies that distribute them. AT&T wants its network to be the shipper.

At least one piece of the network strategy has turned into its own juggernaut of a business within AT&T. The company's network construction group—responsible for building and maintaining AT&T's network—is fast becoming the prime contractor for the building of information highways by other companies worldwide. No group is considered better at assembling and integrating advanced networks for megamedia than the people at AT&T. Other AT&T branches build and supply much of the advanced technology, such as ATM multimedia switches and software to make the network run.

In May 1994, AT&T won the prime contracting job for Bell Atlantic's big push into megamedia—an $8.5 billion project over five years, one of the biggest telecommunications contracts ever. In the weeks before that, AT&T landed a $4 billion contract to rebuild Saudi Arabia's phone system with digital technology, and a $1 billion contract from Southern New England Telephone for information highway technology. A few months earlier, Pacific Telesis hired AT&T for a $5 billion project to build a California high-tech network. That's a total of $18.5 billion in contracts, and more like that are coming, says Rich McGinn, president of AT&T's Network Systems division. "We expect to be the market share leader" in information superhighway deals, he says, and the deals could generate $30 billion a year in contracts for AT&T by 2000.

"We want to build the infrastructure," says Allen. "All these players from various industries are converging, and they all can use the technology we can supply." That brings up one of the interesting dilemmas of the newly competitive communications world. "No question we're selling technology to companies [such as Bell Atlantic] in this country that have designs on what is currently our market," Allen says. "Yet if we don't sell it to them, somebody else will. Why not sell them AT&T's?"

Besides, the beauty is that building these local networks helps AT&T in two ways. First, it's a money-making business all by itself. Second, the networks will prod people and companies to use multimedia communications, sending more traffic over long-distance networks to friends or family or coworkers. It's the core strategy.

One of AT&T's biggest efforts for the rest of the decade will be in wireless communication. AT&T finally closed its $12.6 billion deal to buy McCaw Cellular, although it had to promise the Justice Department it would operate McCaw as a separate business and give McCaw customers the right to link to any long-distance carrier, not just AT&T. Still, wireless will be a great business for AT&T. The market is growing around 40 percent a year and should keep up that pace for a while. AT&T will lend McCaw its clout and brand name to help aggressively market cellular services. The company will buy cellular properties in cities not covered by McCaw, or bid for PCS wireless phone licenses in those areas. The goal is to create a nationwide wireless system. That would allow AT&T–McCaw to go to a big company like Procter & Gamble and offer to be its one wireless communication provider for all its operations in the United States at a bulk-rate price. If the industry ends up being a handful of nationwide wireless competitors, the powerful AT&T–McCaw brand will have a distinct advantage.

In wireless, too, AT&T gets added benefits. Not only will it be a good business, but if AT&T can expand and improve wireless communication, more people will use it. Wireless usually adds new phone traffic, beyond the traffic generated by wired phones, because people make calls when they otherwise wouldn't—in cars, at parks, in restaurants. Some of that traffic will wheel onto AT&T's network. Plus, if AT&T can connect long-distance calls it carries to customers via its own wireless network, AT&T will save a ton of money on access charges. Right now, every time AT&T connects a long-distance call through a local phone or cellular company, AT&T keeps about 55 percent of the fee for the call and the local companies on each end get about 45 percent in access charges. If AT&T manages to connect the call on both ends using its wireless system, that's an immediate 45 percent increase in revenue from that call.

One other important area for AT&T in the next decade is overseas growth. For all of its first 100 years, AT&T was almost entirely a domestic company. In 1984, at the Bell breakup, AT&T employed 5,000 people overseas. Today, it has almost 60,000. It sees a huge opportunity to build networks for foreign governments, help provide communication services in joint ventures, and connect all of a corporate customer's operations worldwide using AT&T networks.

Allen believes there is no better time to expand overseas. As the Communications Age rolls in, "most countries around the world—even Third World countries—are understanding that they must build communications capacity or they won't be able to compete in the global economy," Allen says. As the leading network builder, AT&T should be able to snatch a big chunk of that developing business. One major push is in China, where AT&T has signed a joint venture with the Beijing government. AT&T says that China, which has only two phones for every 100 people, wants to increase phone service twentyfold by 2020. That means installing 15 million to 17 million lines annually for almost three decades. "If we're really successful, we could essentially build a new AT&T in China over the next 25 years," Allen says.

Again, if AT&T can stimulate foreign markets, people there who never before made phone calls or sent e-mail would start to do so—and some of that traffic would move on AT&T's network.

Out on the horizon, look for more of the same from AT&T. It will add to its network and improve the technology. It will go after more information superhighway construction projects. It will invest in start-ups and try to create new megamedia products and services. It will work hard to make its McCaw acquisition pay off and develop a nationwide wireless business. And it will continue its overseas thrust.

What AT&T won't do is buy or make a major investment in a content company. Allen says there are no movie studios or TV networks or publishing companies in his future. "We want to understand the entertainment industry and people who are creative and who are content providers," Allen says. "We might have to have some interest and involvement to understand or learn. But it doesn't mean we're going to go buy a Paramount or other studio or feel we have to own a content business."

AT&T's problems look pretty wan next to its successes. The company's biggest single challenge is probably how to make NCR into a useful part of AT&T. Ever since AT&T bought the computer maker in 1991 for $7.5 billion—at the time, AT&T's biggest acquisition—NCR has been a strategic dud. It has stayed narrowly focused on computers for automated teller machines, retail stores, and other business services. What AT&T needs is a broad multimedia computing division that can build anything from video servers for movies-on-demand systems to home computers capable of handling video telecommuting. In late 1993, Allen put Jerre Stead in charge of turning around NCR, now called Global Business Communications Systems, and he took the division a long way before leaving to run a small software company in January, 1995. So far, though, few hot new developments have come out of that division.

On an almost comical note, AT&T has a truly horrible record when it comes to creating new kinds of consumer and business devices. Flops go back to its personal computer line in the 1980s and run through the EO. AT&T was one of the major investors in Trip Hawkins's multimedia video game company, 3DO, launched in 1992. 3DO never caught on with consumers or game developers, and it's sinking fast. AT&T introduced a Videophone in 1993. For $1,500, users could see herky-jerky images of the person on the other end, as long as that person also had an AT&T Videophone. Few have been sold.

Such pratfalls aren't going to bring down the company. The investments are a sliver of AT&T's overall business—the 3DO investment was only $2.5 million. Once in a while, the company lands on something that works, like its investment in the ImagiNation Network, a California-based on-line game system that has been gaining popularity.

CEO Allen is convinced that the company's most dangerous devil is deep under its own skin. He fears the company's old non-competitive, bureaucratic culture, which still lurks in some office hallways and factory floors. Banishing that devil is Allen's passion.

"The biggest risk we have is getting comfortable where we are," Allen says. "It's a risk I fight every day."

To get a picture of Bob Allen, imagine Jimmy Stewart if he were starring in a modern-day movie called *It's a Wonderful Communications Company.* Like Stewart, Allen is tall, lanky, soft-spoken, easy-going, likable, and brimming with an unmistakable integrity. Colleagues say he rarely displays anger, though his fuse gets short when, for instance, his executives get into turf battles when they should be getting on with business. Allen is not much of a joker, but he does have a laconic sense of humor. He certainly doesn't lead through sheer force of personality. He's not a Ray Smith or John Malone. He's more a behind-the-scenes coach, cheerleader, and team builder. Some of Allen's closest friends say he doesn't even understand a lot of the technology and potential of the information superhighway, but he knows how to assemble people who do, and then lets the best ideas bubble up. He is quick to say that none of AT&T's more celebrated moves of late—the purchases of NCR and McCaw, and the launch of the highly successful Universal Visa Card—was his idea. Allen is a good listener. And then he is decisive. Once his direction is set, Allen can become almost dictatorial: sign up or get out.

Allen's ongoing focus is on the organization around him and how to make it tick, not on the day's developments or the next new product. He usually gets into the office at 7 A.M., works until 6:30 P.M., goes home for dinner, then works a few hours more at home in the evening. He says he always looks forward to coming to the office each morning. On weekends, he plays golf whenever possible. He's very good at it for some of the same reasons he's good at his job: he stays absolutely focused on the shot he's making and tunes out extraneous noise.

Allen was born January 25, 1935, in Joplin, Missouri, grew up in Indiana, and would've gone to Indiana University but for a scholarship from Wabash College. He graduated with a B.A. in 1957 and went right to work for Indiana Bell. The company paid for the up-and-comer to attend Harvard Business School, from which he graduated in 1965. From there, Allen scaled the Bell corporate ladder. He was AT&T's chief financial officer at the time of the Bell System breakup, and then became chief operating officer. In 1988, Allen's friend and AT&T's chairman and CEO, James Olson, died of cancer after a brief illness. Allen was handed Olson's job.

The company was a mess. Olson had started layoffs and was fighting AT&T's bureaucracy, but much more had to be done. Management was political and stagnant. Corporate structure was tangled so badly that if something went wrong, Allen says, he had a hard time determining who was responsible. The long-distance unit was hemorrhaging market share, and other divisions, like office equipment, were losing money.

That's when Allen decided the enemy was within. One of the first things Allen did when he became chairman was call Donald Peterson, who had turned around Ford by emphasizing quality and pushing decisions down the corporate line. Allen wanted to do the same at AT&T.

Allen began by dividing AT&T into 22 units, each responsible for its own success or failure. He created executive teams that would force the different units to think and work together when it made sense. An overall Operations Committee was made up of the five top group executives, which forced them to strategize as a team. He has tried to "depoliticize" AT&T and turn the organization upside-down. One Allen tactic was to start having managers be evaluated by their subordinates—and the first manager to get appraised was Allen.

Maybe the most important change was bringing in top managers from outside, a rarity in the old AT&T. Allen didn't go after just anyone. He wanted people who had been CEOs of other companies. He wanted leaders. Allen recruited Stead, who had been the dynamic CEO of Square D, an electrical equipment maker. Stead was at first put in charge of the ailing office phone and equipment division in 1991. He turned the group around in months. Allen also brought in Alex Mandl, who had been CEO of Sea-Land, the $3 billion shipping company. Mandl now runs AT&T's long-distance business and he negotiated the McCaw merger. Allen gives his executives unusual autonomy, and so far he has shown a remarkable ability to spot and lure top talent. AT&T's executive ranks are rich in world-class managers.

That's one reason no one flinched when Kavner, AT&T's multimedia chief, left to join Hollywood superagent Michael Ovitz in 1994, or when Stead departed.

Thanks to Allen's moves, AT&T is now considered one of the best-managed companies in the world. It is competitive, tough, and surprisingly quick: only two months after EO's founders first met with AT&T executives, AT&T put up money and EO started developing its product. Change is likely to be an opportunity to AT&T, not a threat.

Allen isn't satisfied, though. He thinks often of IBM at its height in the mid-1980s, when mainframe computers were king, and rivers of money flooded the company. IBM got so good at what it was doing that it couldn't believe it had to change to keep up with the times. Now that battered company is trying to get up off its knees. "Look, I'm very proud of AT&T, and I think we're the leader in our industry," Allen says. "But don't think I or anybody else can be complacent in that regard. Otherwise we'll become a slow giant who gradually fades into the background and has to go through a real bootstrapper operation."

Allen sees his job, in fact, as setting up an organization that can respond to change. That's the key, he believes, because trying to foresee the future would be silly. "I thought divestiture was a major change," Allen says. "It certainly was the largest change any corporation has ever gone through. But what's happening now, has happened the last couple of years—you'd have to question the sanity of anybody who says they know how it's going to come out and what their particular company is going to look like.

"It's hard for a company that has a large market share to possibly believe they are vulnerable," Allen says. "But every day I read something in the newspaper that gives me pause, because everybody's got wonderful ideas, they're making deals, they've got new products and new ways to play in our sandbox. So it's a real challenge for us to assess change and try to stay abreast of it. I don't profess to know how it's all going to sort out. AT&T could be 10 years from now a very different company than it is today."

That doesn't mean Allen ignores the future. He says he spends a lot of time peering out there, trying to see what might be coming for AT&T. He is certainly a believer in the information highway, multimedia, interactive TV, video phone calls, and all that megamedia is about. Interestingly, though, Allen is not a megamedia evangelist. "It's going to happen, but it's a question of when and how," he says. Applications so far have been disappointing, he adds, and failures like EO show that finding products and services that consumers will pay for won't be easy. "The potential for the information highway is just that right now—potential," Allen says.

In other words, poor Bob Allen is going to spend the rest of the 1990s feeling uneasy and unsatisfied about how AT&T works and where it's going—and that may be the best thing that could happen to a company of 300,000 people. I don't think an Allen-led AT&T could fall behind. Allen told *Fortune* in 1993 that AT&T could, just possibly, more than double its annual revenue to $150 billion or $200 billion by sometime next decade. That's an amazing statement coming from a man not given to hyperbole. Yet, if you look closely at the company Allen has built, you just might believe him.

MCI: A COMPANY OF BUNGEE JUMPERS

At any other company facing so much fundamental change, the atmosphere might be tense or tentative. A touch of fear would be etched into employees' faces. But MCI is the corporate equivalent of people who like bungee jumping. There's a feeling of glee at the prospect of diving headlong into a megamedia world that will be, for the company, equal parts exciting and dangerous. MCI could end up soaring or dashed on the rocks below. Says chairman and CEO Bert Roberts, "A lot of people can't survive in this company, because we're strange."

MCI is going to have a challenging decade. Since its inception in 1968, the company has been almost purely a long-distance communications concern. It has been stupendously successful, growing into a company with more than $12 billion in annual revenue, all but a sliver of it from long-distance tolls. MCI is the number-two long-distance carrier in the United States (behind AT&T) and one of the top four in the world. It has built one of the most impressive high-tech networks on earth, again behind only AT&T's and probably on a par with Sprint's. The network, almost all fiber-optic, is ready and able to carry video phone calls, multimedia services, interactive TV, and everything else megamedia will bring.

But that's not enough anymore. Not in the converging, increasingly competitive communications industry. Long-distance alone is too narrow and vulnerable. AT&T already surrounds its core network with businesses that enhance and draw strength from it. By contrast, MCI has a superb core network, but it stands there nearly naked. If MCI were to stick strictly to long-distance, strong new competitors—mainly the seven regional Bells, which will eventually be allowed into the industry—could easily damage the company by hacking at MCI's one reason for being.

So MCI has embarked on a mission of change, a mission wrapped up in a strategy called networkMCI, launched by Roberts in January 1994. The plan calls for MCI to shell out more than $20 billion through the 1990s "to create and deliver a wide array of new branded services to telecommunications users," says a company document. The bulk of the strategy calls for MCI to venture far beyond its core long-distance business, getting into local phone service, wireless communication, electronic computer communication, international partnerships, and perhaps even investments in cable-TV operations. Most of the moves are gutsy gambles that are anything but sure winners. One way or another, by 2000, MCI is going to look like a very different company.

This is not window dressing. Roberts and his managers firmly believe that, for the first time in its history, MCI can't go it alone, stay focused on its one market, and continue to be successful. There is a sense of urgency, too. The stuff of megamedia, Roberts says, "is coming at us very fast. Industries are changing very fast. It's a situation where the dynamics of everything that's going on as we've known it to date will be restructured by the end of the decade."

That prospect doesn't scare Roberts. He is confident to the point of sounding cocky, which is part of MCI's way. "With our marketing and merchandising skills and our tenacity and culture and our vision of the future, we can react to changes that are going to be forced upon us," he says. "It's hard to envision us not being a winner in this."

The networkMCI strategy has a lot of pieces, some in place and others in the distance. Here's an overview.

British Telecommunications

One big initial chunk of the plan is MCI's headline-making alliance with London-based British Telecommunications (BT), announced in 1993. BT bought a 20% stake in MCI for $4.3 billion, and the pair have jointly put up an additional $1 billion to form a joint venture called Concert, which is marketing worldwide telecommunications services to corporations.

More than anything, the BT deal gives MCI cash to spend on the other parts of networkMCI. Beyond that, joining with BT was a quick way for MCI to go global. It should now be easier, for instance, for MCI to offer a single package of communications services to a corporation that has offices in the United States and Europe. And expect BT to help guide European-based companies to MCI. The partnership gives MCI a head start on long-distance rivals AT&T and Sprint, which are still struggling to put together partnerships with European telephone companies.

The question is whether the relationship can ever really blossom into more than an investment for BT. The two participants have very different cultures and agendas. Roberts says he and BT Chairman Iain Vallance are personally involved in trying to make the deal into a working partnership. They meet at least once a month and they push other executives to interact. BT, which is making a transition from monopoly to competition in a newly opened communications market in the United Kingdom, says it needs to learn from MCI—an attitude that may help prim BT executives keep their patience with their overenergized partners. Even Roberts says MCI's way sometimes unnerves the BT people. "I think we're moving toward an increasingly common vision, but it's not 100 percent smooth," he admits. "I mean, . . . we have the kind of culture that, since we announced the deal, we've reorganized three times."

If BT and MCI can integrate, they'll be a powerful force. If not, the money will help MCI, but the partnership and the grand plans for global marketing could turn into duds.

Wireless

In March 1994, MCI announced it would pay $1.3 billion to buy 17 percent of fledgling Nextel Communications, which is building the first national digital wireless communications network. Nextel was to be MCI's wireless strategy. It was MCI's way of matching AT&T's purchase of McCaw Cellular. By the fall of 1994, the investment was dead. Squabbles between MCI and Nextel's other partner, Motorola, and MCI's concerns about the quality of Nextel's network convinced MCI to pull out. It was a painful decision because Roberts is convinced that MCI absolutely has to have a wireless component. As 1995 rolled around, MCI still had no dance partner in the wireless world.

That's a big problem. MCI wants wireless because it's a fast-growing market, and also because it's a way for a long-distance company to get into the local telephone market. AT&T, with McCaw, is way ahead. Sprint has created a partnership with cable companies to build new wireless PCS networks. Most of the obvious wireless partners for MCI are now unavailable.

At the end of 1994, Roberts hadn't said what MCI might do. The key may be Timothy Price, an aggressive executive named, in November 1994, to the number-three job at MCI. He is in charge of MCI's long-distance business and he'll supervise entry into new businesses, including wireless. Price seems to be exactly what the wireless effort needs. He's known for finding innovative solutions to tough problems. He was a key creator of MCI's fantastically successful Friends & Family marketing campaign, for example. He's also known for getting new businesses up and running. Price launched MCI's on-line computer businesses while other long-distance companies were only testing the market. MCI is counting on him to do the same in wireless.

Local

One of MCI's most audacious plans is to spend $2 billion to barge its way into the local phone business. It is going to simply build new local phone networks in select cities to compete directly against the local Bell company. The networks will be fiber-optic and coaxial cable, so they can carry megamedia programming and services. First stops: Atlanta and Chicago, where the networks are already being built. After that may come New York, Los Angeles, Dallas, and Washington, DC.

MCI reasons that its megamedia-ready long-distance network is largely wasted as long as the old twisted-pair local phone lines can't deliver much more than a voice conversation. A network, to quote an old saw, is only as powerful as its weakest link. If local phone companies won't rush to put in broadband phone lines, MCI will come in and do it ahead of them. Not only will it be a good business by itself, but it should stimulate megamedia applications and eventually help add megamedia traffic to MCI's long-distance network. Plus, MCI would find another way to save on those pesky access charges.

MCI hopes to frighten local phone companies into moving faster on megamedia—again, helping stimulate traffic that would move over MCI's long-distance network. "We're going to force competition," Roberts says. "We have to either make it happen or be there, and we've cast that die."

One wild card here is a cable-TV link. Roberts says that investing in cable companies, which plan to offer local phone service over their networks, "may be the quickest road to competition." MCI will consider taking that road, he says; in fact, MCI has obviously made some efforts in that direction. "Doing deals with cable companies is an interesting exercise, sometimes in futility and sometimes in success," he says, hinting that he has negotiated with the industry. So far, futility has won out. Sprint cut the big deal with cable companies, not MCI. Sprint even stole away MCI's closest cable ally, Comcast, which joined Sprint's partnership along with TCI and Cox. That had to hurt.

Electronic

In an office in Atlanta, MCI vice president Brian Brewer shows off his work on networkMCI Business. It's an electronic communications and software package for companies that already use PCs connected internally to a network. Without the MCI package, employees could only send or receive e-mail or share files with others in the building. With the package, they can connect to the outside world to use e-mail, get into the Internet, find news reports through an MCI service or buy products through an electronic MCI shopping mall. Soon, the package will also let users make video phone calls. Price is about $100 for the software and $50 to $60 a month for the services.

The offerings are a new area for a long-distance company, but they play into an MCI strength. Long before e-mail was widely used, MCI created MCI Mail, one of the first electronic mail services. It has long been one of the biggest carriers of data and messages for the Internet. As computer communication takes off, MCI may profit most among long-distance companies. "We wanted to hit our competition where it wasn't," Brewer says.

Those are the main parts of networkMCI now. MCI is open to broadening the plan as megamedia develops and the industry changes. "Will we have to be in entertainment? I don't know. I don't know. But we're going to have to know," Roberts says. He's also asking whether MCI should be aligned with a software company such as Microsoft or Novell. "All the answers aren't out now."

The most important leg of networkMCI is a commitment to continue to expand and improve the core long-distance network. After all, it's MCI's crown jewel. It cost about $10 billion to build, and is among the most technologically advanced commercial networks in the world. It gives MCI a national presence and a strong brand name, which the company can use to boost its other businesses, including wireless phones and local phone service.

Outside of the core network and the grand strategic plan, MCI's chief asset in these turbulent times has to be its culture. The street-fighting, little-company-that-could spirit is at the heart of MCI's history, and it nourishes every molecule vibrating inside Bert Roberts.

MCI was born while Roberts was still a young upstart at Westinghouse Electric Company. MCI was officially founded in 1968 when crusty, scrappy Bill McGowan joined what was then a mobile radio company and helped it get financing to build a series of microwave towers between St. Louis and Chicago. The towers would be the first system to carry long-distance communication in competition with

AT&T. Ma Bell repeatedly tried to crush the company. MCI, taking cues from McGowan's personality, developed its guerrilla-warfare style to survive and battle back. MCI spent so much time fighting AT&T in court through the 1970s that McGowan gave his company the famous label of "a law firm with an antenna on top." By 1982, MCI's efforts had helped force the breakup of the Bell System—the equivalent of a pee-wee football team forcing the breakup of the NFL. No wonder MCI learned to be cocky.

Roberts, educated as an engineer at Johns Hopkins University, bounced around at Westinghouse and then at a computer leasing firm before joining MCI in 1972 in the sales and marketing department. Over the years, Roberts ended up running just about every department at MCI. McGowan named him president and chief operating officer in 1985. Roberts was made CEO in 1991 and took on the chairman title after McGowan died in 1992.

Sitting in his bright corner office, lined with windows overlooking downtown Washington, DC, Roberts appears and acts like a regular guy you'd meet at a neighborhood bar. He's dressed in a neat white shirt, black pinstripe suit, and purple tie, but his belly strains against the waistband and he wears an almost perpetual mischievous grin. A hearing aid nestles in his right ear. He talks fast and is perfectly willing to make dry, sarcastic comments about anyone outside of MCI—especially companies he perceives as monopolies. "We have companies out there announcing that *their* goal in life is to have 500 channels of cable TV," Roberts says, aiming at TCI. "*Our* goal is to satisfy the customer. One is a *presumption* of what the customer wants or needs. The other is a *question* as to what the customer needs. One is a monopoly approach and one is bred in competition."

One of his private passions is technology. He calls himself "a PC groupie." He says: "One of the advantages of the position I'm in is I can get the latest new snazzy small PC hot off the press." He fanatically uses electronic mail—specifically, his company's MCI Mail. When he travels, he takes a laptop and plugs it into the phone jack as soon as he arrives at a hotel so he can send and receive e-mail messages. He uses e-mail to communicate not only with others at MCI, but with his new allies at British Telecom.

Roberts spends his work time molding MCI's strategy and looking for the deals and moves that will make the networkMCI plan work. But his obsession is preserving MCI's culture, mainly because he believes the culture—not any one person or strategy—gets credit for everything from winning market share from AT&T to foreseeing trends in megamedia.

"The biggest thing, the single biggest challenge, is we have to not let our company's culture change," Roberts says. He goes into a long discourse on IBM and General Motors and how they lost their focus and sense of purpose when they got too big and successful. "If we can't keep our company thinking small, entrepreneurial, keeping the distance from the customer to decision makers short, we're going to fail. We're one of the top 50 companies in the United States but we can't talk about that around here. We've got to talk about how we only have 20 percent market share [in long-distance] and there's all this opportunity out there."

When looking at the megamedia future, Roberts says MCI is good at three things that should prove particularly useful. One is that the culture has always been geared toward starting with no market share and clawing for a little at a time. That's what MCI will have to do, for instance, in the local phone business and the wireless business—and perhaps someday in TV or entertainment. The other talent embedded in MCI's culture is a lust for competing against monopolies—kind of handy, considering many of megamedia's competing companies have long been monopolies.

Finally, there's that idea that MCI flourishes amid change. "We've dealt with change and dealt with change," Roberts says. "Monopolies tend to be companies that don't change. If you have a culture that has dealt with change, I think you can be more sensitive to changes as they occur. You can be more innovative. Maybe we don't have a lot of experience in things, but we also don't know that things can't be done."

Keep in mind that MCI has never dealt with so much change and so many risks all at once. It has always been a one-business company. The simultaneous drives into local phone service, wireless communication, and global marketing will stretch MCI's personnel and resources—and its culture—to limits the company has never seen before. Any other culture would surely snap.

It's an even bet whether MCI crash-lands before the decade's out, or whether all the strategic moves click and the company turns into a rip-roaring megamedia success. If MCI does come through a winner, it will be because of its heart and soul.

SPRINT: GONE WITH THE WIND?

"I don't think you'll recognize Sprint five to seven years down the road," says Ted Schell, the number-three long-distance company's senior vice president for strategic planning.

No doubt he's right. Schell believes Sprint will become a one-stop global communications powerhouse. But there's another version of what Sprint will be by the turn of the century: gone.

A quick look at Kansas City-based Sprint reveals a fairly impressive company. It has all the right pieces assembled to launch itself into megamedia ahead of its competitors. Other companies would kill to put together Sprint's list of assets: a world-class long-distance network with some of the best technology in the business; the ninth-largest local phone company; the eighth-biggest cellular provider; and announced alliances with European phone giants. Sprint's ads, featuring Candice Bergen, the lead on the popular "Murphy Brown" sitcom, have vastly boosted Sprint's brand name.

Yet a host of insiders and industry watchers believe Sprint is bungling its future. The company suffers from a lack of leadership and focus. It doesn't have a cohesive vision. It moves too slowly. It makes big mistakes. Sprint management simply cannot translate the company's great technology and promising mix of assets into a strong strategic advantage. The company is often crippled by internal turf fights, say executives who have left Sprint in recent years.

Put it all together and Sprint looks vulnerable. By the end of the decade, chances are Sprint will no longer be an independent company. It will either be broken up or sold.

History is part of the problem. The company is a schizophrenic conglomerate that can't seem to get all its horses pulling in the same direction. Take a look at Sprint's pieces.

Local

The company's roots go back to 1899, when Jacob and Cleyson Brown strung wires around Abilene, Kansas, to start one of the earliest independent phone companies. In 1911, they and other independent operators in Kansas merged to form United Telephone Company. Over the next seven decades, the company's fortunes meandered up and down, and it got into and out of a string of businesses, including nuclear power plants and cable TV. By 1971, the company was renamed United Telecommunications and owned local phone companies in mostly rural areas dolloped across the Midwest and South.

The local part of the business hasn't changed much. It is regulated, slow-moving, and monopolistic. Because it operates in few major markets, it hasn't had to take action to get ready for near-term competition from cable companies or alternate access phone providers. The technology in United's local networks is often a few grades below that of the regional Bells. The division has been content to spend little and rake in lots. In 1993, revenue from local operations was just two-thirds that of Sprint's long-distance business; yet local operating profits were double long-distance operating profits.

Long-Distance

In 1970, Southern Pacific, the railroad company, started a competitive long-distance company. In 1983, just as long-distance was turning into a real industry in the United States, GTE bought the Southern Pacific brainchild. GTE Sprint quickly developed into the number-three long-distance provider, behind AT&T and MCI. In 1985, United Telecommunications bought 50 percent of Sprint, renaming the service US Sprint for a while.

United and GTE set up Sprint as a separate entity, largely free of parental strings. The joint venture developed an independence and a technology-driven culture. Engineers ruled. The goal was to build the best, most advanced communications network anywhere; surely a market would follow. In the 1980s, Sprint built the world's first 100 percent fiber-optic long-distance network.

United bought out GTE's interest in Sprint in 1992 and renamed the whole company Sprint. In its new setting, Sprint has continued to stay ahead of competitors in technology, adding high-speed SONET data networks to its system and putting in computerized "intelligence" that allows such applications as voice-dialing (say "Mom" into the phone and Sprint's system looks up and dials your mother's number).

To date, Sprint has never effectively used its technological advantage to create great products for consumers and businesses. One famous example is that Sprint finished its sparkling fiber-optic network, then installed a faulty billing system that drove away customers. In another example, a group at Sprint had developed a calling plan similar to MCI's hugely successful Friends & Family campaign more than four years ahead of MCI. The plan was shelved, then resurrected only after Friends & Family took off. "Their tendency, as opposed to being a trendsetter, has been to respond," a former Sprint executive says.

Long-distance profits have been soaring, but that's mostly because the whole industry is way up and Sprint has cut costs to boost the bottom line. A more telling measurement: since 1988, Sprint's share of the long-distance market has changed little, hovering around 9 percent.

Wireless

United Telecommunications had owned cellular operations, then sold out. Under the Sprint banner, the company got back in, buying Centel in 1992. Renamed Sprint Cellular—a more powerful national brand name—the company has been growing in step with the wireless industry (about 40 percent a year). The division operates as yet a third fiefdom within the overall corporation.

Sprint is creating what could become a fourth unit competing for resources and power: the partnership with cable companies TCI,

Comcast, and Cox. If the venture gels, it will become another local phone business for Sprint. The plan is for Sprint to lend its technology, expertise, and brand name to the cable companies, helping them offer local phone connections over cable lines. The service would compete against established local phone companies, and the venture plans to launch new PCS wireless services. In return, Sprint would get a bigger piece of the local phone business and cut down on the access charges it pays to connect local customers to its long-distance network. Sprint also gets, through the cable lines, broadband connections to homes and businesses, a possible pathway to new kinds of megamedia offerings.

The plan has merit, but the venture implementing it will be a separate company from Sprint, guided as much by TCI's John Malone, Comcast's Brian Roberts, and Cox's Jim Robbins as by Sprint's Esrey. That's a lot of head-butting potential, both within the unit and in the venture's relationship with the rest of Sprint. Without a doubt, the cable companies will benefit from Sprint's help, especially since the Sprint brand name will help legitimize cable's nascent phone service. Less obvious, though, is whether Sprint can make its connection to cable pay off.

In megamedia, the various kinds of telephone service—local, long-distance, wireless—will cross and converge. Sprint's range of assets could, in theory, give it a head start, except that Sprint's divisions don't interact well. (To be fair, in some cases they can't because of regulations.) They don't plan together, don't seem to see the future in a cohesive way, and tend to fight turf battles to gain an upper hand in how the company will develop.

Sprint's chief executive, William Esrey, hasn't helped matters. Wall Street analysts have praised Esrey's short-term performance. He knows how to cut costs, boost profits, and get stock prices up. As for the long term, Esrey doesn't seem to be a visionary. He hasn't shown he can rally the troops for a charge into a new era. Esrey illustrates the importance of bold leadership during a time of upheaval. Sprint has just about everything but leadership, and so it has stalled.

In 1994, Sprint took a couple of shots at major deals that would vault the company to a higher level. Both moves ended up showing

Sprint's inability to get things done. The first, in May, was the announcement of merger talks between Sprint and Electronic Data Systems (EDS), the huge computer services company that's part of General Motors. The merged company would have had an intriguing mix of computer and networking capabilities. Officially, the deal fell apart because the two sides couldn't agree on price. Insiders say the problem was that both Esrey and EDS's Les Alberthal wanted control. Sprint and EDS have since put together some joint marketing efforts.

In June 1994, Sprint announced a plan to sell 20 percent of the company to a partnership of France Telecom and Germany's Deutsche Telekom for $4.2 billion. The deal would give Sprint cash for U.S. expansion and a link with two of the strongest phone companies in Europe, a big step toward making Sprint into a global communications giant. As of this writing, the deal has not closed, and it may not for some time. The U.S. government is threatening to block the deal unless France and Germany open their telecommunications markets to U.S. companies.

The deal might not be such a blessing for Sprint. The French and German telephone companies are two large, government-owned, monopolistic organizations that have very different and often conflicting agendas. A partnership with both is a recipe for bureaucracy, infighting, and sluggishness. The deal would not be like MCI's hooking up with British Telecom, which is a single entity battling in a newly competitive market. I have heard BT officials titter with glee over the idea that a potential competitor will get mired in a partnership with the French and Germans. That deal is not likely to be Sprint's key to the future.

None of this negative talk goes down well with strategist Schell. He says the company has big plans for the next decade, and they don't have anything to do with selling out.

Schell believes the communications industry is moving toward one-stop shopping, both for consumers and business. Instead of choosing a local phone provider, a long-distance service, and a cellular service, consumers will want to go to one company and get all of the above in a package—one phone number, one bill, one customer service office to call about problems. Businesses will want the same treatment *and* they'll want the communications company to be able to link computers in networks and provide computer services such as worldwide electronic mail.

Sprint is working to become just such a one-stop shop, Schell says. To get there, Sprint is moving in a handful of different directions.

First, there's a push to go global. To be a competitor in the next age, Sprint will have to offer communication services that "look, smell, and taste the same no matter where you are in the world," Schell says. The deal with the French and German phone firms will help do that. The three partners plan to set up a separate, well-funded venture that will knit together a global network. "Nobody's kidding themselves—it's going to be tough to meld the cultures," Schell admits. But the partnership will work for two reasons. One is that all three have a similar vision for the future. The other is that all three know the partnership *has* to work if the companies want to survive. "It creates a sense of mutual dependence," Schell says.

A second Sprint push is to expand across technologies. That was the rationale for talking with EDS. Sprint believes it needs "a tight relationship with the information processing industry," Schell says. The company can then sell souped-up communications and information services to businesses, instead of just selling plain vanilla long-distance connections. Schell says Sprint is talking to a number of companies. It is also looking to expand further into wireless technologies.

Sprint's third front is the drive to add more local business to Sprint's menu. Sprint may assemble a patchwork of partnerships—some with local phone companies, others with the cable partners—so Sprint can resell local service as part of a complete communications package.

"One thing I never said we'll look at is content," Schell notes. "We're not buying movie studios and publishing houses."

Schell argues that having long-distance, local, and wireless under one roof has already given the company a competitive advantage. Outsiders just can't see it yet. "It's a learning experience," Schell says. "And it's extraordinary."

What about talk of dissent and lack of leadership? Schell acknowledges that there is "jockeying and politicking" going on, but strongly states that, at the management level, executives have signed on to the same vision and are working together. As for Esrey, Schell says the CEO has a "sense of balance" about megamedia—an ability to move toward the future while strengthening the company today.

Still, the company's plans sound good, but they're a long way from execution. Time may turn out to be a critical factor. Can Sprint build global networks and computer alliances and local links before the industry changes and competitors close in and gobble the company up? Probably not, unless Sprint's culture and management change drastically.

What's likely to become of Sprint? It will move along on its own for a while, probably turning in decent financial results as Esrey works at the numbers. But sometime in the 1990s, the regional Bell companies are going to be allowed into the long-distance business. Sprint, in the industry's third spot, will be vulnerable. Cable companies might start getting into the local phone business, competing against Sprint's local operations. Enormous competition is coming in cellular. Sprint will get bombarded on every side of its business. The cable alliance will help a little, but not enough.

Sprint's long-distance network—the jewel of the company—will become a tempting takeover target for one of the regional Bells. In one shot, an Ameritech or BellSouth could become a long-distance powerhouse and blast far ahead of the other Bells. Or, two or more Bells might team to buy Sprint and jointly operate the long-distance network, spinning off the rest. One way or another, Sprint's future is a question mark.

BRITISH TELECOM ET AL.: THE GLOBAL FACTOR

In the U.S. market, only three long-distance communications companies matter: AT&T, MCI, and Sprint. Smaller players will find niches and prosper, but they're not going to be important factors as megamedia unfurls—unless or until the regional Bell phone companies buy them.

The big three aren't sitting on their U.S. market shares anymore. They can't afford to. They are increasingly playing a global game, in large part because multinational corporate customers would prefer to buy all their long-distance services from one source. The global telecommunications market is only now developing, and it's there that AT&T, MCI, and Sprint may run into competition—although probably not much.

Just about every overseas communications company is a state-owned, protected, bureaucratic, slow-moving, monopolistic blob. The United States was far ahead of the world in unleashing competition in communications. As a result, AT&T, MCI, and Sprint are today far nimbler and more innovative than any possible international competitor. (Most telecommunications markets remain closed to foreigners or limit their role, so the U.S. companies aren't yet able to use their competitive advantage to win loads of new business in other countries.)

The one company emerging as a worthy global communications competitor is British Telecom (BT).

BT's home market, the United Kingdom, has been peeling back regulation over the past decade. In just the past few years, the United Kingdom has become an even more open communications market than the United States. BT now faces local phone competition as well as long-distance competition. Cable-TV companies can offer phone service over their networks, and they have been siphoning off up to 15,000 BT customers a month. Several of those cable companies are owned by U.S. firms such as US West, Comcast, and NYNEX.

BT stumbled when it first lost its monopoly status, but now it's following AT&T's playbook for getting competitive. It has cut more than 70,000 jobs in three years, paring down to about 170,000 employees—and it's still cutting. It has pumped its network full of fiber-optic and digital technology. It forged an alliance with MCI. It installed a young chairman, Iain Vallance, who is far different from past BT executives. He likes change and independent thinking, and he relaxes by heading up to Scotland for a bit of rock climbing. Under

Vallance, BT has begun thinking in terms of megamedia and the new markets that will emerge in the next decade.

"Competition is very healthy. It focuses the mind quite well," says Michael Hepher, the number-two executive at BT, inside the company's modern-looking headquarters in downtown London. He adds, though, that BT has work to do to get to the level of the U.S. companies. BT hopes the MCI link will help. "They're sort of a role model in some respects," Hepher says. "They are fleeter of foot than we." The close ties with MCI should give BT a window on the U.S. market, where new communications technology, strategy, and marketing tactics are usually born.

If BT can get competitive and responsive, it could be a formidable player. It is one of the top five in communications traffic worldwide. (AT&T is the leader.) It is the largest company in the United Kingdom and the twelfth-largest in the world. Its research labs are almost as revered as AT&T's Bell Labs. BT has plenty of resources to pump into megamedia and global markets.

First, though, it is concentrating on the United Kingdom, trying to stop the loss of market share at home, Hepher says. Besides competition from U.S.-backed cable companies, BT's only long-distance competitor, Mercury, is getting more aggressive and working with US West on a wireless phone venture. "We feel strongly that we've got to be a success in our home market first," Hepher says.

As BT reforms, its biggest handicap will be government regulations that limit businesses BT can get into. The regulations were set up to promote competition and make sure BT doesn't hold on to its monopoly. But they prevent BT from getting into some of the hottest advances in telecommunications, such as transmitting TV signals and interactive entertainment, for up to eight years. That's another reason the link with MCI is valuable. BT can work on megamedia in MCI's markets to get a head start.

Most importantly for BT, MCI represents BT's push into the U.S. market, the richest communications market in the world. "MCI gives us a presence there that we could never have gotten to organically. It would have taken the rest of our lives to get to that kind of presence," Hepher says.

Next, BT will aim at Europe, where protectionist telecommunications barriers are beginning to come down. "The French and the Germans are where we were a decade ago and they don't know what they've got facing them," Hepher says. BT plans to invade Europe, and will represent MCI's push on the Continent as well.

MCI and the move into Europe "are clearly not the last things we'll do," Hepher says. "We'll need to think more about the rest of the world—particularly Asia." All in all, BT certainly has a shot at becoming one of the great communications powers of the next decade.

Not so much can be said for any other national communications company. Anywhere else in the world, the behemoths are still state-owned, protected monopolies that are miles from being able to compete in the world market. Here are the companies that might be worth watching.

NTT of Japan

Its home country has one of the world's strongest and most technologically advanced economies. That should count for something. NTT is poking into the U.S. market with small investments. It put money into high-profile software start-up General Magic, for example. But the Japanese communications market remains highly protected, so NTT remains a bloated monopoly that won't be allowed into other nations' markets until Japan opens its own doors to foreign competitors. Some observers expect NTT to form an alliance with Sprint and Sprint's new European partners, France Telecom and Deutsche Telekom, which might give NTT a jump-start. In its home market, NTT is in the middle of a two-year project to explore interactive TV and other megamedia services. It signed up a U.S. firm, Silicon Graphics Inc., to help, but NTT is far behind companies such as Bell Atlantic or AT&T.

France Telecom and Deutsche Telekom

The two companies, now aligned in Europe, will buy 20 percent of Sprint if U.S. officials let the deal go through. But France and Germany don't plan to begin opening their voice communications markets until 1998. Alignment with Sprint may help, but neither company looks much like a global competitive player.

Deutsche Telekom is particularly bloated with people and burdened with high costs of doing business. One positive note: the company is learning high-tech cable TV in its home market. As Germany's only major cable operator, it has about 13.5 million customers—on a par with TCI. It is beginning to experiment with digital transmission of TV signals, and it plans to offer megamedia services in 1997.

Deutsche Telekom, which had 1993 revenue of $38 billion, will offer shares to the public for the first time in 1996—the biggest privatization in German history. Public ownership should force the company to get into better competitive shape.

France Telecom, like NTT, has been cautiously investing in U.S. megamedia start-ups, including General Magic. France Telecom has also tried some innovative services. Its Minitel, a cross between a phone and a computer, can send and receive text information and messages. A pioneering venture when it was introduced more than a decade ago, the service has turned into a big hit in France, with 6.5 million terminals in use and 23,000 on-line services available on the system. But it may not translate into a business elsewhere. US West worked with France Telecom to put in a version of Minitel in its region. In May 1994, when users had dwindled to fewer than 500, US West shut down the service.

What is the most likely scenario for the Japanese, French, and German phone companies? They'll have to suffer through years of painful downsizing and cultural change at home before becoming honed competitors who can make a mark on the global megamedia industry.

7

MAKING IT WORK

THE SOFTWARE INDUSTRY

LEADERS TO WATCH: BILL GATES, NATHAN MYHRVOLD, AND MICROSOFT

Nathan Myhrvold sits down in a conference room at *USA Today,* asks me for a Diet Coke, folds his hands on the table. He has a big beard, unruly hair, a suit that can't cope with the rolls around his body. His watch is thick, digital, and spiked with buttons. His hands are milky, small, fine. They look like they've never worked outdoors or grasped a baseball bat or guided a power tool.

But, hey, that's what a genius is supposed to look like.

Myhrvold, in his mid-30s, is Microsoft Corporation's big thinker. He is master of the company's push into megamedia. Yes, Bill Gates is Microsoft's chairman and five-star general—the grand strategist and sharklike competitor who keeps the giant company blasting ahead in the computer wars. But Myhrvold is the advanced technology guru—the person who will lead Microsoft beyond the boundaries of personal computers and into what sometimes sounds like science fiction. "Other than myself, Nathan has more impact on our long-term strategy than anyone else," Gates told *Scientific American* magazine. What's neat about Myhrvold is he just might have more raw brainpower in his skull than anybody in the computer industry.

Myhrvold graduated from high school at age 14. Before joining Microsoft, he worked with legendary cosmologist Stephen Hawking and wrote a doctoral thesis titled "Vistas in Curved Space Quantum Field Theory," which dealt with some of the more difficult problems confounding scientists in their search for the origins of the universe. He sits at the table, sipping his Diet Coke, and tosses out stray thoughts that go far beyond operating software, market share, or next quarter's earnings. He mentions that personal computers by 2000 will have 100-gigabyte hard disks, which is more than 1,000 times the storage in today's PCs and enough to save and replay 100 full-length movies. He says that the price-performance of communications will drop by a factor of 1 million in 20 years, which basically means that if, by then, there is a means of recording in virtual reality the experience of seeing and holding a newborn son, the event could be sent to a relative in Tokyo over high-speed fiber-optic lines for a couple of bucks. He notes, for no apparent reason, that computers will never do some things. They won't print out the gargantuan mathematical calculation 100! (pronounced "100 prime"), because that would take all the particles in the universe.

Myhrvold is known for writing 100-page memos describing his vision of the future. In 1990, he wrote a thick memo to Gates explaining why Microsoft needed to get into software for coming high-tech televisions and information highways. Gates agreed, and Myhrvold's future-driven Advanced Technology Group was born. It now employs more than 500 people and has an annual research and development budget of $150 million. Its success or failure will define whether Microsoft makes the leap from the PC age to the Communications Age.

Everybody knows about Gates and Microsoft. It is the most astonishing American business success story in history. Gates dropped out of school in 1975 to start creating one of the first operating systems for PCs. Five years later, IBM licensed Microsoft's MS-DOS operating system for its foray into PCs. Fifteen years after that, Microsoft is a dominant business empire unlike anything since John D. Rockefeller's Standard Oil days. It is the world's strongest marketer of operating software (programs such as MS-DOS and Windows, which tell computers how to work and juggle information) and applications software (such as word processing program Microsoft Word and database program Excel). About 90 percent of the world's IBM-compatible computers run on MS-DOS. Windows is installed on 80 percent. About half of all applications software sold is from Microsoft. Microsoft's ubiquity means that almost any piece of PC software from any company has to be compatible with Microsoft products—or else all those people running Windows or MS-DOS won't buy it. The entire PC software universe dances to Microsoft's beat.

Among other measures of its success, the company brings in almost $5 billion in annual revenue. It has 15,000 employees and spends $600 million a year on research and development. The total value of the company is greater than that of Ford or General Motors. Gates is the U.S.'s second-richest person. His net worth is more than $7 billion, most of it in Microsoft stock.

But the company's future could yet crumble away. Gates himself says so. The technological landscape is shifting. Microsoft's entire business is built on desktop computing—mostly office-type information work done on stationary or laptop PCs. The next age is taking computing in every which direction, making it part of TV sets, cars, phones, games, home appliances, and maybe even wallets. Computing and communicating are becoming forever intertwined. The stuff of computing and information is evolving from text and two-dimensional graphics into a world of multimedia information, sometimes delivered in three dimensions. Computer software is forever becoming obsolete because of advances in technology, but now the 20-year-old *concept* of computer operating and applications software might be heading out the window. It is no less than one era giving way to another. The whole computer software industry will struggle to make that leap. And for the leader—for Gates—nothing is more scary.

"No high-tech company has ever made the transition from one era to the next," Gates told *USA Today.* He cited IBM, which got lost in the change from mainframes to smaller machines. Digital Equipment, creator of the minicomputer segment, didn't negotiate the change to PCs. Gates is determined not to have the same thing happen to Microsoft. "Somewhere in there is a demarcation between the PC era and an information highway era. If we have an important position in that era like we did in the PC era, that would be a pretty phenomenal thing."

To veer from destiny, Microsoft has turned up the product-development throttle to full speed and handed the steering wheel to Myhrvold.

Although Myhrvold likes to pooh-pooh the hype and hysteria that have driven so many megamedia megamergers and wild product announcements, he clearly feels a need to move quickly. He almost casually says that, by 1997–1998, "millions" of people will be hooked to high-tech networks, using newfangled multimedia interactive devices and services. He said in 1994 that Microsoft's push into information highways was "three years to significant revenue; five years before *real* revenue." He said then of his Advanced Technology Group: "Hiring all these people now is risky, but we think it's the right thing to do."

He's a believer in much of the megamedia stuff that gets talked about—maybe more of a believer than most. He has no doubt that people will be calling up TV shows on demand. "Ten years out, people are going to laugh at the idea that you had to be home at 8 o'clock to watch 'The Simpsons.'" He talks about sending video postcards and carrying wallet-size computers and shopping via interactive TV. All were part of a multimedia presentation Gates gave, in 1994, at the giant Comdex computer show in Las Vegas. Myhrvold scoffs at people who look at today's megamedia technology or programming experiments and say they're terrible.

"The first TV shows were corny. The first PCs were amazingly primitive. But from those early beginnings were built industries of incredible strength and reach," he says.

Myhrvold is also a believer in today's personal computer hardware industry—the companies that make the computer chips and guts (such as Intel) and the companies that make the finished products (Compaq, Apple). Those companies may become a key to whether Microsoft does well in the next era or not.

Microsoft has always written software for devices made by PC companies. It knows its way around that kind of hardware and knows how to sell to people who buy that industry's products instead of the hardware associated with high-end computer makers such as Silicon Graphics or IBM's mainframe division. When Microsoft has ventured outside of the PC world, it has stumbled, as it did when creating high-end computer server software called Windows NT. Microsoft has to hope that Intel chips or Compaq-made boxes evolve into the smarts controlling the information superhighway—whether PCs, set-top TV boxes, handheld communicators, digital appliances that do everything from take phone messages to control the central air conditioner, or servers dishing out video on demand and on-line information for the local cable or phone company. If the PC industry makes that transition, Microsoft will be there. If other kinds of companies become megamedia's hardware makers, Microsoft is in deep doo-doo.

One of Myhrvold's first big ventures into megamedia is an attempt to win a place in interactive TV for PC-based devices running Microsoft software. The product, called Tiger, is a video server program designed to let a modified PC dish out movies on demand to hundreds of customers at the same time. Compaq and Intel are building the first hardware.

Until Tiger was unveiled in 1994, all other means to handle video on demand involved million-dollar supercomputers or modified mainframes. Video takes up huge amounts of memory and computer power—one film would eat up all the memory in a top-of-the-line desktop PC. Many people may want to call up the same movie a few minutes apart, and each may rewind, pause, or stop and then continue watching hours later. One way to handle all that traffic and billing is to overwhelm the problem with the sheer braun of supercomputers, such as those from a company called nCube.

Tiger takes a different approach. Store all the movies on laser disks or stand-alone hard-disk drives; then let a single powerful PC shuffle among them to grab small chunks of the movie a viewer has ordered. The PC sends the chunks down the line to a computerized box on top of the TV, which stores them and plays them on the screen. Every few seconds the host PC sends updated chunks. If the viewer pauses, the chunks stop coming until the restart signal comes in. In the meantime, the host PC keeps finding and sending chunks of movies to other viewers who have ordered them. The selector dances among files and customers in nanoseconds, all guided by Microsoft's program. Supercomputers, Myhrvold says, "are designed to let people create a single big problem. We're instead dividing it up into lots of separate problems. You don't need some crazy nCube machine."

No doubt Microsoft's approach is less expensive. The company figures that Tiger and its hardware would cost $200 to $300 per TV set served. Systems developed by Oracle, the software company whose CEO also owns nCube, would cost about $500 per TV. In all likelihood, Tiger and its hardware would get cheaper and more powerful at a faster pace than any other technology, simply because today's PC industry is geared to mass manufacturing and intense price-per-performance competition. Because the technology would be pretty much off-the-shelf, a cable operator could buy a starter set now, and add more pieces or upgrade the technology later. Cable-TV operators, who have generally felt the supercomputer solution would be far too costly, find Tiger seductive. At the cable industry's national trade show in 1994, for instance, Microsoft's Tiger display was the hottest exhibit—outside of Arnold Palmer signing autographs for The Golf Channel.

The big question for Tiger is: Can it scale up to handle big jobs? For now, one PC can serve only about 100 users. A rack of eight might handle a couple thousand. A 200,000-customer system would need a closet full of PCs. Tiger is based on Windows NT, and that software can be slow and clunky when running big systems. Some analysts believe Tiger will always be a "low end" interactive TV system, serving small cable operations or individual office buildings. Microsoft is shooting higher, though. It is just beginning to test Tiger with TCI in Denver and Seattle, with Rogers Cablesystems in Canada, and with Southwestern Bell in Richardson, Texas.

If Tiger works and TCI, Rogers, and Southwestern Bell use it for their megamedia roll-outs, Microsoft would get a huge boost in its effort to become as dominant in interactive TV as it now is in PCs. On the other hand, Oracle is working on Bell Atlantic's megamedia system, Silicon Graphics is doing Time Warner's Orlando project, and Hewlett-Packard is also in the game. If Tiger sputters, any of those competitors will be ready to rip past Microsoft in the video server market.

Myhrvold's group is working on far more than just Tiger. It wants Microsoft to be a part of the whole megamedia concept. So it is helping develop one of the many contenders for the home end of the information superhighway. Microsoft, Intel, and cable TV equipment maker General Instrument are building a digital set-top box for interactive TV, also likely to be tested by TCI. Many other companies, including IBM, Hewlett-Packard, and Scientific-Atlanta, are building similar boxes.

As an aside, Myhrvold isn't so sure a separate box will run the TV. In the future, a single PC could be powerful enough to run all megamedia functions within a home. The cable or phone line would come into the PC sitting in the den, and another line could run out of the PC to TV sets or display devices elsewhere in the house. That master PC would, presumably, run on Microsoft software.

Microsoft has also worked on an interactive TV operating environment—software that could manage content for TV the way Windows manages software for PCs. Myhrvold demonstrated an early version in 1994. If anything, it showed that Microsoft doesn't have any particular advantage in that field. The system had a cartoonish interface and featured most of the usual suspects: home shopping, extra information and statistics that could be called up during a baseball game, movies on demand. One playful addition on the test system was a fishing guide, which Myhrvold jokingly dubbed "trout on demand."

Other than Tiger, most of Myhrvold's megamedia work remains secret. One of Gates's pet ideas is the wallet PC, which would hold electronic money, digital plane tickets, photos, addresses—everything people now carry, but in computer form. Myhrvold hasn't said whether he's actually working on such a device. He does promise this, though, about Microsoft's efforts: "It's not just video on demand. If it were, Microsoft would not be interested."

On a very different front, Microsoft is also broadening its aim at megamedia by getting deep into content, a fairly new area for the company. So far, the effort looks promising.

Patty Stonesifer is head of the new Consumer Division. Her main mission for now is to create a humming CD-ROM publishing business. It started with *Encarta,* Microsoft's multimedia encyclopedia, which has sold an amazing 300,000 copies. Other successful titles include *Multimedia Beethovan, Musical Instruments,* and, more recently, *Microsoft Baseball,* a multimedia baseball almanac. The company is intent on creating a multimedia publishing empire. "We have 500 people working on these products, teaming with all different specialists," Stonesifer says. She is trying to squeeze the time it takes to create a high-quality CD-ROM. *Encarta* took five years. Most today take nine months. She's pushing for six months. Costs are dropping and profit margins are soaring.

The CD-ROMs are only a beginning. They form a cornerstone of a whole information-provider strategy. *Baseball* is the first example. The CD-ROM contains biographies and statistics on every major-league baseball player ever. But some players are traded, others are called up from the minor leagues, and stats change all season long. Along with the CD-ROM, Microsoft will start an on-line computer service called Baseball Daily. Customers could tap in for $1.50 a day and get up-to-the-minute baseball data to complement and integrate with the information in *Baseball.* The service may eventually include computer forums, games, or other features. "Now, we don't update averages on the CD-ROM," Stonesifer says. "But that's where we'll head. This is where information and the power of computers and the information highway all come together."

Microsoft will do more of the same. For example, Stonesifer hinted at a CD-ROM and on-line service dedicated to the Middle East. Another twist: Microsoft and TCI are jointly creating a PC television channel, which would include home shopping for PCs and software and how-to segments about using a computer. A new mass-market on-line service, The Microsoft Network, could conceivably tie into the channel, adding forums and a way to send messages to hosts on the TV shows.

All of the plans described in this chapter are peripheral to Microsoft's real business. It sells personal computer software. No company is better at it. Microsoft may or may not always have the very best technical product, but it certainly has high-quality software—and no one beats it at global marketing and outmaneuvering competitors. Desktop PCs are not going to go away in the foreseeable future. That market will be there for Microsoft. And Microsoft seems set to hold onto its dominance in that part of the business, thanks in no small part to its latest version of Windows, called Windows 95.

Yet desktop PCs as we know them today are going to become only one part of computing—a niche, albeit a very large niche. The question for Microsoft is whether it can reach beyond its niche. Can it win customers who don't know Windows from a hole in the wall? Can it compete against companies it never battled before? Can it make its magic work for machines that don't necessarily have a keyboard, mouse, and monitor?

All Microsoft's plans—from Tiger to wallet PCs to the Microsoft Network—are part of the drive to take Microsoft to the next level: the mass consumer market. Microsoft has already taken serious steps to get there. In the fall of 1994, it launched a $100 million ad campaign, it's first aimed at everyone, not just computer users. The goal is to make Microsoft a brand name as recognizable as Nike or Sony. In November, Gates hired Robert Herbold, from consumer product powerhouse Procter & Gamble, to be executive vice president and chief operating officer. Robert Herbold, Bill Gates, Steven Ballmer, and Mike Maples make up Microsoft's "office of the president," which guides the company. Herbold had run P&G's computer departments and also created marketing strategies for P&G brands. "My primary job will be to help sort out the strategic plan," Herbold says. "It's more important than ever that the [software] business rely on consumer marketing."

The Microsoft Network will help the company chase consumers. Scheduled for introduction in 1995, it is supposed to compete against America Online and the other broad services. Microsoft also bought Intuit, the maker of hot personal finance software Quicken, in a move to get into home banking. Again, that could become a service that appeals to a broad consumer base.

The transition to the new era won't be easy. The job of making it happen falls to Gates.

Gates is no accident. He is rich and successful because he is so good. He's the Wayne Gretzky of business, standing above all others in his field. At this writing, Gates is 38 years old. According to Jeffrey Sonnenfeld at Emory University's Center for Leadership and Career Studies, Gates is the youngest person ever to reach his level of wealth, power, and status in American business—ahead of Rockefeller, Henry Ford, and Andrew Carnegie. One implication is that Gates could be around and running Microsoft for a long, long time. In 25 years, he won't even reach most companies' retirement age.

Gates says that his skill is understanding both technology and business. He started making money at computer programming when he was in eighth grade. He reads about biotech discoveries for pleasure. He claims he finds business boring because it's too simple.

Business is clearly his strong suit. He can grasp the most complex technological concepts, but he has never been a great technologist. In 1980, under pressure to develop the operating system for IBM's PCs, Gates and partner Paul Allen didn't whip up the legendary MS-DOS program. They bought an existing operating system called QDOS from a Seattle programmer for $50,000, tinkered with it, and renamed it MS-DOS. That illustrates Gates's abilities. At 24, he recognized the software that would work, bought it cheaply, then used it to launch his empire. And at that young age, he negotiated with the old pros at IBM to get a deal that let Microsoft license MS-DOS to other companies. When all the IBM clone PCs popped up, Microsoft licensed MS-DOS to run on them. That made Microsoft an integral part of almost every computer on the market, and formed the foundation for the company's dominance. That kind of business sense infuses everything Gates does today. It will be needed as Microsoft moves into megamedia.

Gates is a battler. He's tough. As a founder and owner of 30 percent of his company's stock, he is devoted to Microsoft. He'll never let it fall behind without a hard, hard fight.

He's also a celebrity, and that has already helped draw megamedia's leaders to him in search of possible partnerships and ventures. He has met often with TCI's John Malone, and says they have a lot in common. He has an ongoing relationship with Michael Ovitz, the top Hollywood agent, who might steer creative talent to Microsoft as computing and entertainment converge. He knows Rupert Murdoch, Barry Diller, and Gerald Levin. Late in 1994, Microsoft announced it added 10 partners to its interactive TV work. They include US West, Deutsche Telekom, and NTT. The only problem here is that Gates has had trouble forming broad alliances with anyone. Gates always wants too much control. Potential partners fear his ambitions. No one wants to be the next IBM, essentially a pack mule carrying Microsoft to the top of the mountain. That could limit Microsoft's reach in early stages of megamedia.

Overall, Gates knows that Microsoft must make the transition to the next age. Gates will pursue that transition relentlessly. Yet, all the while, a small voice seems to be reminding him that the whole era is changing and that companies in Microsoft's position have had a bleak history. "IBM is one to remember all the time," Gates told *USA Today*. "A lot of smart people work there. It's a fine company that lost its way."

Gates knows the facts: Microsoft is a powerful and seemingly invincible player today, but it might not be tomorrow. In megamedia, Microsoft's success is not assured.

SILICON GRAPHICS: YOU HAVE TO SEE IT TO BELIEVE IT

The outside of the headquarters of Silicon Graphics Inc., in Mountain View, California, is a low-rise building in a nondescript corporate park. Inside, it's one funky place. The decor is industrial high-tech, with exposed steel beams and holograms on the walls.

Up a staircase is the company's demonstration area. It has eight tables, each holding a different Silicon Graphics computer loaded up with the company's software. Some group from somewhere in the world is always there, getting a taste of what the company's systems can do. What they see usually flies beyond what they'd ever imagined. The images on the computer screens are amazing and inspiring. Of all the places and companies I've visited to learn about megamedia, this is the one stop that made me simply say: "Wow."

Silicon Graphics makes the hardware and software for "visual processing workstations"—a fancy name for superfast desktop computers that can create 3-D, realistic, full-motion images. The demo area offers a glimpse. Call up a program storing 200 years of U.S. per-capita income figures by state. On the Silicon Graphics machine, a 3-D map of the United States pops up. A state's per-capita income is represented by how tall or short that state is on the map. Toggle through all 200 years (it will take only 10 or 15 seconds). The states rise and fall, showing changes in their stature compared to other states, in a fluid motion. The information is as clear and easy to watch as an animated cartoon. Zero in on when California's rise to riches began. Or look for the poorest state during the Civil War. Imagine searching for the same data in tables of numbers, and trying to spot trends.

Try some other demo programs. One is a multimedia Boeing manual for repairing jets, including text and 3-D graphics showing parts and how they fit together. Another shows an image of a martini glass. It is photographic quality. Reflected in the glass is a bar scene, as if you are looking at the glass and the bar is behind and around you. Rotate the glass or spin it around with a toggle switch. The reflection in the glass changes just as it would in real life! It is the closest thing to "virtual reality" that I've ever seen.

Words can't adequately describe all that can be seen at Silicon Graphics. Visitors come away thinking that computers will be able to do a lot more a lot sooner than most people realize.

That might be moderately interesting if the machines were running through carefully constructed calisthenics that only the computer elite could ever set up and run—or afford. But Silicon Graphics has bigger ambitions. It is driving to put this kind of power on top of everybody's TV set for a few hundred bucks.

This relatively small company could pull it off and jet past huge rivals such as Microsoft and Oracle in the megamedia race.

Silicon Graphics began when Jim Clark left his job as a professor at Stanford University to start the company in 1982. His goal was to make 3-D computer workstations for engineers, car designers, and scientists who, for instance, might want to assemble and manipulate molecular structures on a computer screen. The company made both the computers and the software that made the machines special. For years, the market was tiny for such high-end workstations and the company was even tinier. In 1987, the market took off and Silicon Graphics started to do well in its high-tech niche. It eventually bought MIPS, the company that makes the chips for Silicon Graphics machines. The purchase turned Silicon Graphics into a rounded builder of chips, computers, and the operating and applications software that makes those computers work.

The company's big break came with the release of the movie *Jurassic Park* in 1993. A few years before, Hollywood special-effects gurus had found that Silicon Graphics hardware and software could produce fantastic, lifelike computer images. The machines had created the water creature in *The Abyss* and the morphing evil robot in *Terminator 2.* But it took the *Jurassic Park* dinosaurs to catch the public's full attention.

The company's revenue had been growing around 60 percent a year. It reached $1.5 billion in 1994, almost all on sales to engineering and scientific users. But Silicon Graphics was quickly making a name for itself in entertainment.

Since then, entertainment has been the company's most visible new direction. And it may be onto something. Silicon Graphics' systems move computing from stiff, keyboard-enslaved, two-dimensional functionality to fluid 3-D that almost makes a computer come alive. It's apropos that Silicon Graphics systems have been used by Hollywood to create beings. The systems have a way of giving technology character. As computing spreads into everyone's everyday life—entertainment, communications, personal business—a little character might make the technology more palatable, acceptable, and friendly. Silicon Graphics wants to start by putting character into TV set-top boxes and megamedia networks. The company thinks that's the key to its future.

"If this works out, the set-top box will become the true consumer computer, the CC," says founder Clark. He argues that it will take a new entrant to create such an era-defining product. "It would be as difficult for Microsoft to make a personal computer into a consumer computer as it was for Digital Equipment to make a minicomputer into a PC. The personal computer has created a whole lot of baggage that it would have to pull behind it," Clark says. "They can't make the leap. There's a new opportunity to step in."

Clark left Silicon Graphics in 1994 to start a business based on the popular Mosaic software, which helps users navigate the Internet. Ed McCracken, current chairman of Silicon Graphics, agrees with Clark's assessment of the company's opportunities. "PCs are old and obsolete," McCracken says. "Our computers are more real and lifelike. They're fundamentally different from PCs and other computers."

People will find it easier to get information from and interact with the information superhighway if they can do it visually and in a more lifelike way, McCracken insists. Someday, maybe a 3-D dinosaur with a sense of humor will appear on a computer or TV, understand spoken commands, and help you to find old tax records or a particular movie. Silicon Graphics is talking about a leap similar to computers' going from a medium of obscure codes to the graphical interfaces on today's Windows programs or Macintosh computers, which opened computing to millions more users. The next leap could open computing to tens of millions more.

The company has started its trek into entertainment and consumer computing with some of the best partners available.

Time Warner

Silicon Graphics is the primary technology company for Time Warner's Full Service Network in Orlando, Florida. A modified version of Silicon Graphics' low-end Indy computer will be the TV set-top box for about 4,000 Orlando test customers. Top-of-the-line Silicon Graphics computers will be at the other end of the network, acting as the servers that dish out interactive video, games, movies, and information services. Most importantly, Silicon Graphics is writing the software that makes the whole network run and gives it a rich, 3-D look and feel.

The Orlando test is high-profile and high-stakes for Silicon Graphics. "I think it's the world's most advanced project in this area," McCracken says. Every other entity considering moving into interactive TV is watching Orlando. If Silicon Graphics creates a whiz-bang system that consumers love, bet on orders flowing in from around the world.

If the company can't iron out bugs or lower costs to consumer levels, potential customers might turn to Microsoft or Oracle. Silicon Graphics had postponed the start of the test for almost a year, to smooth the technology. "We have to make it right," McCracken said soon after announcing the delay. "We're trying to make a very sophisticated digital network seem to the viewer like it's a nice little smart television." The company can't afford to make any more apologies out of Orlando.

Nintendo

In August 1993, leading video game maker Nintendo signed Silicon Graphics to help develop Nintendo's 64-bit "Project Reality" system—its next-generation video game box, which promises 3-D, full-motion, photographic-quality images. The system has already appeared in arcade games and will be marketed to the home in 1995 under the name Ultra 64. The home machine is expected to cost around $250.

The Nintendo alliance has gotten less attention than the Time Warner project, but it may be nearly as important for Silicon Graphics. Nintendo should introduce Silicon Graphics technology into millions of homes and put it in touch with a broad consumer base. The expanded audience should help Silicon Graphics, which has always been a specialty-market and high-priced business, learn how to do high volume at a low price. As founder Clark points out, Nintendo machines should end up being compatible with Silicon Graphics' computers. The possibilities for linking the two, or selling computers to developers, or allowing Silicon Graphics to develop software for Nintendo machines would be "a tremendous advantage," Clark says.

AT&T

AT&T signed Silicon Graphics, in June 1994, to add computers and software to AT&T's technology in order to boost AT&T's ability to build interactive TV systems—for itself or for other companies. AT&T is great at building broadband, digital transmission networks, but lacks the servers and graphic capabilities that Silicon Graphics can supply.

The alliance could turn into a way for Silicon Graphics to spread its technology across the high end of megamedia—a nice complement to Nintendo on the low end. AT&T is the biggest builder of megamedia networks. It has won multibillion-dollar projects from Bell Atlantic, Pacific Telesis, and the government of Saudi Arabia, among others. Now that it has Silicon Graphics on board, AT&T hopes to win even more interactive TV projects from cable and phone companies.

Other Contracts

Electronic Data Systems, the biggest computer services company, has signed Silicon Graphics to develop systems that would handle computer databases in a 3-D, friendlier, easier way. NTT, Japan's telephone monopoly, has brought in Silicon Graphics as it builds its first interactive TV system. Moviemaker George Lucas's company, Lucasfilm, hired Silicon Graphics to help build a digital production facility called the Joint Environment for Digital Imaging, or JEDI, a reference to the Jedi knights in Lucas's *Star Wars* films.

Silicon Graphics' own core workstation products continue to do well. The company is number-one in its niche and still taking market share from Sun Microsystems and Digital Equipment, its main competitors. The company's grand megamedia push at this point relies on success with its partners. Silicon Graphics' goal is to use those successes to turn Silicon Graphics into a brand name in megamedia,

McCracken says. He clearly is thinking of a brand as strong and widely known as Microsoft.

A few obstacles stand between Silicon Graphics and that vision.

The first is price. Silicon Graphics' machines cost customers a lot. The low-end Indy and its software—Time Warner's set-top box—costs about $2,000. The cost of the whole Silicon Graphics-run system in Orlando is $6,000 to $7,000 a subscriber, a company official says. That's an impossible amount of money for a TV-based consumer product.

McCracken is unfazed. "If you're not putting in something that's expensive today, it's not worth your time," he says. "It's important with these experimental projects to really stretch." Then he points to Nintendo, where Silicon Graphics is learning to fit its software and technology into a $250 box. Still, the company has a big cost and margin chasm to jump. It won't be easy.

The second problem will be managing growth. McCracken says the company is hiring more than 100 people a month. The company's management style is barely controlled chaos anyway. "One thing we're trying to build is a culture that loves change and eats it up," McCracken says. "If you mind having your desk moved three times in a year, you don't belong here." He also says, "My management philosophy is to let our people run. Our people are not good at being controlled." That style has certainly worked well for Silicon Graphics so far. But as the company's personnel list and number of businesses and projects explode, might the chaos get out of hand? Keeping control on everything from finances to product quality will be one of McCracken's biggest challenges.

Silicon Graphics, like many megamedia companies, is entering brand new worlds. It will be trying to sell to customers it has never known anything about. It will compete against companies that were never before on its radar screen. That creates a dangerous time for any company.

Yet the one thing that can't be ignored is Silicon Graphics' technology, especially the way it takes computers to a new level of—well, *likability*. If McCracken can deal with the issues of price and control and keep his company on track, Silicon Graphics may indeed turn out to be the next Microsoft—or like Apple, in its heyday.

Jim Clark is proud of his baby. He says, "Now the world is beating a path to their door."

ORACLE: SMART, LUCKY, OR BOTH?

Larry Ellison, chairman and founder of Redwood Shores, California-based Oracle Corporation, has been deadpanning a favorite phrase lately: "Better to be lucky than smart."

The information superhighway has practically rolled out like a red carpet at Oracle's feet. By happenstance, the company's software, originally created to run gigantic corporate databases on high-end computers, seems to be ready-made to function as operating software for multimedia information superhighway servers. Just tweak the programming a little, make it work on a couple of different kinds of machines, and *zoom!*—Oracle's at the front of the mega-media pack. Right place, right time. Ellison has moved quickly to take advantage of his good fortune by retooling the entire company to aim at multimedia and lining up an impressive list of partners ranging from Bell Atlantic to Capital Cities/ABC.

For the moment, Oracle looks both lucky *and* smart, although that image could change.

Oracle is not what anyone would call a household name. It's one of those companies that has long operated in the bowels of industry, making products that are absolutely essential to everyday life, yet never selling to consumers, never advertising, never becoming well known. Oracle is the third-largest software company in the world. It built its business on relational database management systems, which store truckloads of information and allow users to access it, sort it, and rearrange it in just about any way imaginable. If a company stored its personnel records on an Oracle-run computer, a personnel director could ask the software to list all employees who make more than $100,000, drive a company car, and received unfavorable performance reviews in the past year. Oracle-run systems are used to operate banks, governments, factories, and airlines.

Ellison, Robert Miner, and Edward Oates founded the company in 1977. Ellison had helped Amdahl build the first IBM-compatible mainframe. He had read that IBM was working on a relational database product, and he thought it sounded like a great idea. He and his cofounders launched Oracle specifically to beat IBM to the market with that kind of software. They did. The company also decided to create a product that could run on all brands and sizes of computers—an unusual strategy at the time. The software was a hit. From 1986 to 1989, Oracle grew an average of 82 percent a year.

The astonishing growth fostered a cocky, hard-driving, damn-the-torpedoes culture. That almost brought down the company in 1990–1991, when the rush to keep up the pace of growth led to product-development blunders and financial fiascos. The stock price dove to one-seventh its all-time high, and Oracle cut workers and regrouped. In 1992, the company launched a new product called Oracle 7, which not only made its databases easier to access, but also connected them to networks, allowing a central computer to dish out information to other computers anywhere. That turned out to be one key of Oracle's future.

The other key dates back to the late 1980s. Ellison got interested in a company called nCube, which makes massively parallel supercomputers. The computers wire together hundreds or thousands of microprocessors (tiny computers themselves) such as Intel Pentiums. Give an nCube machine a big, tough problem, and it divides it up into many little problems that all the microprocessors work on at the same time. Traditional mainframes or supercomputers have one big memory and one big processor, and they tend to work on a problem linearly—from beginning to end. By dividing up problems, nCubes can often perform a task much faster than any other kind of computer.

Ellison forced Oracle to write all its software so it would work on nCube and other massively parallel machines, even though the task would be extremely difficult. Ellison got even more deeply involved in 1989, when he privately bought a controlling interest in nCube, which is based in Foster City, California.

As the story goes, Oracle was pretty much oblivious to multimedia technology, interactive television, and similar developments until early 1993, when Bell Atlantic and British Telecom started looking seriously at building megamedia networks. No software existed that could operate a multimedia server feeding video and data into thousands of homes at once, so each company started looking for likely developers. One stop was Oracle.

"Some of the folks here said, 'We could solve this problem without a whole lot of additional effort,'" says Jerry Held, now Oracle's senior vice president for multimedia products, a position that did not exist at that time. "So we responded to the proposals."

Oracle 7 was database software created to serve thousands of users on networks. Interactive TV systems would essentially be huge databases—they just had to handle information in video form as well as text and graphics. Video takes a lot of speed and power to process, but by putting Oracle's software on something as powerful as an nCube machine, users could start to get a solution—here and now, not sometime at the end of the decade. BT and Bell Atlantic bit. Ellison treated it as a revelation. He swung the whole company around to address multimedia, set about repositioning Oracle as the number-one software builder on the information superhighway, and even renamed Oracle's main product the Oracle Media Server.

"We don't want to be known as the leading relational database company," executive Held says. "We want to be the leading provider of systems managing all kinds of information, whether it's text, documents, audio, or video."

By 1994, Oracle appeared to be at every signpost on the information superhighway. Besides BT and Bell Atlantic, it had announced deals to create software for network builders such as BellSouth, US West, and Pacific Telesis. It also signed to make its software work on servers from Hewlett-Packard; TV set-top boxes from General Instrument, Scientific-Atlanta, and Apple; game units from Sega and 3DO; and portable devices from Motorola. It began working with content providers building links to information highways, including Capital Cities/ABC and *The Washington Post.*

According to Held, here is Oracle's pitch to potential customers.

First, Oracle is a proven operator of large systems. That's been the company's forte for years. Not only do Oracle-run computers shuffle, search out, and deliver information to many users on a network, the software keeps track of transactions for billing and other information. Neither Silicon Graphics nor Microsoft, for example, has a history of providing software that handles all those functions. Oracle products, the company says, can be trusted. Businesses have so far bought that argument.

Oracle has no proven record for video transactions. The company, for instance, is only now testing software that can reliably serve 10,000 customers at once, far below what's needed to serve a major metropolitan area. But Oracle says it can increase the number of simultaneous customers served by two to three times a year and not jeopardize reliability.

Oracle's software is meant to run on big-muscle computer systems that can be "scaled up"—putting in more processing power and memory—as demand for megamedia services increases. The software runs on nCube and Hewlett-Packard machines, with more to come. Oracle likes to slam Microsoft on this point. Held says Microsoft's Tiger is "PCs slapped together with duct tape trying to run a metropolitan network. It won't work."

One last part of the pitch is that Oracle is "open systems" software. The company is trying to make its software communicate with any network or any computer that might someday plug into the information superhighway. That's tantalizing to companies making big investments years in advance, such as Bell Atlantic. "If you choose a set-top box that doesn't work out, you can change. You're not stuck with the hardware," Held says. "We give you the leverage Oracle has traditionally done by making software that can run on different computer systems. It's something of an insurance policy." By comparison, Silicon Graphics' software is meant only for its machines; Microsoft's will work only on Intel-based personal computers.

Add up all that, and Oracle's big chance is in big systems. It figures it may lose smaller megamedia networks, such as local cable-TV systems or internal corporate multimedia networks, to Tiger or Silicon Graphics or a host of other contenders that might enter the field. But nobody else has the big-systems software, the experience, and the flexibility to handle, say, Bell Atlantic's system serving all of Philadelphia.

Not surprisingly, one other little piece of Oracle's strategy is to try to make the information superhighway happen as quickly as possible. Oracle, thanks to its good luck, has a lead. Potentially powerful competitors are getting off the ground, ready to move toward Oracle's part of the business. If Oracle can hustle megamedia along, more companies will feel the need to jump into it. They'll look around for software that can support their efforts, and they'll see that Oracle has a good, proven product that seems to be ahead of the others. Customers won now might tend to stay with Oracle even as new software comes to market. Today's lead would get leveraged into tomorrow's strong market position.

On the other hand, if megamedia dawdles, potential Oracle customers will be able to wait to commit to a software supplier. Competitors will have time to close Oracle's lead. Oracle would find it harder to nail down a dominant position.

"Our bet is it happens faster," says Held. "We're doing everything we can to make it happen. Others are focusing on later and out at the turn of the century." The beauty of that part of Oracle's strategy is it doesn't have to sound self-serving. The company pitches it as a benefit to society.

Yet the "sooner, faster" strategy also points up Oracle's weakness. It's likely that megamedia won't develop fast enough to cement Oracle's lead. It's very early in the game to say that Oracle's many partnerships translate into guaranteed later business; much of what Oracle is doing now with partners is development and testing.

Competitors might, in some ways, catch up with Oracle within a year or two, and they may offer some compelling advantages. Silicon Graphics' software may make digital systems more friendly to average users than ever before. Oracle makes no such leap. Microsoft's PC-based software could offer cost advantages. PC power is almost always cheaper than equal amounts of power on big computers. Can strung-together PCs handle a big megamedia network? Maybe not today, but the power of PCs is increasing exponentially. By the late 1990s, a desktop PC will have the power of one of today's supercomputers. It's certainly conceivable that such PCs, driven by Microsoft programming, could eventually serve a metro area. Even Held tips his hat in Microsoft's direction. "They're not a real player yet," he says. "But they will be."

Where might Oracle realistically be in five years? If it can continue to be both lucky and smart, its software could wind up being something of the MS-DOS of the information highway—an unglamorous but huge business of providing the software that makes a lot of megamedia go 'round. But luck is luck, and it may not hold. In that case, Oracle's smarts will likely make it the leading software company for the really big networks. Held compares that future market to today's market for high-tech telephone switching gear: only a few companies worldwide (AT&T, Northern Telecom, Alcatel, Fujitsu) make them, and only several dozen companies worldwide (major telephone companies) want to or can afford to buy them. "It's big but it's not that many deals," Held says. In any case, Oracle should play an important role in megamedia for the rest of the decade.

By the way, Oracle's other business isn't going away. It still writes software for big corporate databases, and the megamedia push may increase those orders. Oracle is making all its software capable of handling multimedia information, so as companies add things like video to, say, personnel records, Oracle's software will be ready. Plus, that will make corporate computers ready to plug into the information superhighway, perhaps giving companies new ways to use or sell multimedia database information over digital networks. In a roundabout way, the information superhighway—and Oracle's role in making it happen as quickly as possible—will come back to boost the company's basic business. A very nifty strategy.

Really, it's better to be smart than lucky.

GENERAL MAGIC: ON A CLEAR DAY YOU CAN SEE THE FUTURE

The atmosphere at software developer General Magic is like no place else. The offices look like a day-care center for child prodigies. Otherwise sterile gray cubicles are stacked with computers and cluttered with toys, a good number of them derived from the Disney movie *Aladdin.* An old Rock 'em Sock 'em Robots game sits on one desk, a train made of Lego blocks is on another, and in the middle of one group of cubicles stands a full-size foosball table. One programmer has built a bunk bed over his desk so he can stay all night. Community futons are piled in hallways in case anyone else wants to sleep over. Rooms have labels such as "Yoda" and "Willy Wonka Chocolate Factory." The chief executive is a Zen strategic thinker and his top designer is a bubbly middle-age kid. Where company-bought boxes of donuts might sit out in other offices, General Magic has heaping plates of fresh fruit. Out in the parking lot, the car of choice seems to be the Mazda Miata.

Maybe the shoe fits. What General Magic is doing is like nothing else. It's creating one software product that would run next-generation mobile computer-communicator devices, and another program that would make the breadth of megamedia networks more accessible to everyone. The challenge is that General Magic is looking so far ahead; neither the devices nor the networks needed to make full use of its software yet exist.

On the basis of total apparent flakiness, it's tempting to dismiss General Magic. Then again, a lot of important corporations seem to believe in General Magic and its products. The software company has put together the most impressive list of financial and strategic backers in all of megamedia. The list includes AT&T, NTT, Motorola, Sony, France Telecom, Philips, Matsushita, Toshiba, and Fujitsu. The company, originally part of Apple, was spun out in 1990. Motorola, Sony, and AT&T have already introduced early versions of products designed to start taking advantage of General Magic's software.

The backers are all betting that General Magic has come up with software that can rev computing and communicating to a new level, integrating it seamlessly with our everyday lives. The software has personality. It's one of the best attempts yet at making high-tech devices and information highways as easy and nonthreatening as the telephone and a copy of the Yellow Pages.

"People are very fuzzy and analog and emotional and irrational," says Marc Porat, General Magic's chief executive, who always speaks as if he's trying to put listeners into a state of hypnosis. "Digital technology is very hard-edged. When digital technology touches people, it cuts them like a knife. The best way to make a buffer is to make something that's emotionally appealing." That's the philosophy behind General Magic's software.

General Magic is really almost two companies sewn together. Its two main products share the same underlying purpose, yet they were developed by different teams with different cultures for different markets. Take a look at those products.

Magic Cap

Andy Hertzfeld, General Magic's top designer, has the official title of Software Wizard. Back in the 1980s, while working for Apple, Hertzfeld was a key creator of the Macintosh user interface, which took a giant step toward breaking down barriers between humans and computers by turning commands into cute icons, adding a mouse to use as a pointer, and generally making PCs simpler and more fun. Now, Hertzfeld has guided what he hopes is an equally impressive next step—a user interface called Magic Cap.

Magic Cap makes computer commands more obvious than anything that has come before. It pretty much eliminates manuals and lengthy learning curves. Say you want to do business-type functions. Magic Cap starts you off in a cartoonish office hallway. By guiding arrows, you "walk" down the hallway past doors marked "library" or "game room" or "desk." Stop when you get to the desk door, and tap the door. Up pops an image of a desktop, as if you were sitting in the desk chair. On the desk, for example, is an image of a Rolodex. Tap it to get into your address book. Tap the image of a paper and pen to write a letter or document. The desk has a calendar book, filing cabinet, "in" mail box, "out" mail box, and so on. All do exactly what you'd think they'd do.

Magic Cap is designed for the megamedia era, when computers will tap into all kinds of networks. A Magic Cap user taps arrows to go out of the hallway and onto the street—something of an information superhighway metaphor. The buildings on the street represent other places to visit on networks: stores for home shopping; news stands for information; a school for educational networks; a travel agency to book flights and plan trips. At each stop, more sets of images and instructions guide users onto and through networks or other functions.

At every level, Magic Cap tries its best to be endearing with funny sounds or images, or deft touches such as a cat that walks across the desk once in a while. "We went overboard making it fun or cute," Porat says. Some critics say the program is so cute that people won't take it seriously and business users won't buy it. Porat disagrees. "We used to be a little sensitive about that, but we're confident we have the right product."

Magic Cap was created for personal digital assistants (PDAs), those mobile computer-communicators that haven't quite caught on yet. Sony and Motorola have both made PDAs that are now using Magic Cap. But General Magic sees a wider market these days. Magic Cap is so easy to use—and does such a good job meshing computing, communicating, and entertainment functions—that it may turn out to be a good operating system for personal computers and TV set-top boxes. General Magic is aiming at those markets, too. Competition will be intense, but the company at this point has a decent shot, especially if its many backers help out.

Telescript

No one has developed anything similar to Telescript. It's one of those products that will either disappear without a trace, like quadraphonic sound, or become part of everyday life, like the Walkman. This is the product that stands a chance of making General Magic into a big, *big* company.

Telescript is communications software with a twist: it creates something called an agent—a personal little software helper. Say you call up the agent on your computer (or PDA or set-top box) and tell it that you want it to buy two round-trip plane tickets to Portland, Maine, on a certain date, plus get a compact rental car and a downtown hotel room. You connect to a travel network, send the agent into it, and immediately disconnect. You don't have to look through airline schedules, hotel listings, and so on. The agent does it for you, inside the travel network's computer. When the agent finds what you asked for, it dials you up, comes back to your computer, and shows you the choices it has found. You check off what you want, give the agent your credit card number, authorize it to make the purchases, then send it back into the network.

Telescript is like having someone to run errands for you, but over electronic networks. Or like having a research assistant at work, or a personal concierge. "The idea is to create an electronic marketplace," Porat says. The general concept of agents has powerful proponents, including Barry Diller of QVC and Scott Case of America Online.

There are a couple of problems. To be truly useful, Telescript would have to be embedded in all networks and all computers. An agent could then travel anywhere to get information, go shopping, deliver messages, schedule meetings with people, and so on. The program was written to be "the lingua franca that could live in all devices," Porat says. That would take a lot of commitments from a lot of companies. AT&T has started the process by putting Telescript on a network called PersonaLink. A handful of other companies are following, but that leaves a long way to go.

The other problem is security, especially when users give these agents their credit card numbers. Network owners will have to feel confident that misprogrammed agents won't become little troublemakers that run amok making purchases or damaging files.

The upside is that, if agents turn out to be a sexy concept that catches on, Telescript has little competition. Imagine the revenue from selling Telescript to every computer user and every network operator.

For the foreseeable future, General Magic will concentrate on improving and marketing Magic Cap and Telescript. At this point, the programs are really only seeds of a business, but a lot of companies and industry analysts believe little 120-employee General Magic will prosper. Part of that belief has to do with the appeal of Magic Cap and the powerful idea behind Telescript. Another part has to do with General Magic's personnel.

Porat, Hertzfeld, and another ex-Apple star, Bill Atkinson (now General Magic's chief scientist), have lured some of the industry's most creative programmers. General Magic has become an "in" place to work, a tightly knit club for the software elite. It offers the thrill of working with software legends like Hertzfeld, the freedom of working for a small company, and the exposure of working for an alliance that includes many of the biggest technology companies in the world.

Like any start-up, General Magic is a high-risk venture. In a million ways, it could sink between now and the end of the decade. But it also has a lot going for it: heavyweight backing, two of the most interesting software products in the business, and a gaggle of supertalented software whizzes. The company is certain that megamedia will develop and change peoples' lives, and it believes General Magic can be in the middle of those dramatic developments.

"That's the plan," Porat says. "Well, unless we get crushed."

ET CETERA

There must be a thousand operating and applications software companies out there that could, potentially, with a little luck or a twist of fate, strike it rich in megamedia. Some are already large successful companies—Lotus, Novell, Broderbound—and others are a handful of whacky college dropouts working in somebody's attic. Most will be lucky if they achieve moderate success in the coming decade. Many will flat out disappear.

I chose to write about the companies above—Microsoft, Silicon Graphics, Oracle, and General Magic—because they seem to have the best chance of making an impact on megamedia. Or, if they fail, they will be spectacular failures.

I know I have left out some important players in other sectors of the software industry. But so far, none is being talked about as a breakthrough company—a name that will be well known five years from now.

More generally, a couple of sectors of the vast software industry seem positioned to find interesting and lucrative ways to migrate into the converging world of computing, communications, and content.

One sector is usually called networking software or groupware. These programs tie personal computers together and give them ways to share information, exchange messages, and work together. Sometimes the computers are in one office; sometimes they're spread around the world. But as more work gets done on PCs, companies increasingly want their PCs to talk to each other. As megamedia evolves, communications will become even more important: remote workers will be able to "meet" via desktop videoconferencing or to work on multimedia files together. When companies like Pacific Telesis build networks that can link PCs for rich, broadband telecommuting, somebody's going to have to write the software that tells the various PCs how to interact with each other and with shared software and files.

The strong companies in this sector should find new markets opening up in megamedia. One of those companies is Novell, long the leader in linking PCs. Considered a strong, sound technology company, it has begun to link up with a few partners, such as Oracle, to move toward megamedia. But the company has stayed focused on its niche and hasn't stated any grand ambitions for the coming age.

Another is Lotus Development Corporation, until recently a fading one-time superstar in PC applications software. Lotus got a boost in 1993–1994 from its Notes program. Notes lets far-flung groups of computer users work together and even send video e-mail. AT&T formed a partnership with Lotus to make Notes available through its global network. Lotus is rebuilding its entire company around Notes. The program may give Lotus a lift into the megamedia race.

A host of other software companies operate in different niches of the networking market. Bay Networks, a merger of Wellfleet and SynOptics, is one hot company. It makes software that links networks to other networks, smoothing a usually incompatible gap between the two. A different kind of company is NuMedia in Alexandria, Virginia. The company makes software that allows video to be distributed on computer networks. It's working with NBC and IBM in a high-profile venture called Desktop News.

A second hot area is multimedia content software, which these days means the CD-ROM business. Computer users can't seem to get enough, whether it's interactive adventure games such as Crystal Dynamics' *The Horde;* self-help programs like *Design & Build Your Deck* from Books That Work; or children's CD-ROMs such as *TuneLand* from 7th Level. In 1994, sales of multimedia CD-ROM equipment for computers doubled. Sales of CD-ROM titles more than doubled to nearly $4 billion.

That's pretty good, considering CD-ROMs are a far-from-ideal vehicle for multimedia content. They are often slow, balky, and difficult to use. CD-ROM drives and CD-ROMs themselves will get faster and better, and that will boost the market.

Better yet, megamedia will open up more ways to pump something like *TuneLand,* which stars comedian Howie Mandel in a romp through a music-filled animated playground, into PCs or computer-driven TV sets. Broadband cable or phone company connections will be powerful enough to deliver multimedia on-line. Users may subscribe to a service that offers, say, educational programs. Tap in and choose from menus of multimedia content. Computer service companies such as Prodigy and America Online are already planning to eventually offer the equivalent of CD-ROM on-line. Multimedia titles may someday be as normal to call up as a TV channel or a computer bulletin board. The new outlets could send sales rocketing for multimedia content companies—as long as the companies remember they're in the content business, not the CD-ROM business.

Who will make it big? Good question. Most of today's CD-ROM companies are tiny, creative ventures. Compton's New Media, part of Tribune Company, is the biggest CD-ROM publisher, although third parties create many of its titles and it operates more like a book publisher. Crystal Dynamics gets a lot of ink. It is backed by HBO and King World Productions, and its CEO, Strauss Zelnick, had been president of 20th Century Fox studios. 7th Level is an interesting company. One founder is George Grayson, who had previously started Micrografx, a leading graphics software firm. Another founder is Scott Page, former saxophonist for Supertramp and Pink Floyd, who went into multimedia programming. The third founder is Bob Ezrin, who produced records for Alice Cooper and other rockers.

There are dozens of other companies like Crystal Dynamics and 7th Level. It's too early to say which ones might win. Besides, the field is fickle—a prediction would be like trying to say which authors will write best-sellers or which band will create a top-of-the-charts hit. Still, it's fascinating to think that multimedia content today might be at the same stage as animation back when Walt Disney first drew Mickey Mouse.

8

GOTTA SEE PAST THE KEYBOARD

THE COMPUTER INDUSTRY

LEADERS TO WATCH: LEW PLATT AND HEWLETT-PACKARD

Drastic change never comes easy to any organization that's more like a good-natured cult than a profit-hungry company. Hewlett-Packard (H-P) was stumbling like a blind elephant when Lew Platt was named CEO in 1992. Platt had to slap the company back to life, yet keep intact the sacred corporate culture, the "H-P Way."

"People had begun to associate certain practices with the core values themselves," Platt told a group at a conference in San Francisco. "And when we changed a practice, they'd say, 'Gee, the core values aren't important anymore. We used to have free coffee and doughnuts for everybody.' You can say it's a trivial example, but free doughnuts had come to be known as part of the H-P Way.

"Well, we don't have doughnuts anymore, although we still have free coffee," Platt said. "But every once in a while somebody will use the disappearance of free doughnuts as evidence that the H-P Way is dead. One of my challenges is to make sure people understand that we can express our values at H-P in many ways. In fact, to stay a viable company that's what we must do—change with the changing times."

In just a few years, Platt has done a miraculous job of making change part of every minute of every day at H-P. The Palo Alto, California-based company has turned into an ultraflexible technology company. It's huge and powerful, yet made up of more pieces than an Erector Set. Pull one piece off, bolt a couple of others together, and *voila!*—the company can quickly change and attack any emerging market.

"The thing that's different now is that it's no longer desirable that you're flexible. It's mandatory," Platt says. "Inflexible people simply don't survive in the current environment. Inflexible companies don't, either."

It's tough to even get a handle on what H-P does, exactly. It makes all kinds of computers, has a huge computer printer division, builds scientific and medical instruments, makes microprocessors, and is getting into interactive TV. Its customers are everybody and anybody: the military, big companies, small companies, governments, and individual consumers. About its only well-known product line is the LaserJet printer. But H-P's mushiness has turned out to be a good thing. The company is healthier than it's been in a decade. Revenue, at $20.3 billion in 1993, is growing around $4 billion a year. From 1991 to 1994, H-P's stock price jumped about 60 percent.

H-P is called the number-two computer company, but it doesn't really consider itself a computer company. For lack of a better term, it's more of a *computering* company—a company that finds ways to use computer technology to do just about anything that needs to be done. That might mean building not a computer as we know it but some other gadget that uses some of the technology from computers.

Here's how they say it at H-P: "The future high-tech world will not be dominated by computer companies, but those that use technology to solve customers' problems," says Jim Olson, general manager of H-P's Video Communications division. "H-P is uniquely suited to that. To our [division's] customers, we're a video company, not a computer company."

Put it all together, and H-P comes out looking like the model for a successful computer company in the megamedia age. Platt has engineered not only a new company but a new way of thinking about the computer business. And it doesn't necessarily include keyboards or hard-drives or Microsoft programs or even the latest whizbang silicon chips.

Jim Olson's story shows how H-P works these days. It begins with John Young, Platt's predecessor as CEO, who belatedly started some of the changes that Platt carried through. In 1991, Young went to a telecommunications show in Geneva, Switzerland. He came back alarmed at how fast the TV and communications businesses were about to converge with computers and grow—and H-P was doing nothing in those arenas. Young put Olson in charge of H-P's oldest division, which made microwave measurement devices, and had Olson move all the division's products and some of its people into other parts of H-P. Olson's group was given the best of all worlds: It had the financial backing of a giant company and could tap the expertise or hire the people in H-P's many divisions, yet the unit was cut free to make decisions and succeed or fail on its own.

Olson simply told his new group of engineers and managers to "scout out billion-dollar opportunities in video," he says. He bought his team plane tickets to visit potential customers. For months, the team traveled constantly to meetings at TV networks, cable companies, production houses, and trade shows.

In those meetings, the team learned that TV and movie companies wanted a cheap, easy way to grab images off a video screen and print them. Olson's unit sought help from H-P's wildly successful printer division, developed some new technology itself, and added some computing power. "We did the VidJet Pro in seven months, start to finish," Olson says—a timetable unheard of at H-P until recently. The VidJet Pro, selling for about $3,500, is a studio tool aimed at the 20,000 video production facilities worldwide. CNN is using it to grab and print images of news footage for cataloging, basically printing on paper exactly what appears on the TV. Movie directors can print a tiny image of every scene change on one poster-size sheet of paper, making editing a film easier. Olson's group built a $300 version that will go into homes as part of Time Warner's test TV system in Orlando, Florida, and a similar US West test in Omaha, Nebraska.

True to H-P's flexible ways, Olson's group didn't decide it was strictly a video printer division. It looked for other ways to make technology that might solve video industry problems. For instance, it came up with a device that monitors the quality of video signals, drawing heavily on H-P's expertise in computerized measurement instruments. In 9 months, the unit had created 14 new products.

Olson's biggest effort shows how H-P is willing to bend its computer-industry thinking. His group had heard from customers that they wanted a video server for interactive television. Most of H-P's competitors were—and still are—pitching their standard computer products to handle that task. Olson's group took another look and decided that desktop machines built to do spreadsheets or word processing, or big computers made to tackle scientific equations or run a company, would not necessarily make good video servers. Those machines have too much costly computing muscle, most of it wasted when handling interactive TV, Olson argues. But they don't have enough "input–output" capability—electronics that quickly shuffle content from one place to another or from a storage disk to an interactive TV network. The best video server, the group decided, would be something totally new, not a modified version of one of H-P's computers. "Here we're the number-two computer company, and we are refuting that," Olson says. In fact, Olson isn't even using H-P's powerful RISC (reduced instruction set computing) computer chips, deciding that a cheaper, older model from another vendor would be good enough and would hold down the total cost of the machine. "We're building our architecture from the ground up."

The result, H-P's Video Transfer Engine, is one of the lowest-cost video servers yet available. It is not really a computer, but a computer-controlled machine tailored for one thing: grabbing multimedia or video out of storage in a "disk farm," sending it out over the network, and keeping track of it for billing purposes. No one's sure yet how the machine will perform once in the market, but Pacific Telesis hired H-P to create the video technology for the phone company's $16 billion megamedia system in California, and CBS is buying H-P's equipment. Lee Camp, the Pacific Telesis executive in charge of the project, says he's happy with H-P's product: "H-P is a terrific company to work with."

Olson is amazed at what his group has done in such a short time. "I'm not sure it could've been done here five years ago," he says. "We're street fighters. We're like a start-up."

Across the computer industry, few big companies look and operate like H-P. That could turn into an industrywide problem as megamedia rolls in.

Since about 1980, computer hardware makers have been at the heart of creative technological change. They've all been on the same road all this time, driving to build machines that are smaller, cheaper, and more powerful than the generation before. Functions haven't changed much: crunch numbers, do documents, store and retrieve information in databases—oh, and play games. Computer companies were out front. They'd improve the machines, then software companies would create applications that fit. In 15 years, a whole empire has grown up around Compaq, Intel, Apple, IBM, and others. Its citizens have all tended to talk among themselves, to look at things from the same computer-centered point of view, and to act in concert. Megamedia is or will be a rude jolt to them.

The center of gravity is shifting. Creative technological change will be led by networks, not individual computers. The hardware focus will be on making networks more powerful, faster, more interactive, and cheaper to use, and on connecting to more devices in homes, offices, and pockets (via wireless networks). The great software developments of the next age will either help the networks operate better or create new applications that take advantage of the growing networks. They won't key just on the computer industry.

The kinds of computers we know and love today will wind up becoming one component piece of a network. The networks will connect to many different things, diffusing computing rather than concentrating it in a box on a desk. It's the difference between getting water from a well and having plumbing.

TVs will contain little computers and will be on the network. So will cellular phones—and, someday, pocket computers, car stereos, home thermostats, and who knows what else.

Desktop computers won't go away. They will, in fact, become even more valuable tools when they are connected with each other over networks and can communicate with other devices to do wonderful new things. Desktop computers will get more amazing. The power of computer chips is increasing at exponential rates. A current top-of-the-line Pentium-based PC has the computing power of a 1988 Cray supercomputer. In a decade, a single PC will be able to store and manipulate whole movies, understand speech, run an entire airline's reservation system, or handle a big corporation's payroll.

Most people who use a Pentium PC already have many times more computing power than they'll ever need. They're not going to keep buying the latest and greatest when it starts getting to be the equivalent of bringing home a 10-ton backhoe to spade the backyard garden.

The current PC market trend will intensify: except for the top end, PCs will freefall toward becoming as much of a low-price, high-volume commodity as home stereo systems or microwave ovens. And then, traditional PC makers may run smack into a nest of new competition when convergence makes devices such as TV set-top boxes and home video game machines more and more like computers. Computer companies would not welcome a mass-market battle against Sega.

From what I've seen, most computer companies remain defiant. They have a highfalutin attitude that says, "We've got the box for the info highway. The PC will win. It can sit on a desk and connect or sit on a TV as the set-top box or work as a video server. All we have to do is stay on the same path—smaller, cheaper, more powerful—and the world will come to us."

For evidence of this attitude, look at alliances. The other industries converging toward megamedia readily say they can't go into the new age alone. They need to tap wide-ranging expertise to create products for new, unfamiliar, hybrid markets. Even AT&T, a rock-solid technology company, is mating. Now look at computer companies. Few have aligned in any meaningful way with anybody.

As of this writing, none has been involved in any of the big megamedia-driven mergers, not even as bit players or investors. The only computer companies busy at all with alliances have been Hewlett-Packard, Compaq, Intel, and IBM. (Most of IBM's have gone nowhere.)

I don't mean to suggest that computer companies are going down without a parachute. Computer companies that get into the game will have a lot to offer; they have some of the best computing technology in the world. PC companies are superstars at packaging and selling low-priced computers. As *Business Week* cleverly put it: "Among the microprocessor and DRAMs and other chips inside [a PC], you get roughly 100 million transistors. Yet the PC costs less than $1,000. You can't buy 100 million of anything else for so little. That many sheets of toilet paper would run more than $100,000."

Yet most computer makers are not in position to take full advantage of megamedia. The companies that will be winners need to become flexible enough to evolve computer technology into whatever works: set-top boxes, palm-top computers, video servers, game machines—maybe even home central computers, analogous to central forced-air furnaces and ductwork, that have wires running through the walls to lend computing power to all sorts of appliances and devices. Computer companies will also need to bring in new skills, whether through alliances, mergers, or hiring of new kinds of people. The insular, one-note mindset of the past 15 years won't be valid in coming decades.

Hewlett-Packard had to learn that lesson, too. But it had an advantage: its history.

Bill Hewlett and David Packard formed their company in a Palo Alto garage in 1938. As James C. Collins and Jerry I. Porras recount in their book, *Built to Last* (HarperCollins, 1994), H-P started with no great idea, no first breakthrough product. Hewlett and Packard were electronic engineers. They simply knew they wanted to start an engineering and technology company. They found ways to put technology into anything that might need it. The company's first products were an electronic bowling foul-line indicator, a clock drive for a telescope, a shock machine for weight loss, and an automatic urinal flusher. Its big break was the sale of eight audio oscilloscopes to The Walt Disney Company for work on the movie *Fantasia.* It was the ultimate flexible technology company, and it formed the foundation for H-P's 57-year-old culture.

As the company grew over the years, it continued to operate that way. It was highly decentralized and rarely dependent on a single product line for profits or identity. It is perhaps the most egalitarian big company. To this day, any building in the company is a vast, open sea of low-walled cubicles. Secretaries have cubicles, managers have cubicles, even CEO Platt has a cubicle, albeit a big one. The idea is to encourage easy exchange of ideas and a feeling of community. The H-P Way has evolved as a culture that gives individuals room to be creative and find new markets and new technology, yet ties together the organization with a set of beliefs and a loyalty to the company. That has let the company grow and change with the times, sometimes making mistakes (a blunder in PCs in the 1980s) and sometimes smashing home runs (the first handheld calculator in 1972). But the company has almost always moved on, changed again, kept going. "It's more like a biological system than a company," says author Collins.

Admittedly, in the late 1980s, H-P lost its way. John Young was named CEO in 1978, the first chief executive who was not one of the two founders. Young took the company from hodgepodge instrument maker to major computer company—an important move for H-P. In the process, Young focused too intently on computer technology and central planning. H-P became too inward-looking and rigid, too caught up in its own processes rather than in listening to customers. It missed new markets and created too many products customers didn't need or buy. The company started looking like a dinosaur in the midst of all the fast-moving start-ups in Silicon Valley.

Platt was named CEO in 1992. Young had started to make changes toward the end of his tenure, like granting H-P divisions more autonomy and starting programs such as Olson's video unit. Platt, who has worked at H-P nearly 30 years, has pushed change further. On the painful side, H-P under Platt laid off thousands of workers in the early 1990s, to trim the corporate bloat that had welled up under Young. Platt's most significant move has been to take the company back to its roots—the days of the flexible technology firm. "Lew moved us back toward the traditional H-P style," Olson says.

Platt started running the company like a conglomerate of little ventures, each responsible for its own success. He steered H-P away from creating technology first and then seeing whether customers would buy it. Instead, H-P now asks customers what problems they have, then says H-P has the talent to create technology to solve those problems. Whole divisions may shift, change, merge, form teams, or do whatever it takes to do the job. "We no longer have a vertical organization," Platt says, "but a virtual organization."

To that, Platt has added a couple of new concepts. One is an itchiness to keep moving, no matter how successful a product is. "Things that work today will not necessarily work three years from now," says Wim Roelandts, an H-P senior vice president and Platt deputy. "You have to continuously rethink yourself."

The other concept is: Work well with others. H-P had long been a company that wanted to create and manufacture everything itself. Now it considers its ability to forge productive partnerships one of its key assets. It is working with Pacific Telesis and Time Warner on video-related systems. It's teaming with Oracle to put Oracle's Media Server software on H-P's video server machine. In mid-1994, it created a stunning partnership with Intel to develop next-generation computer chips. "We can't do it all ourselves," Platt says. "We need partners. We need to form alliances."

Platt sees himself as working for the rest of the company, not the other way around. He looks for new opportunities, looks for ways H-P divisions could work together, then leads by persuasion. "In the H-P environment, you really can't order people to do anything," Platt told *Fortune* magazine. "The best I can do is sort of bring people together and hope they mate."

"I've known Lew Platt for many years," says John Logan, executive vice president at Aberdeen Group, a Boston-based market research firm. "He has a style of being able to take criticism as constructive, even from competitors. That's a management style you don't see in many high-tech companies, which are always trying to sell their products and vision."

Logan says of H-P, "It's the way a business should be run. With a tremendous amount of modesty and an interest in what the future should hold."

The company today is a set of sometimes-intersecting businesses. In desktop workstations, it is number-two in the market (behind Sun Microsystems), selling about $2.5 billion worth of the machines a year. It has another $2.5 billion business building midrange computers often used as servers. It was the eighth-biggest PC maker in 1994, up from seventeenth in 1992. In the past few years, the printer division has been H-P's star—growing every year, dominating the market, and hitting $7 billion in revenue in 1994. Outside of those big divisions, H-P makes handheld computers (great-grandchildren of those first calculators), medical instruments, electronic measurement devices, and, now, interactive video equipment.

H-P is not perfect. Its RISC chip business, for instance, has been lackluster. One of its first ventures into interactive TV was a partnership with EON, then called TV Answer. It was a dud. Although H-P has been more aggressive about moving into megamedia than most other computer companies, it has been tentative compared to the likes of Oracle or Motorola or AT&T.

Still, H-P's flexibility and its focus on computering instead of computers should carry it into new, emerging markets ahead of the computer-industry pack. In the company's Santa Clara building, Laurie Frick, marketing manager for the interactive TV group, has a theory about where H-P is heading. "Fifty years ago, we built technology for engineers," she says. "Then we built technology for businesses. I think the future of H-P is technology for consumers, for our everyday lives."

Across most of the computer industry, that's a rare way of looking at what's to come.

INTEL: COMPETITIVELY PARANOID

Andrew Grove's entire strategic plan for Intel, written out, looks exactly like this:

1. Job 1.
2. Make the PC "IT."

Cryptic, yes, but typical of Grove, CEO of the biggest and most powerful computer chip maker in the world. He is a man who acts like he barely has a second to tie his shoes, and he drives his company at full throttle all the time. In a secret decoder-ring sort of way, those two lines manage to capture all of Intel's hopes, dreams, and fears as it races into a new age. The lines also say something about why Intel may succeed in megamedia even if its main customers—traditional PC makers—slip behind.

When asked verbally about the goals, Grove puts them into slightly more human terms—a complete sentence, in fact. He says: "Our charter is to build faster microprocessors and find applications that use them."

The best way to look at Intel is to jump right into its goals. "Job 1" refers to Santa Clara, California-based Intel's main mission ever since Grove rescued the company from near-death in the mid-1980s. Job 1 is the drive to make the best-selling microprocessors in the world. The company starts by creating new chip technology at an absolutely manic pace.

Intel got to be number-one by investing heavily in research and development (R&D). In the mid-1980s, the company was making relatively low-tech DRAM memory chips and turning out new generations of microprocessor chips—the little internal computers that give PCs their processing power—at a fairly slow pace. That approach proved disastrous. The Japanese got into DRAMs and crushed Intel. Clone companies had plenty of time to copy Intel's microprocessors and eat at its market share. Intel fizzled, losing $183 million in 1986.

Grove, one of the company's three founders, turned things around. He pulled Intel out of DRAMs and threw resources behind R&D in an effort to make new generations of microprocessor chips faster and faster, eventually leaving clone makers in the dust. The R&D budget soared. In 1993, the company had $8.8 billion in revenue and $2.3 billion in net income. It spent $1.1 billion—almost half its profits—on R&D. The company's Pentium chip, out in 1993, took about four years to create. It processes information at twice the speed of the chip it replaced, the 486. Intel's next chip will double the speed again and will take only two years to get to market. Starting in 1990, the company began to overlap development of its chips. (It used to do them one at a time.) These days, Intel is working on five generations at the same time. No other company comes close to that kind of aggressive chip development.

A smaller but important part of the Job 1 effort is marketing. Through most of its history, Intel rarely advertised. Now it spends $100 million annually on commercials and brand awareness. It wants consumers to demand that little "Intel inside" sticker on their computers. As a result, Intel has turned into a brand name on a par with Microsoft or Apple.

Intel has been extraordinarily successful at Job 1. It has around 80 percent of the market for microprocessors for PCs. It sells to 400 computer manufacturers. Intel is probably the single most important force in the entire PC industry; its chips dictate nearly every computer maker's product line. For that matter, with around 75 percent of all personal computer programs written specifically to run on Intel's chips, the company also calls the shots for the software business.

For the first time in years, Intel is facing reenergized competition. The biggest threat is the PowerPC chip, unveiled in 1993, from a consortium of IBM, Apple, and Motorola. The chip is based on RISC (reduced instruction set computing) technology, which is speedier and easier to make than Intel's chip technology, called CISC (complex instruction set computing). RISC chips also handle multimedia more smoothly than CISC chips do. Most analysts agree that the PowerPC is a better-performing chip than Pentium.

Scary for Intel, yet PowerPC or any other competitor will have a long and tough fight. Most offices and computer owners have software that runs best on Intel chips, and all of Microsoft's programs are developed specifically for Intel machines. PowerPC will run Intel-based software, but not as well, and little software is on the market yet for PowerPC chips. Another plus is Intel's brand name. It will be hard to get PC buyers to switch. Intel's monumental blunder in December 1994 didn't even crack its hold on the market. Intel tried to down play a minor flaw in the Pentium and caught a lot of heat. But sales of Pentium PCs never slowed, frustrating Power PC and other competitors.

Keep in mind that Intel doesn't just want to beat PowerPC, it wants to bury it. Attacking competitors like a swarm of mad hornets is a corporate compulsion. Employees describe Intel's culture as "competitively paranoid." It is hard-driving, fast-moving, and geared toward winning at all cost. It's a direct reflection of Grove, who, as legend has it, escaped his native Hungary in 1956, carrying just $20 in his pocket. He helped Silicon Valley entrepreneurs Robert Noyce and Gordon Moore start Intel in 1968, when Grove was 31. Small, sun-tanned, funny, sarcastic, highly impatient, and packed with explosive energy, Grove has proven he will do whatever it takes to keep Intel on top. Outside of the computer industry, Intel is admired. Inside, it is feared.

Few people doubt Intel will slip anytime soon. More than likely, it will start to move to RISC chips, maybe lose a little market share, but generally continue to be the company that makes personal computers ever more incredible. Job 1 will likely be a success.

Is that enough for the megamedia age?

Intel's answer is: No.

That's where the second part of the strategy comes in: "Make the PC 'IT.'" The phrase calls on the company to find any means possible to make the personal computer the single most significant appliance on the information superhighway. If the PC is "IT," by extension so is Intel, the supplier of the most important component of the huge majority of PCs. And if the PC or PC-based products can drive everything from desktop multimedia to TV set-top boxes, handheld communicators, videophones, and more, PC sales—and sales of Intel's chips—should rocket. Grove's goal is to drive the global market to suck up 100 million PCs a year by 1999, double the pace of 1994.

"PCs are the most powerful computing elements around," says Grove, explaining why he believes PCs should take over the information superhighway. He adds that PCs have an open, multivendor architecture, which means many companies develop PCs or PC equipment and software. That creates a fiercely competitive industry, so the technology "makes progress more rapidly and it's more Darwinian," Grove says. By contrast, many high-end computers and cable-TV set-top boxes are closed, single-vendor technology.

That part of Intel's strategy is a bald-faced move to spur its own growth. But it's also a hedge against competing chipmakers such as PowerPC. If Intel is going to lose market share, it might as well do all it can to make the overall market bigger, so Intel's take would continue to grow. Beyond even that, Intel's strategy is a first-strike attack on future possible competitors in a future probable market. Those competitors are the makers of TV set-top boxes (such as General Instrument), video game machines (Sega, Nintendo), high-end computer workstations (Silicon Graphics, Hewlett-Packard) and anybody else who might attach to the information superhighway digital appliances that traditionally have *not* included Intel's chips. As the future megamedia market develops, Intel doesn't want to see non-PC and non-Intel devices take a slice of the business and perhaps even start usurping some tasks—and sales—of personal computers.

Avram Miller is the lonely guy charged with making this second part of Intel's strategy work. The whole company has long known how to chase faster microprocessors, but Intel had never veered from its computer-chip focus until Miller came along. "My job is to go where no one dares go—to make Intel do things it doesn't want to do," Miller says.

Miller is not a typical Intel employee. Far from getting a grounding in the complexities of engineering, he studied music at the San Francisco Conservatory and is now an accomplished jazz pianist. He went on to teach at universities in Holland and Israel, and spent the 1970s trying to apply computer technology to medical care. Miller eventually wound up as president of Franklin Computer before joining Intel in 1984. Now he's the company's director of business development.

Miller and others at Intel are frustrated with the PC industry. A few years ago, the Intel folks saw megamedia coming and saw the opportunities for Intel-based PCs. Intel wanted PC makers to start forming alliances and restructuring their products for the information superhighway and for use in everybody's everyday lives. Most PC makers didn't share the vision. Many still don't. The industry has been slow to take action. "We began to realize we're moving faster than anyone else," Miller says. "We had to take care of our own destiny. The future is too important to be left to chance."

Intel never had to worry about anything like this before. It just made the chips. PC companies made the market, advertised, responded to consumers, and did all the rest. Even Grove was nervous about veering at all from Intel's well-trod course. At a meeting of 200 senior Intel executives in 1992, the discussion turned to spurring home and multimedia markets for Intel-based products. Grove told only Miller to work on it and said to the others, "Forget about it."

"It's hard to move Intel off whatever it's doing," Miller says. "You have to be willing to stand up to people and you need some evidence." The company came along slowly, but Miller's push eventually became part of Grove's official mantra. In 1994, 20 percent of Intel's whopping R&D budget went to developing what Intel calls "enabling" products.

Intel has by now unveiled a number of alliances and new products for megamedia. All of them have been aimed at protecting the company's markets, expanding uses for Intel-based products, or nudging the PC industry into the future. Some could prove to be important new businesses for Intel. Here are a few of the company's moves.

ProShare

Intel wants the PC to become the telephone of the future by siphoning videophone capabilities into the PC box. "There will never be videophones in offices," Miller says. "It will be over computers." PCs are already sitting there on desks. They have screens that can show video. Once broadband phone connections become available, a top-notch multimedia PC would need only specialized software and a little video camera. PC makers, though, have been slow to develop videophone products. Intel has stepped in with ProShare, developed in the company's Hillsboro, Oregon, research lab. A $200 version of the program lets two computers share software over a regular phone line. A $2,000 version, with a tiny camera, uses souped-up, digital ISDN phone lines to deliver video images as well. The next step is ProShare for broadband lines. Intel is marketing the product with help from regional phone companies such as Ameritech. ProShare seems to have become a hit.

Cable Connections

Intel wants to marry the PC to television and, it hopes, makes Intel-based PCs the "engine" for multimedia, interactive information, and entertainment. There are two ways to do that. One is to make a "cable modem," which allows PCs to hook to cable-TV lines much the way they now link up with phone lines. That would allow PCs to send and receive information 1,000 times faster than via a standard telephone modem. PCs could instantly get TV shows, videophone calls, graphics, photographs, video games, or just about anything else. That capacity would make PCs more useful and marketable, especially to home markets, where entertainment will be a key selling point. Intel has been developing cable modems in a venture with General Instrument (GI), the big cable-TV equipment maker. The modems began to trickle into the market in 1994.

The other path to TV is also through GI. Intel, GI, and Microsoft are working together to essentially put PC technology into TV set-top boxes. It's a very interesting move. GI, the leading maker of cable-TV converter boxes, has strong ties to cable giant TCI. GI has never made a personal computer. But traditional PC hardware companies have been slow to develop a new kind of box aimed at TV and entertainment. Powerhouses Intel and Microsoft, usually dependent on PC hardware makers to expand their markets, have gone outside the industry for help. Along the way, they are turning GI into a specialized PC maker and converting it into an ally instead of a likely competitor.

Content

These days, Miller must be making Intel traditionalists very, very anxious. "The biggest thing I'm spending my time on now is: Where is new content going to come from?" Miller says. Imagine Intel starting to rummage around in Hollywood or poking into TV networks. It's like trying to picture Ross Perot at a Grateful Dead concert.

Yet that's Miller's big push now. The reason: The better the content, the more reason consumers have to buy PCs or computer-driven set-top boxes.

The working projects so far aren't too drastic. One is Intel's venture with CNN. The two are creating a system that delivers CNN news stories to a computer network. The network stores individual stories, and users can call up the video news on demand—even search for key words or headlines. The system was being field-tested at San Francisco-area companies in early 1995.

Intel is working with at least a dozen companies in the development of multimedia content, whether on CD-ROM, over on-line services, or via any other medium. The company has helped America Online, Compton's New Media, and shopping service CUC International, for example.

Miller hints that Intel will also help creative content companies develop megamedia programming, as long as it somehow helps drive the market for digital hardware. "We're toolmakers, not artists," Miller says. "So we're looking at how we can do that. Donate equipment? Finance companies? That's what we're doing."

Overall, Intel's terse two-point strategy awes most industry observers. It's exactly what Intel needs to do to defend its position and continue its amazing growth. The only question may be execution.

It's hard to doubt Intel's ability to keep making groundbreaking microprocessors. Yes, rivals will turn up the heat. But Intel is the fastest and most determined chip designer in the world. It can make hard decisions to scrap an entire line if it no longer makes sense, as it did with DRAMs in the 1980s. If, for instance, its CISC chips drift out of favor, bet on Intel's dumping them for RISC architectures. Intel is already working on RISC chips in a joint venture with Hewlett-Packard.

Intel's biggest challenge will be making sure PC-based equipment wins a major role in megamedia, especially since the PC hardware companies have shied from helping much. Intel should get a huge amount of credit for attacking the issue, even though it cuts hard against the corporate culture.

Intel's potential achilles heal is arrogance. The company, sated by success, often believes it can do no wrong. That attitude damaged Intel's reputation during its Pentium mess.

In November 1994, mathematician Thomas Nicely posted a message on the Internet saying he'd encountered a flaw in a Pentium-run PC. The news ripped through the computer community and made headlines. After all, more than 2 million people had bought Pentium PCs. Many were concerned that their PCs might make errors.

For weeks, Intel insisted there was no problem. It said the flaw would only effect intense, sophisticated math calculations, and could cause an error once every 27,000 years. The company would only offer fixed Pentiums to people who could prove they were doing high-level work.

Computer users were furious. Who was Intel to decide who should get a new chip? Then IBM announced it stopped shipping Pentium PCs, saying its labs had found that errors could occur as often as once every 21 days. Animosity toward Intel piled up. On December 20, Intel relented. It offered to replace any Pentium, no questions asked, and apologized to customers.

But even then, Intel couldn't hide its impudence. In a conference call to analysts and reporters that morning, Grove sounded like a kid whose mother was making him say he was sorry. "To some users, our policy seemed arrogant and uncaring," Grove sputtered. "We apologize for that. We were motivated by a feeling that it was not necessary for most people (to replace the chip). We still believe that, but want to stand behind our product."

By stonewalling so long, Intel came close to doing itself in. The apology and full replacement policy eased tensions and kept Pentium sales on track. The worst damage to Intel was to its pride. But a failure to admit mistakes and deal with them can be a dangerous attribute in the competitive, fast-moving world of megamedia. Grove says he learned from the Pentium fiasco. He better hope so.

COMPAQ: WORKAHOLIC, INC.

Bob Stearns is full of PC industry hubris. Informal, likable, voluble, Compaq's executive vice president for business development delves into his vision of the future. Boiled down, it's pretty simple: the PC wins.

"I don't think the set-top box exists in the future," he says. "It will be a cable modem with a PC-like device. Today's TV occupies a space that will be displaced by computer devices. People will still call it TV. They won't be aware that it's a PC."

Stearns goes on. His viewpoint is fairly typical of executives at just about any PC company. They reason that the PC industry alone builds the most powerful technology for the cheapest price. No electronics maker or game company or defense contractor or anybody else can put out a $2,000 machine with the awesome capability of a PC. Besides, they say, the worlds of communications and entertainment are moving in the PC's direction by going digital. The other industries converging into megamedia will be grateful for PC technology. How, the execs ask, can the PC *not* win?

The attitude is too smug, too dangerous, and has already cost most PC companies critical time in getting into megamedia. But Compaq, at least, is doing more than bragging. Without ever abandoning a PC-centered point of view, the company has been by far the most active in its industry at cutting deals, entering alliances, and working on new office and consumer products aimed at megamedia. Competitors such as Dell, Gateway 2000, and Packard Bell have been idle in this area. Compaq has at least shifted out of park and hit the gas.

Stearns is the guy in the driver's seat. He joined Compaq in 1993 after a stint at consultants McKinsey & Company, and has since been charged with guiding Compaq toward the information superhighway. "I have the neatest job. I think that a couple times a week," Stearns says. He usually meets with four or five companies a week, mostly listening to their ideas. He also gets together with customers and Compaq employees just to kick around thoughts about the future. If a particular investment or project looks like a good one for Compaq, Stearns finds a way to support or finance it. He says he does this 14 to 15 hours a day, 7 days a week—and absolutely loves it.

Stearns's efforts have taken Compaq into some new businesses, often crossing into megamedia. One of the most interesting is Compaq's role in Microsoft's Tiger program. Tiger is software that lets slightly modified personal computers act as servers for interactive TV. Tiger is still an embryonic product, but cable and phone companies like it because it should prove far less costly than other multimedia server systems that use mainframes or supercomputers. Microsoft wrote Tiger around Compaq's ProSignia servers, and Compaq plans to use the tie to Tiger to sell computers for interactive TV.

"Tiger is experimental," Stearns is quick to say. "But it makes a whole lot of sense and is an attractive business for us."

Compaq has also dived into desktop videoconferencing, which allows PCs to handle video phone calls, usually in a baseball card-size window on the screen. The video is crude when using regular phone lines, but when hooked to broadband wires or internal computer networks, the video can be TV-quality. "It's the next big thing," Stearns says. To back up that statement, Compaq signed a five-year alliance with PictureTel, a Danvers, Massachusetts, company that has been a pioneer in PC video technology. The two will jointly develop and market products. Compaq believes the PC will be the telephone of the future.

Stearns is high on CD-ROM multimedia content. He has Compaq backing KidSoft, a children's CD-ROM marketer, and Books That Work, another multimedia developer. Compaq believes multimedia—especially for children—can drive demand for PCs in homes. That would certainly help Compaq, already a force in the home market.

Stearns promises a continuing flurry of announcements of alliances and projects with phone companies, cable companies, software companies, and even a toy maker. None of those is likely to be a merger or major investment. "We don't think we have to do that," he says.

Basically, Compaq is striving to get PCs into every nook and cranny of megamedia. The company has a number of things going for it: a solid reputation, a well-known brand name, and Stearns's alliances. It also has a couple of other weapons.

One is manufacturing. The company may be the most efficient maker of high-tech products in the world. Since 1992, the company has worked to change the way computer factories operate. Some of the moves have been simple, like operating factories 24 hours a day, 7 days a week, instead of the more usual 60-hour week. Others are more complex. Compaq has adopted all the latest "design-for-manufacturing" techniques. When creating a new PC, Compaq's engineers simplify parts, cut down on screws, and make the machine fast and easy to build. The company is switching to a "build-on-order" system—factories don't build a computer until a retailer or consumer orders it. That cuts down on computers that have to be stored in warehouses. From 1992 to 1994, the combined cost of labor and overhead per computer at Compaq fell 75 percent, according to *The Economist.* Quality has not suffered. Compaq's machines continue to get some of the highest marks in consumer polls and in tests by magazines such as *PC Week.*

Compaq is already using its manufacturing strength as a competitive weapon. The company can make competitively priced PCs and still build in plenty of leeway to cut prices to beat other PC makers—without wiping out profit margins.

Compaq's other weapon is a tireless, go-go, change-is-good culture—a trait shared by many companies that are expected to lead in megamedia.

Nobody sits still at Compaq. Regardless of how a job description reads, the drive is to try something new all the time. Employees at all levels are given the power to act, and act they must. "At Compaq, it's better to ask forgiveness than ask permission," Stearns says.

Employees work their butts off and, like Stearns, seem to enjoy it. Parking lots at the company's Houston headquarters are full at 8 P.M. The mostly young workers joke that none of them may live to retirement. The stress of change is everywhere, but nobody complains. "The reason Compaq is number-one today is it doesn't take anything for granted. We're always running scared. Lack of change frightens this culture," Stearns says.

That's probably because lack of change nearly killed Compaq in the early 1990s. The company had been the most successful start-up in history in its early years. Rod Canion helped found Compaq, in 1982, to make 30-pound, suitcase-size portable PCs. By 1988, the company had $2 billion in revenue. It had hit its stride as a maker of high-end, high-quality PCs for corporate customers. The company became fat and cozy, then got clobbered when computer price wars broke out. Dell, in particular, ate up Compaq's market share. It built

PCs good enough for those corporate customers and sold them at much lower prices. Compaq couldn't respond. In 1991, net income dove to one-fourth that of the previous year. Chairman Canion was ousted. The one-time star company seemed to be in serious trouble.

Canion's replacement was German-born Eckhard Pfeiffer, who had been chief operating officer. Pfeiffer cut prices, told engineers that Compaq's PCs would have to be cheaper to make, and told factories to lower costs. He didn't tell them how. In general, he pushed decisions down the ladder and told people to innovate constantly. Good ideas bubbled up. Costs came down. Compaq's machines started catching on again. The company smelled blood and kept cutting prices while making better PCs. By 1994, the company was on course to be the nation's top PC seller, ahead of Apple, IBM, and Packard Bell.

"Eckhard Pfeiffer has little ego, he treats people well, he's a colleague," Stearns says. "Empowerment—he's the walking encyclopedia entry for what that means."

Stearns is quick to add that this is why Compaq can be successful in the next age: "The secret of Compaq is not its technology, not its market—it's the culture. And I don't know how it happened."

One problem looms. So far, the culture hasn't been able to move beyond the PC universe. For instance, Compaq launched a computer printer division in 1992. By December 1993, it was dead. The company's engineers had designed, tested, and readied a handheld Newtonlike computer/communicator for introduction in 1994. When Newton bombed, Compaq took another look at its product and canned it. Another version may come out in 1995.

For all of Stearns's effort, not much of it goes very far toward rethinking PC technology or markets for a new and different time. Tiger, PictureTel, and the CD-ROM moves are all geared toward boosting sales of traditional desktop or laptop personal computers. They're not about adapting PC technology to fit everyday life, which will be a great new opportunity as megamedia evolves.

On the other hand, Compaq seems to be thinking about the consumer market in ways that are foreign to most PC makers. For example, the company has built a prototype of a computer the designers call Mr. PC Head. It's an 11-pound, $600, portable PC for kids, with purple feet and ears added to make the device more attractive to its target audience. Meanwhile, Compaq marketers have launched a campaign to get Compaq products on movies and TV shows. Compaq PCs have shown up on "Seinfeld" and "NYPD Blue" and in movies such as *The Santa Clause* and *Father of the Bride.* The move is aimed at making Compaq more familiar to consumers.

PCs will be a great market for a long time; no doubt about that. If I had to bet on a PC company doing well through the 1990s, I'd bet on Compaq.

Can Compaq make a splash in the broader megamedia market? Hard to say yet. Compaq is taking the lead among personal computer companies, but that's a lead among one of the slowest groups in the race.

IBM: CAN BIG BLUE PULL ANOTHER IBM?

IBM has never been a bold innovator and it is terrible at transitions from one technological era to the next. The company was originally built in the 1930s and 1940s on sales of electric tabulating machines, time clocks, and electric typewriters. Thomas Watson Jr.'s move to computers in the early 1960s was excruciating and put the entire company at risk, until the System/360 became wildly successful and made IBM the computer giant it is today. In the 1980s, IBM fought the shift from refrigerator-size computers to desktop PCs, and hasn't yet recovered.

Nothing much has changed. A new technological era is on its way. Computers will no longer be just for computing. They'll be part of multimedia communications networks and they won't necessarily sit on desktops or look at all like today's computers. Facing this transition, IBM has seemed as flummoxed as ever.

However, there are signs that IBM may pull another IBM—a leapfrog move reminiscent of the 1960s. In the summer of 1994, IBM began moving the pieces into place to change the corporate focus from computers to what it calls "network-centric computing"—the stuff of megamedia. The concept has the backing of new CEO Lou Gerstner and chief technologist James Cannivino. It's a significant bet on the future. The plans are in place. "It all depends on execution," says David Harrah, a spokesman for the group guiding the strategic shift. "That's where the warts will show up."

The group is planning nothing short of an internal coup, vaulting the minority futurists over the entrenched computer hardware culture. The company doesn't want to abandon its computer base; it hopes to put it at the beck and call of those developing the multimedia, information-highway products and services for the next generation. Expect big battles to be going on inside IBM through 1995.

IBM's megamedia plan has three layers. The bottom layer, the foundation, is a communications network. Much to almost everyone's surprise, IBM is building its own. Sounds ridiculous, but it's true. IBM already has a high-tech, worldwide computer network that it uses for internal communications and information services for some of its customers. By an MCI or AT&T standard, IBM's network is tin cans and string. But the company says it is going to "beef up" the network, link it to the Internet, and make it the backbone of the company's network-centric computing strategy.

The next layer involves creating hardware, software, and integrated systems that make use of IBM's network or other megamedia networks. That will be a broad division throwing its arms around all the ragtag multimedia projects IBM has launched during the past few years, from building TV set-top boxes to developing General Magic-style digital agents or helping IBM's customers create services for the Internet. An important point: From here on out, all megamedia products and services IBM develops will be aimed at business users. Moreover, the company will concentrate on big, integrated systems for big customers—a way for IBM to leverage its size and expertise in everything from microprocessors to supercomputers to software.

The top layer will lie within IBM's sales force. Gerstner reorganized that unit to sell by market segment (versus by geography, as in the past). One sales group, for instance, sells to health care companies around the world. Under the new plan, the health care sales force might identify a possible megamedia application for its customers. It would then go back to IBM, work with technologists to pick and choose from IBM's products, and create a complete, one-stop, all-inclusive IBM package that could handle the application. It marks an important shift in focus from selling rigid lines of computers to selling IBM's ability to create technology that can do almost anything—the Hewlett-Packard model.

For now, these changes and layers supposedly apply only to IBM's multimedia and networking efforts. But they really involve the entire company, people at IBM say. In time, they are intended to change IBM.

Before we get too upbeat here, it's important to say that these are only *plans*—very intriguing plans, but miles from execution. There seem to be a few troubling holes in the strategy. A big one is IBM's determination to go it alone. "We don't need an alliance to do this thing," spokesman Harrah says. Funny, but just about every other company, including fellow giant AT&T, has pointedly said alliances are necessary in megamedia. No single company can know all the converging pieces. IBM may be shutting itself off from needed help.

Another problem will be the task of wrestling all of IBM's current megamedia efforts into something that resembles a coherent whole. The company has not been sitting still the past couple of years: IBM is involved in a fairly long list of megamedia projects. But they are scattered across the company, lacking in any singular purpose or vision. Most have been minor side projects, orphans among the bigger tasks of developing new computer lines or, for that matter, keeping afloat a company that recently lost $16 billion in three years. IBM has started and discarded a number of megamedia strategies since 1990. Two previous multimedia chiefs have left the company—Lucie Fjeldstad, now a multimedia consultant, and Robert Carberry, now at Blockbuster. The whole effort has something of a Keystone Kops flavor.

IBM is the only company described in this book that refused requested interviews with executives running multimedia or information superhighway efforts. Part of that distancing seems to have come from a reluctance to talk; another part is that IBM's plans were still being worked out. Fernand Sarrat, the IBM executive in charge of megamedia, has been tied up in meetings formulating the company's strategy, I was told.

Here's a quick scorecard of some of IBM's ongoing megamedia projects, many of which will fold into the new strategy.

Apple Alliances

IBM and Apple formed a handful of multimedia ventures in the early 1990s. Kaleida was created to develop broad software standards for multimedia, but has since been scaled way back to work only on a multimedia software authoring program called ScriptX. Another joint venture, Taligent, was supposed to be creating a next-generation operating environment. It has barely been heard from. (IBM's hyped alliance with Apple to build a common PC is more about survival in the PC business than megamedia.)

Set-Top Boxes

IBM is one of three companies developing and building TV set-top boxes for Bell Atlantic's coming megamedia network. IBM is also developing and building set-top boxes for Le Groupe Vidéotron Ltée, which operates one of the most advanced interactive TV cable systems in the world in the Montreal area.

Blockbuster Alliances

One is called Fairway, the other NewLeaf. They are creating technology that would allow consumers to walk into a record or video store, find the product they want on a kiosk's computer database, call it up via fiber-optic networks, and "print" it on a compact disk or tape right there in the store. The technology might someday allow consumers to do the same thing using devices in their homes.

Desktop News

IBM is working with NBC and NuMedia to develop a system that would deliver interactive video news reports to PCs on office desktops.

Servers

Various parts of IBM—including those making mainframes, massively parallel supercomputers, midrange computers, and desktop workstations—have been trying to pitch their computers as ideal interactive video servers. So far, only a couple of major network builders have turned to IBM for video servers. For the most part, potential customers say IBM's machines are not well suited to the task.

CD-ROM

The company has an IBM Multimedia Publishing Studio making consumer CD-ROM games in Atlanta, Georgia. Titles include *Mad Dog McCree, Star Trek Personal Multimedia Collection,* and *Karaoke Shakespeare.*

Prodigy

IBM's joint venture with Sears is one of the three biggest mass-market on-line computer services. The service has been facing ever-hotter competition, but it has pushed aggressively toward a next step for on-line services. It has developed a high-speed multimedia version of Prodigy aimed at PCs that connect to Prodigy using cable-TV lines instead of phone lines. Prodigy has also worked on adding interactive information services to TV broadcasts. Prodigy has about 3 million users and could become a powerful link to consumers for IBM.

New multimedia chief Sarrat is apparently trying to rope all of those unconnected efforts into one organization moving in one direction. Sarrat is expected to focus IBM on building the guts of the information superhighway, selling to commercial customers. That probably means, for example, marketing IBM's computers as video servers for interactive TV networks, making TV set-top boxes for phone or cable companies, and developing computers that would operate an interactive multimedia home shopping service for a major retailer. Consumer-oriented ventures such as CD-ROMs and Prodigy might not last in the new atmosphere.

At this point, no one knows for sure what IBM's overarching strategy might be, or how much weight it will carry within the company. It's possible IBM itself doesn't know yet.

About the information superhighway, Gerstner hasn't said much. He wants IBM to "be an infrastructure provider," he told *USA Today* in 1994. "We want to be a provider of technologies to everyone." He also said IBM will "make bets earlier on some new technologies. IBM invents almost everything, and then others exploit it." One ironic example: IBM helped build the original network that became the Internet, but has done little to capitalize on its early contribution.

It's important to keep in mind that any strategic shift decided today will take a long time to have a solid impact on IBM. The company is gigantic and so are its troubles. IBM had $62 billion in revenue in 1993. It brings in more than $7 billion a year just on fees for computer maintenance, and $4 billion a year from its computer financing division. It is the world's biggest computer hardware company, making everything from supercomputers to notebook-size ThinkPads. It is the biggest software company (most of its software is written for big computer systems), the biggest computer services company, the biggest peripherals maker, and one of the three biggest PC manufacturers. IBM also makes computer chips and data storage devices to go inside computers.

As for its well-publicized troubles, IBM stuck to rigid, old ways of developing, marketing, and selling computers, and has paid dearly for it. The company went through a high-profile and unflattering CEO search in 1992–1993, and hired Gerstner to turn things around. During 1993 alone, IBM lost $8 billion. The company is bureaucratic, slow-moving, and conservative. Gerstner cut 45,000 jobs and tweaked IBM's operations enough to stop the losses in 1994, but he hasn't set IBM on any kind of path toward regained glory. He has just kept the company alive.

Can Gerstner help IBM pull another IBM? Can he do what Watson Jr. did in the 1960s and swing the company from one era into another? Can IBM use its incredible size, its broad range of talent, and its strong presence in the marketplace to thunder into the Communications Age?

The history of IBM suggests that it's possible. The current mess at the company might make observers wonder, but no one argues that IBM doesn't have smart people or solid underlying technology. It needs a culturectomy—the kind Robert Allen performed on AT&T. Then IBM could make some noise in megamedia.

Here's an interesting key to look for: The name of the company is International Business Machines. It prospered for eight decades by following its name, applying the latest technology to create whatever "machines" businesses needed. The name of the company is *not* International Business Computers. Right now, the company is completely focused on computers. When the company stops thinking in terms of computers and starts thinking in terms of how to apply technology to make all kinds of next-generation machines that will help businesses function better—then the IBM of history will be ready to stand up and win back its crown.

APPLE, DEC, AND THE JAPANESE: TRYING TO SURVIVE IN AN INSANE INDUSTRY

The computer industry is a crowded and chaotic arena. Hundreds of companies from around the world compete to put digital hardware on desktops and in home offices. The industry has gone through its own brand of convergence: companies can no longer be sorted by old market sectors such as mainframes, minicomputers, and personal computers. IBM and Hewlett-Packard make PCs; Compaq sells servers that compete against minicomputers; and Intel makes a microprocessor that's as powerful as the mainframes of just a few years ago. Even the old Apple–IBM dichotomy in the PC world is going away: new machines run software for both camps. Many companies are slamming together, creating much the same product, fighting for the same customers.

Where are these masses of computer companies going over the next decade?

The answer, for a lot of them, is: down the tubes.

The computer industry is already insanely competitive, more so than any industry coming into megamedia. The competition will only get tougher. As the computer industry converges with communications and entertainment, change will come faster and faster. As computers become even more of a consumer product, price battles will intensify. Any company that can't react like lightning to new technology, new markets, and new price points is going to get stomped. It will not only lose ground in its traditional computer markets, but will also fail to win a place in emerging megamedia markets such as interactive television.

Predicting who will survive and play a role in megamedia is a tough sport. Hewlett-Packard, Intel, and Compaq all came back from the brink of disaster. They rebuilt their companies in just a few years' time and now look like the leaders for the next age. Apparently, recovery can be learned. One of today's dogs could be tomorrow's comeback story.

At this writing, no computer companies outside of H-P, Intel, and Compaq look poised to become megamedia stars. More commonly, computer companies look poised to become megamedia victims.

Let's start with Apple Computer. A lot of smart people think Apple will be gone as an independent company by the end of the decade. In the predicted scenario, Apple continues to lose market share and bungle new products until it is forced to merge into another company to stay viable.

Sounds strange. Apple seems like a national treasure. But it's essentially a one-product company. That product is the Macintosh, now more than 10 years old. Its only other break-out success was the PowerBook laptop computer, which started off strongly but quickly became an also-ran when other laptops caught up to PowerBook's technology and beat its price. A sign of the times.

Apple prospered for years because its proprietary technology—the Mac—was easier to use than other PCs and won devoted customers. That let Apple charge high prices for its machines and stay above the battles in the IBM-compatible market.

These days, Microsoft's Windows makes all PCs as easy to use as a Mac. As megamedia emerges, the proprietary technology is a handicap. People want PCs to talk to each other, and Mac computers can't talk to the vast majority of other machines out there. (Apple has about 10 percent of the PC market.) Apple's new PCs, based on its PowerPC chip, are more compatible with other personal computers—but that eliminates Apple's old one-of-a-kind edge. The company will increasingly have to compete on price and features in the down-and-dirty PC market, something Apple has never had to learn to do. It doesn't react quickly to change, and it doesn't have Compaq's lean and low-cost manufacturing. The company's successful past has left it unprepared for the future.

In John Sculley's last tumultuous year at Apple, he began to push the company into megamedia. Most of what he started has gone nowhere. Sculley's pet project, the Newton, became Apple's most famous flop. It was certainly a visionary product, one of the first to try to take computing out of computers and push it into everyday life. It is where computing is headed—eventually. Newton simply didn't work well enough and it cost too much. Sculley staked Apple's reputation on Newton, and lost.

Sculley wanted Apple to become the foremost maker of TV set-top boxes for interactive video. Apple has a couple of trials going, including one with British Telecom, but it's a weak effort. Apple has been passed by H-P, General Instrument, IBM, and Silicon Graphics. Apple's other forward-looking products, including a combination Mac and TV and an on-line service called eWorld, haven't set off any fireworks. Its best megamedia product is software, not hardware. The company's QuickTime multimedia software, which lets users see and edit video along with music and text, may be incorporated into a number of interactive TV systems, including those developed by Bell Atlantic.

Current CEO Michael Spindler, a pragmatic engineer who took over from Sculley in June 1993, is more intent on boosting Apple's profit margins than charging after The Next Big Thing. He may keep the company from getting buried in the current PC market, but he's not likely to send Apple flying into the future. It would be a shame if he were Apple's last CEO.

Sadly, on a list of top computer companies, none of the rest looks like a real megamedia contender.

The number three computer maker (behind IBM and H-P) is Digital Equipment Corporation (DEC). Around 40,000 people, one-third of its 1992 work force, are being laid off. It has bungled a switch to a new product line based on its high-powered Alpha chip. The good news is that after all these years, DEC seems to have finally created a PC division that works. Its HiNote notebook PC has been a hit. Still, DEC may be lucky to survive, much less cash in on new developments.

In the workstation market, Sun Microsystems, hasn't shown any particular imagination in moving outside its market for desktop workstations and has lost market share to H-P and others. In the personal computer market, most of the rest of the companies are focused on the here and now—the struggle to stay ahead in the competitive PC business. Dell, Gateway 2000, AST, and Packard Bell have all waved off the information superhighway. At least those companies have built responsive, low-cost manufacturing operations and innovative marketing departments, which could help them stay abreast of changes.

Some people think massively parallel supercomputers are the hot video servers of the future. If true, companies such as nCube, owned by Oracle, and Thinking Machines, which ran into financial trouble in 1994, would get a boost. Massively parallel computers wire hundreds of microprocessors together. Those machines will probably turn out to be too powerful and too costly for most megamedia systems. Simpler computers from the likes of H-P, Silicon Graphics, and Compaq seem better able to handle most interactive TV tasks.

How about the Japanese? They have huge computer-making companies. The biggest are Fujitsu, NEC, Hitachi, Toshiba, and Matsushita. But the Japanese have fallen horribly behind. Innovation has been slow, and manufacturing costs are high. Fujitsu, NEC, and Hitachi are dinosaurs that are already having a tough time keeping apace of change. Matsushita's most interesting move was having its Panasonic division climb in bed with upstart game maker 3DO. But 3DO has been a dud. Toshiba may qualify to play a role. It has been a success in the laptop computer market and is part of the Time Warner partnership building interactive systems in Orlando, Florida, and elsewhere.

If established companies don't adapt to megamedia, the computer industry always has room for entrepreneurs. Somebody new may come galloping out of a garage and into an unoccupied niche, creating an Apple for the next age to replace some of the tired companies of the last one.

9

CUTTING THE CORD

THE WIRELESS INDUSTRY

Wireless communication is the hottest business in the world. The industry's revenue is growing at a mind-boggling 40 percent to 50 percent a year. The number of users in the United States alone, about 15 million in 1994, is expected to hit nearly 90 million by 2004—and those are the realistic predictions. A typical user is now on his or her wireless phone 80 to 100 minutes a month. Calling time is nearly doubling every couple of years as prices of calls continue to fall. Look for wireless calling time to come close to the 1,000 minutes a month of use common to a wired phone.

Worldwide, the numbers are even more breathtaking. Hungary, stuck with a rotting old Communist-built wired phone system, is rushing to build cellular phone systems that will, for many people, completely replace the wired phones. Other emerging countries, including China, are doing the same.

More astonishing, the soaring forecasts are based largely on today's wireless paradigm: the two-way voice conversation via analog cellular telephones. Over the next decade, new kinds of wireless communication will emerge and converge and drive the industry to greater heights. At least two new digital voice-telephone technologies are in the process of being built around the United States. Those systems will compete against cellular, no doubt driving prices lower. They will better accommodate new kinds of wireless computing devices, such as Motorola's Envoy, unveiled in 1994. Such devices will be the beginning of anytime, anywhere electronic mail and other computer-related communication. Wireless interactive video is a much more difficult technology and is at least a decade away, yet GM Hughes Electronics is starting up an early piece of it: nationwide wireless cable TV.

Wireless will be an important part of megamedia, extending its reach everywhere. And megamedia will dramatically change the wireless business. Here are profiles of companies to watch in four very different parts of the wireless universe.

NEXTEL: DEFINITELY NOT FAINT-OF-HEART

"No question, the first time I met Morgan, I thought, 'This guy's got the most grand plan, and either he's P.T. Barnum or he's Craig McCaw or Bill Gates at the beginning.' And so far it's leaning toward McCaw and Gates."

That's from Brian Roberts, president of Comcast, which is a major investor in a company called Nextel. Roberts is talking about Morgan O'Brien, chairman and founder of Nextel, one of the most audacious communications ventures ever.

Nextel has said it is seriously gunning to become one of the biggest phone companies in the United States. So far, the promise has far exceeded reality.

By late 1994, the company could count its phone customers only in the thousands. This start-up, this pip-squeak of an operation, plans to build an all-wireless, all-digital network that transmits calls and data over radio frequencies once reserved for taxi dispatches. The system is supposed to blanket the entire nation by the late 1990s. Then Nextel figures it will begin challenging not just cellular phone operators, but the likes of AT&T and Bell Atlantic for communication dominance.

Sounds crazy, except that some very impressive people have believed in the dream. Nextel's investors include Comcast, Motorola, Matsushita, and NTT—players who can help Nextel pull off its plan. Some analysts and competitors say the company has a shot. A lot of others say that, long before the nationwide system is completed, we'll be reading Nextel's obituary.

O'Brien is the tireless, driving, smooth-talking, sharp-as-tacks key. He has no doubts about where Nextel is heading. "Here's the way I see the future," he says. "There will be not more than five and not less than three major global telecommunications players. Clearly there's going to be convergence of what used to be separate. All the different services have been isolated by separate technology. But digital is different. Everything's the same when it's digital, just ones and zeros. We're going to spend a couple million dollars a day to build our infrastructure. We're committed to spending billions. And since wireless is such an integral part of where communications is going, we'll be one of those three to five players. There will be a shake-out and other alliances down the road. But it's clear to me that's what will happen."

O'Brien is a lawyer by training. He spent a number of years at the Federal Communications Commission in legal and managerial positions. Next stop was the prestigious law firm Jones, Day, Reavis & Pogue. O'Brien was partner-in-charge of the firm's telecommunications section. Throughout his legal career, he specialized in wireless communication. At Jones, Day, he spent about half his time representing cellular phone clients and half on clients in specialized mobile radio, or SMR. Cellular was the glory industry. SMR, those static-filled two-way radios used by taxis and delivery vans, was a low-tech, scattered, mom-and-pop business.

"It occurred to me in 1985–1986 that the same thing that happened in cellular and paging and cable—consolidation—would take place in two-way radio," O'Brien says. "If I didn't make it happen, it would happen, and not the way I wanted it to."

O'Brien wanted to aggressively buy SMR systems to create a national company—at the time, all he was thinking about was a national mobile radio company. O'Brien talked to investment banker Peter Reinheimer, who had helped several early cable and cellular companies get started. Reinheimer introduced O'Brien to Brian McAuley, an investment banker with experience as a communications industry manager. In 1987, McAuley joined O'Brien and started raising money while O'Brien identified buyout targets and worked the FCC, which would have to approve any SMR purchases. They named their company Fleet Call.

Through 1991, the company went on a shopping spree. All the deals were as secret as possible—otherwise, SMR owners in key markets might pump up the price when they heard a company was trying to assemble a nationwide system. "It was round-the-clock, seven days a week, buying like crazy," says O'Brien, slim, bespectacled, and looking younger than his 50 years. "We were doing like 75 to 80 acquisitions in secret, operating in so many parallel ways. We'd say to a seller this is confidential, we're moving quickly, here's our proposition and we need an answer immediately."

By 1990, Fleet Call had bought about 100 SMR systems—and 100 different names, 100 different accounting systems, 100 different ways of doing business. O'Brien was getting his nationwide network, but it was a zoo. He and McAuley started trying to mesh the systems into one company by putting in standard operating practices, creating a single brand name, and building a professional, up-to-date two-way radio company. During this phase, O'Brien hit on the next idea.

"One day it came to us," he says. "Just the whole idea. I was worried we had this beautiful SMR business that was going to be wrecked. I get my best ideas when I'm worried." While consolidating his SMR operations, O'Brien saw that cellular companies were getting ready to change their analog systems to digital systems. Computerized tricks can pack cellular radio frequencies with many times more digital calls than analog. It would take years, but once digital was in place, the cellular systems would have huge capacity—enough to also handle mobile radio calls. "The cellular companies were not going to stay out of our business. We could see that," O'Brien says. "We were going to be isolated—marooned here unless we leapfrogged *them!*"

O'Brien paid a visit to Motorola, the top supplier of mobile radio equipment. He asked the company if SMR systems could be converted to digital, and if so, why couldn't SMR systems add switches and then have the capacity to start carrying phone calls and other traffic—competing against cellular companies, pre-empting their move to digital? As it turned out, engineers in Motorola's Land Mobile Products Sector were working on such technology. Motorola liked the idea of applying it to a national network. The two started working together.

At the time, in 1990, O'Brien realized what a huge project he was talking about. His company would have to build, from scratch, digital radio systems in hundreds of U.S. cities. It would have to create a brand and then market it to whole sets of customers it didn't know. It would have to race to get its business up and running before cellular could go digital, and before new PCS digital wireless phones made it to the market.

"The only way to succeed," O'Brien says, "was through alliances. We made a list of all the companies in the world we thought would be good partners. There were, like, 200 on the list. We approached them all. We started with our A list. MCI was near the top from the start. A natural. We talked with AT&T, but they said, 'We like wireless but we don't like you.'"

O'Brien called on MCI three or four times. MCI wasn't interested. It was working on other wireless strategies. In the meantime, Comcast got involved. O'Brien called on Comcast in 1992 because "they were a good fit, and they were still run by the entrepreneurial team that created it. They were able to identify with us." Comcast invested $70 million in September 1992. Then, in 1994, Comcast's Brian and Ralph Roberts called on MCI Chairman Bert Roberts. They had never before met. The Comcast Robertses told Bert Roberts of the progress O'Brien had made. Comcast offered to transfer to MCI options it held to buy additional shares in O'Brien's company, renamed Nextel Communications. In 10 days, MCI committed to pumping $1.3 billion into Nextel.

The MCI deal gave Nextel instant credibility and publicity, but MCI's support may never materialize. MCI and Nextel called off their deal in August 1994 because of disagreements over how to value

MCI's stake and how much power MCI would have over Nextel. Talks have continued on-and-off, mainly because MCI and Nextel badly need each other. At this writing, the two seem unlikely to get together—a blow to Nextel.

By mid-1994, Motorola had signed a long-awaited agreement to take a stake in Nextel. In the complex deal, Nextel transferred about $1.7 billion in stock for dozens of SMR licenses Motorola had held. The same day, Nextel agreed to buy rival SMR firm Dial Page for another $700 million in stock, though that deal has run into trouble. Nextel added Japan's Matsushita and NTT among its investors. The company potentially held radio licenses covering 85 percent of the U.S. population and 47 of the top 50 U.S. communications markets. Put another way, Nextel could eventually sell wireless service to around 210 million people. The biggest cellular operator, McCaw, has a potential market of 60 million.

Nextel has hired a new CEO, Wayland Hicks, former executive vice president at Xerox. Hicks knows how to run large operations. He had been in charge of operations bringing in about $8 billion in revenue.

Nextel, which set up headquarters in Rutherford, New Jersey, is aiming high. People *want* wireless phone service. At the right price, they'll take it over wired phones. Nextel's digital system should have the capacity and the economies of scale to offer aggressive prices and, perhaps, lure millions of customers from traditional phone companies. The systems are not compatible with cellular, but Nextel's service works the same and uses very similar phones—in fact, the phones offer some additional features. Consumers would not have to adjust to something entirely new.

The digital system could also handle certain computer communications better than some wired networks and gives Nextel a shot at that emerging market.

If Nextel can put together its national digital system and market it as an alternative to the old telephones, maybe it could rocket to the top of the communications industry. But at this point Nextel is still not much more than an analog two-way mobile radio provider that owns a lot of attractive licenses and has big-name backing. The company is a long way from a national, digital, megamedia communications superpower.

Nextel's digital network start-up is a huge and difficult undertaking, and it has hit its share of potholes. Nextel built its first digital system in communications-intensive Los Angeles, and it is supposed to be the proving ground for everything from hardware and software to marketing approaches and customer service. By late-1994, the system was battling bugs that would lose calls or knock out service to part of the market. The inconsistent quality troubled early customers (it had been one of MCI's concerns) and delayed roll-out of Nextel systems in other cities. "About 85 percent of what we do is the same as cellular systems we built 10 years ago," says James Dixon, a Nextel executive who has started up cellular phone operations for the likes of McCaw. "The next 15 percent, though, requires a new level of attention."

Trouble is, if Nextel slows too much, it'll lose its surprise-attack advantages. Nextel saw an opening because cellular was moving tortoiselike toward digital networks. But cellular owners—mostly deep-pocketed companies such as GTE and BellSouth—have stepped up the pace to digital. If there's little difference in offerings and price between newcomer Nextel and proven cellular companies, customers are going to stick with the known brands.

To add to the crunch, PCS wireless phone service, which will be digital, is finally getting moving after years of delays. Some markets will see 7 to 10 wireless competitors within a few years. Nextel has to get in early and establish itself, or risk getting lost in the clutter.

In the face of such odds, what does Nextel have going for it? Most importantly, it has what's known as a "nationwide footprint"—radio frequency licenses in enough cities to give it almost coast-to-coast coverage with its service. No other wireless operation has that. Such total coverage will allow Nextel to market itself to corporations as the only one-stop wireless provider that could serve offices and factories anywhere in the country. Individual Nextel customers could easily use their phones almost anywhere—"roaming," in cellular lingo. They'd still be on Nextel's system and wouldn't have to dial in special codes or pay high fees, which cellular roamers often have to do. A call placed to a Nextel phone that's usually in, say, New York would bounce around Nextel's network until it found its destination—even if the phone were taken to Miami or Dallas or Bloomington, Illinois. Those are powerful concepts that will give Nextel a chance even if it fails to get a head start.

Another important factor is Nextel's partners. They have invested a great deal in the company, and not just billions of their dollars. Motorola, especially, has created a product around Nextel's service and is counting on Nextel's huge potential market as another way to sell wireless phones.

Finally, don't forget about the wireless market numbers. Demand for all kinds of wireless communication is going through the roof. Through the 1990s, there might be enough wireless growth to pull along almost anybody who comes into the industry. Nextel's system is, so far, the only one set up to tap into demand for any kind of wireless communication: two-way radio, paging, phone calls, messaging, and computer communication for everything from laptops to handheld Newtonlike devices. Nextel may be able to fall back on other kinds of services if its voice phone service doesn't catch on.

Some say Nextel is a clever scheme destined to shatter when it hits real-world problems such as serving customers and battling competition. More likely, Nextel will spend the next few years dancing along the edge of disaster before getting its systems built, its bugs worked out, and its marketing plans in place. MCI or another company like it has to come aboard for Nextel to have a more certain shot at success. Nextel would then have a sexy and competitive wireless business—though probably not a communication company to rival existing phone giants.

No matter how others see it, O'Brien says this of his venture: "It's not a business for the faint-hearted."

MOTOROLA: DOUBLING REVENUE EVERY FIVE YEARS—FOR ETERNITY

Motorola is a weird company. Managers verbally abuse one another in meetings. Teams of employees work to destroy competing teams from other parts of the company. Individuals who feel their ideas are ignored routinely go over their bosses' heads. Small surprise that Motorola's megamedia strategy is to sow discord and warfare in wireless communications and then reap the rewards of supplying the combatants.

Don't get the impression that Motorola is an evil company. It's one of America's best-run corporations, employees consider it a great place to work, it invests in communities that are home to its offices and factories, and customers and suppliers think of the company as a partner and friend. Yet Motorola believes that conflict and a certain amount of chaos bring out the best in business. Since Motorola is the most powerful shaping force across the breadth of the wireless industry—well, you can see where this is leading.

"Our fundamental strategy is to create new technology platforms that seed new businesses," says Keith Bane, Motorola's strategic director. If that means the new businesses compete against Motorola's current businesses or against some of its best customers, tough bananas. The best technologies will win, and Motorola will be ready and able to quickly switch to whatever is winning. It's no fluke that Motorola is supporting or trying to build a gaggle of competing wireless communications platforms, including paging, cellular phones, PCS phones, digital phones that work over mobile radio frequencies, wireless electronic mail, and global satellite phones. "We anticipate that 20 years from now we'll be in 10 other businesses that don't even exist today," Bane says.

The approach drives a lot of people in the wireless industry crazy, but it has definitely been good for Motorola. In mid-1994, Motorola was America's fastest-growing major corporation. How fast? In the second quarter of that year, revenue surged a whopping 63 percent and profits were up 38 percent over the previous year. Annual revenue, which was $17 billion in 1993, has been growing 25 percent to 30 percent a year for the past few years.

The company gets 31 percent of its revenue from making computer chips, including the bold new PowerPC microprocessor. It is the number-three maker of chips in the *world* (behind Intel and NEC). It gets another 15 percent from businesses such as defense electronics. It is starting to make PCs.

But Motorola's home base is in wireless communications, which brings in 54 percent of the company's revenue. More importantly, it is the industry where Motorola can make things happen.

Motorola-made cellular phones, such as the little flip MicroTAC, hold down 45 percent of the global market. The company has 85 percent of the global market for pagers. It is the leading maker of two-way dispatch radios and of all sorts of wireless communication innards, such as the SC 9600 Base Station System. In most of its markets, Motorola is gaining share, not losing.

For most companies, that would be enough. After all, the cellular industry is growing more than 40 percent a year and should be a great business for a while. Paging is a recent hit in China, where only a few million people out of a potential market of a few *billion* have so far been able to get their hands on pagers made at Motorola's new Tianjin plant. Why rock the boat?

"Our philosophy within the company is one of constant renewal," says Bane, who comes across as stiff and straitlaced but preaches something closer to rebellion. The company line is that it plans to obsolete itself before somebody else does. "If you look at everything IBM did, it was to remain centric around the mainframe," Bane says. "We hope not to do anything like that. We hope we are a very different-looking company in five years."

Smart enough to see that megamedia could change the company, Motorola plans to get to the information superhighway first and shape megamedia—at least the wireless portion of it.

How? Take a look at Motorola's involvement with Nextel. For years, products for consumer and business wireless voice telephone calls were made in only one part of Motorola: the General Systems Sector. Its analog cellular phones were sold to work with the cellular systems built over the past 10 years in most cities and towns in the United States and in many areas overseas.

A different part of Motorola, the Land Mobile Products Sector, had long been making low-tech two-way radios for use on dispatch systems known as specialized mobile radio (SMR). Around 1990, engineers from that sector started tinkering with the idea that SMR frequencies could carry high-tech digital communications, whether phone calls or computer data or electronic mail. That year, Morgan O'Brien, founder of Nextel, started talking to Motorola about his dream of building a nationwide wireless phone system using SMR frequencies, competing against existing cellular operators. The mobile products people went to work and developed the technology and phones that will make Nextel's service a reality. Motorola even ended up taking a stake in Nextel in 1994, exchanging SMR licenses owned by a Motorola division for $1.7 billion in Nextel stock.

Nextel may be an important next-generation wireless service. If so, it will slice into existing cellular companies' business and, by extension, into Motorola's sales of cellular phones. On the other hand, that prospect has goosed Motorola's cellular phone group to more quickly create digital technology for its customers, the cellular companies. It's a retaliation against the division's brothers and sisters on the other side of Motorola's organizational chart. The battle is on. But one thing is assured: Motorola will end up on the winning side.

There are more than two sides to this story. For instance, Motorola is busy creating phones and technology for coming PCS systems. PCS is supposed to be a less expensive, low-powered form of cellular phone service. It's also digital, which could make the service attractive for messaging and computer communication. The FCC is awarding seven PCS licenses per city. That's seven new competitors for the cellular companies, and for Nextel. Motorola hopes to be supplying phones and equipment to them all.

Another part of Motorola has created the Envoy handheld computer-communicator. Envoy is something like Newton: a small personal PC that can store phone numbers and calendars and such and also send and receive electronic mail or faxes over wireless networks. Envoy is really a new product for a new niche, but in some ways it competes against pagers, a big Motorola business. (Envoy is driving the paging division to try to pump new life into its technology.) Motorola hopes to develop Envoy into a line of devices that can do things like electronic shopping and tapping into on-line computer services via digital wireless networks. It could be an important line of business over the next decade if the devices catch on.

And then there's Iridium, which sounds like the most lunatic project any major corporation has announced in recent years. A small group in a remote Motorola research center started developing the idea in 1987 and got it approved by going over the heads of bosses who shot it down. As the plan has evolved, an international consortium run by Motorola will launch 66 low-orbit satellites, beginning in 1996. Their signals will cover every square inch of the earth's surface, allowing an Iridium customer to connect with the system from absolutely anywhere. Ground-based antennae and switches that link Iridium to local phone systems will have to be built around the globe. To put up the satellites, construct ground stations, and connect phone calls, Motorola will have to get permission and cooperation from hundreds of countries, probably cutting many of them in on a piece of the system's profit. The phones at first will cost $3,000 each and calls will cost $3 a minute, although Motorola predicts 2 million users by 2002, which should pull down the cost of phones and calls. Customers will be, for instance, businesspeople who travel to countries that have terrible phones, scientists who go to remote areas, and the military. Service is expected to start in 1998.

Iridium is an unbelievably huge undertaking. Just getting it built and launched will cost more than $3 billion. Operating it for the first five years is projected to cost another $3 billion. Motorola has at least 14 partners so far, and they will help defray the cost. Iridium Inc. has been set up as a consortium. Still, Iridium will soak up huge amounts of Motorola's capital and resources for at least the rest of the decade.

Iridium sounds like a wild plan to turn Motorola into a global wireless telephone service provider. But guess what? Motorola doesn't care about being a phone company. "Keep in mind that we're an electronics company and primarily a manufacturer," strategist Bane says. "That's what we're good at." Instead, Motorola is playing its familiar game of stimulating a new communications business so the company can supply the industry with phones and other gear.

Motorola saw a market for inexpensive global satellite telephone services. (At $3 a minute, Iridium would be a fraction of the cost of current direct-to-satellite phone calls, which can cost $15 a minute and require bulky equipment.) The digital system would be a whole new level of service, competing in only minor ways against existing wireless operations. No other company seemed ready to create such a service, so Motorola got things started. The company may, someday, get out of the business of running Iridium and providing service. What really counts is that Iridium should create a worldwide market for a new generation of Motorola wireless phones. In fact, phones may only be the beginning of Motorola's Iridium business. "Iridium is a satellite system today, but it will move to broadband down the road," Bane says. "It will get us into the whole area of multimedia and wireless data, which we've invested in for 20 years and it's still not a market." In the next decade, Motorola may be selling Envoy-type devices that connect to Iridium, or interactive video units, or some other machines that haven't been thought of yet.

Can Motorola pull it off? It has the resources and technology. The major snag will be getting international cooperation, although Motorola has shown it can be remarkably savvy when dealing with even the most difficult nations. After all, it pried open Japan's wireless phone market and now dominates there, and it is selling pagers to the Chinese. Motorola may indeed get Iridium built. In fact, Motorola has a much better shot at creating such a system than would-be competitors, including Hughes and start-up Teledesic. A decade from now, Iridium may look like a bold stroke that helped create a new era of communications.

Oddly enough, within Motorola, Iridium is not talked about as if it's some make-or-break gamble. The project is almost business as usual for a company that has been built around change and intrepid moves. Paul Galvin started the company in 1928, at first making "battery eliminators." At the time, radios only ran on batteries. Galvin's product let people plug the radios into wall sockets. Yet Galvin knew that radios would soon be made to work off household current, making the battery eliminator obsolete. He was already working on his next market. The company was the first to see that everyone would want radios in their cars. By the 1930s, the company changed its name to Motorola and became a car-radio maker.

The company has been shifting markets ever since, remembering that it's an electronics and manufacturing concern, not a maker of a specific line of products. In the 1960s, for instance, Motorola was a leading maker of radios and TVs (under the Quasar name). By 1974, it had sold all those businesses to move into its current lines: computer chips and wireless equipment.

Motorola today is stronger than it has ever been. In 1987, the company's chairman was Robert Galvin, founder Paul Galvin's son. Robert Galvin was horrified at the poor quality of products coming out of Motorola's factories. He and other executives launched the company's now-famous quality program, which is the envy of companies everywhere. Productivity is way up: since the program's inception, revenue per employee has more than doubled. The program has made Motorola into one of the most cost-effective, highest-quality manufacturers in the world. That alone gives Motorola a huge edge in the next decade. In whatever business it enters, the company can make world-class, aggressively priced products.

The quality movement has changed the way Motorola is run. It created self-managed teams and gave individuals the power to do something about problems, criticize management, and chase their own ideas. The company has long had a macho, freewheeling culture, but the empowerment part of the quality movement turned Motorola into a business that thrives on dissent.

At the top, Motorola's management is deep and strong. The company spends more per employee on training and development than any major corporation. That pays off in a thousand ways. It trains and percolates up great managers. There is no better example than the events surrounding the departure of CEO George Fisher in December 1993. Fisher was considered one of America's best chief executives and was given a lot of the credit for Motorola's fantastic performance in the early 1990s. Fisher left to turn around ailing Eastman Kodak. At most companies, the loss of someone like Fisher would be devastating. At Motorola, it was barely felt. "It was clearly without the skip of a heartbeat," says Bane, who is a close friend of Fisher's. New CEO Gary Tooker has a different managing style than Fisher—more impatient, perhaps. But he's a product of Motorola and is generally running things the same way, with the same kind of leadership. After Tooker, the next CEO will likely be Christopher Galvin, grandson of Paul Galvin, son of Robert Galvin, and already Motorola's president and chief operating officer. Leadership will not be a problem for a long time.

Motorola's ambitions are huge. It wants to double revenue every five years—for eternity. It wants to grab and hold the lead in every form of wireless communication hardware, from pagers to multimedia of the future. It wants to be the daring player, launching more Iridium-scale projects in coming years.

Not much is in Motorola's way. The company seems to be up to dealing with its biggest challenges. One of those challenges is an ongoing shift from selling mostly to other businesses and governments to selling to consumers, as wireless communication becomes more of a consumer business. It's a different kind of marketing and a different mindset, yet it's part of Motorola's history. The company has made changes from top to bottom that seem to be helping it cope with the switch. One example at the top: Motorola has formed what it calls the Virtual Consumer Group—so named because Motorola has no actual consumer division. Senior executives from all the company's divisions get together regularly to talk about consumer products and ways the divisions could work together to address consumer markets.

Motorola's other big challenge will be complacency. "If you look at major corporations, so many times they get to the $40 billion sales range and stall," Bane says. At its present rate of growth, Motorola could hit $40 billion by 2000. Bane says the company is already thinking about ways to make sure that's not a barrier. Executives literally try to make the troops unhappy and unsatisfied with Motorola's rampant success.

So far, that seems to be working. The company is pressing harder now than ever. It is positioned to ride the communications wave right into the next century—although anyone who said that to somebody at Motorola would probably get an argument.

DIRECTV: IN A MAKE-OR-BREAK SITUATION

Eddy Hartenstein is quite a character. His features are dominated by silver hair, a silver beard, and crinkly Santa Claus eyes, yet he has the attitude of a prankster and frequently makes points by being either sarcastic or just a little bit crude. His office, in a tower bumping up against Los Angeles International Airport, has a panoramic view of runways and jets taking off and landing. Hartenstein jokes about a friend who told him that if there's ever a plane crash, the friend wants to come up to the office and rubberneck.

Hartenstein is president of DirecTv, a $1 billion gamble on television's future.

DirecTv is a somewhat independent unit of GM Hughes Electronics, which in turn is a somewhat independent piece of General Motors. DirecTv, or any other entry in megamedia, is not going to make or break the auto maker. But DirecTv is such a high-profile and expensive venture that it's worth a look, especially since it's the first serious attempt to take mass-market TV beyond the decades-old broadcast and cable model.

The delectable quickie sales pitch goes like this. DirecTv is 150 channels of digital, wireless, satellite TV, available using an 18-inch dish, not a backyard-dominating monster. It's available to consumers anywhere in the nation *now,* not when some cable company gets around to putting in new technology.

Sounds great, except that DirecTv is probably about five years too late. Developments in megamedia will likely swamp the venture before it can win a strong place in the market, leaving DirecTv to become a TV delivery system for rural areas and rabid sports fans.

Here's how DirecTv is presented to consumers. If you can't get cable TV, or if you're sick of your cable company, head out to an electronics store and buy an RCA pizza-size satellite dish, decoder box, and remote control for $699. You can install it yourself and aim the dish (which is tricky, no matter what the salesperson says), or pay someone to come out and do it. Then, sign up for a service that's available nationwide. DirecTv has a 150-channel capacity, but subscribers don't get 150 channels. They get selections of channels, mostly the same ones that are on cable, plus a big selection of pay-per-view movies, events, and sports. Depending on the level of service chosen, subscribers probably spend $30 a month to receive DirecTv—more, if they watch many pay-per-view offerings.

A few things a salesperson probably wouldn't mention: DirecTv doesn't get local stations or network TV, so subscribers have to switch out of the DirecTv system to watch shows such as "NYPD Blue" or the Super Bowl. Also, the DirecTv converter box has to be plugged into a phone jack—the box keeps track of pay-per-view purchases and periodically calls the DirecTv billing center to update the charges. If there's no phone jack near the TV, one has to be put in.

Add up the positives and negatives and it's feasible that a decent number of people in today's TV market would sign up for DirecTv, especially those who live in areas that don't have cable TV or those whose cable companies are particularly expensive or bad at customer service. The first dishes were hot sellers during the 1994 holiday season. Hartenstein says DirecTv needs 3 million subscribers to break even, not a lot in a nationwide market that includes 12 million homes in areas where cable TV isn't available. "Our chances are extremely good," he says.

That would be true if the TV market was not going to change. Cable companies, which too often annoy their customers, are vulnerable to just such an attack.

But the television market *is* changing—rapidly. Phone companies are moving in, forcing cable companies to become more competitive. Even if new megamedia technology doesn't rush into the marketplace, evolving competition will push cable TV prices down and service up. Many disgruntled cable subscribers will have an alternative: the phone company—a known, trusted-name utility that won't demand $700 for hardware up front. DirecTv won't be as attractive a choice.

If DirecTv could offer a price advantage or breakthrough programming, consumers would pay attention. But neither seems to be on the horizon. For now, DirecTv subscriptions cost more than cable-TV service in many areas. About programming, Hartenstein says: "We're going to offer something of the familiar and something of the different." The familiar includes many of the usual suspects on cable—C-SPAN, CNBC, Court TV, and USA Network. The different includes Bloomberg Direct, an exclusive DirecTv business news channel; 25 to 30 pay-per-view movies at one time; and pay-per-view sports offerings. (Pay a fee to see your favorite NFL or NBA team, no matter where you happen to be tuning in at game time.)

Bloomberg Direct is interesting, but that alone is hardly going to persuade people to buy DirecTv. The pay-per-view movies are a draw, but the same kind of pay-per-view is now on cable TV—it's *not* video on demand, nor does it allow viewers to pause or rewind. And sports? It's a key draw for DirecTv, but the premium service can be expensive. On top of all that, consumers will resist subscribing to a service that doesn't bring them local or network TV.

Now, add in megamedia. Some cable companies are already building systems that have 500 channels of capacity, giving them the ability to offer far more pay-per-view movies or events and other programming than DirecTv. Cable companies have long-time ties and interests in programming companies; DirecTv does not. Cable has a much better chance of being first to create niche or breakthrough content. Going a step further, phone and cable companies are beginning to build interactive television systems, which would allow viewers to order movies anytime, pause them, rewind them. Viewers could play interactive games, hook computers to the systems to get on-line services, make phone calls or send messages, and more. DirecTv will offer none of that. It can offer rudimentary interactivity through the phone line connected to the converter, but nothing that could compete with a broadband cable or phone company network. DirecTv is a one-way broadcaster, and that's going to hamper the operation.

DirecTv cost as much as $1 billion to start up. Its chief asset is a pair of $200 million satellites built and launched specifically for direct broadcast satellite (DBS) TV, the generic name for DirecTv's technology. The satellites are the most advanced Hughes has ever built, and Hughes is the world's number-one satellite company. DirecTv spent another $100 million to build a ground facility in Castle Rock, Colorado. It converts feeds from cable TV programmers such as CNN and ESPN into digital form and sends them to the satellites.

The key to DirecTv is digital compression, which squeezes 8 channels of programming into the broadcast space normally taken up by a single channel. The satellites are the first that can bounce compressed digital signals back to earth. That means DirecTv can offer 150 channels using just two satellites instead of 8, 10, or more. The satellites are unusually high-powered—120 watts per channel versus 5 to 45 watts for most TV satellites. The high power is the reason the home satellite dishes can be so small.

Hughes has been fidgeting around with DBS plans since 1985, but couldn't find a way to make them work until digital compression technology emerged. By 1990–1991, Hughes started forming DirecTv and looking for strategic partners. Hughes owned some licenses for

DBS satellite positions and service over the United States. Another company, Hubbard Broadcasting, owned five more key licenses. Hughes brought Hubbard aboard. Hubbard contributed its licenses and $100 million, and gets to use part of a DirecTv satellite to offer its own DBS programming service. Other partners include Sony, Digital Equipment Corporation, and Thomson Consumer Electronics, which is making the RCA converter boxes and dishes. The first satellite went up in December 1993; the second, in August 1994. Service started in 1994 and lured an initial trickle of customers. DirecTv and Hubbard have only one DBS competitor: a service called PrimeStar, launched by a group of cable-TV companies. PrimeStar has also won only a smattering of customers so far.

Hartenstein's faith is unwavering. He figures DirecTv can grab its first million subscribers pretty quickly. Then the price of the dishes and converters will start to drop, helping to bring in more customers. Cable and phone companies will slow construction of new networks, giving DirecTv a bigger window of opportunity, he believes. "Our forecast is that half the homes get 200 channels of capacity by 2000," Hartenstein says. "People will get tired of waiting for their cable companies to do this." His goal is 10 million subscribers by 2000, each paying about $30 a month, generating $3 billion in annual revenue. "If we get 10 million homes, that's not a home run. That's a grand slam," he says.

Hartenstein's basic strategy from here: "We need to grab our market share over the next six years and hold onto it with quality. If we can do that, we'll be successful."

No less than John Malone believes direct broadcast television can succeed. He's a backer of the PrimeStar DBS venture, but also the biggest competitor for DBS systems. He says the whole DBS industry can eventually draw 8 million to 10 million customers.

Still, it just doesn't look like wireless satellite television is the wave of the future, say most executives who have watched the industry. If DirecTv had started service five or six years ago, it might have, by now, grabbed enough customers to make money and it might've been in position to hold them through the decade. But now, too many megamedia missiles will be heading straight for DirecTv's service before it can get a solid start.

AIRTOUCH: STRANGE JOURNEY

The decade-old cellular phone business is in the middle of upheaval. Oh sure, times are great. Cellular industry revenue has been growing at 40 percent a year. New customers are flooding in, and existing customers are using their wireless phones more. Cellular is catching fire internationally, and most of the big U.S. cellular providers are charging into overseas markets.

And yet, it's ulcer time in the industry. When cellular was first set up, the Federal Communications Commission (FCC) licensed two providers in each city and town. One provider would always be the local wired phone company, such as Ameritech or Southwestern Bell. The competitor could be owned by anybody—a cable company, an independent businessperson, another phone company. No other wireless technologies were around to challenge cellular. The industry grew up as a comfortable duopoly. And now that neat arrangement is going to hell.

New competition is coming. Nextel's wireless phone network may be up and running in many large cities as early as 1995. Around 1997–1998, PCS phones—another wireless contender—will be operating in most major markets. Up to seven competitors will be able to start PCS businesses in every region. The hordes will attack traditional cellular operators, aiming for a piece of their market share.

That's not all. In the next decade, competitive wireless companies will have to have a strong nationwide presence. Today, none does. They'll also have to offer digital service, which can more easily handle computer data and messaging and expands a cellular system's capacity. Today, few cellular systems are digital.

To rebuild systems, expand nationally, build brand names, and acquire the economies of scale to withstand price wars and fend off newcomers, cellular owners launched a merger frenzy in mid-1994. AT&T got the go-ahead to buy the biggest cellular company, McCaw. Bell Atlantic and NYNEX merged their cellular holdings. So did AirTouch and US West. Everybody else has been talking to everybody else. Don't expect it to stop until there are only three or four national cellular powerhouses dominating the industry. The rest will be scattered niche operators.

One company that should be interesting to watch as this process evolves is AirTouch. Most major cellular operations are part of a larger telecommunications company—some of the biggest providers are GTE, Sprint, the regional Bell companies, and AT&T–McCaw. AirTouch, based in Walnut Creek, California, is the biggest independent cellular company.

It has had a strange journey. AirTouch had been the cellular arm of Pacific Telesis. On April 1, 1994, Pacific Telesis spun off AirTouch as a separate company. Sam Ginn, who had been CEO of the parent company, jumped ship and became CEO of AirTouch.

Parent Pacific Telesis wanted the spin-off for a handful of regulatory reasons. For AirTouch, the move has meant a chance to try a variation on the strategy theme of the phone company-owned cellular units. The new strategy can be summed up in one word: focus.

"Look at the financial side," Ginn says in his Alabama drawl. "When you spin off, interesting things happen. You can now raise money solely for wireless and you don't have to pay dividends." AirTouch is operating as a growth company, and its investors don't expect dividend payments. Pacific Telesis, like all regional Bells, has shareholders that expect large, stable, utilitylike dividends, which ties up money that could be spent building new businesses. As Ginn says, "Not every Bell can build the information superhighway *and* do worldwide wireless expansion."

Focus will be AirTouch's advantage from a service point of view, too, Ginn says. The company is aiming at one target: getting and keeping wireless customers. No distractions. That plays out noticeably in employee motivation. When employed at Pacific Telesis, workers at AirTouch (a name the company took after the spin-off) never saw their efforts pay off in the company's stock price. But at the spin-off, employees were given restricted stock worth 10 percent of their salaries. When the initial public offering price doubles, employees get the shares. You can bet that helps focus them on cellular service. "I'd say the morale here is as high as anyplace I've ever seen," Ginn says. "I hope we can keep it that way."

The focus should help AirTouch fight for customers when more competition comes to its markets. The ability to raise money should help it build digital systems or do whatever else is necessary to defend itself.

The other drive at AirTouch is to expand. At the spin-off, the company owned systems throughout California and in Michigan, Georgia, and a few other areas. In mid-1994, AirTouch announced a merger of its cellular operations with those of US West. AirTouch will own 70 percent of the venture. The merged operations will cover just about every region west of the Mississippi River—a step toward national coverage. The merged company has allied with the NYNEX-Bell Atlantic cellular arm to further expand coverage.

AirTouch will also continue to chase international business. It already owns a huge cellular operation in Germany, plus systems in Japan, Italy, Belgium, Sweden, Portugal, and South Korea.

"At the end of the day, if there are going to be four or five wireless companies, I'm going to be one of them," Ginn says.

For Ginn, the pace will be very different from the more stable, phlegmatic cadence atop a giant regional Bell company. But he sounds up to the challenge. "Am I happy? Absolutely. I didn't know I'd be so fortunate after 30, 40 years in the industry. And I'm away from all that detailed regulation and Judge Green and all that stuff that'll really give you ulcers."

TELEDESIC: WHERE DOES THE LINE FORM?

Bill Gates and Craig McCaw are visionary entrepreneurs, two of the most successful of their generation. Gates built Microsoft from nothing into a company that has a market value greater than IBM. McCaw just sold the cellular business he started to AT&T for more than $12 billion. Both are brilliant, competitive, and ahead of the technological curve.

But they aren't miracle workers. And anybody who believes in Teledesic, the satellite communications venture they've backed, must truly think Gates and McCaw walk on water.

Teledesic strains common sense more than any megamedia venture so far pursued. It is so expensive and relies so heavily on unproven and apparently uneconomical technology that the project is unlikely to ever be built. Yet, just because Gates and McCaw each put up $5 million of their own money to back Teledesic, a lot of people and even companies such as Hughes have taken the venture seriously. More than likely, five years from now Teledesic will be a trivia question on "Jeopardy!" "I'll take 'Business Boondoggles' for $100, please."

Teledesic's plan, as detailed to the FCC in 1994, would put 840 satellites into low orbit, forming a digital wireless network that could transmit phone calls, computer data, and possibly multimedia, anywhere on earth. Target customers would be in areas too remote to be part of the wired information highway. Monks in Tibet might use TVs attached to coin-size antennae to conduct interactive videoconferences with followers around the world. Other users would include international business travelers and the military. Teledesic would not sell services directly to users. Instead, it would plan to build the system, then lease it to other entities, such as phone companies in different nations, which would in turn create and sell services.

The 840 satellites would spread across the sky 435 miles up. Each would be the size of a refrigerator, bigger than many of today's communications satellites. The low orbit would make communications clear and instantaneous, eliminating the delay that can come from bouncing phone calls off satellites stationed 23,000 miles up. On land, Teledesic would have to build relay stations in every country and region to connect the satellite system to regular phone lines. The company would have to get regulatory approval from every country it operates in.

Neither Gates nor McCaw is the brain behind the project. It was designed by Edward Tuck, who founded Magellan, which makes handheld "global positioning" devices that bounce signals off satellites to determine the holder's exact location. Tuck borrowed the concept for Teledesic from Reagan-era Star Wars plans—specifically, the idea of "brilliant pebbles" that could watch for missiles coming in from space. Tuck owns 10 percent of Teledesic. The company's CEO is Russell Daggett, an international lawyer specializing in regulatory matters—a skill Teledesic will need.

What's wrong with this picture? Why is it any more outrageous than Motorola's Iridium project?

Start with the pricetag. Teledesic says it will cost $9 billion to develop and build its system. That's three times the cost of Iridium, and Motorola, a $17 billion company that has an excellent international reputation for building partnerships, is having trouble raising all the capital it needs for the Iridium project. Teledesic is starting from zero to fund its system, and the company has to bank on its association with Gates and McCaw to open doors.

Daggett defends the cost by saying that $9 billion is "a drop in the bucket compared to what's expected to be spent on telecommunications the next 10 years." It may also be a drop in the bucket compared to what Teledesic will really cost. I asked Alan Parker, a senior vice president at satellite-launching company Orbital Sciences, to work out some numbers concerning Teledesic. He says that if 840 satellites cost $9 billion, that comes to $11 million each, and that's not even close to what it would cost to build and launch satellites less sophisticated than those Teledesic requires. By comparison, each of Iridium's satellites will cost $56 million. "Something is amiss," Parker says. He worked through the problem and came up with a more likely figure for the cost of Teledesic's system: $45 billion.

There are more snags. The satellites, each of which would have to contain a digital asynchronous transfer mode switch, would require lots of technological breakthroughs to handle the tasks Teledesic proposes. The Ka band signals used by the satellites would too easily be disrupted by weather. The low-orbit system would suffer from "satellite churn"—satellites regularly falling out of the sky and burning up on re-entry. Some estimate that Teledesic would have to replace up to 10 percent of its satellites a year. That's 84 satellites—and a lot of money.

Politics will be a minefield. Teledesic is counting on unprecedented international cooperation. "What we seek to offer is something desperately needed by every country in the world," Daggett says. "We're hopeful we'll be able to get broad cooperation and partnerships across the globe." That's nicely worded, but almost impossible to do. Motorola already operates around the world, and it considers regulatory hurdles to be among its biggest challenges in creating Iridium. Teledesic has no such international base.

Teledesic is aiming to have its system up and running by 2001. Most observers say that *if* the system can ever be built, it won't be ready until at least 2005. By then, a wide range of digital wireless communications systems should be in place, further squeezing Teledesic's chances. Several other companies are moving ahead with plans to build ambitious yet more pragmatic global wireless networks. Besides Iridium, there is Globalstar, headed by Loral and Qualcomm. A third possible competitor is a system from Hughes, a division of General Motors.

What about the formidable presence of Gates and McCaw? First of all, their presence is overstated. Teledesic has not been a priority for either of them. Gates is a passive investor. McCaw is the company's chairman, but he's been focused on getting into the PCS business on his own. Second, contrary to popular belief, there are limits to their talents and resources. Is Gates ready to put up his entire personal fortune of some $9 billion to get Teledesic started?

As of this writing, no other company has announced an investment in or alliance with Teledesic. If it was such a hot idea, there'd already be a line forming behind Gates and McCaw.

10

THE GRAB BAG

The companies coming into megamedia don't always fit into neat industry segments. What the heck are on-line computer services, anyway? They're some kitchen-sink combination of print media, entertainment, computer software, and communications, and they really have no precedent.

A lot of outsider companies are doing some very interesting things. They may play major roles in megamedia or die trying. In this chapter, I profile those that should be interesting to watch.

AMERICA ONLINE: "I WANT MY AOL"

Steve Case doesn't look a day over his 35 years. The cofounder and CEO of America Online is wearing jeans and a long-sleeved knit shirt in his cramped and inglorious office at AOL's Vienna, Virginia, headquarters. He sits in one chair at a tiny round conference table and throws his legs over the chair next to him. He's wearing white Rockport sneakers. Case talks in a high-speed, rhythmic lilt, almost like an auctioneer. As he fires off thoughts about the future of his on-line computer service, he sounds confident, even cocky, about leading AOL through coming years of intense competition and impending quandaries about how a business like AOL fits into the megamedia marketplace.

"I think, in 5 years, 10 million subscribers will rely on America Online," up from 1.5 million in 1995, Case says. That's not ridiculous. America Online's annual subscriber growth rate lately has been about 200 percent. "I think there will be a handful of services with millions of subscribers," Case predicts. "I don't think anyone will run off with the game." As a clue to how he thinks about AOL's future market position and customers, Case says, "In the '80s, it was 'I want my MTV.' In the '90s, it's going to be 'I want my AOL.'"

Case started America Online in 1985 with James Kimsey, 20 years Case's senior and now AOL's chairman. Kimsey was a restaurateur. Case had worked in marketing at Pepsi and Procter & Gamble. Their on-line computer service, then named Quantum, was launched in 1989. In 1991, the company changed the name to America Online and became the first on-line service to adopt the point-and-click interface of Microsoft's Windows. By 1993, AOL became known as the easiest on-line service to use. It scored points with consumers by adding name-brand services from the likes of *Time* magazine and the ABC television network and by becoming the first Windows-oriented service to give users access to the Internet.

At the same time, PCs were flooding into homes like never before. By early 1995, up to one-third of U.S. households had a personal computer. Most new PCs were being packaged with modems, a necessity for connecting to an on-line service. Some PC makers even started preinstalling software to run America Online—all a buyer would have to do is dial into AOL's computer and sign up.

So America Online took off in 1993–1994. In terms of subscribers, it quickly caught up to the two other major on-line services, CompuServe and Prodigy. By mid-1994 it had passed 1 million subscribers. It has room to grow—only 5 percent of U.S. households subscribe to on-line services. The number of employees at the company doubled in a year to more than 600. America Online became a media darling. As the only independent, publicly traded on-line company, AOL got a lot of attention as *the* on-line stock play. CompuServe is owned by H&R Block. Prodigy is owned by Sears and IBM. Those two services are also improving their offerings and growing quickly, but these days America Online has the momentum.

Stunning as America Online's story is, everything to this point has probably been the easy part.

The company is now chasing two different and very tough goals at the same time. The first is to get ready for Microsoft.

AOL will have to survive the next few years if it wants to emerge as a major megamedia player. Microsoft is creating a new on-line service, which will debut within the next year or so. It will be packaged as part of Windows 95. Called the Microsoft Network, the service is expected to be a formidable entry, especially now that John Malone is playing a role in it. It's also possible that AT&T will introduce its own on-line service. "Microsoft and AT&T—that's daunting for little America Online," Case says, not sounding like he really means it. "But we have a shot at beating them."

Case's plan is mostly based on sheer brute sales force. AOL already has a popular system. For a monthly fee plus charges for time spent on-line, users can send and receive electronic mail, get programming and music news from MTV Online, get news and stock information, join electronic forums (something like clubs), and jump into the Internet. The company is on a crash program to get as many people as possible to try the current service before new competitors come along. If those recruits like AOL, they'll stay, they'll get used to how AOL works and get involved in forums, and they'll develop a loyalty to the service. When Microsoft or anyone else marches into the market, AOL's theory goes, people may try those new services but they'll come back to America Online. "After all, this is about retention," Case says.

He's confident AOL can offer the best and most innovative service because that's all the company does. To Microsoft or AT&T, online services are a baby niche business—supplements to the bigger businesses of selling software or transmitting phone calls. To America Online, on-line is everything. That should mean AOL will stay more focused and drive innovation harder than big-company competitors, because company survival is at stake. History is on AOL's side. Big TV networks tried to unseat Ted Turner's CNN, but never could. IBM couldn't crush upstart Apple's personal computers. No doubt AOL is in for a tough fight, but never count out a single-minded entrepreneur.

The second big goal for America Online is to define its service for the next age. "This is really about the emergence of a new medium," Case says. "We want to be an interactive service that you can use on your PC, your TV, the phone, a PDA, whatever. What you'll really want to do is get your mail, update your stock portfolio, get news, talk to friends, and you won't care what you do it on."

As Case sees it, AOL will develop into a trusted guide, helper, and "aggregator," to use his word, on increasingly confusing and information-soaked digital networks. Case cites the Nordstrom department store chain as a model. Consumers might find more choices and better prices if they searched thousands of stores and catalogs and wholesalers for every shirt, bra, or pair of shoes they'd buy. But many consumers would rather walk into one Nordstrom, knowing they can trust the store to have good products at decent prices in a single place. Clerks are friendly and helpful. You only go to one cash register, or one desk to return products. And the whole place has a personality and familiarity that Nordstrom's customers like.

AOL wants to play the same role with information. As interactive networks propagate, consumers might be able to link up on their own to every conceivable information source, but each will work differently and charge differently. AOL will be the one-stop department store. As an aggregator, it will form partnerships with media outlets and assemble on-line versions of MTV, *Time, The New York Times,* NPR, and C-SPAN, plus shopping services, forums, and more. Everything accessed would work the same way using AOL's software. One bill would be delivered. "Consumers don't like complexity," Case says. "In a sea of choices, brands become more important. You'll go to America Online and trust it as a brand."

As megamedia evolves, AOL will too. In three to five years, Case believes, a good many people will be accessing on-line services using PCs connected to cable TV or other broadband lines. That will let on-line services add video and multimedia to what is now mostly text. Plus, as TV sets start to be hooked to computerized set-top boxes connected to those same broadband lines, subscribers could use AOL on their TV screens. And as Newtonlike personal digital assistants catch on and wireless networks go digital, users might be able to get AOL while walking down the street.

A scenario from Case: A user tells AOL it wants the service to find news on certain topics. At midday, she checks her PDA and it flashes headlines. The user picks stories she'd like to see later. She gets home, calls up AOL on her TV, and receives video clips of the news stories she had selected. She watches those but wants to know more. She sits at her PC and tells AOL to find the full text of any stories published during the past two months on the topics she is interested in.

In Case's vision, AOL will become a friendly medium that 10 million people will rely on as an intimate part of their lives.

OK, so that's what AOL wants to be. The problem is, it's only one version of how things might turn out. AOL is guessing at how consumers will react to the many megamedia offerings coming their way. Bell Atlantic's Stargazer will start as a TV and entertainment service, but it could also assemble information services and function as a mirror of AOL. On the other hand, consumers may decide they don't want least-common-denominator aggregators like AOL when they can roam networks to find anything they want. No one yet knows where the market is heading, or how big it might get. Case thinks the market for on-line services will grow from 5 percent of the population today to 25 percent by the end of the 1990s, but even that's not assured. "The market is a work in progress," Case admits.

It's interesting, too, that Prodigy and CompuServe are taking somewhat different paths than AOL. Prodigy believes that a mass-market interactive service has to be closely tied to television, so it's moving fastest to become something people would use while watching TV. CompuServe, the oldest on-line service, is sticking to its professional, serious, research-oriented approach. It has made no links to TV and few to mass-market magazines or newspapers.

America Online's one other big enemy may be itself. "A lot of companies stumble when they grow fast," Case says. "We did stumble, and it taught us to be careful." Early in 1994, as subscribers signed on to AOL in droves, the service's computers faltered. They couldn't keep up with the demand. Some customers got busy signals when they tried to dial in, and those who were connected found service to be painfully slow. Word got around quickly, and AOL's reputation was damaged. The company can't let anything like that happen again—not a computer problem or a software glitch or screw-ups in customer service. Another major incident and AOL's exceptional word-of-mouth-driven sales could be quashed.

To help manage growth, Case split America Online into four divisions in mid-1994. The domestic service group is run by Ted Leonsis, founder of multimedia firm Redgate Communications, which AOL bought in early 1994. Case is spending a lot of time with an Internet division, trying to devise fresh ways for AOL to use the global computer network. A third division will take AOL international, and a fourth will concentrate on technology.

Will the great success story of 1994 be around in 2004? That's a tough one. The on-line market is still very young and AOL's place in megamedia is still in flux. Case is smart and has proven himself to be a world-class marketer. The service is hip and popular and still growing. As more computers make their way into more corners of our lives, on-line services will probably be something we'll want and AOL will be one of the top choices. But, as Case points out: "The good news is there's going to be a mass market. The bad news is, others have noticed." Big companies are coming in with big bucks. AOL may outinnovate its competitors, but it may not have the money and clout to stick it out by itself.

The company has so far fought hard to remain independent, but chances are good that a MCI or Comcast or Viacom will someday buy America Online.

GENERAL INSTRUMENT: SURVIVAL OF THE FITTEST?

Daniel Akerson, CEO of General Instrument, is blunt, impatient, hard-driving, and, in an interview, about as warm and fuzzy as one of his company's transient voltage suppressors. "I literally view business as not unlike war," he says. "We all want to win, and if you consistently win, the competition will not survive."

Lovable or not, Akerson is changing Chicago-based General Instrument (GI). After 10 years at the top levels of MCI, including the posts of president and chief operating officer, Akerson was named to run GI in 1993. The company had a long history of being an insular, nerdy maker of cable-TV industry hardware—everything from coaxial cables to modulators and amplifiers, cable-TV head-end systems, TV signal scramblers, and set-top cable boxes. Akerson's goal is to steer GI out of the just-cable business and into the great wide megamedia world of the next decade. The company, for starters, won a position in 1994 as a supplier for Bell Atlantic's new high-tech networks—a deal worth up to $1 billion for GI. As Akerson points out, with some disgust, GI didn't even have anyone marketing to the regional Bells when he came aboard.

GI is still the cable industry's number-one technology partner, and that puts the company in an interesting position. Akerson sees it as a launch pad for becoming a powerful and broad force, setting standards for megamedia and helping all kinds of devices communicate over all kinds of networks. Down the road, GI could even turn into a maker of the next-generation version of the home computer. It's a long view that GI rarely thought about before.

"At MCI we always looked at the long-term trend and laid the groundwork to get ahead," Akerson says. "That's what I'm trying to do here. I wake up every morning and wonder what it's going to be like in two years, three years."

GI started making a high-tech mark before Akerson joined the company. It worked closely with TCI to develop and implement digital compression for cable-TV systems, which led to TCI's earthshaking "500 channels" announcement. GI was the company that developed technology that would allow high-definition television (HDTV) to be digital instead of analog. The United States has been pursuing the more advanced digital HDTV, while Japan has been stuck chasing analog HDTV. GI helped the cable industry develop ways to scramble and unscramble TV signals, and that's made GI a leader in encryption technology. More recently, GI has developed technology that would allow cable operators to add PCS phone service to their networks and to connect cable lines to personal computers.

All that has led to a good business for GI. The company had $1.4 billion in revenue in 1993, turning its first profit in years. In most products, GI has a lead over its only big competitor, Scientific-Atlanta. GI has developed a reputation as a can-do technology partner. The company has a huge installed base and tight relationships throughout the cable and satellite TV industries.

But all of that is TV-centric. It ties GI's fortunes directly to those of the cable industry. That's what Akerson is trying to change. "Traditionally we've marketed only to cable companies," he says. "But the PC is becoming more televisionlike and the TV is more PC-like. We've got to cover both bases, to hedge on whether the PC-centric view prevails or the TV prevails." The company is hedging on another important bet: whether cable companies or phone companies prevail. GI wants to be on all sides, supplying technology that makes the networks go.

As Akerson sees it, five years from now, GI will be known not as a cable equipment maker but as a local distribution technology company, making anything that delivers megamedia signals into homes or businesses. It will sell to phone, cable, and satellite companies in the United States and around the world.

Akerson admits it will be a tough transition, like a good college athlete moving up to the pros. But he says GI is making headway. "The Bell Atlantic deal was hugely important to GI," he says. "It showed that the architectural solution we proposed is good, our technology is first-rate, and GI can sell into markets it has not sold into before."

To expand its horizons, GI has entered into a number of cross-industry alliances. It is working with Intel to develop technology that will let PCs plug into cable lines and exchange multimedia information with other computers. It jumped in bed with Microsoft to develop TV set-top boxes. It has licensed interactive video technology to Motorola and Hewlett-Packard. Each will build the technology into computer chips.

Most of GI's business is and always will be on the unglamorous and unseen side, making cables and electronics that go underground, on telephone poles, and in TV industry back-offices. But one product may end up on the high-profile side of things: the TV set-top box. GI now has about 60 percent of the market for analog cable boxes. It hopes to turn that base into a huge market for coming digital, computer-powered set-top boxes that can handle digitally compressed video signals plus store and manipulate information the way PCs can. GI is making such boxes for Bell Atlantic and TCI, and they cost twice as much as current analog set-top boxes. In the future, the boxes, sitting next to TV sets and capable of playing games, keeping financial records, or handling interactive home shopping, may compete against PCs to become the widespread home computer. Someday, GI may even find itself marketing set-top boxes directly to consumers.

It most ways, megamedia seems to spell huge opportunity for GI. Here is a company that was already developing a lot of the technology for megamedia and selling it to a limited market, which happened to be the only market interested in its products. Now, all sorts of new industries from phone companies to computer companies are developing needs for the same kind of technology GI has always sold only to cable firms. How can GI lose?

A couple of problems could get in GI's way.

One is a long-standing reliance on proprietary technology. GI's systems, from cable head-ends to set-top boxes, run on GI software and work only with other GI products. That's the old model for the computer industry—the structure that got IBM in trouble. The "closed" model simply doesn't work in a highly competitive market today. Customers want "open" systems, so they can buy any component from any manufacturer and know it will work with the system. In that way, customers can always buy the best and cheapest technology, no matter who makes it. They don't want to be stuck with one manufacturer. Also, outside software developers and entrepreneurs often create the most ingenius new applications and products for open systems, making the systems more useful and valuable than closed systems.

Akerson is trying to break through GI's closed-system mentality. The Microsoft alliance is part of that effort, Akerson says. Microsoft makes software for open systems, mostly those based on Intel's microprocessors. Licensing technology to Motorola and H-P is another move in that direction. Tellingly, in a corporate financial document dated September 29, 1993, GI's proprietary systems were listed as a strategic advantage. By the time GI's 10-K came out in March 1994, that language was cut.

Still, GI has only begun the move to open systems. Because the closed systems have served the company so well for so long, making cable customers dependent on GI, change will come hard. Yet if GI doesn't change, its effort in set-top boxes will be doomed. Companies such as Compaq and IBM are also coming after the set-top market. They're making open, Intel-based boxes, and they know how to make them cheaply and upgrade them quickly when technology improves. GI won't be able to keep up.

In fact, GI's other hurdle will be competition. Not that GI isn't a competitive company, but it has always fought on home turf against familiar adversaries. Now GI is trying to move into markets it doesn't know. It will find itself battling bigger and richer companies, such as PC makers and AT&T's network-building division. What's more, some of those companies will move into GI's cable-TV market. As GI's opportunities increase, so will its risks.

Akerson, though, is taking a hard-nosed view of increased competition. "So what?" he says. "It's good for business."

Can GI make a transition to the future? "I'm a corporate Darwinian," Akerson says. "I think GI is strong and reacting quickly. The computer industry is a good model for us. I believe in evolution."

If GI doesn't evolve, it could end up in the high-tech tar pits.

DISCOVERY COMMUNICATIONS: A REFUGE FROM CACOPHONY

John Hendricks was skiing. Down the slopes. Up the ski lifts. It was December 1991. The founder and CEO of The Discovery Channel kept thinking about the 40,000 people who had sent $19.95 to buy Discovery's documentary *In the Company of Whales.* That was a lot of money to spend and a lot of trouble to go through to get a tape that they might watch a few times. On Discovery's end, it cost $4 to package each tape and pay the postage. Hendricks knew that, someday soon, cable was going to go digital and send hundreds of channels into homes. If people could click one button on their remote controls and spend $1 to see *Whales,* delivered right then over TV lines—wouldn't that be better? Hendricks spent the next two days of his vacation working through his thoughts, outlining ideas for Discovery on demand, making plans that were ahead of the rest of the programming industry. "At the time, I was just thinking of Discovery," he says.

These days, Hendricks is thinking far more broadly. His company in 1995 is launching Your Choice TV (YCTV), an ersatz video-on-demand service that is the most plausible link between today's linear TV technology and tomorrow's high-tech, high-choice TV systems. Hendricks hopes YCTV turns into a brand-name packager of TV shows on demand, much the way HBO is a well-known movie packager, giving YCTV a long life once megamedia takes hold. If Hendricks has his numbers right, YCTV could bring in revenue of $400 million a year by the end of the decade. "I think it can be big," he says. "Bigger than Discovery is now."

Hendricks is not a technologist. He's not a lifelong media guy. He spent the 1970s raising money for universities—first at the University of Alabama (his alma mater), then the University of Maryland. But Hendricks has always been someone who could think outside his little box and then run with an idea. During his academic fund-raising days, Hendricks started seeing an inevitable link between education and television. They were meant for each other. The powerful medium could spread knowledge, and universities could use TV to expand their reach—and bring in more money. Hendricks started a consulting firm, the American Association of University Consultants, which specialized in TV distribution and marketing of educational programs.

By 1982, Hendricks was looking at the emerging cable-TV medium and seeing better possibilities there for educational shows. He founded Cable Educational Network, started working toward a documentary-heavy channel, and in 1985 junked the original name and launched The Discovery Channel. Along the way, a consortium of cable companies, including TCI and Cox, bailed the network out of financial disaster and got 56 percent of the company in return.

Discovery is soaring now. It reaches 62 million cable subscribers, 1 million more than CNN. Its viewers are more upscale and educated, and older than those watching most cable networks, which helps Discovery lure advertisers. The network sells millions of dollars' worth of videotapes of its documentaries every year. Discovery also owns The Learning Channel, an educational network that reaches 29 million homes, and is launching four niche channels (focusing on nature, science, history, and home life). Discovery and The Learning Channel have a secure place on any cable or other kind of TV service because they are "good" programming. TV operators want to air them to parry potential criticism that television is a hotbed of sex and violence.

Hendricks, in his mid-40s, didn't need to do something else. He could've tinkered with Discovery, moving it into new media. He's already putting documentaries into CD-ROM form, and educational shows will be prime material for megamedia. He's starting an on-line service. Hendricks could've ridden through the next 20 years as a respected, successful, wealthy programmer.

But then he got that idea on the ski slopes. It kept growing, and he couldn't resist it. He needed a new challenge. "I just saw this as an opportunity," he says. So he went to work on YCTV.

YCTV makes more sense when it's seen firsthand; reading about it doesn't work as well. Hendricks' favorite analogy for YCTV's ultimate goal is the best-seller rack in a bookstore. A bookstore offers thousands of choices. Sometimes, customers want to browse through them all; sometimes, they know what they want and will go and find it. Often, though, they want a good recent book and don't want to hunt for it. They go right to the best-seller rack, look at 25 or so titles, grab what they want, and head for the cash register.

A 500-channel interactive TV service is the "bookstore," offering thousands of programming choices. YCTV is the place to go to quickly find the best stuff. On the YCTV rack would be the top-rated network shows of the previous week—"Home Improvement" or "Fresh Prince of Bel Air." The show would air at its regular time on its broadcast-TV network, then land on YCTV for the rest of the week. Anyone who missed the show could find it on YCTV, call it up on demand, and watch it for maybe 69 cents. YCTV's menu would also include high-quality but perhaps more obscure programming from other networks: a PBS documentary, a hot debate on C-SPAN, a sports highlight show from ESPN. The menu will only have around 24 choices. "Less is more for us," Hendricks says. If Hendricks is successful at selling YCTV to TV service operators, YCTV might pop onto the TV screen when viewers hit a preset button on the remote control, or it might be on the first general menu on an interactive service.

The idea is to make YCTV a known and trusted place to turn to find a manageable number of high-quality TV choices, all available on demand for not much money. In the cacophony of megamedia, the service is intended to be a refuge.

Test runs on 8 cable systems around the country have shown that viewers spend an average of $8 a month on YCTV when it's made available, or around $100 a year. Hendricks is aiming to have YCTV in 40 million households, either through cable service or, possibly, services offered by phone companies. That would add up to $4 billion coming in. No on knows yet how the money would be divided among programmers, networks, and cable operators, but if YCTV gets just 10 percent as its cut, Hendricks would have that $400 million business.

Anyway, that's where YCTV is going. Today, it's a little less graceful. Digital interactive technology is not in place, so YCTV has to run on regular cable systems. In the tests—all on systems with capacity of 100 or more channels—YCTV has run on around 24 channels.

At a test in Syracuse, New York, the YCTV menu screen ran on Channel 54 and YCTV offerings were Channels 55 to 78. On each channel, one offering ran continuously in a loop. The week's episode of "20/20" would start on Channel 55 the day after the show aired, then run its full hour—ads included—before starting again each hour on the hour. For each household, selections were scrambled until a show was ordered by pressing a button on a special YCTV-supplied remote control. The cable converter box would unscramble that channel for the week; the show could then be watched anytime. A signal would travel back through the cable line to record the choice and add it to the cable-TV bill. Sample charges in Syracuse were: 69 cents for "20/20"; 99 cents for "All My Children" (soap opera); 49 cents for a half-hour "Sesame Street" special.

The key here is that YCTV is real. Hendricks is the only one thoroughly working through the technology, concept, and snags in offering video on demand to a national market now, not sometime after high-tech networks roll out. YCTV has a shot at becoming viewers' first taste of a premium video-on-demand service, much as HBO was the first premium movie channel two decades ago.

Being first and figuring everything out from scratch "is a lot of work," says Nancy Stover, general manager of YCTV. "But it's probably our best competitive advantage."

Why? Because YCTV is opening a new can of worms at every turn—all issues that every video-on-demand service will have to tackle. And guess what: none of them has to do with technology.

One of the biggest problems is getting the four big broadcast networks to contribute shows to YCTV. The networks have lots of reasons not to. They're wary of turning over control of their programs to a third party that would mix programming from many sources. And, like Capital Cities/ABC, they may want to offer their own on-demand services someday. Also, the networks don't want to risk eroding some of their prime-time audience by letting viewers too easily watch shows at random times. Maybe the networks wouldn't lose any money because they'd get a cut of YCTV's revenue. But the network affiliate stations, which air the shows in the first place, might lose audiences and revenue, and raise a stink.

Hendricks is still working out those issues with networks. He is trying, for instance, to price the YCTV shows high enough so viewers don't automatically decide to watch shows on demand instead of during the regular, free time. He's also trying to convince networks that it would be a good thing to get their premier shows on YCTV's best-seller rack. "I think the networks see the value of getting their good products next to other people's good products," Hendricks says.

Another tough knot is protection of and compensation for intellectual property. "Basically, we're defining a new right," Hendricks says. "When Discovery was launched, nobody had thought about cable-TV rights for documentaries. Now we're talking about a seven-day window right" for shows, and how payment for that right will be split.

Another esoteric issue: How will viewers find YCTV on future television systems? To go back to the bookstore analogy, YCTV wants to be at the front of the store—a menu on the first screen that appears when a 500-channel interactive TV system is turned on—or one button away, at most. But lots of other services and programming will want to be at the front of the store, too. If viewers find YCTV a helpful way to cut through the 500-channel clutter, YCTV may get its wish.

The issues go on and on. What about marketing? YCTV is trying a fun, hip approach. One flyer says: "Hello in-laws! Good-bye favorite TV shows!" It explains how YCTV gives a second chance for seeing missed shows. Other questions: How does YCTV sell this to cable operators? How does it charge for advertising?

Networks, programmers, and cable operators see YCTV as one of the best ways to get a version of interactive TV up and running, find out how audiences react, work out business models that make sense, and so on. They'll help YCTV get going, which is all the start-up can ask for. Audiences will decide whether YCTV succeeds.

Another key to YCTV is Hendricks. He is everybody's programming good-guy—the Colin Powell of television. The Discovery Channel is Hendricks' foot in the door. Just about every TV executive loves the channel. They're impressed by its success. They'll talk to Hendricks. Then they'll find that, in person, Hendricks is as warm and mellow as an old sweater. He's a good listener, yet he's brimming with ideas. As he has done with YCTV, Hendricks will thoroughly research new projects, then go with his gut feeling. "If he just knows, that's enough," says Nancy Stover. "He has a history of building companies out of things nobody thought would work. He's just perfect for this."

YCTV will become an intriguing and important megamedia business in some form—maybe or maybe not as it exists today. YCTV has evolved from its earliest concept, and it will probably continue to evolve. It could become a subscription service—pay one monthly fee, then get any of the best-sellers any time. It could cater to narrower audiences, like Discovery's upscale crowd. Or it could go down other paths. Hendricks is smart enough and flexible enough to take the research and experience gained creating YCTV and mold it into a service that works.

Down the road, YCTV could stay a part of Discovery or spin off as a separate company. Hendricks acknowledges that his programming networks and YCTV have little in common.

Some powerful executives believe in YCTV, including TCI's John Malone, who is trying out the service on some of his company's cable systems, and ABC multimedia chief Bruce Maggin. Best of all, Hendricks believes in it. In the past, he has seen opportunity in concepts that only made most people scratch their heads. There's a good chance he's done it again.

SONY: TOO FAR FROM ITS CORE

Sony is the most important single company in Japanese history. It was started by Masaru Ibuka and Akio Morita in defeated, devastated, rubble-filled downtown Tokyo in 1945. At the time they called their company Tokyo Telecommunications Engineering, and it operated out of a rented room in a bombed department store. Start-up funding was $1,600 from Morita's father's sake business. To survive in its early days, Sony made electric rice cookers, heating pads, and even sweetened bean paste soup.

But Ibuka and Morita had a vision. They wanted to create a company that would elevate the image of Japan in the world's eyes. Its core would be built on technology and on being uniquely Japanese. As described in *Built to Last,* Sony's "Purposes of Incorporation," drawn up by Ibuka, read, in part, like this:

- To establish a place of work where engineers can feel the joy of technological innovation, be aware of their mission to society and work to their heart's content.
- To pursue dynamic activities in technology and production for the reconstruction of Japan and elevation of the nation's culture.

- To apply advanced technology to the life of the general public.

Nowhere in those principles is there any mention of making movies with Arnold Schwarzenegger.

That's no facetious comment. By sticking close to its core purposes, Sony became a great company. Over the decades, it altered the life-styles of people worldwide. Sony built the first transistor radios in 1955, the first transistor TV in 1959, the first home videotape recorder in 1964, and the Walkman personal tape player in 1979. It created and popularized the audio compact disc in the 1980s. Along the way, Sony erased the stigma of the stamp "Made in Japan." Sony became one of the most recognized brand names in the world.

And then, in 1988, Sony ventured into software. It bought CBS Records for $2 billion. A year later, Sony paid $4.9 billion for the Columbia Pictures and TriStar movie studios. Though Sony is a huge company, bringing in more than $30 billion a year, the purchases were a sharp turn away from the company's core. CBS Records and Columbia create entertainment programming, not technology. They are distinctly American, not Japanese.

The purchases have been a disaster. Sony has poured another $3 billion into Columbia, yet the studio is considered one of the worst run in Hollywood. Its market share has fallen, its hits come sparingly and its management is in turmoil. CBS Records, renamed Sony Music Entertainment, has been profitable. But it hasn't done the job Sony had hoped. Sony had figured that its engineers could create new technology for music delivery, and Sony Music would help ensure the technology's success by creating software for it. That hasn't happened. Sony Music's support, for example, has so far failed to make Sony's MiniDisc format a hit.

Meanwhile, the U.S. software divisions keep pulling Tokyo-based Sony further from the technological and cultural strengths that built the company.

"If I were sitting down with Sony," says *Built to Last* author Collins, "I'd tell them that if they can't make the entertainment divisions Sonyesque, if they're not going to pulverize the divisions into the core (of Sony), there's little reason to have them. It's probably harmful to have them."

Sony is a great technology company. It's a lousy software company. By trying to be both, it's doing neither well, and the company is losing its edge.

Sony, though, strongly says it plans to keep the U.S. record and movie operations. By itself, that may diminish Sony's impact on megamedia.

Then again, it's hard to count Sony out. It is a gigantic company. Sony is the world's biggest maker of video camcorders, personal stereos, CD-ROM disks, professional broadcast equipment, cordless phones, and airline video systems. It makes monitors for Apple Computer and Silicon Graphics. Sony makes TVs, compact disk players, car stereos, batteries, videotapes, VCRs, computer chips, and portable multimedia CD-ROM players. Sony is a world leader in consumer electronics and a top supplier of components for the computer industry.

Innovation is part of the company's fabric. Sony is willing to take major chances on entirely new products. In the past, it was personal stereos, compact disks and numerous other devices that had never existed before. Now the company is hanging out there with the MiniDisc, a re-recordable compact disk format. Its Data Discman is a carry-around multimedia player, and there is nothing else like it. In 1994, the company introduced the Sony Magic Link, a hand-held computer-communicator that's one of the first to run on General Magic's software.

Some of the products may become huge sellers. Some may be dogs. But by taking big chances and sometimes winning, Sony has consistently pushed electronics and technology deeper into the lives of people around the globe. The company's engineering side will no doubt continue to try to do that in the decade to come.

On the software side, there is no question that Sony's holdings have value. Columbia and TriStar, for instance, have a combined library of 3,400 films and 25,000 TV episodes. Sony Music pumps out albums by stars such as Billy Joel, Dolly Parton, Mariah Carey, and Barbra Streisand.

By all rights, the combination of hardware and software assets along with such a strong global brand name should be the envy of the megamedia universe. Sony management gets a gold star, in fact, for understanding that technology and entertainment would converge long before most executives even thought about it.

Sony's Morita, who was chairman until ill health forced him to leave in November 1994, wanted to create a company in which hardware and software worked together to march into the future. If Sony created new hardware, his thinking went, the software side would make content to support it. Sony would never again have to beg outside companies to create programming for new formats—a lesson learned from the bitter days when Sony's Betamax videotape system lost out to Matsushita's VHS format. Another advantage of meshing technology and content is that software creators should get early insights into new technology so they could be first with new kinds of programming.

In theory, it all made sense. In reality, it hasn't worked so well.

For starters, the old Sony's spartan, reserved engineering culture has not found common ground with the more bombastic, free-spending, ego-driven entertainment side. Studio executives had given themselves enormous salaries and spent millions just redecorating offices. It was quite a shock to old-line Sony employees.

In the 1980s, Morita co-wrote a controversial book entitled *The Japan That Can Say No*. In it, he depicted the United States as an inferior society. Morita has always been stridently pro-Japan, even while understanding America better than any other top Japanese executive. Given that, how could Sony merge its culture with a movie industry that is quintessentially American? If Sony tries to impose Japanese style on a Hollywood studio, the studio would surely whither.

Sony-Tokyo and Sony of America, run by ex-physicist Michael Schulhof, are more like two separate companies under one flag. The "S word," as they refer to "synergy" around Sony, hasn't happened. In the best case, Sony's hardware side will continue to be a world leader while the software side gets its act together and performs well as a fairly independent unit.

The worst case, though, is that Tokyo gets caught up trying to fix the software side, even if it means making changes to Sony's core hardware business and culture. That could cripple Sony and leave it limping while U.S. companies pass it in megamedia.

Sony was early to see convergence and early to act on it. Some other companies are now similarly putting together hardware and software sides—Bell Atlantic moving into programming, for instance. Sony may be an unusual case, given its strong Japanese bent and technical core. But any company looking to follow the path it blazed ought to look closely to see if Sony becomes a warning sign on the road to megamedia.

SEGA: THIS AIN'T NO GAME

Stan Thomas, chief executive of The Sega Channel, grinned from his seat at a table in a nearly bare conference room. The Sega Channel had moved into the new offices in New York just a few days before, and the interactive game channel's launch was only a month away. Thomas, remarkably, showed little stress. A big, affable man with a face as warm as a sunrise, he chatted about his teenage son, Chipper, and a recent speeding ticket before talking about the plan for The Sega Channel.

The channel is a way to play Sega's videogames via cable TV lines. Pay a subscription fee of about $12 a month, snap an adapter into your Sega game machine, plug in the cable wire and you can choose from 50 games. The games change each month. Play any of them as often or as long as you'd like.

It's Sega's first big move into megamedia, with help from The Sega Channel's other equal partners, TCI and Time Warner. Sure, the start-up of the service will absorb Thomas for the next year at least. But Thomas is already starting to think about what's next, and it says a lot about where Sega is heading. "The reality is that through the Genesis game and The Sega Channel, we are supplying data," Thomas says, his words echoing among the unadorned walls and the two Sega games in the room, one set up at each end. "Right now, the data is games. But it's not inconceivable that we could supply other kinds of data. We have no particular plans right now, but we recognize we are a provider of data."

Thomas smiles and breezily moves onto another subject. He doesn't want to ruin Sega's image as a hip, wild, escapist company by attaching too many words like "data" to it. At least not quite yet.

However, if anyone in megamedia thinks Sega is nothing more than a harmless Japanese videogame company, they risk getting their backsides blown to smithereens, like an evil spaceship in the Sega game *Taz in Escape from Mars.*

Think about Sega's position right now. Its game machines are in about 18 million homes. The machines don't have the power of a personal computer, but they are most certainly digital, interactive devices that could handle a lot more than just *Sonic the Hedgehog.* Sega is a stronger brand name among teenagers than any brand in megamedia. Its only branding competition in that age group is MTV. Sega has a fanatical following among the generation that is going to lead the world into mass-market uses of the information highway.

Beyond that, Sega knows how to make both hardware and software. It makes all of its own game machines. Unlike PC makers, Sega has experience making inexpensive, consumer-electronic devices for home markets. (A Sega Genesis costs less than $100.) The company also creates and makes up to 85 percent of the games that run on Sega machines. About 40 percent of the company's 5,000 employees are devoted to research and development, spending a budget of $200 million a year—more than Microsoft is spending on megamedia research.

Sega is a global company—another strength. It was started by an American in Tokyo. It's still based in Tokyo, but it's most important division, Sega of America, is based in Redwood City, California, and is run almost autonomously by an American former toy company executive named Thomas Kalinske. Sega's president in Tokyo is Hayao Nakayama, a charismatic Japanese techno-wiz. The cochairman is Brooklyn-born David Rosen, who founded the company. The new executive vice president is Shoichiro Irimajiri, who previously helped make Honda cars a booming success in the United States. That team is marketing Sega products on every continent.

And now, through The Sega Channel and a similar service being tested in Japan, Sega will create one of the first widespread interactive TV services and link those once-isolated Sega machines to the developing info highway.

Add up the pieces, and Sega seems to be ready to become an important player in megamedia. If it can grow up along with its core audience, Sega could be in position to offer things like shopping, interactive dating services, on-line music videos, news or anything else young adults might want from their TV sets in the coming decade. If megamedia executives don't pay attention, phone companies and computer companies might come knocking on consumers' doors a few years from now and find Sega already there—a comfortable part of every family.

Sega, of course, isn't the only videogame maker out there. Nintendo is big. Sega has around 55 percent to 65 percent of the market; Nintendo, 35 percent to 45 percent. Nintendo is not as aggressive or innovative as Sega. Instead of having a smart global team guiding the company, as Sega does, Nintendo is run with an iron hand from Japan by founder Hiroshi Yamauchi. And Sega is finding ways to reach beyond teens to young-adult audiences while Nintendo seems perpetually stuck in the pre-teen market. Besides Sega and Nintendo, a few other companies are getting started in the business, most notably 3DO and Sony. But their chances are slim.

Sega's history helps explain its drive. In 1954, David Rosen was 20 years old. He had spent some time in Tokyo with the U.S. Air Force, and went back to the Japanese capital to get into business there. He started a company called Service Games and imported arcade games to install on U.S. military bases in Japan. But Rosen found most of the games from U.S. manufacturers boring and decided to develop some of his own. He bought a Tokyo maker of jukeboxes and slot-machines. When Service Games shipped a machine, it stamped it with the acronym SEGA—using the first two letters of each word in the company name, SErvice GAmes. Rosen later adopted Sega as the company name.

In the late-1960s, Sega invented a game called Periscope, which let players shoot torpedoes at electronic images of ships. The game was a hit and Sega took off in both Japan and the United States. In 1971, Rosen sold Sega to Gulf & Western Industries. Rosen stayed on as CEO.

Then the story gets complicated. Sega did great as an arcade game maker for a decade. But in the early 1980s, the technology ran out of steam. Arcade game players were tired of the same old thing. Home games weren't going anywhere. The electronic game market crashed. The shattered remains of Sega's U.S. operations were sold to Bally Manufacturing. Back in Tokyo, Rosen joined with Nakayama to buy the Japanese portion of Sega for $38 million.

The two men started rebuilding the company, sticking with arcade games but also making a run at the home market, then dominated by Nintendo. In the 1990s, thanks to better and faster machines and in-your-face advertising, Sega came from behind to dominate the videogame business.

From that messy struggle, Sega learned two lessons. One is to have the best technology. The other is to keep moving, keep creating new products, keep going after new markets. Sega had almost disappeared once because it had stagnated. Rosen and Nakayama vowed it would never happen again. Today, Sega has more than $4 billion in annual revenue. And it is certainly not sitting still.

The Sega Channel is one of the company's most interesting moves. In the early 1990s, Sega researchers had started talking about linking their machines on-line. About the same time, executives at Time Warner's Home Box Office premium movie channel began discussing a video game service that worked something like HBO. They wanted to make it a monthly subscription service and offer access to lots of games. "HBO took a medium that existed—movies—and brought it into the home in a more convenient, efficient, and exciting way," says Sega Channel's Thomas, who worked at HBO 11 years before launching The Sega Channel. "We wanted to do the same with videogames."

In the boiling pot of megamedia in the early 1990s, Sega and Time Warner eventually talked. They added TCI to the discussions. What came out was The Sega Channel. Time Warner and TCI would distribute it using their cable systems. Sega would provide the software and name brand. The three companies would be equal partners in the channel. General Instrument and Scientific-Atlanta were signed to make adapters that would link Sega games to cable lines.

The beauty of The Sega Channel is that it doesn't need to be on a high-tech cable network of the future. It can run on a small slice of spectrum between other cable channels, so it doesn't eat up even a channel's worth of capacity on a cable system. Most up-to-date cable systems could add The Sega Channel by investing a few thousand dollars in a personal computer. The service will likely be available to millions within a few years. Thomas expects to have up to 1 million subscribers by the end of 1995—and make a profit.

For videogame consumers, the channel is almost a no-brainer—just the kind of evolutionary step that will begin to pump life into megamedia. Owners of a Sega machine would get an adapter from their cable companies. Plug a few wires in and it's ready to go. Turn on the TV—it doesn't matter what channel it's tuned to—and turn on the Sega machine and The Sega Channel comes on automatically. It offers categories of games. Some are "Test Drives," which are chances to play games not yet on the market. Others are "Classics" or "Sports Arena." Choose a category, then see a selection of games. Pick one, click a button on the Sega machine, and the game downloads over the cable network into the Sega machine. The game then plays exactly as it would if you put a cartridge into the machine.

As a vehicle for games, the channel is considered by industry observers to be a sure-fire hit. Customers in test markets are enthusiastic. "Outrageous! Right on time! Saves my parents a lot of money!" a 7-year-old in Buffalo, New York, wrote to Sega. "It is probably the best idea Sega has ever had," wrote a 12-year-old, also from Buffalo.

The channel is also showing signs of what it could become. Subscribers can pull down news about coming Sega games and can get tips on how to play existing games better. If Sega can deliver that kind of information into homes, it can deliver anything. Thomas adds that The Sega Channel is looking at ways to connect point-to-point, so a player in one home could compete against someone in another home. That would add to Sega's information-delivering ability.

"It's more than a great business," says Sega of America's Kalinske. "It's a wonderful test ground for the future. We have hands-on experience operating what everyone else is dreaming about."

Beyond The Sega Channel, Sega is making a number of other thrusts at the future. In Japan, it's launching an interactive karaoke network to take advantage of the popularity of the sing-along pastime there. Users will see a menu of songs, choose one, then get the background music plus a video showing the words to the song. Sega may try the service in the United States.

On a different front, Sega is charging hard into amusement parks. But not just your typical amusement park. Sega is building virtual reality parks. They are entirely made up of the most advanced electronic games, several steps up from an arcade game. One is a virtual reality space ride. Customers get into a pod, on a moveable platform, that holds 16 people. The riders don helmets that have goggles and earphones. As the ride begins, images and sounds and the motion of the pod make riders feel as if they're in space. Then, as Kalinske puts it, "lo and behold you end up in a space battle and you've got to fight the bad guys. You have control of rockets. The winners get to land the spacecraft."

The space ride is in Yokohama, Japan, in the first of Sega's parks, called Joypolis. Such a park occupies about 3 percent of the land of Disney World in Orlando, Florida, and costs about $25 million to build. EuroDisney cost billions. Yet the parks are big enough to include restaurants and enough attractions to keep a visiting family busy for a couple of hours. At Joypolis, visitors are spending $40 to $50 a person; profit margins are around 30 percent. No wonder cities and business people have been besieging Sega with requests to get in on the action.

In the United States, Sega is considering building up to 50 virtual reality parks by 2000. An intriguing thought: "When we get a lot of parks built, we might tie them together via phone lines and let visitors in several parks play against each other," Kalinske says.

The parks should strengthen Sega's brand and software, just the way Disney's parks bolster its other products. Users of Sega at home will be pulled to the parks. Park-goers may get glimpses of coming Sega home products, generating excitement. And importantly, adults are a big part of the parks' visitors—a way for Sega to reach that market.

That would help Sega with one of its biggest weaknesses. Though it's doing far better than Nintendo at reaching older customers, Sega is still primarily a teenage pastime—for that matter, most Sega players are teenage boys. If the company wants to be a major player in megamedia and move beyond games, it will have to widen its appeal.

Also, it will likely become important for Sega to move beyond games. The company gets almost all of its revenue from game sales. But even the company's executives have admitted that creativity seems to have stalled in the home game business. There are few new ideas or game plots and Sega worries that demand may sag if there are no breakthroughs soon. At the very least, the game business relies on the fickle nature of public taste. To become a broader, more stable company, Sega will have to move in new directions. Kalinske says he's trying.

"We have a mission statement," he says. "We want to lead in interactive entertainment whether in the home or out of the home." The statement purposely doesn't use the words "video games." In November 1994, Sega opened a digital studio, where it can film actors or record music to help the company go beyond computer animation. Kalinske wants to develop educational programing. Sega machines "could be the greatest Trojan horse for enhancing education that the world has ever seen," he says.

What might Sega become? Some say it's a future Disney, and the parallels are interesting: Sonic the Hedgehog as the next Mickey Mouse; loads of entertainment software; a kid-dominated customer base; theme parks. Yet Sega is also a technology company, making machines that go into homes and now hooking them to megamedia networks. It makes for a brand new combination—just the kind of company that megamedia is all about. Sega is a hard-charging company that is going to be a strong player in the next decade, one way or another. Its advertising slogan is, "Welcome to the next level." The ads refer to games. But Sega seems headed for the next level of megamedia.

MIKE MILKEN'S EEN COMMUNICATIONS: A MILLION MILES FROM WALL STREET

The house, just inside the sign that says "Bel Air" and a few hundred yards from one of Los Angeles's busiest freeways, looks like it could be a doctor's office. It is well-kept, good-sized, but fairly plain in a neighborhood of similar unexceptional houses. There is no sign on the house, just a set of glass double-doors. In the foyer sits one security guard at a lonely little table. On the table are three monitors, showing what the video cameras placed around the house are picking up.

Through another doorway, in cluttered, cramped, not very nice offices is Mike Milken's venture into interactive television.

Not many people know about the venture, EEN Communications Network. Milken has kept it low-key, almost secretive. Talk to others in the TV or software industry and they're often not even aware Milken is in the business. Yet the man often called the most brilliant financial mind of our time says he'll pump "hundreds of millions" of dollars into the venture—apparently his own money, if necessary. That alone says something significant about megamedia: if Milken's doing it, there's money to be made.

Milken is the famous junk-bond king of the 1980s who wound up going to prison for securities fraud. His high-rolling, innovative, Beverly Hills-based unit of brokerage firm Drexel Burnham Lambert virtually created the 1980s corporate takeover boom and financed a number of industries that were then on the brink of disaster—including, not coincidentally, a good deal of the cable-TV industry. One year alone, he was paid $550 million. Milken is now in his late 40s and is banned from the financial industry. He is also suffering from advanced prostate cancer. When I saw him briefly at EEN, he did not look well. He is not expected to live a long life.

Milken, wearing a bright, geometric tie and no jacket, and looking a little pudgier than he used to, said little more than hello and talked about the importance of using emerging new media for education. He left, and Lorraine Spurge outlined Milken's plans for EEN. Spurge, a small woman with the personal force of a pile-driver, had worked with Milken through the 1980s glory years. Now she is managing director of EEN's first project, dubbed EEN Business Network.

The business network aims to take advantage of Milken's fame to launch a business education network. The plan is to start small and low-tech, then ratchet up to become a full-fledged interactive TV network on future megamedia systems. The start will probably be a series of videotapes on different topics, such as corporate finance or investments. Milken would be featured on the tapes, along with some of the nation's best professors and financial professionals. "Mike's vision is to make education entertaining," Spurge says. The tapes, she promises, will be lively and engaging.

The next step would be putting the same kind of programming onto CD-ROM and adding interactive elements. Users might play a financial game against Milken, or Milken will get one of his pals to be part of an interactive game—anyone from Carl Icahn to Henry Kravis. It's easy to see how EEN could leverage Milken's name and reputation to create business software. As Spurge explains it, by moving into content this way, EEN will be ready to create an interactive TV network by the time megamedia systems are up and running.

Milken's contacts can also make sure EEN gets a slot on new networks. In the 1980s, Milken's outfit financed the likes of TCI, MCI, Turner Broadcasting, Viacom, Oracle, McCaw Cellular, and many other players coming into megamedia. A lot of those companies would help a Milken-backed venture any way they could.

In the grand plan, EEN Business Network would be one of a full range of interactive networks created by EEN Communications. "First we'll do business, then maybe we'll try kids," Spurge says. Again, Milken has his contacts. It might sound like an unlikely pairing, but Milken has talked to singer Michael Jackson about doing something for EEN. "We talked about filming a tour and doing geography lessons along with it," Spurge says.

EEN is a start-up. It had only about 20 employees when I visited. It has no sales yet and doesn't plan on having much of a product for another couple of years. But it does have a lot more going for it than just any interactive programming start-up. It has Milken's name and cachet, which will help win customers and lure top talent to the company. It has Milken's considerable money and his ability to get much more. And it has Milken's worldwide contacts.

A wild card is Milken's health. If he can't be on the videotapes or CD-ROMs, the products might not have as good a chance in the marketplace. If he's not there to call on his contacts, EEN might not be able to raise as much money or get the same level of help. But don't underestimate the kind of people working at EEN. Some are ex-Drexel types who have Rolodexes almost as impressive as Milken's. Others are top business school graduates. They'll carry on Milken's enterprise with or without the founder.

EEN is a mighty long way from getting anywhere. Of all the companies profiled in this book, EEN is the most likely to disappear without a trace. But again—it's Mike Milken. What he's doing and thinking about in megamedia is worth a look. There's a chance that Milken can make EEN into a legacy that outdistances the man's infamy.

11
OUT ON A LIMB

Making predictions about megamedia is like trying to pinpoint the next place lightning will strike. Educated guesses may get close, but the only way to hit it on the nose is through sheer luck.

Over the past two years, I've talked with many people about what they think will happen in megamedia through the 1990s. The people included CEOs, inventors, stock analysts, consumers, regulators, and citizens of Hill City, Kansas, a small town worrying about being left off the information superhighway. Add up everything they've said, mix it with the facts of what's been happening at the various companies, and the patterns of what's going on come into clearer view. Based on that information, I think I can make megamedia predictions that will at least get close.

WINNERS

There aren't any sure things in megamedia. From what I've learned, the five winners listed here have the best chances, if not guaranteed success. I'm not trying to discover the one little company operating in somebody's basement that's going to become the next Microsoft. These players are well positioned today to lead the way into megamedia and reap the full benefits of the communications boom.

1. AT&T

By 2000, AT&T will be the most powerful company in the world. It is simply the best communications company anywhere. It owns and operates the biggest and best broadband, global network. It is the world's leading builder of megamedia systems and networks. It is positioned to be in the middle of everything that happens in megamedia. AT&T has turned into a competitive, determined company. If there's a reason to think AT&T might stumble on its way up, I don't see it.

2. The Walt Disney Company

Disney is the world's premier software creator. Two of its animated features—*Aladdin* and *The Lion King*—were $1 billion businesses by themselves. Its characters and copyrights are known and desired across borders and across all media. As megamedia develops, the market for top-quality software will rocket. Disney will be at the top. It doesn't need to own a piece of the information superhighway, although the company could probably make good use of something like a major TV network. Management troubles may be the only hitch, but CEO Michael Eisner has lured the best people to Disney in the past. He should be able to do so in the future.

3. Motorola

The business of wireless communications is growing more than 40 percent a year, and the only company positioned to reap the rewards no matter how the industry develops is Motorola. It is the world's biggest seller of wireless phones and equipment, and will likely keep that position even as the wireless service industry goes through turbulent change. Just to make sure, Motorola continues to drive the creation of new wireless services, such as global satellite phones, so it can sell equipment for them. Competitors would typically come into those markets later. Finally, Motorola is so good at reinventing itself to keep up with the times that I'd vote the company a winner even if I thought the wireless industry would disappear tomorrow.

4. Hewlett-Packard

H-P is today what every other computer company will have to become. It is a flexible, morphing company that is able to deploy computer technology in any conceivable way. It doesn't think in terms of desktop machines with keyboards and screens. It thinks in terms of what people need and how technology can meet those needs. In megamedia, that will be key as computing diffuses into everyday life. H-P, the second-biggest computer company, is already on a roll, growing more than 20 percent a year. It should keep on rolling right through the 1990s.

5. John Malone

Notice this doesn't say TCI. Malone is the smartest, boldest, toughest, bravest individual anywhere on megamedia's radar. His loyalty is also first to himself, not to TCI. Malone is always ahead of the curve and in with the right people. He is one of the few executives who intimately knows all the keys to the entertainment side of megamedia: technology, content, and consumer markets. He is a leader willing to trek into uncharted territory, then make it work by the sheer, mighty force of his will. Wherever megamedia goes, I'm sure Malone will be there, probably out front. It may or may not be with TCI. Malone is a builder, not an operator. If TCI runs out of steam, don't be surprised if Malone finds better things to do.

Missing

Bell Atlantic is not on this list for one reason. Ray Smith may be among the most aggressive megamedia CEOs, but too much of Bell Atlantic is still a slow-moving, mushy, monopolistic old phone company. To make it in megamedia, it will have to become a fast-moving, hardened, competitive operation. Bell Atlantic may be further along that path than any regional Bell, but, by Smith's own admission, it has a long way to go.

Viacom is also not in my top five. It probably has potential to be more exciting than Disney, after Viacom, Paramount, and Blockbuster are all merged and working together. But that blend is a couple of years and a lot of work away. I don't doubt Viacom will be good. The question is whether it can be great.

LOSERS

It's pretty hard to call any multibillion-dollar company or top executive a "loser." In a strict sense, it's rarely true.

But some major players simply don't seem likely to do well in megamedia. Their strategies for the coming years seem questionable, or their leadership is weak, or they don't seem able to live up to expectations. In a relative sense, they will be losers.

Again, I'm not looking at little companies that might fold before the next payroll is due. These are the major players that look like they're heading for trouble.

1. Pacific Telesis

Of all the regional phone companies, PacTel is most at risk. About 98 percent of its revenue comes from operations in California, and that state is going to become the most competitive communications market in the world within a few years. Cable, wireless, and long-distance companies will be trying to take slices out of PacTel's business there. The company is pouring all its resources into protecting itself in California, but putting none toward moving into other markets. It has done little to get into software. PacTel could soon find itself isolated and embattled in its big state. Beyond that, PacTel got rid of its fastest-growing business: cellular phones. It's now the only regional Bell that has no wireless capabilities. PacTel is the contrarian phone company. At this point, the strategy looks like a dead end.

2. Sprint

The number-three long-distance company has a major high-tech global network, and it's the only company that has long-distance, local phone, and wireless businesses all under one roof. But the pieces don't work well together. The company can't seem to muster the resources and drive to effectively chase new markets or back new ideas. (Its deal to work with cable companies is an exception worth watching.) It has not united behind CEO William Esrey, who seems to be managing for the short term, failing to articulate a long-term plan for Sprint. As number-three, Sprint's long-distance business will be vulnerable once regional Bells are allowed into the industry. Sprint may wind up as a takeover target before the decade's out.

3. DirecTv

Direct broadcast satellite television—basically, wireless cable TV—is coming about five years too late. DirecTv's service, launched nationwide in 1994, costs too much and doesn't offer enough unique programming to lure mainstream consumers during the next few years. After that, there's a good chance most areas will have two or three wired TV choices superior to DirecTv, so most consumers won't even consider the satellite service. DirecTv isn't interactive. By 2000, it could be left in the dust. DirecTv, a unit of GM Hughes Electronics, cost as much as $1 billion to launch. The venture hopes for 10 million customers by 2000. It might end up with one-quarter of that goal—enough to possibly break even.

4. Apple Computer

John Sculley ruined Apple by thinking too brilliantly about markets and technology too far into the future. He focused on products whose time will not come for years, and forgot about the ongoing business. When Sculley left, the pendulum swung way back to the short term. As a computer maker, Apple is in trouble today for a lot of reasons. For the future, Apple no longer seems to have the leadership, talent, or cultural will to create breakthrough products, à la the Macintosh. From what I hear, the magic is gone. It left with Steve Jobs, Sculley, the people of General Magic, and others who moved on. Apple is another candidate for being bought by someone else before the 1990s end.

5. Barry Diller

After joining QVC, Diller was proclaimed king of new media, and an interactive TV visionary. He's neither. He is simply one of the greatest mass-market, traditional programming executives of our time. Period. Diller really didn't do much of anything to drive QVC into the future. He was thought to be a builder of empires, but it didn't turn out that way. Now QVC is being sold to Comcast and Diller is expected to look for something else to do. Nobody would be surprised if Diller ended up successfully running a TV network or Hollywood studio. But a lot of people are disappointed that he's not going to be the megamedia messiah.

Missing

The really big losers are not any of the companies above. At least they're on the right playing field. The companies to really worry about are those that are in the communications, technology, or media industries, yet don't seem to be ready for the coming changes. On that list, I include many computer companies, much of the broadcast TV industry, the music industry, and many of Japan's big electronics companies.

There's another group of companies I'd put in the loser category: the ventures that jumped in with early versions of interactive TV that turned out to be clunky, crude, and unappealing to consumers. Names include Interactive Network, EON, and NTN Communications. Their services have gone nowhere despite high-profile backing.

FIVE COMPANIES TO WORK FOR IN MEGAMEDIA

Whenever I visit a company, I meet executives, walk the halls, talk to people, see what everyone is doing. One thing I always ask myself is: Would I want to work here?

Based on that criterion, here are five companies, in alphabetical order, that are involved in megamedia and seem to be the best places to work.

1. Comcast

This Philadelphia company has a peculiar outlook on management, compared to most companies these days: it wants employees to feel like partners or part of a family. It wants to earn their loyalty and be loyal to them. The atmosphere at Comcast is friendly and supportive, but not overly cozy. Many of the company's top managers are young and aggressive—a new generation of cable-TV and communications leaders. This is a company with energy. Comcast is still small enough to feel like a family business, yet big enough to make exciting moves into new markets, such as buying QVC or backing Nextel. Seems like a good place to build a career.

2. Compaq

In Houston, the lights burn late into the night at Compaq headquarters. People work hard and long—and they love it. Individuals are given a great deal of responsibility and freedom. They are encouraged to try new things and are supported even if their ideas flop. As a result, Compaq has become the best and most innovative PC company, and it has the brightest future in megamedia. Employees have to like stress and change to work at Compaq, but the opportunities to grow and get ahead are humongous there.

3. General Magic

This company is more like a playground than an office. Toys are everywhere—videogames, a foosball table, electric trains. Software engineers Rollerblade together at lunch time. Everyone wears jeans or shorts to work, at the California headquarters. Managers are just as childlike as their underlings. Yet serious business gets done. The company has developed groundbreaking software. It has backers like AT&T and NTT. The futons in the halls are around because people working on intense projects spend the night in the office. Other positive factors: General Magic is still small, but, thanks to its many big-name backers, it is high-profile. It's a place that could lead to bigger things. The company employs some of the PC industry's legendary software developers—a chance to work closely with the best. Not for the risk-averse; General Magic could make it big, or not make it at all.

4. Hewlett-Packard

H-P is the most egalitarian, normal, comfortable, honest workplace around. People who work there love it. Most become loyal to the company and find career-long challenges in its many different and constantly changing businesses. Top H-P managers often get recruited to run other companies—a case in point is former H-P executive Ed McCracken, now CEO of Silicon Graphics. H-P is on the rise, creating a new brand of flexible computer company. After years of struggling and dipping morale, H-P is once again a great place to be.

5. Viacom

I don't know whether all of Viacom is a great place to work. In fact, the merging of operations may make employees in some parts miserable. But two pieces of Viacom seem to be wonderful workplaces.

One is Blockbuster. The company is about fun and entertainment, and employees take that to heart. They enjoy themselves. The company has an interesting attitude. It knows its business of renting videotapes may fall victim to movies on demand in the future, so it wants to reinvent itself as an entertainment brand name. Blockbuster also has huge amounts of cash, generated by its currently booming video rental business. Managers are given big globs of capital to chase all kinds of possible new businesses for Blockbuster. They and their employees have a blast.

The other neat workplace is MTV Networks, the cable programming division. It may be a little too hip, young, and freewheeling for everybody, but it is certainly one of the most innovative programmers in the business. Plus you might get to mingle with Janet Jackson and Pearl Jam.

TO BE CONTINUED: PREDICTIONS AND TRENDS TO WATCH

Here are some (gulp!) predictions and trends to watch for as megamedia unfolds.

Vertical integration will fizzle. Many companies charging into megamedia seem to be crazed about vertical integration, the concept of owning all the parts of a business from beginning to end: creation, distribution, and end-user sales.

Programmers say they feel a need to tie up with a distribution company so they can make sure they always have an outlet for the shows and movies they produce. Even Disney is looking to buy a major TV network. The phone and cable companies say they want to own software so they can be assured of having content to pump over their pipelines. Phone companies are hooking up with Hollywood agent Michael Ovitz to gain access to talent.

Vertical integration, by itself, will turn out to be a bad reason to merge and form alliances. As megamedia settles out, content creators will want to sell their work to as many outlets as makes sense or to the highest bidder among competing outlets. The more outlets clamoring for software, the more money content creators can make. At the same time, distribution owners—cable companies, phone companies, TV networks, and other such organizations—will want to be able to buy from a wide range of programmers. In that way, they can find the best content at the best price.

Vertical integration has never worked. As Viacom's Frank Biondi has pointed out, movie companies scrambled to buy chains of theaters in the 1970s. They figured the move would ensure outlets for their films and would add up to a more efficient operation. "The investments turned out to be disasters," Biondi says. Biondi insists that Viacom's purchase of Paramount was not about vertical integration but about building a software giant. Biondi is selling Paramount's movie theater holdings to help pay off debt from the merger.

Panic is driving the vertical rush. Programmers, for instance, are afraid they might find themselves locked out of distribution channels if they don't buy into them. That's silly. The panic will eventually subside and companies will get back to cutting deals for better reasons.

Brands will be a battleground. All kinds of companies are crashing together into the megamedia business. They're creating new layers and amalgamations of services and content. Expect confusion to reign.

In that atmosphere, brands become hugely important. New kinds of services will more easily lure consumers if they come packaged under a strong, familiar brand name.

To companies that have them, brands will be a competitive weapon—something they'll want to both wield and protect.

When Nextel was building its new kind of wireless phone service, it wanted to hook up with MCI in large part to get MCI's brand name, which would have given the service legitimacy in consumers' view. MCI got skittish about putting its name on service it wouldn't control. The brand problem helped nix the Nextel—MCI deal.

In interactive information services, several brands may wind up nesting together. Viewers may turn on a computerized TV and get Bell Atlantic's Stargazer, then use that to hook into America Online, which in turn will link them to interactive versions of *Time* or *The New York Times.* Each of those brands will vie for attention. Each will be concerned about losing identity to other brands in the lineup. People today usually don't know the names of wire services that pump stories into a newspaper. Similarly, consumers may start thinking of America Online as the news source and consider *Time* and the *Times* as often-anonymous feeders for AOL. AOL would probably like that outcome. *Time* and the *Times* would hate it and would fight for better positioning. Similar tensions will mount across megamedia.

What brands will be known and trusted 10 years from now? Sprint? Comcast? MTV? Microsoft? Intel? Your Choice TV? US West? They'll all be in the same business. Which names rise and which fall is completely up for grabs. Through the 1990s, brands will be a powerful enough force to help shape strategy and deals.

Dealmania will continue. Companies in every industry joining megamedia perceive that they must be bigger and broader to compete. A lot of companies will be looking for a lot of deals. The pace of deals has been frenetic since 1993, but it's only the beginning. Many more mergers, investments, and alliances are to come.

Some deals seem certain: continued consolidation of the cable industry; consolidation of the cellular industry; phone company investments in content; long-distance company alliances with cable TV and the sale of part or all of NBC and CBS, Sony's Columbia Pictures, America Online, Prodigy, and, somewhere further down the road, maybe Apple and Sprint.

Regulation will be a defining issue for a long time. Congress promises action to cut through the tangle of regulation governing most industries converging into megamedia. But it faces an incredible mess. Even if good laws are passed, years will go by before regulation is cleaned up. One example: Phone companies have to answer to state commissions and the FCC. Cable companies answer to community governments and a whole different set of regulations at the FCC. They are getting into each other's businesses. Yet, when phone companies offer cable TV, they won't have to go through community governments. When cable companies offer phone service, they may be able to skip state regulators. It hardly makes for fair competition, but that's the way it will probably stay for several years.

Megamedia will run hot and cold with the public. Microsoft's Nathan Myhrvold says he's braced for several cycles of hype and backlash over the next decade. There have already been a couple such cycles in the past few years. Some days, megamedia will be all the rage. It will drive CEO strategies, blare from newspaper headlines, and lure investors. Other days, it will be dead, usually after a couple of highly touted deals fall through or some promised technology gets delayed. CEOs will publicly scoff at the concept, newspapers will write emperor-has-no-clothes stories, and investors will turn elsewhere.

As usual, the truth will lie somewhere in the middle. Megamedia will move ahead in fits and starts—but move ahead it will. It won't stop. It is being driven by the most powerful force in American business: competition.

As megamedia blurs lines separating industries, the phone companies, cable companies, computer software makers, movie producers, hardware companies, and other players will find they have to compete in new, more ferocious ways—either to defend their turf or to make a grab for new markets. It doesn't even matter whether the competition is real yet. Fear of future competition is what has driven many of megamedia's developments so far. As long as those fires burn—and there's no reason to think they will be extinguished—megamedia has to happen, probably more quickly than we think.

The United States will kick butt. A Communications Age is dawning, and U.S. companies are so far ahead it's not even funny. Megamedia will create powerful worldwide demand for America's technology and software. The potential for international growth for U.S. megamedia companies is phenomenal.

Every square inch of megamedia will be dominated by U.S. companies. American local and long-distance phone companies are far more competitive and advanced than any other phone companies in the world. The United States is the leading developer and manufacturer of key communications hardware such as fiber-optic cable, digital switches, personal computers, and microprocessors. It is the most advanced developer of communications networks, whether computer networks or cable TV systems. Software companies such as Microsoft are the world's best at writing the computer code that makes systems run. Only a handful of companies outside the United States can run with that pack.

At the same time, the United States is unequaled in producing the content that will fill megamedia networks: films from Hollywood, CNN, America Online, "The Simpsons," CD-ROM educational programs, NBA and NFL games, and university research databases. The United States gets a built-in bonus because English is increasingly becoming the international language of commerce and entertainment. It's hard for the Japanese to beat that.

Nearly every other nation is saddled with a lumbering, state-run monopoly phone company and a handful of state-run TV stations. Even Japan, which has a more freewheeling communications sector than most, is crawling along. Only about 3 percent of the population there has cable TV. Per-capita cellular phone use is about one-fourth that of the United States. The big, bloated state-run phone company, NTT, is only beginning to get into fiber-optics and digital communications. "Nations that have stuck to old monopoly models of telecommunications have quite frankly fallen behind," says Anne Bingaman, who has been immersed in international communications issues while running the Justice Department's antitrust division.

Megamedia is a powerful technology, as significant as the coming of the computer. Domestically, it will help U.S. companies become more competitive and improve peoples' lives. Around the world, other nations will want and need to catch up. And they will buy from the likes of AT&T, Microsoft, Hewlett-Packard, Motorola, Viacom, Disney, and Time Warner.

AT&T thinks it can build in China an operation the size of another AT&T. NYNEX and a US West–TCI partnership are the leading cable operators in the United Kingdom. Motorola has crushed the Japanese in cellular phones and has become the world's number-one supplier. In Russia, Vietnam, and Saudi Arabia, people treasure their bootleg videotapes of Hollywood movies such as *Aladdin* and *The Fugitive*.

This is big stuff. As the coming decade unfolds, megamedia will surely be an exciting game in our own backyard. On the world's playing fields, megamedia could take the United States somewhere almost beyond imagination.

INDEX